Janie Hampton

Janie Hampton is the author of a dozen books and the editor of *Joyce and Ginnie*, the letters of Joyce Grenfell and Virginia Graham, and *Hats Off!*, a volume of Joyce Grenfell's poetry and drawings. She has been a BBC World Service producer and planner of health projects in Africa. She and her husband have four grown-up children and live in Oxford.

JOYCE GRENFELL

Janie Hampton

JOHN MURRAY

First published in 2002 by John Murray (Publishers)
A division of Hodder Headline

Reprinted 2002, 2003

Paperback edition 2003

The moral right of the author has been asserted

A CIP catalogue record for this title is available from the British Library

ISBN 0-7195-6490 5

Typeset in Monotype Bembo by
Servis Filmsetting Ltd, Manchester

Printed and bound in Great Britain by Clays Ltd, St Ives plc

John Murray (Publishers)
338 Euston Road
London
NW1 3BH

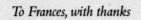

To Frances, with thanks

Contents

Illustrations ix

Preface xi

Acknowledgements xiii

Family Tree xvi

Joyce Grenfell 1

Appendices

   Joyce Grenfell's Homes 341

   Stage Shows 342

   Films 344

   Books 345

   Monologues 346

   Songs 348

   Selected BBC Radio Programmes 351

   How BBC Radio Programmes 353

   Selected Television Appearances 354

   Selected Articles 355

   Selected Charities 356

Bibliography 358

Index 363

Illustrations

1. Joyce Irene Phipps, aged three, 1913
2. Joyce's grandmother, Mrs Wilton Phipps, 1884
3. Joyce's mother, Nora Langhorne, with Aunt Liza Pie, 1891
4. The Langhorne family home
5. Tommy Phipps and Joyce, 1925
6. Tommy at Eton College
7. Joyce and her father, Paul Phipps, 1936
8. Joyce and Nora by Cecil Beaton, 1928
9. Cliveden
10. Cousins at Cliveden, 1939
11. Mr and Mrs Reginald Grenfell, 1929
12. Reggie and Joyce opening a chrome mine in Yugoslavia, 1934
13. The Grenfell family, 1935
14. Joyce at Cliveden, 1935
15. Virginia Graham and Joyce in New York, 1935
16. Elliot Coleman
17. Entertaining a party in Connecticut, 1934
18. Reggie at Parr's, 1936
19. Nancy Astor
20. August bank holiday at Parr's, 1938
21. Who's for tennis?, 1939
22. Ruth Draper
23. Joyce in her first revue, 1939
24. Harold Lindo and Joyce
25. The Canadian Red Cross Hospital at Cliveden, 1940
26. Transmitting a 'Transatlantic Quiz', 1941
27. Joyce, Myra Hess and Howard Fergusson
28. Joyce and Viola Tunnard on tour for ENSA in Persia, 1944
29. ENSA poster, 1944–5
30. Viola and Joyce in Iraq, 1944
31. Prince Aly Khan and Rita Hayworth, 1949
32. Joyce posing for Victor Stiebel, 1947
33. Joyce in Noël Coward's revue, *Sigh No More*, 1945

34. Joyce as Dr Barrett in *The Lamp Still Burns*, 1943
35. Richard Addinsell and Joyce in New York, 1946
36. Stephen Potter and Joyce, 1948
37. Little Orchard, North Carolina, 1946
38. Joyce and her niece Sally Phipps, 1955
39. Long Island, 1963
40. Daphne Oxenford and Joyce on television, 1956
41. Joyce in her attic study at Elm Park Gardens, 1957
42. Joyce at a nursery school in Oldham, 1952
43. George Henry Clews presents Joyce with a bouquet, 1958
44. Joyce in *The Belles of St Trinian's*, 1954
45. Joyce in *Blue Murder at St Trinian's*, 1957
46. Athene Seyler and Joyce rehearsing for *Happy is the Bride*, 1957
47. Roy Boulting and Joyce
48. Reggie and Joyce on holiday, *c.* 1960
49. Joyce and her new Ford Corsair in Cumbria, *c.* 1965
50. William Blezard composing for Joyce, 1967
51. William playing Chopin, 1972
52. Stage manager Diana Lyddon, 1967
53. Joyce in her kitchen at Elm Park Gardens, *c.* 1970
54. Rene Easden at Parr's, 1941
55. Mrs Gabe at Elm Park Gardens, by John Ward, 1963
56. Mrs Agos, by John Ward, 1979
57. 'The Magic Circle' celebrating Christmas, 1961
58. The Anderson family and the Grenfells, Christmas Day, 1962
59. Benjamin Britten, Joyce and Peter Pears at the Red House, Aldeburgh, 1964
60. The wedding of Verily Anderson and Paul Paget, 1971
61. Joyce's favourite *Face the Music* team, 1976
62. Joyce at the Cowans' bookshop, Aldeburgh, 1979
63. Joyce and Reggie's golden wedding party, 1979
64. Joyce in Loweswater, Cumbria, 1963

The author and publishers would like to thank the following for permission to reproduce illustrations: Plate 16, Carley Dawson; 31, © Hulton Archive; 40, Daphne Oxenford; 44, London Films/British Lion, courtesy of The Kobal Collection; 45, British Lion, courtesy of The Kobal Collection; 46 and 47, Estate of Roy Boulting; and 64, Ivor Nicholas. All other illustrations are held in private collections.

Preface

On Friday 13th January 1939, Joyce Grenfell and her husband Reggie went to supper with the radio producer Stephen Potter in Chiswick. After an informal supper with poets, publishers and BBC types, everyone was expected to do a 'turn'. Stephen Potter gave a spoof lecture on 'Eng. Lit.' and his wife Mary sang a bawdy song to her ukulele. Joyce was used to playing the comic in the school dormitory or at family gatherings, and she volunteered a song about the eight-year-old Princess Margaret Rose. At a dinner party a month before, she had mimicked a lecture at the Women's Institute in her Buckinghamshire village and Potter now asked her to repeat it. In a dainty accent and clipped consonants, she embellished on the 'gifts that are not only easy to make, but ever so easy to dispose of', such as 'a boutonnière from empty beech-nut husk clusters'. The guests loved it and she became carried away, improvising on 'unusual mod-ernistic furniture' such as waste-paper baskets they could create from biscuit tins, obtained by 'having first made love to your grocer'.

When the laughter stopped, a tall man in his fifties approached Joyce. Herbert Farjeon was the director of a West End revue called *Nine Sharp*. He asked her if he could use her monologue and a week later, after hearing her again, invited her to appear herself. At first Joyce was reticent. She had other commitments: her garden, two dogs, writing radio reviews for the *Observer*, presiding over the local WI, and welcoming Reggie home from his office each evening. But her three favourite men – Reggie, her father and the editor of the *Observer* – encouraged her, and after a month of letters and phone calls from Farjeon, she finally agreed to perform in public. Her conditions were stringent: she would only come to the rehearsals of her own spots, she wouldn't join the chorus, she must have a wireless in her dressing-room and she had to catch the train home before the final curtain call.

Joyce Grenfell made her professional stage debut in Farjeon's *Little Revue* at the Adelphi Theatre on 21 April 1939. She had spent five months writing her monologue and a month rehearsing it. Performing in front of a packed audience was 'astonishing and thrilling'. She woke the next day to rave reviews, many comparing her to the American monologuist Ruth Draper.

For the rest of her life Joyce Grenfell told the story of the extraordinary coincidence of being discovered by Herbert Farjeon at the Potters' party and referred to it as 'what can happen to a housewife when she isn't looking'. But Joyce had been invited especially to meet Farjeon, who auditioned and rejected hundreds of hopeful entertainers. Letters, diaries and archives show that all her life Joyce had been determined to make a career in writing or entertaining, and her career as an entertainer actually owed little to chance. As a child she knew Noël Coward, Ruth Draper and Ivor Novello and wanted to be like them. For two years she had been asking producers at the BBC for work as an actress, and the bandleader Carroll Gibbons had already auditioned and rejected her as dance-hall singer. For several years she had been sending short stories to British and American magazines – with no success – but her poems had been published in *Punch*. Her family background was rich in potential. From her Virginian grandfather came energy and ambition; from her mother a talent to entertain and an extrovert personality; and from her father discipline and determination. The lack of children after nine years of marriage, together with a supportive husband, gave her both freedom and opportunity.

If she had only appeared in the *Little Revue*, Joyce would have been quickly forgotten. But she spent the next fifteen years writing for radio, newspapers and magazines; appearing in films and on television; and entertaining in Nissen huts and hospital wards all over Britain and the Middle East. She performed in five more West End revues before her first solo show in 1954. Her career extended over a further twenty-five years of hard and dedicated work, ending, after retirement from the stage, as a best-selling author. Yet Joyce always managed to create the illusion of being just a housewife who had wandered out of her kitchen and onto the stage. She is still well remembered nearly a generation after her death, not because of a happy accident in 1939, but because she was both talented and determined.

Acknowledgements

Joyce's life was so full and she made so many friends all over the world that it was impossible to do them all justice in one book; my apologies to anyone who feels inadequately treated. Nearly everyone who ever met Joyce has a story to tell about her, and I had to select only a few of these.

Every reader will have their own version of Joyce Grenfell, and writing a biography is about seeing someone through other people's eyes, while working out what spectacles those eyes are wearing: some are rose-tinted and others have become frosted with time. With a life as complex as Joyce Grenfell's it is inevitable that there will be discrepancies in stories: even when she told them herself, they varied. Her autobiographies are not reliable as a source for dates or facts: she changed stories to protect people alive at the time, forgot dates or muddled place names. I have chosen the versions which match most closely with contemporary primary sources.

I take full responsibility for this portrait of Joyce, but I could not have done it without her relations, colleagues and friends who have generously given me their time. The co-operation of so many has been both inspiring and tremendous fun. It also gave me the opportunity to make new friends in Somerset, Kent, Chelsea, Norfolk, Buckinghamshire, Surrey, Suffolk, Boston, New York and the south of France.

Thank you to the following people for all the information given me in interviews and letters: Sir Alistair Aird, Cass Allen, Janet Anderson, Verily Anderson, Luciana Arrighi, Alice Astor, Richard Baker, Frith Banbury, Nicholas Barter, Margaret Baxter, George Bauer, Leon Berger, Oliver Bernard, William Blezard, Svend Bok, Hilary Boyes, Betty Brooks, Judy Campbell-Birkin, Dame Frances Campbell-Preston, Ian Carmichael, David Chance, Joan Chandler, George Cole, Lady Silvia Combe (née Coke), Phillip Cotton, Jean and Christopher Cowan, the Dowager Countess of Cranbrook, Priscilla Cunningham, Pam and Terry Curry, Johnny Dankworth, Artillery Gunner Frank Darns, Irving Davies, Carley Dawson (née Robinson), the Duchess of Devonshire, Clive Evans, Michael G. Falcon, Tanya Fletcher, Margaret Flory, James Fox, Richard Garnett, Leonard Gershe, Dione Lady Gibson, Celia Goodman, Nadine Gordimer, Charlotte Gray, Kate Grimond, John Guilleband, Valerie Hadley, Philip Hale, Roberta Hamond, Tony Hampton, Judy Harris, Muffet Harrison, Anne Harvey, Tim Hely Hutchinson, Wynford Hicks, Arthur Hiller, Bevis Hillier, Richard and Mary Hoggart, Lady Rosamund Holland-Martin, Leslie Humphrey, Lady Susan Hussey, John Hutchinson of dresscircle.com, Jonathan James-Moore, Beryl Kaye, Nadine Lady Killearn, Cleo Laine, Daphne Lakin, Philip Lane, Lionel Larner, Brian Levison, Roy Loring, Andrew Lycett, Candida Lycett Green, Diana Lyddon, Katharine McCellan, Alan MacLean, Hugh Martin, Trevor Milne-Day, Sheridan Morley, Diana Lady Mosley, Norman Newell, Robin Nicholson, John Julius Norwich, Melita Norwood, Mary O'Hara, Marian O'Hare, Michael Olivier, Daphne Oxenford, Henry Paget, David Paramor, Graham Payn, Lang Phipps, Mary Phipps, Sally Phipps, Tommy Phipps, Julian and Valerie Potter, Helen Raikes (née Campbell-Preston), Bridget Reiss, Jennifer Rose, Sally Rose, Gwen Rosswick (née Cooke), Ken Russell, Anne Ryan, Julia de Saint Sauveur (née Fitch), Mr Michael Sanders, Paul Scofield, Denise Silvester-Carr, Richard Simon, the Earl of Snowdon, Raymond Stanley, Susan Stranks, Margot Strickland, Wendy Toye, Freda Troup, Peter Tunnard, Signalman Alfred Turner, Peter Ustinov, Alex Walker, John and Alison Ward, Keith Ward, Merlin Waterson, Eleanor Whitcombe, June Whitfield, Professor Bertram Willis, Mary Wilson, Elizabeth Winn, Mr John Winstanley, Norman Wisdom, Dr Patrick Woodcock, Bruce Woods-Jack, Geoffrey Wright, Joyce Young and Philip Ziegler.

Joyce left an amazing number of letters, manuscripts, radio and tele-vision programmes, notebooks and diaries in Britain and the USA. Thank you to the staff at the following archives for their invaluable help: Graeme Powell, Australian Collections and Services; Dr John Jones and Alan Tadiello, Balliol College, Oxford; BBC Written Archive Centre, Caversham; Bodleian Library, Oxford; British Film Institute; Chris Mobbs, British Library Sound Archive; Judith

LeGrove and Keiron Cooke, Britten Pears Library, Aldeburgh; the Burma Star Association; Rachel Wells, Central Chancery of the Orders of Knighthood; Pam Chance, Christian Science Publications Committee, London; Yvonne C. von Fettweis, Church History Department, First Church of Christ, Scientist in Boston, Mass.; Angela Steph, Clerk of the First Church of Christ, Scientist, London; Claremont Fan Court School, Esher; Cliveden Estate and House, Bucks; Ditchley Park, Oxfordshire; Penny Hatfield, Eton College Archive; Sally Bassington, Francis Holland School; Holly Callahan, Johns Hopkins University, Baltimore, MD; Lucy Cavendish College, Cambridge; Claire Brown, Middle East Centre, St Anthony's College, Oxford; Museum of Fine Arts Library, Boston, Mass.; National Museum of Performing Arts, Covent Garden; National Museum of Television and Radio, New York; Tim Knox, National Trust; Public Records Office, Kew; Spotlight enquiries; and University of Bristol Theatre Collection.

Thank you to the following for permission to quote material: Kate Fleming, for her mother Celia Johnson's biography; Clive James, for excerpts from his letters; the estate of Joyce Grenfell, for excerpts from her songs; and the estate of F. Scott Fitzgerald, for the quote from 'The Intimate Strangers', published by Quartet Books in *The Last Uncollected Stories*.

Practical support came from Rachel Anderson, Marie Baines, Mr and Mrs Baubus d'Uccles, Carole Bidder, the Rev. Jane Butterworth, Patricia Davies-Gilbert, Petra Dubilski, Rachel Hamdi, Joe Hampton, Vicki Harris, Tim Miller, Sally Phipps, Tommy and Mary Phipps, Bill Powers, Teresa Thompson, Simon Trewin and Amir Yasin of MCM Computers. Last but by no means least, Charles Hampton for his editorial, emotional and culinary support.

I dedicate this book to the memories of David Astor, Herbert Axell, Roy Boulting, Archbishop Donald Coggan, Joseph Cooper, Gervase Farjeon, John Grigg, Sir Rupert Hart-Davis, Katherine Moore, the Right Rev. Simon Phipps and Alice Winn, all inspiring people who shared their stories of Joyce with me before they died.

Janie Hampton
Oxford, 2002

Joyce Grenfell's Family Tree

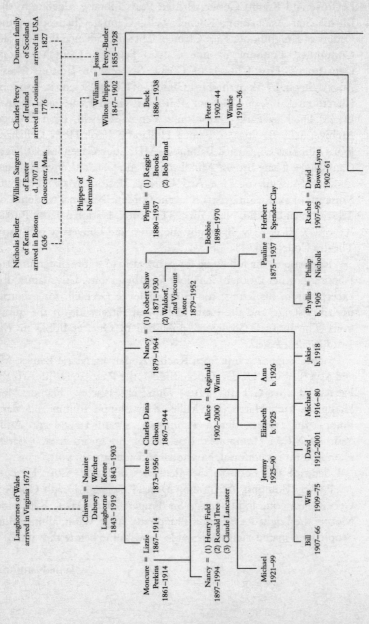

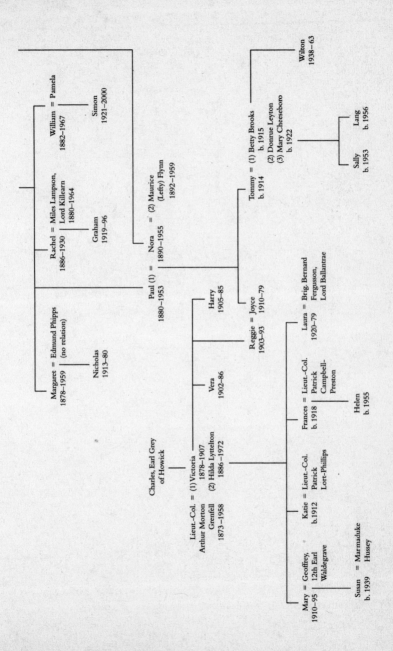

– 1 –

'I was born into a not-so-well-to-do family who had a great many
well-to-do relations. We only had titles by marriage. But not by birth.'

Joyce Grenfell

JOYCE GRENFELL'S FAMILY tree included American governors, transatlantic merchants and British landowners. Her mother, Nora Langhorne, was the youngest daughter of a Virginian millionaire and sister of Nancy Astor, the first woman to take her seat as an MP in Britain. Her father, Paul Phipps, was the eldest son of a British coffee merchant and a society beauty from New York. Both the Phipps and Langhorne families were in the exclusive New York 'Blue Book'. They went to society balls and the theatre and took care to marry their daughters to young men of social standing and wealth, preferably English aristocrats. The Phippses and Langhornes were enthusiasts for the special relationship between the USA and Great Britain as far back as the 1880s and were active in international events and politics into the mid-twentieth century.

The Langhornes went to Virginia from Wales in 1672 – ten years too late to qualify as a 'First Family'. Some of them lived in the Mississippi area, and Joyce's grandfather may have been a cousin of Samuel Langhorne Clemens, alias Mark Twain. Certainly the Langhornes of Virginia shared the same quick wit, wry sense of humour and ability to tell a story.

Joyce's grandfather Chiswell Dabney Langhorne, known as 'Chillie' and pronounced 'Shillie Langan', was born in 1843 and brought up on his father's plantation in Virginia. During the American Civil War he fought with the Confederates and when it was over, the Langhornes' slave labourers were released and the tobacco estate fell into ruin. Chillie was large, energetic, a ready mixer, well dressed and full of good stories, a man who could make any party go with his plantation songs and dancing. Near the end of the Civil War he married sixteen-year-old Nanaire Witcher Keene, a Virginian of Irish extraction who was gentle, artistic, musical and interested in people. For the first fifteen years of their marriage Chillie was employed as a night watchman, a piano salesman and an auctioneer of tobacco and horses. Nanaire's growing family and various relations were crammed into four rooms in a clapboard house in Richmond, the capital of Virginia.

In 1890, when Nora, the youngest of eleven, was still a baby, Chillie went completely bust. The family were sitting on their packing cases in the street when General Douglas rode by and offered Chillie work on the new Chesapeake and Ohio railway line. In only three years, Chillie used his charm to make his fortune as a railway contractor. By the time Nora was four years old, Chillie had made enough money to buy a large estate near Charlottesville in the foothills of the Blue Ridge Mountains.

Mirador was an 1825 colonial red-brick house to which Chillie added wide porches and two new wings. It was a house from *Gone With the Wind*, with white pillars, green-shuttered windows, a cobbled stableyard, and flowerbeds edged by box hedges. The Langhorne children led an idyllic country life. They shot squirrels and migrating bull-bats in the nearby woods and bullfrogs in the Mirador millpond. On the back line of the grass tennis court grew a cherry tree which Chillie refused to cut down. 'If they can't play well enough to negotiate the tree, they had better give up,' he said. The girls were brought up tough – they had to break their own horses, ridden side-saddle, for fox-hunting and show-jumping.

At weekends the Langhornes and their friends danced in the parlour to hired fiddle and banjo players; they sang, mimicked each other and told stories. One friend observed that 'The Langhornes are like street musicians – they entertain you whether you ask them or not.'

The Langhorne children learned their humour from the African-American staff employed at Mirador, most of whom had been slaves. To show respect, children always addressed the adult servants as 'Aunt' or 'Uncle'. There was Uncle John Pate the coachman, Aunt Ann Broady the housekeeper, and Winston Fountain, who wore a tailcoat and top hat when he drove the horse and carriage along the red clay road to Mirador. Aunt Veeny was born at Mirador before the Civil War and had escaped capture by the Yankees by hiding in a hollow log. When Chillie asked her who the father of one of her children was, she replied, 'If a jig-saw hit you, would you know which tooth it was?'

The Langhornes and their staff went to the local Episcopalian church. None of them was allowed to drink at home, so the sons made up for it after work and in later life, while the daughters all remained teetotallers. Keene, the oldest son, once bet he could charm his way across America on one dollar. He did – all the way from Virginia to California and back. His brother Buck had so much charm that it was said he could 'get on chatty terms with a tombstone'.

Lizzie, the eldest child, was closer in age to her mother than she was to her youngest siblings and resented her marriage to a poor Virginian before her family became wealthy enough to seek richer, more interesting husbands further afield. Her four younger sisters had the wealth and beauty to impress high society and they cultivated a mystical image of glamour and excitement which entranced men for miles. Each girl was different, with her own strong sense of identity, but all shared a tough upbringing and the determination to make the most of life. Young men flocked to Mirador to court the beautiful sisters, but had to contend with Chillie roaring at them. According to Nora he said: 'Etiquette is for people with no breeding, fashion is for people with no taste.'

Nora, Joyce's mother, was the baby, twenty-two years younger than Lizzie and spoiled by everyone. Her nanny was Aunt Liza Pie, who was born a slave and could neither read nor write but taught Nora the Negro-spiritual slave songs of her ancestors. She smoked a corncob pipe and completely trusted 'Mr Jesus' to protect her and her small charge. When she retired she was offered a house, but she said she would prefer a store, "cause I could git what I wants when I wants it'. Nora was good at boys' games, especially baseball. Lizzie's daughter Alice Winn was only ten years younger than Nora, and was fascinated by her aunt's mimicry and stories:

> Nora told Uncle Remus stories in the rural Virginian accent of an elderly ex-slave with stumbling gestures. Sometimes she mimed a 'Fairy Tailor', fitting an imaginary coat, measuring our

arms and placing the buttons. We squirmed with delight and interest while Nora laughed as much as her victim. Or she pretended we were chickens being prepared for the oven – sprinkled with salt, bay leaves under the arms, and finally trussed up by the legs. If you had an hour to spend with anyone in the world you'd have spent it with Nora. When Nora came into a room she made you feel as if you were the only person on earth. Mind you, as soon as she left, you were forgotten.

She sang delightfully, playing a guitar hung with coloured ribbons, and although she could only play in one key, she looked enchanting. However, she rarely got to the end of a song, for she was a compulsive giggler and every song ended in laughter.

One of Nora's party pieces was an imitation of her tall and beautiful sister Irene singing, 'Go tell Ant Nancy the old grey goose is dead.' It began in her schoolgirl Virginian accent, but halfway through the song her posture, breathing and enunciation changed as Nora imitated Irene after she had had singing lessons from the great opera trainer Jean de Reske.

Nora's mother died when she was thirteen years old and after that her father spoiled her even more. She changed school every time she told him she was unhappy, so she got little education; and anyway, Nora was too busy mimicking the teachers to learn much. Chillie bought everything Nora wanted, so she never learned the value of money and was always in debt. But she had an infinite capacity for laughter, generosity and sympathy which made it impossible to dislike her. She was vague, lacked concentration and rarely told the truth – she said later it was so much more fun to make things up.

In 1908, Nora was sent to stay in England with Nancy, the most energetic and powerful of the Langhornes. Desperate to escape the constraints of the family, she had married handsome, rich New Yorker Robert Gould Shaw when she was only eighteen. He drank heavily, they had nothing in common and Nancy finally divorced him when he threatened to commit bigamy by marrying another woman. That winter of 1905, Nancy and Phyllis took their children and nannies across the Atlantic for the fox-hunting season in Leicestershire. They both enjoyed the physical danger and made an impression on the hunting-field. Nancy returned the following season with her own hunters and on the boat home met millionaire's son Waldorf Astor, a handsome and charming bachelor. The Astor wealth was founded on fur and property-dealing in the early 1800s; after inheriting over $100 million – the equivalent now of £3 billion and all untaxed – Waldorf's father, William, had emigrated to Britain, where he bought several newspapers and two stately homes: Hever Castle in Kent and Cliveden in Buckinghamshire. Waldorf, the oldest, was sent to Eton and New College, Oxford, where he rowed, played polo, scraped a fourth-class degree in history and became the epitome of an English gentleman. Out of all her suitors, Nancy chose Waldorf for his wealth, kindness and his suitability as a stepfather for her son, Bobbie.

As a wedding present William Astor gave them Cliveden, the large Italianate mansion redesigned by Sir Charles Barry in 1850. Beyond the south-facing formal gardens, beechwoods drop sharply to the Thames, which winds and glints between the woods and fields, the town of Maidenhead a gentle blur in the distance. The head gardener worked with fifty men and boys on the 375 acres of park and garden, and outdoor staff included coachmen, chauffeurs and a dozen stable-hands. The one hundred indoor staff included three footmen, a full-time carpenter and a dozen house and laundry maids. The house was so large that coal and laundry were transported on a narrow-gauge railway in the basement. The heating consumed one hundred tons of coal a year, all carried upstairs in buckets by parlour maids.

While Waldorf concentrated on racehorse-breeding and politics, Nancy threw herself into modernising Cliveden and raising four more sons and a daughter.

Nora, aged eighteen, had recently tried to run away with an unsuitable man called Baldwin Myers and it was hoped that a quiet time in the English countryside would calm her down, and that she might even find a suitable husband.

'She couldn't meet a man without making him fall in love with her,' said Alice Winn. They often proposed and she usually accepted. She admitted she had 'a heart like a hotel, with all the lights blazing' and she felt it was rude to refuse a proposal of marriage. Consequently she was often engaged to several men at once and at one time was engaged to two brothers and their friend simultaneously. When they found out they sent her a friendly telegram signed 'Whitney, Webb and Whitney'.

On a previous visit to England, she became engaged to a Mr Valpy, from Dawlish in Devon, who travelled all the way to Virginia to claim his bride. Nora was terrified when she saw him and hid in a cupboard. After that, whenever the family wanted to frighten a child they would say that 'Mr Valpy of Dawlish' would get them.

Like her father, Nora could make any party a success. But she could never refuse an invitation and often accepted several for one evening. She was beautiful in an unusual way and was often asked to sit for her portrait. John Singer Sargent and Charles Dana Gibson both drew her, and Cecil Beaton photographed her. Nora had pale, flawless skin, with blue eyes, a good straight nose, smiling lips and fair, wild hair. Joyce described her as looking 'more eighteenth-century than twentieth; high cheekbones with apple rounded cheeks when she smiled; small pointed chin, and a curling mouth'. She remained slim and elegant all her life and her face barely aged. She also never grew up.

'It's not that Nora had no sense of right or wrong,' her sisters would say; 'she's just got no proper sense at all.' As long as everybody was laughing, then it must be all right, and it never occurred to her that her actions might make other people unhappy. Her older sisters thought she was going too far when she had her photograph taken wearing men's clothes *with her legs crossed*.

Nora wasn't interested in a husband for jewellery and large houses, but she did crave romance and excitement. So at Christmas Nancy and her sister Phyllis organised a family holiday to the Swiss skiing resort of St Moritz, inviting Lord Elphinstone in the hopes he would propose to Nora. But she was still in love with Mr Myers of Virginia so, in order to keep her sisters happy, she told them that Elphinstone had proposed, but wanted to keep it a secret. She moved the proposal from the slopes of St Moritz to the conservatory at Cliveden, and the 'secret' soon spread.

Chillie was delighted when he heard the news – a middle-aged peer was just what Nora needed. But Nora said that she could not take any man seriously who proposed on one knee, even if he did own a castle in Scotland.

By this time Nora's love for Myers was wavering and she agreed to stay in England for the London Season. Within a month her attentions turned to Paul Phipps, a thirty-year-old architect who had been at Eton and Oxford with Waldorf. Nancy wrote to her father, 'He is clean minded, high minded and clever and charming. I don't think she could have got a nicer man.' He was also well-educated, polite and had a promising career ahead of him. He was articled in the practice of Sir Edwin Lutyens, then Britain's most eminent architect. Paul Phipps was not brilliant – at Eton he only just passed his leaving exam, with 16 per cent in maths and 35 per cent overall, and at Balliol he scraped a third-class degree in classics – but he was kind and honest, with a quiet sense of humour. With his large ears and long, wide jaw, he was not traditionally handsome, but he dressed with style, and on the dance floor he spun with agility in his patent-leather dance pumps. Nancy reckoned that if anyone could tame Nora, Paul Phipps could.

His only defect was that, as a junior architect with no private income, he had little money, and her family knew that Nora would need plenty. Nancy pleaded with her father to approve, and to settle at least enough money on her to pay for her clothes and her own maid. Nora told her father that as she already knew her weak points, she had somewhere to start improving. She was determined to be 'good and true and square. If good doesn't come out in me at this time when I am so happy then there isn't any in me.'

Paul described Nora as 'clever in the cleverest way. Very original . . . has her own ideas and looks at things from her own point of view . . . extremely sensitive and artistic person, she has an observation which is quite uncanny. And what is not "harvested" by her "quiet eye" is not worth garnering. In fact she is the jolliest woman with the nicest point of view and the best companion I know.'

Chillie found it impossible to approve – he was in complete confusion. One minute Nora was engaged to a peer and the next to someone described only as 'the lantern-jaw boy'.

Paul Phipps may not have been rich or titled, but he was quite respectable. The Phipps family tree goes back to William the Conqueror's invasion of England in 1066. Since the seventeenth century Phippses had held positions of authority as MPs and landowners and ten Phippses were High Sheriffs of Wiltshire. In the eighteenth century, three Phipps brothers were respectively MP for Westbury, Governor of Bombay and Governor of Cape Coast Castle, now in Ghana.

Paul's beautiful and intelligent mother, Jessie Percy Butler Duncan, was brought up at No. 1, Fifth Avenue, New York, where her father was a wealthy banker and railroad magnate. The Butlers had been in America since they left Kent for America in 1636. Other American ancestors included a governor of Martha's Vineyard in the seventeenth century, and in the eighteenth century a governor of Mississippi and a pirate in the West Indies.

Three of Joyce's grandparents were American, but even her British grandfather thought little of crossing the Atlantic for work or pleasure. Wilton Phipps, a tea and coffee merchant from London, met Jessie in New York. They married there in 1876 and for the next ten years they travelled frequently between New York and London. In 1884 they took 3 Culford Gardens in Chelsea and with their four children soon became part of the London social scene. Paul's prep-school report said he was 'idle at first' but had a 'good perception of idiom and could with care write an excellent piece of prose'.

Among the Phippses' transatlantic neighbours in Chelsea were Henry James and Jessie's third cousins Emily, Violet and John Singer Sargent. John, the painter, was not sure whether to settle in London: although Henry James said he had 'an insolence of talent', the English critics regarded his portraits as 'reprehensibly audacious' and he had to make do painting friends and relations. Joyce's grandmother Jessie Phipps was painted by Sargent in 1884 when he was twenty-eight and wondering whether to continue as an artist at all. In the painting *Mrs Wilton Phipps*, her pale skin glows against the background, into which her dark hair blends. It is in the same style that Joyce adopted sixty years later – swept up above the ears, with a short, curled fringe. Her long face, large, deep-set eyes, small nose and straight back were all inherited by her grand-daughter. Sargent exhibited the portrait in New York and London and it helped launch his career as a society painter.

Nancy was sure that Paul Phipps was just the man to help Nora settle down, and that with a dowry from Chillie it could work. Bombarded with so many letters from Nancy, Phyllis and Nora about the wonders of Paul Phipps, Chillie lost his patience. He was being asked to stump up $4,000 (the equivalent now of over £100,000) to support a daughter he knew might change her mind any minute. Paul was not easily rebuffed, and after writing to Chillie himself, he took Nora back to America to convince him. It can't have taken long to win Chillie over, for in April 1909 the *New York Times* reported the marriage of Paul Phipps and Nora Langhorne in New York. They returned to Cliveden for their honeymoon, where Nancy decided to give Nora an allowance for her clothes and rent for a home in Knightsbridge. Chillie can hardly have believed Paul when he wrote that Nora 'takes tremendous interest in everything to do with the house & is a most excellent and *economical* housekeeper. She goes about in omnibuses all the time. She is excellent with the servants too & so dignified! We hope you will soon come over & see us & our home.'

– 2 –

Joyce Irene Phipps was born at 29 Montpellier Square, Knightsbridge, on 10th February 1910, three months before the death of Edward VII. When she was a month old, the first silent film was made in Hollywood and five months later Edison demonstrated the first talking motion pictures. Paul and Nora were thrilled to have a daughter but, like all parents of their class, had no intention of looking after her themselves. Lucy Sampson arrived as Joyce's nanny when she was a month old. She was pretty, with bright blue eyes, short legs and splayed feet. She wore a grey coat and skirt and starched white pinafore. When she bent down to kiss Joyce good-night, there was a comforting creak of whalebone. She had a special 'nanny' language: 'Hurry up now, you're all behind like the cow's tail'; 'Now up the stairs to Bedfordshire'; 'Don't care was made to care.' Lucy's father was a non-conformist lay preacher and she sang Joyce hymns while washing her with plenty of soap and elbow grease. Joyce recalled that Lucy was 'reassuring, comfortable, kind, good, cosy, loving and *always there*'.

Joyce's first cousin Alice remembered her as a baby. 'Joyce was the prettiest little thing. Everybody adored her. She was very intelligent and doted on by her parents. I remember the day when she learned to walk – we all sat around her applauding as she took her first steps.' Nora enjoyed dressing Joyce up in the finest tucked and smocked lawn, white socks and kid gloves. Her clothes were always simple, stylish and beautifully made.

Paul, however, was struggling to find enough architectural work. Waldorf Astor commissioned him to design Rest Harrow, a seaside house in Kent, and to modernise No. 4 St James's Square, Piccadilly. But that and other work from relations was not enough to maintain his family. When Joyce was nearly one, Paul decided to try his luck in

Canada. The family moved with Lucy and her sister Aggie as Nora's maid, to Winnipeg. Despite the recent construction of the Canadian Pacific Railway, which had transformed the small trading-post into a bustling boom-town, Paul failed to find enough work and they moved further west to Vancouver, a larger and more attractive city. Every afternoon Lucy took Joyce to the beach, where native Indians pitched their tents and fished for salmon in English Bay. One day Joyce decided to visit Granny Phipps who, she had been told, lived across the sea. She set off, and her clothes were soaked before Lucy pulled her out. The next day Lucy drew a line around Joyce's legs and told her not to get it wet – but the temptation to see the ink change colour was too great, so then a length of string was tied to Joyce's ankle. If she went too far, she received a gentle tug back on to dry land.

Although wealth was pouring into Vancouver, Paul just did not have enough ambition to make the most of it. There were three theatres in Vancouver and a burgeoning social life, but Nora, still only twenty-two and pregnant again, was homesick and lonely. At bedtime she sang Joyce the plantation songs Aunt Liza Pie had taught her, and by the age of three, Joyce could hold the tune while Nora sang the harmonies.

To cheer Nora up, Paul suggested that she take Joyce to Mirador for a holiday. Her Aunt Phyllis had recently modernised it with running water, a new tennis court and a swimming-pool. Here, in the summer of 1913, Joyce found her first hero – Phyllis's son Winkie. He was three months younger than her, but could run faster and jump higher. He could even climb trees. After the summer at Mirador, Nora could not face returning to Vancouver, so they all moved to New York in time for the birth of Thomas Wilton. Joyce's reaction to her new brother was to lean into his pram and bite the end of his nose.

'She hadn't done it to be cruel or mean,' said Tommy. 'It was simply her not very subtle way of putting me into the picture. And the picture was that she, Joyce Irene Phipps, was The Boss, that she wasn't going to put up with any nonsense, and that if we were ever going to establish any kind of working relationship for the future, I might as well understand, right from the start, exactly how things stood.'

Paul was optimistic he would find work in New York, but even with Astor connections he failed, and when war between Britain and

Germany looked likely, he enlisted with the regiment due to leave for Britain soonest – Princess Patricia's Canadian Light Infantry. Soon after this, Nora met a tall, handsome twenty-two-year-old called Maurice 'Lefty' Flynn, who had just divorced a chorus girl after only thirteen months of marriage. He was immensely handsome and charming, with a deep, resonant voice. As a student he had been one of the best Yale athletes, an all-American footballer, and had beaten all the records on the track and in swimming. His nickname came from his footballing skills. Nora and Lefty sang close harmony together, accompanied by their guitars. They were both natural entertainers, both romantics, and they fell in love. When they decided to run away together it didn't seem to occur to Nora that Paul would mind.

When Chillie Langhorne heard about the elopement, he threatened to shoot Lefty. The couple had been spotted in a small town in the Midwest, still singing, and Nora's brother-in-law Charles Dana Gibson was dispatched to retrieve her. When she was found, she did not appear concerned that she had no money and had abandoned her two small children. Gibson realised that shock tactics would be needed and told her that the police were coming and would arrest them both for bigamy. Nora left immediately, not waiting to consider exactly what bigamy was. Gibson delivered her to Chillie in New York, who put her on the next boat across the Atlantic, pointing out that she could not desert Paul and her babies during an international crisis.

There are no records of where Joyce, Tommy and Nanny Lucy were at this time, but they had probably been sent back to England with Alice, aged twelve. Her parents, Lizzie and Moncure Perkins, had both recently died, and she was to live with her aunt Nancy Astor at Cliveden.

It was on board the liner crossing the Atlantic that Joyce first became aware of an audience. She found herself alone in the passengers' lounge, dancing solo to the teatime orchestra. She was not exactly dancing but revolving, very slowly, with her eyes shut, and occasionally kicking up one leg. She realised that the grown-ups were watching her, and laughing, and she liked it.

When Nora finally reached England, Paul was waiting for her at Liverpool dock. He didn't mentioned the episode, preferring not to make a fuss. This may have been a mistake, for if he had, she would have known how much he loved her.

Nora was reunited with the children in Inverness-shire, where the Astors were on a grouse-shooting holiday. It was August 1914 and, with war imminent, Paul returned to London. The grown-ups appointed Alice 'Sergeant of the Glencoe Guards', with instructions to keep her dozen cousins in order. 'The worst soldier was Joyce Phipps as she reacted very slowly to my word of command. She didn't seem to have her heart in the business.' Maybe even at four years old Joyce was dimly aware of the chasm between her parents. After all this excitement Lucy decided she had had enough. She was replaced by Mary Edwards, and although she was kind, Joyce always felt that Mary preferred Tommy.

For the next four years, Joyce saw little of her father. Princess Patricia's regiment decided that, at thirty-five, he was too old to go into action. Paul disagreed, volunteered for the Third Sherwood Foresters and was sent to Ypres as a second lieutenant. At the start of the war, the highest casualties were from German snipers. Paul, with his skilled architect's eye, was promoted to captain as a musketry instructor, training soldiers to aim rather than just to fire wildly. As an example to the men, he gave up smoking his pipe and drinking alcohol, a pledge he kept for the rest of his life. By 1916 he was invalided out of the trenches with a damaged knee and promoted to major in the War Office as Assistant Director of Movements and Railways.

Meanwhile, the rest of the Phipps family joined their cousins and aunts at Cliveden, where the male servants had been replaced by female parlour maids. A Canadian Red Cross hospital was constructed in the grounds, and Nora became a Voluntary Aid Detachment nurse, with a starched white ankle-length uniform. It is unlikely that Nora took this, her first and last job, very seriously, but she enjoyed organising entertainment.

To help cheer up the wounded soldiers, a pantomime of *Hansel and Gretel* was improvised and Joyce, aged five, was a cast as a fairy. This exacting role involved her walking onto the stage, placing a single leaf to hide the sleeping Gretel and then exiting. Joyce was so thrilled by her costume – a silver star in her hair, wings clipped onto her Liberty bodice and her first ever long, white cotton stockings – that once on the stage she refused to come off again. She liked the people looking and laughing at her, and ignored the hissed instructions to come back. Eventually she had to be picked up and carried off the stage, protesting loudly.

Two years later, Nora invited professional dancers Irene and Vernon Castle to perform for the patients. Joyce was so enthralled by the sight of an adult woman with bobbed hair wearing black satin trousers that she decided to be a dancer. In her mind she was slim, and she wanted to leap and spin with light and grace, but she had a square body with matching legs: a healthy, solid child. Her greatest joy was the daily removal of the stiff, leather gaiters that protected the shins from cold, while leaving the knees exposed to biting winds. Newly released legs could feel the air and were suddenly able to jump higher, skip longer and dance perfectly. However, Paul was concerned about the structure of the house, which shook whenever she jumped, so Joyce's bedroom slippers were replaced with a pair of blocked satin ballet shoes. She practised in secret with the wind-up gramophone, though never progressed much beyond wobbling, in great pain, around the table edge.

Nora was too busy to pay Paul much attention, and their marriage was not helped when he accepted a post in the British War Office in Washington, DC. Nancy tried to keep her sister in line, but Nora was constantly distracted by men. She took advantage of both Paul's absence and an atmosphere of jollity occasioned by young men such as Nancy's eldest son Bobbie Shaw, now a handsome subaltern in the Royal Horse Guards, on home leave from the Western Front. Bobbie took a malicious delight in upsetting family life at Cliveden, so was quite happy to introduce his fellow-officers to Nora and even to chaperone her while they canoodled on the sofa. Her niece Nancy Lancaster claimed, 'Nora went through the Guards like a knife through butter.'

Waldorf Astor's sister, Pauline Spender-Clay, and her family lived at Ford Manor in Surrey, which became the next home to the Phippses. Ford, a Jacobean manor which Paul had renovated, was large enough to become a convalescent home for wounded soldiers and to house the Spender-Clay and Phipps families in the servants' quarters. Every day Joyce rode her bicycle slowly and carefully to Miss Griffith's dame school in the next village. She was a very safe child, and never took risks or enjoyed jumping off haystacks. She learned to read with *Reading Without Tears*, written in 1861 by Mrs Favell Lee Mortimer, the author of a series on religious instruction for infants. Joyce wept through the Victorian horrors: 'A coach ran over Jack and crushed him. He was not killed. When he got well he was not as rude as he used to be', which led on to 'Sally was three. Yet she was a thief. Sally stole a pat of butter. Nurse said that Sally was a thief,' and bigger ideas: 'God is on high. He can see you. You will die. Men sin. God cannot sin.' In spite of Mrs Mortimer, Joyce adored reading, but adults frowned upon too much: children might get 'ideas', and it reduced their intake of fresh air. Fiction before lunch was especially bad for them.

When the war ended, Paul returned from Washington and Nora decided that she would try harder to make the marriage work. 'I know I must stick to Paul if it is possible and I am going to, but it isn't easy,' she wrote to her sister Irene.

Both Paul and Nora were urban people – the countryside was all right for short holidays packed with rural pastimes, but not for living in – so they moved back to Chelsea. Chelsea in the 1920s was a mixture of elegance and poverty. In the Regency squares such as St Leonard's and the Paultons lived well-off people with artistic leanings. Within shouting distance of Joyce's home there were families of seven living in one-room tenements with no running water, let alone gas or electricity. The houses were bug-ridden in summer, freezing in winter and infested with rats all the year round. The public baths opposite Chelsea Town Hall were called 'the sheep dip'.

The Phipps family took public service seriously. Jessie, Joyce's grandmother, was a London County Councillor and the first woman chair of the Education Committee, and was created a dame in 1926. Aunt Margaret Phipps became Chelsea's first woman mayor, and her husband Edmund was knighted for his work at the Board of Education. Nora's style of philanthropy was more spontaneous. One chilly Saturday she met a woman in the street who had no blankets for her children, so she rushed home, took the blankets off all the beds and gave them to the needy family. Joyce knew that she ought to admire this act of generosity but, given that the shops were closed until Monday, found the weekend very cold.

Paul set up an architectural practice and the family moved first into a flat and then round the square to 28 St Leonard's Terrace. The early-nineteenth-century house had four storeys plus a basement, and attic rooms for servants. The front rooms had wrought-iron railings and a small paved front garden overlooking the cricket pitch of Burton Court. On the back of the house was a studio, in which a previous owner had painted live horses and the Phippses kept their piano and gramophone. It was a short walk to Ranelagh Gardens, next to the Royal Chelsea Hospital, where Joyce played with her friends while their nannies chatted on benches. As anxious as any eight-year-old to conform, and obeying her plump friend Flavia, she became a founder member of the Followers of Bonnie Prince Charlie. She never understood why Bonnie Prince Charlie needed following, or which way he had gone, but the Followers spent many afternoons plotting under laurel hedges. Joyce was sadly lacking in loyalty and the allure of Maisie, who had founded the Brown Beans, was too great. The Brown Beans were more up to date – their purpose was not to support a long-dead, faraway prince but to Help Others. This involved much discussion, and the wearing of a brown pinafore with yellow blanket stitch around the hem. She didn't stay long with Maisie, either, before she was compiling the rules of the Happy Hours Club, which met under another bush. They promised, *in writing*, not to tell lies, sneak or to use rude words such as 'Dam, Ass, Lord, Gosh, Devil, Dash, My stars and stockings, Drat, Golly my aunt, Bally and Mercy on us'.

Presumably, the Brown Beans were inspired by the Brownies, which Baden-Powell had begun only four years before. As soon as they arrived in Chelsea, Joyce became a keen Brownie and made friends with another stout member of the Pixie Six, Penelope Chetwode, daughter of the Commander-in-Chief of the Army in India. Having earned their 'Brownie wings', they flew up to Girl Guides together on the same day.

Joyce attended Miss Burman's dame school nearby, where, aged eight, she had her first speaking part, as a starving burgher of Calais. This plump child with pink cheeks was determined not to forget her immortal line. She wrote it in black ink on her hand: 'Bread bread give us bread or we shall surely starve.'

Sundays were usually spent with Granny Jessie Phipps, who still lived in her seven-bedroomed house in Chelsea, with six indoor staff and a chauffeur. Although small and feminine, she was no longer the beauty painted by Sargent and, in her black widow's weeds, Joyce found her hard to love. She taught Joyce not to whistle or run down a passage, to be polite to servants and how to enter a room quietly. She was very self-disciplined: after her morning cold bath she always put her buttoned boots on first, so that she could do imaginary skipping in her bedroom.

Conversation at Sunday lunch in the dark, panelled dining-room was limited to certain topics – which certainly excluded God and Drains. Children were not encouraged to speak, let alone have ideas of their own. Tommy remembers the house as dark and stuffy and that his grandmother drank whisky with every meal.

The highlight of Sunday came after luncheon, when the children were dismissed to the basement to entertain the senior servants. Whether they really enjoyed it or not, Mrs Creed the cook, Mr Parker the butler, Mr Leach the chauffeur, Miss Griffin the lady's maid and Miss MacDonald the housemaid laughed at the children's jokes, riddles and conjuring tricks. The kitchenmaid and the odd-job boy had to stay outside. Although small, Joyce found it a gratifying audience: Miss Griffin mouthed the words of each song and clicked her tongue in amazement and the cook laughed loudly, while Miss Mac slapped her knees with joy. Mr Parker played the flute and sang 'Cavalleria Rusticana', which he called 'Cavalry Rusty-can-opener'. Joyce thought that very witty.

For country air, Jessie Phipps rented a small house in Chorleywood, Hertfordshire, then in the depths of the countryside. On summer weekends, Joyce picked blackberries and learned how to milk a cow.

In 1919, Mary Edwards moved on and Lucy Sampson returned, not as a nanny but as 'nursery-governess'. Joyce was thrilled. Lucy replaced her grey uniform with a maroon tailored suit and accompanied Tommy and Joyce to school, supervised their homework and bedtime, took them to their weekly piano lessons at the Wigmore Hall and even learned to play too. She gave her charges undivided attention and a regular supply of wholesome food and warm clothing, and instilled in them a lifelong concern about regular bowel habits. Lucy's philosophy embraced socialism, royalism and a strict adherence to table manners: 'Sing at the table, die at the workhouse' was one of her mottoes.

Between social engagements, Nora loved visiting the nursery and entertaining the children with stories of her day. She would use the voices of all the women she had met – on trains, in shops, and particularly American women with tired feet. One day on her way home, Nora heard a mother yelling from her window, down to her small daughter below, 'Ruby! RUBY! Rubay-ay-ay! Put down that cat! Put down that cat, I say! You don't know where that cat's nose 'as been!' After that, whenever something seemed a little dicey, they would say, 'You don't know where that cat's nose 'as been.'

Nora invented a game called 'Ladies': Nora as 'Mrs Jones' and Joyce as 'Mrs Brown' went out shopping, aired their babies in Kensington Gardens and discussed life, their children and their friends. Mrs Brown and Mrs Jones had a variety of accents to suit all occasions.

Joyce was not so amused when Nora used her talents in public, especially on trains where there was no escape. Nora would suddenly become French or speak in an imaginary language with Balkan-style rhythms and vowels. Joyce and Tommy would squirm with embarrassment as the passengers puzzled where she came from. Worse still, she sometimes forgot who she was supposed to be, and reverted to her own accent. Even as a child, Joyce often felt towards her mother more like an elder sister than a daughter.

Chillie Langhorne died in 1919, when Joyce was just nine. This seems not to have concerned Joyce, but it had a disturbing effect on Nora. Chillie had left $1.3 million, held in a trust for his twenty or so descendants, but Nora had no direct access to these funds. She went shopping anyway, and within a year Paul was forced to ask his in-laws to pay off her debts. In one year she spent over £5,000 – equivalent in 2002 to £200,000 – on clothes and taxis alone. She took so many taxis that most of London's drivers knew her by name. She bought four new pairs of silk stockings a week, at a cost of £365 a year. Her brothers-in-law sympathised with Paul and considered Nora a 'dipsomaniac in clothes'. Paul's only complaint was that, whenever Nora's suitors took her to the Ritz, the bill was sent to him. He still adored her, and whatever she got up to, he did not want to lose her. Nancy was infuriated to hear that Nora claimed to friends that she made all her own clothes. Maybe they were harsh on Nora – she neither drank nor gambled, and it would have taken a lot more silk stockings to make a dent in Chillie's trust, worth over £100 million today. Nora's real failing was her inability to see cause and effect – on either relationships or spending sprees. Waldorf threatened that if the spending at couture houses continued, he would place an advertisement in a newspaper warning against Nora's debts, and the Phippses would be forced to move from the temptations of London to a cottage in the country. Nora fainted at this news, and promised to try harder. That was one thing she *was* consistent at – promising – and somehow everyone forgave her because she was such fun.

Nora entertained her children so delightfully that they forgot that she was not there all the time. She often told a long-running saga about a fictional family called the 'Buttonhooks', who had adventures to suit all ages and tastes. In her autobiography Joyce recounts in detail how her mother went to tea at Buckingham Palace to show the Queen of Romania how to make a dress out of one piece of fabric. The story is very plausible – Queen Marie was a friend of the Astors who often stayed at Cliveden, and Nora would have happily gone to tea at the Palace. But the story has all the hallmarks of the Buttonhook family. It is the details, so masterfully chosen for an eager child waiting at home, that give it away. Is it likely that princes in their mid-twenties would throw scones in the presence of their strict parents and royal visitors? Or that Nora left her old woolly jacket with the footman rather than let the Prince of Wales see it? Far more likely that she left it at the Ritz while visiting a male friend. It was so much more fun to turn an illicit outing into a royal adventure.

If Joyce and Tommy had been good, such as going to the dentist, they would be rewarded with a surprise from Nora's present cupboard – silk flowers, a notebook or a hat ribbon. These small gifts meant far more than conventional presents from their rich aunts.

'The nearest person I ever met to Nora was Marilyn Monroe,' said her nephew David Astor. 'They had the same innocent, flirtatious way of moving. She used to wear a pleated skirt and twirl it the way Marilyn Monroe did. Aunt Nora was very cheeky – she was the grown-up that all children loved to play with. She would happily get down on all fours and play bears behind the sofa. We adored her visits to the nursery.'

Although both parents encouraged their children to believe in themselves, Paul's influence on Joyce was of a different kind. He taught her self-discipline and, at weekends, an appreciation of art and music. From the top of a no. 11 bus he pointed out interesting buildings as he took her to the National Gallery and to concerts in Queen's Hall. Joyce later recalled how, when she was about nine, 'My father and I were looking at a wall in Hampton Court. He said, "Look at the colour in those bricks," and I said, "Yes, they are red." "No, look again." I looked and suddenly saw all these different colours coming out, that I had never noticed. They were waiting there to be discovered and seen.' Paul had three cardinal pieces of advice which Joyce never forgot: 'Always wear wool next to the skin; never stand up in an open boat; and never get funny with a man wearing a peaked cap.'

Sixty years later Joyce looked back on her childhood and said:

There's no denying my privileged background. I was never cold, I had holidays, fee-paying schools, marvellous hand-me-down clothes from generous cousins. The real privilege was having a family of encouragement and affection, and there was always an ear ready to listen. My father taught me self-discipline and true values from a very early time: a powerful feeling that good overcomes evil. If you are brought up like that, that is the privilege.

Every Christmas the children went to the pantomime at the Chelsea Palace Theatre. Outside, pedlars sold hot chestnuts, baked potatoes and toffee apples while buskers entertained the queues shuffling towards the stalls or the gods. The audience booed the wicked barons, sang the words printed on a fly-screen and admired the lines of girls tap-dancing in red shoes. Joyce had first fallen in love with the theatre when, aged seven, she was taken to see *A Box of Tricks*, a wartime revue at the Hippodrome. She was sure that the chorus girls were children because they had skipping ropes and ankle socks.

When Joyce was ten, she and Nora joined a crowd in Knightsbridge to see the film star Mary Pickford and director Douglas Fairbanks, who were on their honeymoon. Nora bought Joyce a Mary Pickford curly wig which she wore all the time, only occasionally lending it to special friends.

Nora and Paul were part of a cosmopolitan, artistic circle, and writers, painters and actors frequently called at St Leonard's Terrace. The actress Gertrude Lawrence, smelling of gardenias, arrived with restless excitement and brought Joyce thoughts of Glamour. Silent-film star Rudolph Valentino came to tea but was a disappointment to both Nora and Joyce – he was so small.

On 10 February 1920, Joyce's tenth birthday, Nora's luncheon guests were the actress Mrs Patrick Campbell and twenty-one-year-old Noël Coward, who had just sold his first play. 'Noël was a rather condescending young man, paper thin, with a faint lisp,' wrote the actress Beatrice Lillie, another regular guest. 'He was already writing songs, songs with a difference. Instead of the usual moonlight and roses, there was a dash of vinegar.'

Mrs Campbell scared Joyce rigid with her enormous black velvet hat and enormous black velvet eyes. In her deep black velvet voice she leaned across the table and asked Joyce: 'Are you . . . harpy?' Joyce was not sure: she didn't always approve of her mother's friends.

The third guest at her tenth-birthday lunch was twenty-seven-year-old Ivor Novello, the author of the song *Keep the Home Fires Burning*, who was about to appear on the London stage. According to Beatrice Lillie, Novello had 'dreamy brown eyes, pale face and jet-black hair' and looked 'absolutely like God's gift to matinee fans'. He sent Nora Parma violets, and Joyce told her friends they were for her.

When Novello appeared in the silent film *The Bohemian Girl* with Gladys Cooper and Ellen Terry, Joyce fell in love with him and decided she wanted to be an actress. It was not the actual job of acting that appealed to her, but the glamorous lifestyle of dancing and chocolates.

After meeting Joyce, Noël Coward sent her *Five Children and It* by his favourite author, Edith Nesbit. The book was a perfect choice – Joyce hated fairy tales, magic and most of all *Alice in Wonderland*, which made her feel as if she had a fever. She liked books about realistic people she could identify with, and E. Nesbit became her favourite author too.

Joyce loved going with Nora to the annual Chelsea Theatrical

Garden Party in aid of the Actor's Orphanage, where for a penny Maurice Chevalier would sing a song, or Marie Lloyd sell you a bunch of flowers. One year, Joyce bought a silk top hat for sixpence, which Tommy wore in the garden all summer.

During her tenth year, Joyce's desires became less glamorous: she wanted red hair in pigtails, a dental plate, freckles and glasses. She discovered that if she walked with her face turned up when it rained, it *felt* as if she had freckles. The novelty of a dental plate wore off after three days, and consequently her bottom teeth remained interestingly arranged all her life.

However, none of these would have been apposite in her role as bridesmaid at the wedding in 1920 of Lady Cynthia Curzon to Oswald Mosley at St James's Palace. According to *The Times*, the seven bridesmaids wore 'palest eau-de-nil chiffon dresses and floral wreaths'. Not mentioned were the silk stockings Joyce wore for the first time. They were attached with tapes to her Liberty bodice, but during the signing of the register one stocking slipped down. She turned to a kindly-looking man with a beard and asked him if he had a safety pin. He hadn't, but he made a sign to someone and a pin was produced. The gentleman helped Joyce to secure her stocking and she rejoined the procession of bridesmaids down the aisle. Years later she learned that the bearded gentleman was George V.

– 3 –

D URING HER CHILDHOOD, Joyce dreamed that she would grow up to be very brave and noble and save many lives. Meanwhile she wanted to go to the sort of girls' school that she read about in *Mona of the Upper Third* and *The Madcap of St Mary's*, with a proper school uniform. She was thrilled when at the age of ten she was enrolled at Francis Holland School, close to home in Chelsea. When the serge gymslip, white shirt and grey woollen stockings arrived, she lovingly placed them by her bed so she could watch over them all night.

The school had been founded forty years earlier to give young ladies an academic education with a Church of England grounding and offered modern subjects such as science and maths. Every morning Miss Carlson, the headmistress, conducted 'Swedish drill' for the girls in the playground. The names of Joyce's classmates evoke the period: Lettice Vivian, Rachel Delmar-Morgan, Nancy Bowes-Lyon, Patience Henn-Collins and Barbara Chetwynd Stapylton. Without working too hard, Joyce remained somewhere in the middle of the class.

Drama was important at the school, a subject which at first disappointed Joyce. In order to give more pupils the chance to act in *As You Like It*, Miss Morrison had allotted two casts of equal status. While cast A performed for the Bishop of London, cast 1, with Joyce as First Lord, performed for the chairman of the School Council. She never forgot the unpunctuated line: 'Indeed my lord the melancholy Jaques grieves at that and in that kind swears you do more usurp than doth your brother that hath banished you.' Distinctive for its lack of depth of character or opportunity for laughs, it seems to have squashed her ambition to be an actress. The brown lock-knit knickers she had to wear cannot have helped either.

Her dream of becoming a dancer came to grief in the gym. She had very little 'spring', and when other girls leaped nimbly over the wooden horse, she lumbered up and then clambered over it.

Surmounting these challenges was made easier by the comforting and reliable presence at home of Lucy, whom Joyce adored even more than her own mother. Lucy taught Joyce how to see the good in people, even those who were unkind. She may not have read many books, but she was wise, steady and could be relied on. When Tommy was eight he was sent to board at Highfield prep school. It was a shock being away from home and he tried to run back, but his school cap was recognised by the local stationmaster and he was returned to school, wiser and sadder. Unknown to either of their children, Paul and Nora had decided that Lucy should stay only until Tommy was boarding and Joyce had begun her periods. 'I didn't even know there was going to be such a thing,' Joyce recalled, 'although there had been woolly little talks about regular times for purifying the blood stream and how wonderfully we are made and there was no need to worry about it: and I didn't. I was surprised by my first monthly, and then Lucy left. I knew it must happen, but when it came it was a misery.'

Joyce came home from school one day to find that Lucy had gone, with no warning. Paul and Nora thought it would be easier for her not to say goodbye. She was heartbroken – Lucy had been her 'ever-fixed star' since she was a month old, and this separation was far worse than the one when she was four. 'The day that Lucy left me I felt a desolation that was hard to bear.' Even though she had gone to a family nearby, and could be visited, she was no longer Joyce's special nanny. Joyce changed from being a quiet, subservient child to an insecure yet bossy adolescent, inclined to mimic the staff behind their backs. She could reproduce exactly Miss Savoury's sarcastic rise of the eyebrow when a girl's Latin prep was not up to scratch. But she had to cope with public humiliation after she wrote, 'This step has not been dusted' on the main stairs. The headmistress called all the girls together and demanded a confession for insulting a maid. Joyce was surprised at the fuss but owned up and was made to apologise to the hurt maid. When Miss Kiddle, her scripture teacher, wrote to Nora complaining that Joyce was not sufficiently interested in her prayer book, Joyce destroyed the letter before it reached home. She then wished she hadn't – her guilt was a worse punishment than her parents' possible disappointment in her poor scripture studies.

From the age of eleven one of Joyce's best friends was Carley Robinson, daughter of an American composer. Joyce and Carley went to the silent movies in King's Road together at weekends and after tea they acted out the romantic films they had seen. 'Joyce's living room in St Leonard's Terrace had French doors leading to the garden, with long curtains to the floor,' remembers Carley. 'One at a time we got behind the curtains and then burst out, depicting Joy – Terror – Anger – Fear, with great passion.' With the gramophone playing Schubert's *Unfinished Symphony*, they rolled their eyes and heaved their non-existent bosoms as they suffered dramatically.

In 1923, Paul was converted by Nancy Astor to Christian Science and thirteen-year-old Joyce soon followed suit. The Church of Christ, Scientist had been established by Mary Baker Eddy in 1879 in Boston, Massachusetts, and the religion soon spread to Britain. With a basis in Protestant non-conformist Christianity, Christian Scientists believe that God is responsible for the good in creation, and that all evil, including bodily sickness, is due to human illusion, 'mesmerism' or 'error'. They recognise Jesus as the Son of God and Saviour, who expressed God's healing power. Christian Science teaches that God is a loving father *and* mother, not an avenger, and that people are created in the image of God with a spiritual rather than material identity. All creation exists as 'spiritual ideas', man and woman being the highest, animals and plants being lesser ideas. Mary Baker Eddy believed in sexual and racial equality at a time when the livelihood of most rich Americans depended on the existence of slavery, and women were subjugated by the state, their fathers and their husbands. She discouraged drinking and gambling while encouraging 'wit, humour, and enduring vivacity', and taught that life should be expressed with active love and charity. Christian Scientists spend some time every day praying and 'Doing the Lesson' – reading selected extracts from the Bible and Eddy's *Science and Health With Key to the Scriptures*. There are no ordained clergy, but there are Christian Science 'practitioners' trained in spiritual healing.

As Nancy Astor's new family with Waldorf grew, she had suffered from 'nervous exhaustion', 'underfed nerves' and even 'organs out of place', but following an abdominal operation in 1914, she found that Christian Science gave her self-confidence and health. It took Nancy a further ten years to convince Nora, Paul and then Waldorf. Nora tried to be a Christian Scientist all her life, but always had great difficulty. Although a teetotaller, she chain-smoked – lighting up as soon as she came out of church, though never in front of her daughter. Paul took Christian Science seriously and was elected as a 'First Reader' in London's First Church of Christ, Scientist, in Sloane Terrace. He persuaded some of his Phipps relations to read *Science and Health*, but they all remained Anglicans.

Paul and Nora decided that Joyce should go to Clearview, a new girls' boarding-school for 'daughters of gentleman Christian Scientists'. Set in a large Edwardian house in Norwood, south London, it was run by Mr and Mrs Gordon Packer, who had a relaxed attitude to academic subjects and soon allowed Joyce to give up algebra.

'Joyce was always very religious, even as a child,' remembered her cousin Alice. 'She was very orderly minded, which helps with Christian Science.' Joyce thought that life was clear cut, and everything was either Right or Wrong, Good or Evil, and all one had to do was embrace the former and reject the latter. Even at Clearview school, Joyce found that many of the girls, and even some teachers, were wanting in their convictions. Joyce was the only one of the thirty-two Langhorne and Phipps first cousins to remain a lifelong Christian Scientist.

Her favourite teacher at Clearview was Miss Hewson, who taught English. 'She was a darling teacher and it was lovely to talk to her about books and the theatre,' said Joyce fifty years later. 'Miss Hewson wasn't the sort of person one would have a crush on, but she was very popular. She was a maiden lady of sensitivity and imagination and we responded to that.'

Joyce was furious when Miss Hewson chose a 'serious and boring play' called *The Golden Doom* for the girls to perform to their parents. She played a sentry who had to stand to attention for two hours. When presented with the costume she wrote in her diary, 'Ye Gods & little fishes, the helmet looks like a treacle tin inverted. Oh awful play. How I do hate you. But I'd rather die than tell Miss Hewson because she works herself to the bone.' Joyce was cast for her height rather than her skills, and usually had to play men. The only female part she had was the manly Miss Poole in Mrs Gaskell's *Cranford*, with the immortal line 'Men? I know all about men. My *father* was a MAN!'

The school was taken to see *Hiawatha* at Crystal Palace and *As You Like It* at the Old Vic. Joyce thought that Edith Evans played 'the most charming of Rosalinds – she was genius. I don't know when I've enjoyed a play more in my life.' This was the moment when Shakespeare's poetry first came alive and suddenly the lines 'glistened and the whole universe was translated into ideas'.

'I really believe I'd rather like to write when I grow up, but I don't think I'm clever enough yet,' Joyce told her diary. A novel soon followed: 'It was the third day of the Lees large house party for the season, and as the weather was warm many of the guests indulged in hammocks.' Gloria, the heroine with violet eyes, wistful smile and pale green chiffon dress, 'stood in front of her mirror and gazed questionably at her reflection therein'. On the night of her first dance, Gloria's rich father learns he has lost his fortune. The shock kills him. Gloria is distraught: ' "I am an orphan and penniless" and she gave a mirthless laugh. When at last Gloria fell asleep, it was through crying herself there.' Undaunted, she set off for Hollywood but fell off a train on the way. A passing cowboy called Brook Gibson (the surnames of two of Joyce's aunts) found her, 'her face deathly white and one leg *crumbled* underneath her body'. In just two weeks the cowboy nursed Gloria back to health. Without a backward glance, she continued on to Hollywood, where she became a film star. Much later, on location, she was reunited with Brook and all ended in happy matrimony. By now Joyce's favourite authors were E. F. Benson and P. G. Wodehouse, but her writing was strongly influenced by the dozens of films she watched.

Joyce looked forward to piano and singing lessons but her music teacher was 'an ass – so sloppy'. She taught herself the ukulele and entertained the dormitory with the latest popular songs. Extra elocution was taken with Miss Avery – a small, deaf cockney lady who taught Joyce about 'Breathing'. There were crocodile walks along the suburban streets and games every afternoon. 'I was completely the wrong shape – big and fat. I had the biggest feet in the school, which at one point seemed to me a mark of distinction.' She rarely hit the hockey ball but she liked netball because she could almost touch the net. In spite of her weight, she could climb up a rope-ladder and she loved country dancing. Joyce cried all afternoon when she and Peggy Beaton were thrown out of the school tennis team after losing to Streatham Girls' College. Friendships were important, but had to be kept in check. When Peggy had a 'pash' on Muriel and Pauline confessed to a pash on Joyce, Joyce remonstrated that 'pashes are not Christian' and they should love each other like sisters.

Every afternoon the girls had Silence Time, followed by hat-making, mending or gardening. Each girl had her own garden and, although Joyce was conscientious, she found it difficult to get the timing right. 'Nancy, Daphne, Evangeline, Bunty, Vallette, Nell and Viv all got prizes – I did not. My garden was chock full of things that don't flower until August.'

On Saturday nights the gramophone was wound up and the girls danced the Charleston and the tango with each other or the female teachers. Sometimes Paul joined his daughter but she had to wait until all the teachers had danced with him. Nora never came too but sent ice-cream instead. Girls who had received too many 'conduct marks' missed this fun, having been sent to bed at six o'clock on Saturdays. Joyce tried hard to be a perfect schoolgirl, but it was an effort not to always know best. 'One Girl, One Basin' was a difficult rule to keep: sharing a basin was so much more friendly.

After she received eight conduct marks in one month she resolved to be more law-abiding. Not long after, she was summoned by Miss Dollamore and warned to 'pull up' as her work was slacking. She had just received two detentions – one for poor scripture and one for saying, 'Blast the clock' when it disturbed her concentration during a sewing lesson. Joyce promised never to talk in the dormitory after lights-out again. Playing the ukulele was different.

Every Sunday morning the school attended the local Church of Christ, Scientist, where girls were encouraged to give personal testimonies about their healings. When 'Betty gave an awfully nice testimony about her foot,' it inspired Joyce to give her first testimony about the healing of her headaches. Sadly, as soon as they left church, the headache returned.

When chickenpox broke out in the school, they stopped going to church and parents were asked to decide whether their daughters should stay. Joyce worried that her parents would not trust her ability to resist the disease, but was also secretly frightened that her faith would not be strong enough. She believed that the girls who caught it were not trying and had allowed 'error' to take over. During the following holidays, Joyce found three spots on her back and went to a doctor for reassurance that they were not the dreaded chickenpox.

For the first half of 1926, Joyce kept a red leather pocket diary. Each tightly written, pencilled page was filled to the bottom right-hand corner. From it emerges a busy girl who is struggling to maintain her own high standards of behaviour. She has plenty of friends, whom she entertains with imitations of teachers, bus conductors and cockneys. Unlike many adolescents, there was never any animosity against her parents, whom she adored and wished she could have been with more. She could not understand rebellious behaviour. Her schoolfriend Val was 'rather stubborn. It seems queer that she should be. I should have thought her mother would have seen to that.'

The only escape from school was going to the dentist – the one form of medical intervention that the Phipps family chose to use. Joyce loved her dentist, Dr Spindels, but more important it was an opportunity to see her mother. However, Nora was liable to forget about dentists' visits. She didn't bother with half-day holidays either. Joyce had to hide her disappointment when Connie, Nora's maid, would turn up instead, bearing sweets and magazines. On her sixteenth birthday Joyce wept because neither her mother nor her beloved Lucy sent her a present. Her father sent her ten shillings, though, and schoolfriends gave her gramophone records and books. The next day she cheered up when she received a pair of gloves from Nora, and was promoted to the second netball team as goalkeeper.

When Nora did come to take Joyce out, she was always late. Sometimes they went to visit Tommy at Eton, or to visit undergraduates at Oxford – it is not clear whose benefit this was for. Joyce was dimly aware her parents led separate lives but tried to think only of the affection they gave her and Tommy.

During the holidays Joyce saw a lot of her cousins in London and at country-house parties. Sometimes Nora insisted that she and Joyce sang duets to the house party, but Joyce did not enjoy it: she felt very self-conscious performing in front of relations.

At Easter the Phippses usually went to Ford Manor. Joyce liked Ford because adolescents were treated as individuals, in a friendly and uncompetitive atmosphere. There was a nine-hole golf course, a tennis court and stables but no one was forced to use them. The spacious gardens were ideal for treasure hunts – organised by Paul and based on rhyming clues and anagrams, anticipating Joyce's fascination with the *Times* crossword puzzles, which were not started until 1930. Joyce enjoyed Nora's youthful companionship in practical jokes, such as apple-pie beds and sewing up the young men's pyjama bottoms.

Ford Manor was where Joyce first met Virginia Graham, who was a few months younger than her. Virginia's father Harry wrote musicals and was the author of *Ruthless Rhymes for Heartless Homes*. The thirty-mile journey from London to Ford took two hours by car; Harry, Mrs Graham and her lady's maid would sit in the front of the Grahams' car while the girls sang in the back, accompanied by their ukuleles. 'There were *some* signs that Joyce was going to be a singer – at least she was always singing,' remembered Virginia. 'She would, at the drop of a hat, imitate any one of the stars at the time – Dorothy Dickson, Evelyn Laye, Jessie Matthews and so on. But I wouldn't say that Joyce impressed me then as someone who was going to be "musical" in the sense that she would ever sing well. She played the piano, but only knew one tune properly.'

Holidays at home in London consisted of shopping at Selfridge's, lunch at Claridge's, tea at Whiteley's, and theatre or cinema every afternoon or evening and sometimes both. When Nora took Joyce to lunch with her godmother Lady Antrim, Prince George and Princess Obelensky of Russia, Joyce thought it pretty dull fare compared to watching Rudolph Valentino in the silent film *Cobra* later that afternoon. Fred Astaire in *Lady Be Good* was 'a marvellous show and the music is gorgeous and the Astairs dancing –!!!!', whilst *The Dixie Merchant* and *The Wedding Song* were 'utter tosh but lovely'.

'Before we went to the theatre or cinema we would keep up our strength with poached eggs at a Lyons Corner House,' said Virginia.

> Of course, we got rather intense and discussed things like God, and 'What's it all *for*?' But so often, just as I was embarking on a profound metaphysical argument, Joyce would suddenly say, 'Sh

sh. Did you hear what she said – that woman behind us?' She
hadn't been listening at all. It used to annoy me rather because I
used to think I was just as interesting as they were. She listened
to everybody everywhere. She was always passionately interested in people; and I don't necessarily mean people she knew,
but people she met on buses or in the street.

Riding on the upper deck home from the theatre, Joyce and her
friends had loud conversations in a bogus language, exclaiming as
they passed places of interest. Someone would usually tap them on
the shoulder and say in a very loud voice, 'Can I help you? Where do
you want to get off? This is Traf-al-gar Square. Battle of Wa-ter-loo.'
The trick was to nod their thanks and continue the cod-conversation
while keeping a straight face.

During the summer holidays Paul took Joyce to the Proms, then
held in the old Queen's Hall and still conducted by Sir Henry Wood.
They stood for two shillings and Joyce could remember the precise
evening when, listening to one of Bach's Brandenburg concertos, she
suddenly understood music. 'As I stood there I knew I was actually
experiencing the music instead of just hearing it. An important break-
through and the opening of a door to a whole new dimension.'

This round of constant entertainment left little time to notice the
worsening economic situation. However, on the first day of the
General Strike in May 1926, Joyce observed with delight a man in a
bowler hat carrying an attaché case and rolled umbrella riding pillion
on a motorbike, and ten people squashed into one Ford. While
Oxbridge students drove the buses, Paul mucked out the dray-horses
at the Paddington goods depot and Nora worked with the actress
Gladys Cooper in a canteen for chauffeurs in Hyde Park.

When Joyce lost her temper during French, Miss Hewson warned
her not to be affected by the 'Reds', who had set fire to a candle
factory in Battersea. On the fourth day of the strike, lessons were
cancelled and the school was sent for a long, rainy walk to calm the
girls down.

Joyce and her friends had no comprehension of the causes of the
General Strike and sympathised with those who wanted to work. She
was well aware of her social class and, when schoolfriend Betty
Langley had her hair shingled, Joyce thought it made her look 'a bit

shop-girlish and tacky'. At the end of term the girls had to clean their classrooms and 'it was rather fun playing housemaids'.

The upper class in which Joyce was brought up despised the language of the middle class – especially 'refined' or euphemistic words such as 'toilet', 'serviette' and 'mirror', defined by Nancy Mitford as 'non-U'.

By 1926 Joyce had had enough of school, hated her brown gym dress and was not looking forward to returning after the Easter holiday. 'Horrible thought it is coming back to school today. Hell. Gee I hate it.' There were some compensations, though, such as directing a play called *The Bathroom Door* and being chosen for the tennis team. 'I almost died when I heard the news. Me, erratic me, with no foot work and a bad backhand. I've decided to write another book. Not the one I was doing – I got bored with that.'

The summer term dragged on far too long, especially when many of her friends had already left school. 'Wiss, Diana Cavendish, Rose McDonell and lots of others are staying at Cliveden for the Eton & Harrow match & I am at this shut up hole. Lessons, lessons, lessons! Bah! How I am dying to leave school.' She would have been even more upset had she known that after the match her mother took Cousin Winkie Brooks, younger than her and still at Eton, to see the new musical *Show Boat* at Drury Lane.

That July Joyce took her last ever school exams: 'Golly I despise exams. They are so fearfully unnecessary.' She finally left school in December, without any qualifications.

The third monologue Joyce ever wrote, in 1940, was called *Head Girl*, about a schoolgirl very like Joyce: full of gung-ho cheeriness, mock-French phrases and earnest appeals for School Spirit: 'Let's pull our socks up, and see if we can't all remember: One Girl, One Basin.'

Every Christmas Eve, the Phippses drove the twenty-five miles from London to Cliveden. As their car approached the enormous Italian marble fountain and they turned the corner of the long drive, the grand Italianate house came into view and the lights of the glass porch came on as if by magic. Years later Joyce discovered that the lodge keeper telephoned to the big house to warn of their arrival. They were welcomed in the large hall by Edwin Lee, the butler. Their suitcases were carried in by footmen wearing brown velvet breeches and yellow silk stockings.

Life centred around the wood-panelled front hall, which was perfect for scooters, roller skates and pogo sticks – Joyce reckoned it was large enough to hold four double-decker buses. A huge Christmas tree stood just inside the front door and garlands of holly, ivy, and yew hung over pictures and wound up the carved banisters. After tea on Christmas Eve, local handbell ringers came, followed by carol singers. Joyce always infected her cousins with the giggles as soon as the tenor began to swoop through his solo verse of *See Amid the Winter Snow*.

The Christmas house party, including the six Astor children, was never less than two dozen. Nancy had replaced the imposing gloom of her father-in-law's taste with bright chintz and fresh flowers from the estate's greenhouses and soon discovered that Cliveden enabled her to invite anyone she wanted, whether aristocracy, film stars or politicians. For Christmas she would invite her relations; a few distinguished friends, such as George Bernard Shaw; and single people with no families. Shaw came armed with a diet sheet: 'Mr Shaw does not eat MEAT, GAME, FOWL or FISH or TAKE TEA or COFFEE.' He would only eat green vegetables, lentils, nuts and artichoke soup. His wife Charlotte sat and knitted the long socks he wore with his knickerbockers while he told stories about his friendship with Mrs Patrick Campbell. One year he gave Joyce seven signed photographs of himself, one for every day of the week, and told her she could sell them once he was dead.

On Christmas morning the maids still had to carry hot water and coal upstairs before the guests rose, though they were relieved of their normal duties of scrubbing and dusting. At nine o'clock Mr Lee struck the giant gong to announce breakfast. Every corner of the hall was filled with piles of presents. One Christmas the young A. A. Milne was horrified when he saw how many presents there were to and from everybody – he had brought nothing. While everybody was eating breakfast he got out his fountain pen and added to the label of one present on each pile 'and from Alan Milne'. The recipients must have been somewhat surprised that this young man seemed to have brought presents in conjunction with such a range of aunts and cousins.

A regular guest was Thomas Jones, miner's son and Deputy Secretary to the Cabinet of several governments. He was one of Joyce's heroes and although he was older than her father, they became good friends. 'The large hall looked like Harrods or Selfridges,' he wrote to his daughter in 1927. 'There were piles of presents of all sorts all over chairs and couches and carpets – the Astor and Phipps children racing round excitedly and the grown up guests distributing their presents from trays and baskets, with contents worth pounds and pounds.' Unable to compete, Jones gave Nancy a sixpenny *Life of Christ* and Shaw a book of nursery rhymes. Joyce spent every autumn making presents of pen wipers, bookmarks and lavender bags. Nora reputedly bought all her presents by pawning her pearls in November. On Christmas Eve, Waldorf would then buy them back, and hang them on the Christmas tree for her. Nora's delight and surprise never waned.

Present-giving continued until it was time for church, where the vicar appeared to have two stomachs – everything he said came out twice, the second time in a deep rumble. Here, too, Joyce could not suppress her giggles, and once she started it set off the others.

There was enough space in the rococo dining-room for all the guests, and Nancy ordered them to use only one plate for all four courses so as to reduce work in the kitchen. Although the Astors were both teetotallers, abstinence was not imposed on guests and Mr Lee maintained an excellent wine cellar.

After lunch, the party stepped out of the dining-room onto the wide, balustraded terrace overlooking the Thames. For Christmas 1927 Waldorf was given a 16mm movie camera, and he filmed Nancy and Joyce dancing the Charleston; Joyce walking on stilts, her hair in a thick plait down her back; and then everyone playing French and English, an energetic team game, on the grass below. Joyce was usually last to be chosen for a team, and tended to hide behind other people rather than be taken prisoner. If it was raining, the children played Hide and Seek all over the house.

Ruth Draper, the American monologuist, was often there to entertain the party after tea. Originally only a drawing-room performer in New York, when she was thirty-six Henry James had encouraged her to appear in public theatres and she had been an instant success in both America and Britain. She had been coming to Cliveden since before the war and had entertained the troops in the hospital. She and Paul were almost related – they shared first cousins and had known each other since they were children in New York. She often stayed with the Phippses in Chelsea, where she entertained Joyce and Tommy in their nursery. Joyce adored 'Miss Ruth' and remembered her as 'faintly governessy, spinsterish and demanded best behaviour from all children. But it was worth behaving well to be entertained by her.' With no props and only a hat or a fan, she conjured up characters ranging from New York dowagers to European immigrants. She was only five feet four inches but projected a huge presence. John Gielgud saw her on stage in the late twenties:

> Ruth Draper's authority and concentration were absolute. How swiftly she transformed that stage into her own extraordinary world, transporting us to other places, other countries – a boudoir, a garden, a church, a customs shed: London, New York, Rome, the coast of Maine – creating in each of those imagined settings a single dominant character and then seeming to surround herself with an attendant crowd of minor figures – children, animals, servants, husbands, lovers. Her wit and imagination could not fail to fascinate and never palled.

Among the Christmas guests there was usually a Langhorne over from America. Joyce's favourite was her Uncle Buck, who as a young man had been expelled from Virginia Military Institute after kidnapping a trained pig from a travelling circus. 'He could mimic anything from a crow to an Englishman,' remembered his niece Alice. 'He spoke like a Southern Negro slave and lived for horses, dogs, whisky and cards.' Buck's constant companion was his African-American butler Clinton Harris, whom he had bought as a child for $1.50. Joyce loved Buck's thigh-slapping stories about slaves and their masters that would shock anyone today.

Anyone under fourteen was not usually allowed to stay up for dinner but at Christmas, children could not only stay up, but were expected to dress up too. On the landing was a huge Chinese chest filled with dressing-up clothes: mandarin coats, real ballgowns, a Parisian Pierrot costume, shoes, hats, fans, flowers and scarves. Another box was filled with masks – girls' faces with pigtails, one-eyed pirates and Hogarthian ugly sisters.

The children became a medley of pirates, gypsies, cowboys and 'grown-ups'. Joyce liked to dress as a 'lady' in high heels, rouge and 1900 French couture ballgowns. Bill Astor, Waldorf and Nancy's eldest son, was always a Chinaman in a mandarin coat who spoke only pidgin English; Bobbie Shaw was usually the Very Reverend Robert Gould, with protruding teeth and a serious line in sermons on topics like 'Is There an Afterlife on the Moon?'.

Nora usually dressed up as a belle of her Virginian youth and Nancy might be a Tsarist Russian *émigré* whose life had been one long disaster, an excitable, persuasive, Jewish businessman, or a brave English lady who rode hard to hounds. 'Lady Astor was an extraordinary figure,' wrote Thomas Jones, 'a racing tout in ill-fitting coat, chequered trousers, field glasses and small bowler hat.' She had all the skills of a comedian – courage, mimicry and perfect timing. Mimicking local characters was part of Cliveden life, both above and below stairs. Waldorf's valet, Mr Bushell, normally silent in stiff shirt and black tailcoat, would for a fleeting instant become the brilliant socialite Lady Desborough, neighbour and adversary of Nancy. The caricature was so brief that afterwards Joyce wondered if she had imagined it. Joyce had to learn when it was appropriate: one day Nancy's maid, Rosina Harrison, took her on one side and asked her to stop mimicking the servants during mealtimes.

Jones described the Christmas meal:

After dinner of Turkey, crackers and plum pudding, we had a characteristic Astor evening of dance and song and all jumbled up in a rollicking way. The carpet was rolled up in the Library, the records turned on, and Nancy did all sort of turns with uproarious results, talking race course jargon all the time. About 10.30 the dancing ceased and Mrs Paul Phipps started Negro folk songs and spirituals with banjo accompaniment, song after song.

On Boxing Day, Joyce helped distribute presents to the staff and then either followed the local beagle hunt or played football in the stableyard with the grooms and chauffeurs. Her cousins did not seek her out to play with: Wiss was only a year older, but much shyer, and the boys had each other. Joyce may not have known quite how rich the Astors were, but she was certainly conscious of being a 'poor relation'.

'I'm afraid Joyce's cousins didn't like her much – she was just too prim,' recalled Alice. 'You could never be rude in front of her. Sometimes she tried to be funny, but she had no natural spontaneity. As a teenager she was also very bossy. I was always very fond of her, even though she was such a prig.'

Joyce celebrated her escape from school by exchanging her black stockings for pale silk ones. Her seventeenth birthday, in February 1927, was celebrated at a 'finishing-school' in St-Germain-en-Laye, a smart suburb outside Paris, where she stayed until July. Finishing-schools were the transition from the schoolroom to the ballroom, when girls were permitted to wear grown-up clothes in public. Joyce was expected to polish the skills needed to acquire a well-bred husband: needlework, opera, hosting a dinner party, good conversation and French. Tutors were hired from among the Parisian intelligentsia, such as professors of the Sorbonne. Classes were small and the teaching good: Joyce learned to speak French with a perfect accent, though her grammar lacked finesse. Conversation was not allowed to flag during meals and anyone caught speaking in English was given twenty lines of French prose to recite the following day. They had lectures all morning and went sightseeing or shopping in the afternoon: buying smart clothes was part of the young ladies' education. In the evenings they were taken to the theatre or the opera, where Joyce put her hair up for the first time, but it was so fine that all the hairpins slowly slipped out. After that, whenever she heard Gounod's *Faust* she was reminded of the sound of hairpins tinkling onto the floor behind her.

There were several finishing-schools in Paris for English girls, each with between ten and thirty students, and they met up with each other when they could, though they were always chaperoned. Joyce often went to visit Virginia Graham and other friends at a school run by the Ozanne sisters near the Eiffel Tower. Joyce and Virginia now became 'staunch and everlasting friends' and remained so all their lives. One afternoon, as Joyce was taking a bus up Regent Street, she made a list of the things that she could not manage without. They were 'Christian Science, Reggie, Virginia's flat, with, of course, Virginia there, a raccoon coat and music.' They were both Christian Scientists and also shared a sense of humour and a love of observing people and singing popular songs. Whereas Joyce liked to be the centre of attention, Virginia was shy and introverted; so there was never any competition between them.

Diana Mitford, later Lady Mosley, was at finishing-school in Paris at the same time as Joyce. 'I remember Joyce as bigger than life size, wearing enormous tulle dresses. She was probably no taller than me but she was huge – body and face and enormous teeth. She was very good-natured and nice and kind, and rather apt to start imitating cockneys. I have always loved imitations but Joyce's were really too unsophisticated.'

When Joyce came home for the Easter holiday, the Phipps family went as usual to Ford Manor – but found that their hostess Pauline Spender-Clay had pneumonia and the usual house party had been cancelled. Reggie Grenfell, a trainee accountant aged twenty-three, was so unassuming that nobody remembered having invited him. Consequently nobody uninvited him either, so Reggie found himself the only guest. He was tall and thin with a long face and high forehead, dark smooth hair and friendly brown eyes. His shy smile stretched between his large ears and his chin melted into a long neck. His large hands and feet made him appear clumsy, but in fact he was good at tennis and an accomplished ballroom dancer. With four younger sisters, Reggie probably found it easier being with Joyce than with sophisticated young women of his own age. Joyce, just seventeen, played tennis with him and thought he was quite pleasant. Fifty years later she claimed that she could not remember the first time she met Reggie – 'Some things are so much part of oneself that it is as if they had always been' – but Reggie knew at once that Joyce was the girl for him.

In the summer, Joyce returned from Paris to a round of pleasure, which she recalled in her song *Time*, written in 1962:

There was always time to sit in the sun.
We were never done with lazing and flirting,
And doing our embroidery, and keeping up our memory books,
And brushing our hair, and going on picnics,
And dancing, dancing, dancing, dancing –
When I was a girl there was always time to waste.

However she had to wait until the following May to 'come out' as a debutante, and meanwhile she wanted to train for the theatre. Paul took this seriously and said she must go to the Royal Academy of Dramatic Arts, the most prestigious acting-school in Britain. He knew Kenneth Barnes, the director, and George Bernard Shaw was a member of the council, which probably helped Joyce get a place for September 1927.

Nine years after the war, girls outnumbered boys at RADA by four to one. Joyce was taught diction, with clear rounded vowels and crisp consonants which could be heard at the back of any theatre. Among her contemporaries was Celia Johnson, who became a close friend. They shared a sense of humour and sparked each other off with hysterical laughter. But whereas Celia wanted to act but was not very interested in Being an Actress, Joyce was the opposite: it was the glamour, the first-night parties and the bouquets that interested her more than learning lines and techniques.

As a student in Mlle Alice Gachet's special French class at RADA, Joyce played a shepherdess in a rustic French play, with Celia in the lead role. In a mob cap Joyce sang in a key 'so high that only a dog could have heard it. I don't believe I was much good at being a shepherdess and I seem to have drifted painlessly away from the wish to be an actress.' After only one term, Paul was relieved that he no longer had to pay the fifteen-guinea fees. Joyce had had enough of acting, especially in French.

In the spring of 1928 she was preparing to 'come out'. The 'Season' ran from May to August, but before it began debutantes had to be fitted for clothes suitable for dances, dinners, luncheon parties and racing at Ascot. Joyce's cousin on her mother's side, Nancy Tree, was married to a millionaire and provided a regular supply of second-hand Parisian *haute couture*. When the suitcases arrived, Nora would turn the occasion into a party, inviting Joyce's friends round to comment and share. They stripped to their crêpe-de-Chine slips and tried on hats, scarves, belts and frocks from Chanel, Lanvin and Schiaparelli. Chests were flattened with a 'bust bodice' – a wide satin ribbon wound tightly round. The style for young women of the late 1920s was flat-chested and narrow-hipped, with cropped hair, which could never have suited Joyce, who kept her hair long, pinned up into 'earphones'. Fortunately Nancy Tree's clothes were so well cut that they usually fitted all shapes and sizes – from Nora's slight figure to Joyce's solid one: five feet ten inches tall with size seven feet, she was wide and shapeless. Other clothes that Joyce needed were made up by Chelsea dressmakers, skilful at copying designs from *Vogue* for only thirty shillings. Silk stockings were coloured 'nigger' or 'honey'; 'beige' was considered shocking – it was too close to nakedness.

The first event to mark a debutante's 'coming out' was presentation at Court, a ceremony begun by Queen Victoria to meet the daughters of her dozen ladies-in-waiting. A debutante could only be presented by a married woman who had been presented herself, and by 1928 there were three hundred upper-class girls at each of the three presentations.

In her regulation headdress of three white ostrich feathers, Joyce was presented to George V and Queen Mary at Buckingham Palace on 23 May 1928. *The Times* reported that

Mrs. Paul Phipps wore a gown of white chiffon trimmed with appliqués of ivory cobweb lace, the tight-fitting bodice finished with a cluster of silver violets and a full skirt made with an uneven hem line.

Miss Joyce Phipps wore an Empire gown of white mousseline and ruched faille, finished with clusters of white velvet roses on the shoulder and hem. A head-dress and bouquet of white flowers. A train of chiffon and tulle.

Both gowns were designed by Norman Hartnell, then at the start of his career as a couturier.

Joyce and Lady Silvia Coke, daughter of the Earl of Leicester, first met in Paris and then came out together in London. 'We queued in our cars down the Mall, with footmen balancing on the running board. The public peered in and made comments about each deb,' she remembered.

Once you got into the Palace you had to wait for hours. Each girl's mother went first, and gave your name card to a flunky who passed it on to the Lord Chamberlain. As the debutante approached the Throne Room, a footman arranged your train behind you. As your name was called out, you had to do a deep curtsey to the King and Queen and then retire backwards, trying not to trip over the train, drop your bouquet or head-dress, or bump into anyone else. Another footman gathered up the train and the ceremony was over. The deb was now a woman, deemed ready for marriage.

There were so many beauties in 1928, it was a bumper year for debs; Diana Mitford was one; and there was Deirdre Hart-Davis, niece of Diana Cooper; Wiss Astor; Anne Wellesley, the Duke of Wellington's daughter; my best friend Penelope Chetwode, who married John Betjeman; Angela Neville, daughter of Lord Cottenham; Georgina Curzon, Lord Howe's daughter; Christabel Burton, who married Bielenberg, the German who tried to blow up Hitler. Oh yes, it was a bumper year.

Life for debutantes was usually 'ripping', 'absolutely marvellous', 'topping', 'divine', 'definitely king', or 'glorious'. On bad days it was 'foul', 'loathsome', 'detestable' or 'perfectly damnable'. A person could be 'an egg', 'top', 'thing', 'fruit', or 'dud', and would be greeted with 'Bung-ho!', 'My dear', 'Top hole' or 'Dahrling'.

Getting enough sleep was a problem during the ten-week Season, when balls went on until dawn. On 7 May 1928 *The Times* announced over eighty forthcoming dances – an average of three a night – from Lady Rothschild's to the Eton Ball. The debs were only just out of the schoolroom and the young men – 'deb's delights' – tongue-tied, so they concentrated on dancing. 'Our standards were very low – we weren't looking for geniuses, just dance partners,' recalls Silvia Coke. 'Two dances with the same young man in one evening was considered very fast and possibly immoral.'

Chaperones – mothers or nannies – watched the debs like hawks to see whom they danced with. Sometimes Reggie was at the same dance as Joyce but she was only allowed to dance with him once. As a big girl, she was hardly the belle of the ball, and neither her boarding- nor her finishing-school had prepared her to socialise with young men. Her dancing-card was rarely filled and she found herself stand- ing on the side, watching everyone else. Being a wallflower however gave her the opportunity to observe and listen to people and, unknown even to herself, she was storing it all up for future use.

'Joyce was not a great success as a deb,' said Sylvia. 'She was too shy and the wrong shape. Balls were very frightening, so most of us spent half the time in the ladies' loos. People have this idea that we were all flappers having a wonderful time. In fact we were shy girls just out of school, never allowed anywhere on our own.'

Cousin Wiss and Joyce shared a coming-out dance at the Astors' London home in St James's Square. Set in the north-eastern corner of the square, it looks like a typical Regency townhouse, but inside it stretches halfway back to Lower Regent Street and has a host of bed- rooms, large reception rooms and vast servants' quarters. Joyce was so naïve about the opposite sex that during a lull in the dance she led her dancing partner up the back stairs to an unused bedroom for a chat. She was appalled when he tried to kiss her.

At weekends everyone who was anyone went to country-house parties; other events of the Season which Joyce enjoyed included the Chelsea Flower Show, the Royal Academy of Arts summer preview and the Fourth of June at Eton. The last event was the Eton and Harrow cricket match, held at Lord's cricket ground, where families could rent stage coaches from which to view the game and eat their picnics.

Forty years later Joyce wrote the song *I Wouldn't Go Back to the World I Knew* in which she describes that time:

Glamorous girls with flattened figures,
Glamorous, bright young men.
Safe, contained, and confident,
Madly cheerful, fearfully gay,
Certain youth would last for ever in an ever better way.
'Let's play tennis!' 'Oh, how topping! . . .
Bags me play with Teddy.'
'Daphne darling, you look spiffing . . .
Service . . . are you ready?'
There we were the lot of us,
Thoughtless, spoilt and young,
When the sun was always shining and the lovely songs were sung.
It was narrow, small and tame, it had to go,
The world I knew, but it was fun then, just the same.

By the end of 1928 Joyce and Reggie were seeing more of each other. Paul and Nora liked him, and secretly thought he would be a suitable husband, but at eighteen Joyce was not yet ready for marriage. After Christmas they packed her off to America to stay with her aunt Irene Gibson in her large house in Upper East Side, New York. Reggie came to see her off at Waterloo but was too shy to tell her how much he loved her, so he hummed instead.

Irene was the easiest of all the Langhorne aunts and, as the wife of the artist Charles Dana Gibson, was the queen bee of New York society. But Joyce thought only of Reggie and came home before the allotted three months. A few weeks later, in April 1929, Reggie wrote to her expressing his concern that, with only a poorly paid job and no future inheritance, he could not support her. He told her not to wait for him.

Joyce would not be put off, and was prepared to wait for ever. Meanwhile, they arranged to see Max Miller at the Holborn Empire the next day. Within minutes of meeting in the foyer, surrounded by friends, they became engaged. According to Alice, Joyce proposed to Reggie. 'He was far too frightened to propose to her.'

At last, after two years of courting, they were allowed to meet alone. To celebrate, Reggie gave Joyce a bag of sticky toffees.

★

Reggie was born on 10 November 1903, the oldest son of Lieutenant-Colonel Arthur Morton Grenfell, a financier, and Victoria, daughter of Earl Grey of Howick and one of Queen Victoria's many god-daughters. Reggie's mother died when he was four, with a younger brother and sister. Two years later Arthur married Hilda, daughter of General Sir Neville Lyttelton, the governor of the Royal Hospital, Chelsea.

Hilda was soon expecting a child and while looking for a larger house they found themselves temporarily homeless. 'Never mind,' said Arthur. 'Rosa will look after us.' As a young man he had visited the Cavendish Hotel in Jermyn Street, a gift to Mrs Rosa Lewis from the Prince of Wales as a place to entertain men away from their wives and mothers. Mrs Lewis treated all her customers as if they were still at Oxford and was inclined to mix up their generations, calling sons by their fathers' names.

Into this somewhat surprising environment Arthur, his pregnant wife and his three children moved for three months. It is unlikely that Reggie, Harry and Vera realised what sort of hotel they were staying in, but their stepmother must have had her suspicions.

Once established in a home of her own, Hilda went on to bear four daughters: Mary, Katie, Frances and Laura. She was tough and slightly eccentric but brought up all seven children with equal love and affection. Arthur's fortunes rose and fell sharply: one month there was enough to maintain a London house with servants, and the next he would be wondering how to feed his growing family. In the crash of 1911 he was forced to sell the family's painting by Titian for well below its value. *The Boy With a Red Hat* ended up as part of the Frick collection in New York.

Reggie was sent to prep school, where he learned to cope without his family, endure regular cold baths and avoid the cane. In 1917 he followed his father and uncles to Eton College, where the fees of £230 per year covered everything except for 'boxing, Jiu-jitsu and use of electric lathes'. Reggie soon absorbed the school culture of 'fags', 'Pop', and 'Oppidans'. By the fifth form he was in the Non-Greek Classical Division, and a History Specialist together with the young Earl of Longford. In his last term the *House Book* related: 'A good [cricket] captain, he has a very graceful style in batting. He is very keen but is inclined to hide his feelings under a mask of gaiety.'

Another contemporary wrote of his prowess at the Field Game: 'Grenfell is rather too tall for a house first. He is not fierce enough to be much good.'

When the First World War ended, Reggie's father formed a company to rebuild the shipping industry on the River Danube, so school holidays were spent in Austria, where Reggie and his sisters learned to speak good German. He left Eton with credits in his School Certificate for French, Maths, Latin and History. In his letter of recommendation to Balliol College, Oxford, his tutor wrote: 'Grenfell is a thoroughly sound boy – quiet. A poor talker in ordinary life – has not yet shown much initiative. But he has a very good brain. He seems to be "coming out" now.'

Reggie sat the scholarship exam for Oxford in March 1922 and was offered a place as a commoner to read politics, philosophy and economics. During this period his stepmother Hilda wrote often to the admissions tutor at Balliol. Her attitude towards attending Oxford University was akin to booking a room in a hotel – you inform them when you want to come and change your mind to suit yourself. Three times she changed the term when he would start, with no explanations, and eventually he went up in October 1923. She never asked about his studies, but was concerned about the linen and cutlery he should take with him. Maybe he would have had more initiative if his stepmother had not taken so much control.

Oxford in the early 1920s was dominated by demobilised soldiers and, according to Cyril Connolly, 'a world of matey young men with their pipes and grey bags'. Among Reggie's other contemporaries at Balliol were the writers Graham Greene and Antony Powell; Crown Prince Olav V of Norway; and the splendidly named Sir Hugh Vere Huntly Duff Munro-Lucas-Tooth and his friend Joseph Edward George Henry Arbuthnot-Quick.

Reggie scraped through Oxford with a third-class degree – the highest qualification any of his family achieved. He was good at figures so, with no possibility of a private income, decided to train as an accountant in London.

Although Joyce's male cousins went to Oxford, there was no question of her following suit. Daughters were expected to marry well and breed heirs. So there were no objections when Joyce, aged only nineteen, told her parents of her engagement to Reggie. At sixteen, she had imagined her perfect husband with 'A sense of humour, good at games, not necessarily good looking but with a nice smile' – a description that fitted Reggie well. He also had perfect manners, a quality that Joyce took very seriously, and was 'one of those naturally good human beings who does it all without thinking: thoughtful, loving, considerate, all those things that I have to struggle to be'.

Joyce found the easy going honesty of the Grenfell family refreshing after the highly charged atmosphere of her mother's family. The Grenfells disliked drawing attention to themselves and were surprised when Joyce's photograph appeared in the *Tatler*. Reggie, his brother and sisters all loved each other in an uncompetitive, relaxed way, without judgement or resentment. Joyce and Hilda skirted tentatively around each other at first, but were soon devoted.

During her six-month engagement, Joyce lost weight, held her head up and learned to control the large feet on the end of her long legs. Falling in love changed her from a plump duckling into an elegant swan.

– 5 –

Nancy gave Joyce and Reggie their wedding reception at St James's Square. She invited the Astors, Phippses and Grenfells to assemble the day before the wedding to help arrange the presents in the dining-room. As the two families moved among the crystal vases and linen sheets, Reggie's younger brother Harry arrived off the boat-train from New York. He was working for the merchant banker J. P. Morgan and consoled Reggie, who had lost his job in the City after the recent Stock Exchange crash. Everyone was astounded when Nancy said, 'Joyce, you've chosen the wrong one. Why don't you marry Harry instead? At least he's got a job.' Frances, Reggie's sister, remembers the occasion:

> The Grenfell family stood rooted to the ground in embarrassment. Laura, our twelve-year-old sister, reached for the hand of our great-aunt, Dame Edith Lyttelton, a formidable lady and a great friend of Lady Astor. 'Aunt Didi,' whispered Laura, tugging urgently at her hand, 'who is that mad old woman who says that Harry is nicer than Reggie? Reggie's *much* nicer than Harry.' Dame Edith broke the ice. 'Nancy', she boomed, 'out of the mouths of babes and sucklings – this young lady thinks you are mad.'

Joyce and Reggie's marriage took place on a cold, windy December day in 1929. On the way from Chelsea to St Margaret's, Westminster, Nora asked Joyce if she knew what a husband and wife did on their wedding night. Joyce confessed she had no idea. Nora hurriedly told her, to which Joyce said, 'That's ridiculous, one of us would have to be upside-down.'

The Times reported that Joyce wore a cream velvet dress, with long, tight-fitting sleeves, and a train falling from the waist. Joyce had designed it herself, but the square neck and complicated draped cross-cutting refused to lie flat.

The nine adult bridesmaids were her friends Rose MacDonell (later Lady Baring); Catherine Fordham (later wife of the Governor of Rhodesia); Lady Margaret Mercer Nairne Petty-Fitzmaurice, daughter of the late Marquess of Lansdowne and stepdaughter of Lord Astor of Hever; Deirdre Hart-Davis, niece of Gladys Cooper; Virginia Graham; Cousins Ann Phipps, Molly Middleton and Wiss Astor; and Reggie's sister Mary. They were all very tall in their medieval dresses with 'Tight-fitting sleeves falling into points nearly touching the ground, lined with leaf-green velvet'. The five child bridesmaids were Reggie's sisters Laura and Frances, Vivienne Mosley (daughter of Oswald and Cynthia), and Cousins Virginia Brand and Elizabeth Winn. The one page was Cousin Jeremy Tree, aged three, in green velvet trousers. Eight-year-old Cousin Simon Phipps remembered the humiliation of wearing a sailor suit: 'I was very jealous of Michael Tree, who was the same age as me, but already in a grey flannel suit.' This was typical of the difference between the traditional British Phipps family and the modern American Langhornes.

The marriage was led by Bishop Perowne of Bradford; and the Rev. Lyttelton, a cousin of Reggie's stepmother, gave a private address to the bride and groom. When asked by his sisters what he had said, Reggie replied, 'Don't drink too much, I think.' There was traditional wedding music – Bach's *Jesu, Joy of Man's Desiring*, followed by the bridal march from Wagner's *Lohengrin*. For a change, Joyce chose a new carol by Alfred Noyes.

Nancy had drawn up the invitation list of four hundred titled and distinguished guests, and never asked Joyce if she wanted any of her own friends, such as Carley. The choice of bridesmaids was also not entirely tactful, with only three of Reggie's five sisters included. Nora invited her favourite cab driver and the one-legged man who sold gardenias outside the Berkeley Hotel in Picadilly.

Following the reception, Mr and Mrs Grenfell spent their first married night at the Savoy Hotel at a cost of £5, where presumably they worked out the acrobatics of married life. Then they set off for their honeymoon in Paris. On their marriage certificate, Reggie gave his 'Rank or Profession' as 'Gentleman', but once the honeymoon was over, he would have to find a job.

Earlier that year, soon after Joyce's engagement was announced, Nora's old flame Lefty Flynn had appeared in London. Cousin Alice described him as 'the sort of man that housemaids fall for' and a homosexual acquaintance said he was 'every gay man's dream'. During the First World War, he had joined the American Air Force, and in 1919 he appeared in the silent film *Oh Boy!* as a cowboy. Over the next eight years he acted in thirty-nine films, starring in twenty-one of them, including *High and Handsome*, *The No-Gun Man*, *The Millionaire Cowboy* and *Omar the Tentmaker* with Boris Karloff. In 1924 Lefty co-starred in *Open All Night*, a comedy set in a French circus with Viola Dana. The beautiful twenty-seven-year-old fell for Lefty. He divorced Blanche, his second wife, and married Viola, who later claimed that he had been drunk for most of their three-year marriage. During the filming of *The Golden Stallion* in 1927 he asked to be excused to go to the lavatory, and eight days later he was found in a hotel in Oklahoma City, painted blue from head to foot, playing a guitar to the accompaniment of a six-piece Hawaiian orchestra. That was the end of his acting career, but he had made enough money to buy a ranch in California and travel to London. Whether he went to find Nora, we shall never know, but when they met all their passion was rekindled and within weeks Nora told Alice that she was 'engaged'. Nora believed her children no longer needed her – Joyce was about to wed and Tommy, then sixteen, was at Eton.

So Nora secretly planned her escape, taking a few clothes at a time from her bedroom to Lefty's hotel. As soon as Tommy was back at Eton after Christmas 1929, and Joyce and Reggie had gone with the Grenfells on a skiing holiday in Switzerland, Nora and Lefty eloped by train to France.

Joyce's letters to Virginia bear no trace of concern or suspicion about her mother. Reggie was keen to show off the skiing skills he had learned in Austria, while Joyce was content to keep the fur strapped to her skis, even when going down, and in the evenings they danced the tango together. Reggie had passed his accountancy exams and was offered a job in his father's investment company, Grenfell &

Co., while Joyce looked forward to a life of rearing more Grenfells. They arrived back in Chelsea late at night and found Paul standing by the fire in the drawing-room.

'Your mother's gone away,' was all he said. Joyce was stunned – her parents had always seemed so happy together. Paul had just kept hoping that Nora would eventually settle down.

A family meeting was called and decided that the best people to persuade Nora back were Joyce, her cousin-in-law Reggie Winn, Nancy and her maid Rosina. After searching the obvious places in Paris, they eventually found Nora and Lefty in the south of France. The rescue party was unsuccessful – Nora would not leave Lefty again: she intended to divorce Paul as quickly as possible and become Lefty's fourth wife. In March 1930 the lovers moved to Paris to await the divorce and Joyce made another attempt to persuade her back, this time with Paul. Once again they failed. Virginia remembered: 'Joyce was pole-axed. She turned to God for help.'

Joyce rarely mentioned the episode to anyone and it took her forty years to admit that

> The break-up of my parents' marriage was the time I was most unhappy in my life. I had just married and it came as terrible shock. It was a moment of total desolation. Nothing has ever been as devastating as that moment. They did a most marvellous thing, they kept together and made a happy family life for us to grow up in. That was the time that I first got a glimpse of confidence that Man is a spiritual entity. I suddenly saw that Man, made in the image and likeness of God, cannot change. This spiritual continuity of Good was going on all the time, whether I could see it or not.

Tommy too was sent to Paris to ask his mother to come back, but all it did was deepen his dislike of Lefty. Nora imagined that she and Lefty could settle down in England and that the family would eventually accept him. She soon realised this was impossible and she would have to leave Britain. This was no great sacrifice – she had never got used to the cold houses and the inability of their inhabitants to throw their arms around each other.

Two years after Lefty had first appeared in London, they were married in Virginia amidst much publicity. Nora was convinced that 'ahead of us lies a bed of roses' and they went to live in Greenwich, Connecticut, where they threw parties and kept horses. Nora succeeded in stopping Lefty from drinking and the parties were all dry. Much to her sisters' surprise, she remained married to him for twenty years.

The Phipps house in St Leonard's Terrace was sold, and Paul moved to Royal Avenue in Chelsea, where he lived for the rest of his life. Outwardly he remained calm, but inwardly he never recovered, nor stopped loving Nora. Tommy, a sensitive sixteen-year-old, was probably the worst affected in the family. In the summer of 1930, a prefect at Eton reported: 'The only time Phipps played cricket he seemed to have lost all his sting. It is to be hoped he will try to *play* the game instead of messing about and trying to look good, his fielding is negligible. He is too inclined to get downhearted.' He cheered up when his father came to give weekly instruction in Christian Science: the classes were 'rather tiresome, but I liked the opportunity it gave me of seeing my father'. Joyce also visited Tommy often, but it was his mother he missed. When he was nearly eighteen, he left the school before taking any exams and joined Nora in America.

For the first few months of their marriage, Joyce and Reggie lived with his parents in Chesham Place, Belgravia. Nancy and Nora then bought them a house and in 1930 they moved to 21 St Leonard's Terrace, a three-storey Georgian house with a basement and an attic, only a few doors away from the house in which Joyce had grown up. They employed a cook called Ada, and Ivy, a parlour maid. Paul designed a self-contained flat for them which was considered to be the latest in comfort, with a bedroom each, a bathroom with running hot and cold water, and their own sitting-room. They could enter it without being monitored by their employers – an independence unusual for the day.

When Ivy became pregnant, Joyce was so shocked she could tell only Virginia. 'It looks so sordid and awful. I expect we've not been strict enough. Oh blast, blow, blast.' Miss Ivy was sent away to get married as quickly as possible and replaced with Mary Bourhill from

Yorkshire, who was properly trained and wore stiff white collars and cuffs. She introduced a new vocabulary to Joyce, such as 'Ooboogersorrymadam' when she dropped something.

Joyce furnished and decorated the house with flowers, pale modern sofas and low lamps on the grand piano. In a letter to Tommy in America, Paul wrote: 'Joyce has gone quite crazy about painting and has a slap at everything – even the walls and doors of the little room behind the Dining Room where she has started a life-size figure sitting on a bank, and a wreath of bright flowers with RG and JG in two hearts pierced by an arrow. She and Reggie are very kind to me and make me come round all the time.'

Joyce's commitment to Christian Science had wavered during her late teens, but she officially joined the First Church of Christ, Scientist in Chelsea in 1933. Though never very successful, Paul's architectural practice benefited from his being a member of the church. He designed several churches for them, such as Wright's Lane in Kensington, a bold building in red brick. He designed small country houses in England and also restored many important houses such as Alderly Park, Ditchley Park and Blickling Hall. Though Lutyens's influence is clear it did not overpower his own feeling for proportion, colour and texture.

The young Grenfells had moved up from the Deb Set to the Young Married Set and were out most nights at dinner parties, the theatre or dancing at the Savoy where they sometimes won prizes. The entertainment of the 1930s was sentimental and escapist: people wanted to forget the dole queues, poverty and the threat of war.

Dinner with Bryan Guinness, brilliant heir to the brewing fortune, and Diana Mitford – married a few months before Joyce and Reggie in the same church – could be a strain. Diana remembers Joyce as 'an ardent housewife' who loved discussing recipes – an unusual preoccupation for a woman of her social class. Joyce remembered Diana as 'clique-y, exclusive & critical with large bovine good looks & blonde voluptuousness & dimples'. She realised that they were in different leagues when she overheard Diana say as she looked in Joyce's direction, 'I *hate* nice, normal, healthy people.'

They preferred dinner with her schoolfriend Carley, now married and living in Hampstead. 'After dinner Joyce asked for some cardboard and quickly cut out some false teeth. She impersonated someone we knew and we were all in hysterics.' Another party trick was a spoof ballet – Reggie as the strong, still hero in the centre and Joyce circling him with much arm-waving and arabesques.

The second verse of Joyce's song *Time*, written thirty years later with some nostalgia, describes her life as a young wife:

> When I was a young woman there was always time,
> There was always time to walk in the sun,
> And we were never done
> With going to weddings,
> Our own and friends',
> And going to parties,
> Away at weekends,
> And talking, talking, talking, talking –
> When I was a young woman there was always time
>   to enjoy things.

The Grenfells' weekends were often spent at country-house parties where they played tennis in the afternoons and sang round the piano after dinner. Joyce was one of the ten 'Bright Spots' who performed at a cabaret at the Pump Room, Tunbridge Wells, near Ford Manor. She designed and made the costumes: the men were dressed as Pierrots and the girls wore tulle frocks with ribbons in their hair and serious expressions. They blatantly copied well-known theatre sketches, such as Beatrice Lillie's woman trying to buy a dozen double damask dinner napkins. Joyce sang a duet, *Lucky Me, Lovable You,* and a trio composed by Virginia called *Gerty*. During supper 'Miss Ursula Preston and Mr. Malcolm Stewart (of Welbeck Street, W.)' demonstrated the New Skater's Valse.

Joyce and Reggie spent most of their holidays with the Grenfell family, often at Nannau, a Queen Anne mansion in north Wales. Joyce took long walks and wrote poetry while Reggie went duck and pheasant shooting. Sometimes she went riding, but only if the horse was slow and did not jump fences. Reggie's sister Frances remembers Joyce being encouraged to trot. 'After a bit Joyce shouted, "Stop. Stop. My bottom's red hot."'

Reggie's job involved a certain amount of travel, and in 1934 he took Joyce by train to Skopje in Yugoslavia, to visit a chrome mine that his father's firm had recently bought. There were no roads for the last twenty-five miles, so they travelled in a rickety wooden railway carriage attached behind open trucks. After a long horse ride further up the mountain, Joyce officially opened a new minehead, named after Reggie's sister Katie. Afterwards peasants danced while sheep were roasted on spits. Back in Belgrade a few days later they took tea with Nancy's old friend Queen Marie of Romania.

With help from Nancy, Joyce was also able to cross the Atlantic to visit America three times during the 1930s. In 1932 she and Reggie visited Mirador in Virginia, Nora in Connecticut, and her Gibson cousins on their island in Maine. In 1933 she and Nora went to a Langhorne wedding in Virginia. Joyce's resentment of Lefty turned to acceptance as she saw how happy he made her mother.

Tommy was by this time working for the *New York Times* and went up to Connecticut often. 'I always resented Lefty for taking my mother away,' said Tommy sixty-five years later, 'but I learned to get on with him. He was a likeable and funny person.' Lefty's son by his second wife, Bud Palmer, was Tommy's age, and when their visits coincided they got on well. Joyce never mentioned meeting either her stepbrother or sister and there is no evidence that she wanted to.

After a couple of years, Nora and Lefty decided they wanted to be in real countryside, where Lefty could hunt, and they chose the small town of Tryon, at the foot of the Smokey Mountains in North Carolina. Nora persuaded Nancy to buy them some land on which to build 'Little Orchard', a white wood-frame house with stables for Lefty's horses.

'Nora is now set up for life in that community,' wrote Phyllis to her husband. 'Lefty is like a Newfoundland Dog around the place, very kindly and harmless; he does a good deal of physical work, clearing the woods, etc. As he appears to make Nora so happy I suppose we ought to be grateful, but how she could have married him I shall never know.'

When Joyce visited America in 1935, Reggie had to stay behind in London to work. Tommy's friend David Niven was also visiting. The year before, he and Lefty had set up a rodeo circus, employing thirty retired cowboys and 150 polo ponies. Despite Lefty's experience as a performing cowboy, they lost $35,000 in only a week. Lefty then encouraged Niven to go to Hollywood and now he was back as a movie star. 'Life member, whether you like it or not,' he wrote in

Nora's visitors' book. Other entries attest to Nora's skills as a hostess. Dana Gibson wrote: 'O fun thrice fun – aye, ye perfect domicile of pleasure giving'.

Another of Nora's friends staying in Tryon when Joyce arrived was F. Scott Fitzgerald. When his wife Zelda was admitted to Asheville mental hospital with depression, Fitzgerald took a hotel room in nearby Tryon and joined in the Flynns' busy social life. For several months Nora stopped Fitzgerald from drinking and probably inspired his short story 'An Alcoholic Case', published in 1937. He also wrote a comic playlet, 'Love's Melody', for their mutual amusement. Nora and Lefty appealed to Fitzgerald – she the runaway daughter of a millionaire, he a former Yale football star, cowboy actor and recovering alcoholic. Fitzgerald's 1935 story 'The Intimate Strangers' was a thinly disguised account of the Flynns and catches the atmosphere of their relationship – two people from different cultures with a shared passion for each other and for singing close harmonies. Nora must have told Fitzgerald how she and Lefty had run away in the summer of 1914, been forced by her family to part and been reunited fifteen years later. Fitzgerald would have witnessed their roller-coaster relationship – alternating between dry parties and Lefty's occasional disappearances. Their story fitted Fitzgerald's desire to portray new social values and alternative sexual roles.

> Sara [Nora] sat beside Killian [Lefty], making a special face of hers that was more like laughing than smiling, fingers pressed to a steeple over her heart, as he meticulously tuned his guitar, then at his nod they began. The Russian gibberish song came first – not knowing a word of the language they had caught the tone and ring of it, until it was not burlesque but something uncanny that made every eye intent on the end of each phrase. Following it they did the always popular German Band, and the Spanish numbers, and the spirituals, each time with a glance passing between them as they began another.

The spirituals were those that Nora's nanny had taught her, and the Russian gibberish and the German Band were comic ideas inspired by Ruth Draper's repertoire. The friendship was not affected when Fitzgerald sold the story to *McCall's* magazine and the following year,

1936, Nora helped Fitzgerald through a particularly bad week when he learned that Zelda's mental illness was untreatable and he was thinking of suicide. On his fortieth birthday she cheered him up at a country dog show. Fitzgerald wrote that Nora was 'a saint, one of the world's most delightful women'. Many years later, Joyce said she believed her mother had had a brief fling with Fitzgerald; both claimed to be loved by the other and Nora certainly hinted at an affair.

Another friend of Nora's made an even greater impression on Joyce. His name was Elliot Coleman, a twenty-nine-year-old school-teacher. They met at a poetry reading in Tryon and Joyce was entranced by his writing. Years later she said, 'The next day every leaf, blade of grass, and face seemed edged in light: every sound rang with meaning. Everything I saw, heard and felt became a poem.' Over the next two weeks they took long walks together through the woods. After six years of childless marriage to Reggie, the excite-ment was probably waning, and Joyce fell in love; but she resolutely maintained to herself that it was with the poetry and not the man. 'I read it, I dreamt it, I lived it, and I found a new door open and life was changed.' At this point her diary is missing several pages, the edges roughly torn. She stopped short of tearing out the sonnet Coleman wrote for her, which ends:

> Then in the starry dawn with birds awake,
> And all the water of the world forsaking
> The sun shall fill one river for her sake,
> And fire and song shall twine when she has found
> All dreams. And Time shall vanish at the source.

On her way home from Tryon in December 1935 Joyce stayed with friends in New York and Tommy gave a cocktail party in her honour. 'If I didn't always hate cocktail parties it might have been a good one,' she wrote at the time. She had never approved of alcohol and the only time she tried drinking a cocktail it made her 'tingle with an alcoholic daze throughout the dinner party – half pleasant and half annoying'. Fifty people, including the magazine proprietor Condé Nast and Aunt Irene Gibson, squeezed into Tommy's one-roomed apartment and Joyce counted seven mink coats on his bed. Tommy was surrounded by beautiful girlfriends, whom Joyce viewed with the disdain of an older sister. 'Joan poses for *Vogue* and has all the scintillating bird-like boniness which is modern beauty. Her conversation was brittle and her eye is hard.' Joyce advised her brother that he wouldn't find her very good on a wet walk – 'too orchidaceous'.

On the last night Tommy took Joyce to Beatrice Lillie's nightclub, Montmartre. Joyce danced 'incessantly' to try to overcome her feelings of separation from her mother and Coleman.

'Leaving America was as unpleasant as all ending pleasures are,' she wrote as she boarded the Cunard liner *Aquitania*. Normally she enjoyed watching the other passengers but this time she tried to regain her composure by remaining in her cabin. However, one evening, leaning against the railing, watching the sun set over America, she attracted the attention of a young man. Owsley Grey was an engineer about to seek his fortune in west Africa. It took him two evenings to persuade Joyce to join him for a glass of lemonade in the smoking-room, where they discussed travel, theatre and Customs officials. She felt very much older than him, even though the gap was only four years. She had matured from a naïve young wife into a woman with a secret.

Her heart was still in North Carolina when Reggie met her in freezing fog at Southampton. 'I found it hard to make the right noises of gladness at being home again,' she wrote. Later she looked back at her time with Coleman as 'very emotional, tense and unhappy – for I did love him terribly'. But unlike her mother she refused to succumb to temptation – her place was with Reggie in London. While Nora acted spontaneously on the desires of her heart, Joyce was more conscious of the effect this could have on others and decided to make her marriage to Reggie work. Her 'Brief Encounter' with Coleman was a crucial point in her marriage.

Nine months later Coleman came to visit Joyce at Cliveden. 'We spent the afternoon walking and talking,' she wrote to her mother. 'For the first time we talked of his work and ourselves and all that sort of thing and you can't think how simple and easy it was and how happy we both feel because it is like that. I really love R more because of it and oh, I've learned *so* much.'

– 6 –

Back in London in the new year of 1936, Joyce realised that the standards set by her relations compelled her and Reggie to live beyond their means. They had to support a seven-bedroomed house in Chelsea, their domestic servants and a handyman on Reggie's salary as a junior accountant. Cousin Nancy Tree was generous with her couture clothes and Aunt Phyllis Brand gave them a second-hand Wolseley car, but still Joyce worried. Dispensing with one of the domestic servants or going to the cinema less than five times a week was not apparently an option.

Joyce decided that she had better start earning. George Bernard Shaw had seen her drawing and suggested that she become a commercial artist, but advised that success required 'either an agent or a Jewish great-great-grandmother'. It was many years before Joyce discovered that one of her great-great-grandmothers on the Phipps side was indeed Jewish, the daughter of a Liverpool trader. W. H. Smith's great-grandson, Jimmie, was an early dancing partner, and with his help Joyce sold six Christmas-card designs to the company. She also designed two posters – one for a private airline, which closed even before the poster was finished, and the other to advertise gardens open to the public. She earned £7.10s. for the posters before abandoning her paintbox.

Next, inspired by Fitzgerald and Coleman, Joyce sent articles and short stories to the *New Yorker*, the *Atlantic Monthly* and the literary agent A. P. Watt, but none of them saw any talent. 'To be a little bit talented in several directions is quite a handicap in the beginning. I sang a little, I wrote a little, I was funny a little. Every time I sat down to write something I thought I'd be better at painting it and if was drawing it I thought I could do it better if I was singing about it.'

That spring Aunt Nancy Astor suggested that until they were better off they should live in one of the cottages on the Cliveden estate. In lieu of rent Joyce would be expected to be 'on call' as a social secretary and dutiful substitute 'daughter'. Joyce and Reggie accepted Nancy's offer, and Paul was commissioned to renovate a cottage on the edge of the estate, a mile from the main house. Joyce wrote to her mother when they moved in at Easter 1936 that Parr's, named after the butler who had once lived there, 'is the most wonderful present and I continue to be incredulous at it.'

Parr's had been built by Waldorf Astor's father, with high gables and small windows. Paul removed all traces of Edwardian gloom by rendering the walls white and installing green metal windowframes. The dining-room was big enough to hold their baby grand piano; there were three bedrooms; and a sitting-room each for the Grenfells and the cook. Paul included his usual trademarks such as windowsills and frames painted black on the inside, in order to frame the view of pastures and woods. The quality of the work was as high as in the stately homes he renovated, and many of the fittings are still in use sixty years later. The sitting-room was inspired by Nora's taste, with books on either side of the fireplace and long, pale-coloured sofas. French windows opened on to the garden, where Reggie planted magnolia trees and a herbaceous border. Nancy gave Joyce a set of china and £100 to spend on furniture at Heal's, where she chose limed-oak furniture.

They were instantly better off by renting out St Leonard's Terrace and only employing a cook and a daily cleaner. Mary the parlour maid had been asked to come too, but she said she 'couldn't stand the idea of all them fields an' that'. Rene Easden from nearby Taplow, aged eighteen, was employed. In 1937 a government Code for Domestic Servants recommended that eighteen-year-old girls should work a maximum fifty-nine-hour week, with alternate Sundays off, for a minimum wage of eleven shillings per week – about 1p per hour. Even on that wage, Rene was so efficient that the cook was dispensed with.

Joyce immersed herself in the life of a busy country housewife. She joined a sewing-circle of young married women, drinking tea while constructing flannel nightgowns for the poor. At the Women's Institute meetings held in the Cliveden recreation hall, Joyce played

Jerusalem on a damp piano – a tricky piece in C sharp major with whole-octave chords. At the WI birthday party she invented games using drinking straws – such as blowing out cake candles from a distance of two yards and moving dried peas by suction. By 1938 she was both WI president and conductor of their choir, but she found it difficult to persuade the women to sing quietly. 'They yell boldly and sound like cracked horns.' She was responsible for organising talks on 'The Uses of Salads' and 'Better Darning', and choosing the songs from the *Daily Express Song Book*. She was delighted when the Cliveden branch came second in the Dainty Tea Competition and the Taplow branch were disqualified for showing nine plates of cakes instead of the stipulated eight. These activities proved a rich source of inspiration for her subsequent monologues.

Joyce was still hoping for a baby, and it was painful for her to watch Reggie's sisters marry and start families; it didn't help that the Grenfells were too tactful to mention it. As a Christian Scientist she would not seek medical treatment, though she did not object to Reggie seeing a specialist. All that is known about the specialist's advice is that he was told to eat more greens. The Eton archives show that when Reggie was seventeen several boys in his House caught mumps: he may have been one of them and as a result had low fertility. Joyce's letters to Virginia often mention her periods, a regular reminder both of her childlessness and the day that her beloved Nanny Lucy had left. Each month she suffered from short sharp depressions, which she called 'little deaths'.

They did, however, have two dogs: a black Labrador retriever, named Nannau after the Grenfells' holiday home in Wales, and a black spaniel called Gary Cooper. At weekends Joyce and Reggie gardened, played tennis and read their library books from Boot's in Maidenhead. Celia Johnson had married their old friend the writer Peter Fleming in 1935, and visited from nearby Nettlebed. Fleming was so impressed by Parr's that he commissioned Paul to design them a neo-Georgian house with a view over the Chilterns. Other friends, such as Virginia Graham, Rupert and Comfort Hart-Davis, and Reggie's brother and sisters, came to stay for weekends of rummy by the fire, swimming in the Thames and walks around the estate. One day Reggie was strolling with his sister Frances when they saw some people in the distance. 'The trouble with this place,' he said, 'is that you never know who you are going to bump into – it might be a gardener, but it could as just as well be royalty or a prime minister. So when I go for a walk around Cliveden I always limp. That way if it's royalty they think I'm bowing, and if it's a gardener they just think I've got a gammy leg.'

One weekend Reggie taught Joyce to drive in an ancient Austin, which she called 'Jane' after her favourite author. This was before driving-tests, and her first solo journey of two miles to Taplow Station took forty-five minutes, stalling at the sight of every bend or oncoming vehicle. After that she became a safe, but always slow, driver. The old Wolseley was replaced by Nancy with a new two-door Ford at a cost of £106.

Next door to Parr's was Triangle Cottage, and most days Joyce popped in for a chat with ninety-year-old Mr Jeffries, a retired estate gardener. At Christmas 1936 she directed the estate workers' children wearing Kate Greenaway costumes in an entertainment featuring songs by Virginia, poetry recitals and carols. This was followed by the estate workers' fancy-dress dance, where one housemaid dressed as a gramophone record and another came as a cracker. Mr Jeffries wore his grandmother's nightgown as Old Mother Slipper Slopper and Arthur Bushell, Waldorf's valet, was a pantomime fairy in the Astor racing-colours.

A year after they moved in, Nora came over from America, but it was neither under happy circumstances nor helpful to her relationship with her daughter. In late 1936 Aunt Phyllis's son Winkie Brooks, the cousin whom Joyce had worshipped as a small child, jumped out of a window in New York. Phyllis lived in Northamptonshire and her only refuge from grief was fox-hunting. After a wet January day in her side saddle, she caught pneumonia and a week later died. Nancy was inconsolable at the loss of her favourite sister and Nora came over to cheer her up. She bought presents in London for everyone, including an expensive ball-dress for Joyce. Over the following year Joyce forwarded many unpaid bills and lawyers' letters to Nora. She became increasingly exasperated and eventually, after fifteen months, paid for the dress herself. She asked Nora never to give her presents again, even for Christmas.

★

Nancy's chief purpose in having Joyce and Reggie living at Parr's was to replace her children. By 1935 all of them had escaped from her overbearing attentions. 'She is such a contradiction of kindness and unkindness; understanding & over powering will that I'm often bewildered,' wrote Joyce in her diary. 'But thru it all I do love her and see her a little lonely thing overpowered by human will & power.' When Nancy gave Joyce frocks and jewellery, she responded with bunches of wild flowers.

By 1936 Nancy was a very busy MP as well as socialite, and she was constantly calling Joyce to come and attend her. One afternoon in her bedroom, Joyce watched Miss Hammond wash Nancy's hair; Miss Brew, a secretary, read out the Child Nutrition Bill; and Rosina, her maid, announce the arrival of a dressmaker. At the same time Nancy's tailor used Joyce as a clothes model.

'I'm always a nuisance, you have to be to get things movin',' Nancy admitted. This was a useful attribute for a politician but hard for those around her. If Nancy had had a hard time in the House of Commons she insisted that they played tennis together, whether Joyce felt like it or not. At nearly sixty she could still beat Joyce in three straight sets.

According to her great-nephew James Fox, Nancy's behaviour 'was always a guarantee against boredom, pomposity, convention. The sheer force of her personality, her humour, her high spirits, her attractiveness, above all her courage, greatly outweighed the negative.' Unlike the Astor children, Joyce shared Nancy's faith in Christian Science, and they went together to church in Maidenhead. Joyce found that one of the biggest tests of her faith was Nancy's driving. 'Aunt Nancy gave an exhibition of the poorest gear-changing I ever hope to witness, it was agony to listen & feel,' she wrote after church one day.

Growing up with Virginian laws and Chillie's domineering treatment of her mother had convinced Nancy of the importance of female suffrage and equality, and Joyce learned from her that women were equal to men. 'I've got nothing against men, in their place,' Nancy said. Many politicians could not cope with her, especially Winston Churchill. In one of their more famous exchanges Nancy said to Churchill, 'If I was your wife I'd put poison in your coffee,' to which he replied, 'And if I was your husband I'd drink it.'

There were times when Joyce felt that the atmosphere at Cliveden was 'so darned poisonous' that she had to leave at once and confide in her diary.

I'm beginning to think that the reason why I find the company of my relations (on my mother's side!) so wearing is that one can never relax in case one gives away one's inner most feelings. I cannot be natural. Perhaps I am too different to play the family game with complete ease. They use their wits but never their minds. Just so much family goes a mighty long way with me and the fact is I cannot sit and rock with any degree of pleasure for more than ten minutes. (The Southern bit left out of me?) The Phipps Yeoman stock drives me into activity – even if it's only writing letters. I can take teasing with better grace than I did but the fact remains: one has not got much humour about one's deep feelings. I believe I am a bit of a prig.

Joyce's duties also took her back to London. At a dinner for League of Nations delegates at St James's Square in March 1936, Joyce conversed in French with the head of Reuters Press Agency and a Spanish official, and found the Soviet Ambassador 'like a small very fat musk-rat' and the Romanian Ambassador 'exactly like a melting candle'. After dinner Nancy thought she would cheer up the humourless German Ambassador, Joachim von Ribbentrop, by playing Musical Chairs. Joyce thumped out a tune on the piano while Nancy whispered to her British guests that if they let the Germans win they would not need to go to war in Europe.

As a politician, Nancy championed the causes that other MPs ignored – slum clearance, the health of women and education of children, often siding with her Labour opponents. In 1923 she had succeeded in getting the Intoxicating Liquor Bill past the brewery lobby, raising the age for legal drinking to eighteen years. In 1937, when she forced through the Ten Year Plan for Children, Joyce attended a reception at St James's Square where the scientist Julian Huxley spoke in support of nursery schools. Joyce told Virginia that after hearing his speech it took considerable self-control not to devote her life to the cause.

Nancy's Ten Year Plan aimed to give British children more light, fresh air and a daily meal. When the Astors visited the Soviet Union in 1931, Nancy told Stalin that she was shocked by Soviet childcare and if he sent over a woman, she could be instructed properly in Deptford. A few months later, Stalin sent not one but a dozen women to be trained in modern methods of child development.

Meanwhile, Nancy volunteered Joyce for Slough Social Centre, five miles from Cliveden, which the Astors had helped to construct. With many new factories, the population of Slough had increased enormously and the families were housed in wooden chalets. Those who joined the social centre enjoyed radio dances, cinema shows and 'glider-skating'. 'No distinction of class, politics or race enters in the Centre Club remit,' stated the first annual report. When George VI and Queen Elizabeth visited, they played a game of darts and watched a keep-fit class. Other visitors to the centre during the first year included Queen Mary the Queen Mother, various peers of the realm and bishops, Rotary clubs, the Slough Chamber of Commerce and the Hitler Youth Movement.

Babies were catered for at an infant welfare clinic, where mothers were taught how to feed and rear their children more effectively. For two years Joyce helped to sell subsidised baby food and weigh the hundred babies who attended every Monday. In the late 1930s, nearly sixty thousand children under five died every year in Britain, mainly from the effects of malnutrition and poverty. Nancy persuaded Buckinghamshire Education Committee to build the first ever state nursery school, for eighty pre-school children from Slough. At the opening on 25 October 1937 Nancy made it clear that, pleased though she was with the county council's initiative, it was her idea and the Astors had contributed £1,025 to the cost of the £5,000 building.

Joyce attended the opening with her aunt and then volunteered to help run it. The model nursery school provided nourishing meals, play equipment and a sleeping area in the fresh air.

'To survey the scene is at once an entertainment and education in psychology,' wrote Mrs Wintle, the play-centre leader, in 1937. 'Some little folk gather together to pore over picture books and comics, while those of a serious turn of mind puzzle over brick constructions. The noise, of course, comes from the merry multitude who rush about, shoot down the slide, or toss balls to one another.' After lunch and an afternoon nap, the children danced, sang, played and did eurythmics as well as 'occupational lessons with plasticene and paint'. Handkerchief drill was followed by nursery rhymes. Each child had their own toothbrush, towel and comb hung up beside the child-level basins. 'All too soon it is time to pack the playthings in the roomy storehouse, and off the children go, once more to worry mother.' It was a revolution in state education. Nancy believed that 'If all the nations and people of the world had attended nursery schools when they were young, everything in the world would be running more harmoniously than it is today.'

The Slough *News Chronicle*'s headline ran SLOUGH'S FAIRY HOME OF HAPPINESS, but not everyone was so impressed. One local paper's editor wrote, 'We hesitate to welcome this unreservedly, for we can see it as the thin end of the wedge for a vast new branch of schooling all over the country which may add enormously to the burdens of the rate-payers without giving any deep-seated advantage to the nation – perhaps quite the contrary.'

Every summer Nancy hired two motor charabancs to bring the Slough Nursery School children and their mothers to Cliveden for the day. A Punch and Judy show entertained them and two Wall's cycle carts provided free ice-creams. Joyce organised games on the polo field and sent each child home with a fistful of flowers.

When Joyce learned of families in Slough who had nothing with which to celebrate Christmas, she organised nursery-school volunteers to take responsibility for one family each. For the family in her own care, she spent £2 on clothes and toys for the three children, a second-hand coat for each parent and a hamper of food. 'You can't think what a good time I had doing it,' she reported to her mother. 'Of all the forms of self-indulgence, giving is the pleasantest.'

Joyce was storing up her impressions of all these activities – Women's Institute, nursery school, committees – for the future. Nursery schools became a leitmotif of her work. Without Nancy's commitment she would never have written the line 'George, don't do that.' It seems she forgot her involvement with the very first state nursery school, for, after the success of her sketches, she claimed that she had never set foot in one. But her inspiration came from the very first state nursery school in Britain, which is still a thriving institution for over one hundred children.

★

Moving to Parr's had been good for Joyce – 'I am very happy these days and feel a very wise and lucky person,' she wrote to her mother in 1937 – but money was still short and Reggie's job was still precarious. Once again Joyce decided that she must get a proper job. She had been having singing lessons for some years, knew all the latest songs and now had the confidence to sing after dinner. While dining at the Savoy, she introduced herself to Caroll Gibbons, the American bandleader, and asked his advice. He invited her to make a gramophone record at the Billy Higgs Studio in Tottenham Court Road, with himself at the piano. She sang *Easy to Love* and believed her voice had a 'rich velvety sound'. Gibbons suggested that she might sing with the orchestra at the Hotel de Paris in Bray. However, when she heard the record, she realised she had a long way to go before she could sing in public. 'My vowel sounds are too open and I'm apt to hit the note instead of letting it flow.' Maybe Gibbons knew this too, and realised that making a record was the most tactful way for Joyce to find out.

In May 1936 she asked the BBC if they would consider employing her. In those days they auditioned anyone who wrote in and asked, so at Broadcasting House she sang Virginia's song *I'm in Love With a Gentleman*, with Virginia at the piano. Joyce told the adjudicators Mr Kester and Mr Mitchie that she could speak French and American and in north, south and west English accents. Mr Kester described her in his confidential report as 'a charming small intelligent voice of the Joan Carr type. Obviously a lady, if that means anything. I could use her.' Six months later Joyce had heard nothing and wrote again, whereupon Mr Mitchie suggested another audition. This time, having forgotten he had already seen her, he noted that she had 'a quite pleasant small voice. Might be used as a rather nice, simple, but cultured girl.' Over the next year Joyce wrote regularly to Mr Mitchie, and each time he assured her that he would use her one day. He never did.

Next she tried again to make money from writing. With Elliot Coleman's encouragement to read poetry, she devoured Housman, de la Mare and Sackville-West. Lytton Strachey, whom she met at Cliveden, encouraged her to join an English literature course run by his younger sister Marjorie. Once a week six women met in Gordon Square, and learned about romantic poetry. Joyce thought Tennyson 'wrote a good deal of complete rot and a certain amount of flat poetry'. Over lunch they discussed psychoanalysis – Lytton and Marjorie's brother, James, had been trained by Freud. Joyce thoroughly disapproved: 'It sounds frightful and altogether wrong. It's all bound up with sex and dreams and those way back terrible nursery days when one was repressed,' she wrote to Virginia. Joyce did not believe in introspection: moods should not be dwelled upon, but cured with activity.

However, the course in Gordon Square did lead her to write her own poetry. She sent 'Air for Strings' to Virginia, whose own work was being published in *Punch* and *Vogue*. Without telling Joyce, Virginia submitted the verse to *Punch* and Joyce was amazed when she received a cheque for ten shillings. This inspired her to write more, and within the next year she was a regular contributor of light and amusing verse – she never called it poetry – to *Punch*, *Country Life* and the *Observer*. Each effort took several weeks of 'long solitary walks, frequent hot baths and a lot of thought'.

Mr Watt, the literary agent, took his shilling commission for the poems but failed to persuade *Punch* to accept Joyce's articles. Edmund Valpy Knox, *Punch's* editor, criticised her attempts at social satire. 'You have been too merciless here – it is hard to write about such people without seeming disdainful, but that's what has to be attempted.' The deputy editor Mr Fougasse decorated her rejected material with drawings and explained to her why some of her poems were ridiculous rather than funny.

'I twist my pen, draw daisies up the margin and go in search of an apple,' she wrote to Virginia in one of her daily long letters. 'But Golly, how I long to do it. I can visualise things and I laugh myself at some of the things I see, but I *can't* tighten it up into words and paragraphs.'

Eventually her tenacity and social connections led to articles being published. Joyce loved listening to the radio, though in her teens this had been considered a terrible waste of time, even worse than reading a novel before lunch. One day in 1936 she was enjoying Bach's Italian Concerto so much on the radio that she was late for a lunch party at Cliveden. She bicycled the mile at great speed and arrived panting. The butler showed her straight to her seat, next to the editor of the *Observer*, James Louis Garvin. Waldorf Astor owned the paper and

Garvin had given it a reputation for both dependable news and coverage of the arts. His uncompromising editorials were known as 'The Thunderstorms'.

'Why are you late?' asked this distinguished man of nearly seventy. Joyce told him she'd been listening to Bach on the radio.

'Do you mean you actually *listen* to the radio?' he said, his blue eyes widening in astonishment. Joyce told him enthusiastically of all the wonders that could be heard: plays, concerts, talks and variety programmes. Already there were eight million licence holders, but Garvin seems to have been unaware of the most popular medium in the country. The *Observer* had featured articles about the *ethics* of radio and its global implications but never mentioned actual radio programmes. He asked Joyce to let him know next time Bach's Italian Concerto was being broadcast: he too liked music. It appears he had never heard of the *Radio Times*, which had, by then, been appearing for thirteen years.

Six months later Garvin sent for Joyce and asked her if she could write. 'Have you appeared previously in print?' (All *Observer* correspondents had to have newspaper experience.) 'Oh yes, in *Punch*,' she said confidently. On the strength of her three published poems Garvin offered her a six-week trial as the *Observer*'s first radio critic. It was to her advantage that radio critics were still rare – Britain's first, Sydney O. Moseley, began writing in 1929, and the *Listener* had only published a radio column for the past two years.

Garvin took personal responsibility for her apprenticeship. She had to write 750 words every week and send it to him for correction. He taught her to avoid the words 'which' or 'and' but to use a full stop. 'Short sentences are more telling. Give facts first and feelings later,' he said.

After only four trial articles, Joyce's first, uncredited, radio column appeared in the *Observer* on 11 April 1937. It praised the first Robert Mayer concert for children, conducted by Dr Malcolm Sargent. There was also a fine recital from a Surrey wood of a blackbird, a robin, a thrush and a woodpecker, in spite of interruptions from a circling plane. 'It was enough that they sang, and sing they did, gloriously.' She was less impressed by Val Gielgud's production of *The Cherry Orchard*, as all the voices sounded the same. Her sentences were so short that some had no verbs in at all. Garvin was impressed.

'You have got the flick of the wrists in writing,' he said. Eight weeks later her name appeared under the column.

Many of the institutions of the BBC were already well established – schools broadcasting, *The Week's Good Cause*, Mr Middleton's gardening talks and Alistair Cooke. Ten years earlier the first live commentaries had been made on the Oxford and Cambridge Boat Race, the Grand National and a BBC Prom concert. With all programmes transmitted 'live', Joyce had to plan her day around the radio.

'I was very conscientious and listened to everything likely to be of interest. Poetic dramas with intoning choruses going on and on in minor keys – "O woe, woe, woe, All is misery and woe" – and talks on soil erosion and sea-gulls, and, for my own pleasure, chamber music.' Her favourite programmes always seemed to coincide with meals, so Joyce and Reggie ate in the drawing-room. Reggie didn't mind – he was as pleased as Joyce not to go out in the evenings. Occasionally she would attend a transmission at Broadcasting House, writing her review in the studio. Even on Christmas Day she was listening and taking notes.

Once Joyce had proved her worth, the *Observer* provided her with the latest Murphy wireless set on which she could even find American programmes. She wrote a column every week for three years and set the standard for the new art of radio criticism. 'She invented the trade,' said theatre historian Sheridan Morley. 'She was the best radio critic I've ever read, her pieces were excellent. Hard-edged and intelligent, she didn't take prisoners: when she praised it was real praise. Joyce Grenfell's radio-reviewing has never been properly acknowledged.'

Without looking for it, a job that combined her two favourite occupations – listening to the radio and writing – had fallen into her lap and she was earning £10 a week – even more than Reggie as an accountant. While working she could continue sewing too – she found it hard to listen without something for her hands to do.

Yet Joyce still hankered after being a voice on the radio and, using her *Observer* connections, she organised an audition with Val Gielgud, head of BBC Radio Drama. He wrote in his confidential report that she wasn't a trained actress and he could see no future for her on radio.

– 7 –

JOYCE WAS THRILLED when in the summer of 1936 her brother Tommy got a job with the *Daily Express* and brought his new Texan wife, Betty, to live in London. Joyce enjoyed having a sister-in-law, who 'was so Southern her voice sounded as if it were lying down'. They went shopping together and the Phippses came to Parr's for weekends. Paul converted Betty to Christian Science, though Tommy could still not be persuaded. Joyce and Tommy did not have much in common beyond a shared sense of humour; she thought he should be more organised, but he took after his mother in his spontaneity. Joyce was determined to improve their relationship and was disappointed that he didn't try harder. She took an active interest in Betty's pregnancy and they were all overjoyed when Wilton – Paul and Nora's first grandchild – was born in November 1937. 'Such a precious baby, pink and curly with square Phippsy hands and a solemn individual face,' Joyce wrote.

When, a year later, Tommy went alone to Hollywood, he did not tell Joyce whether he planned to return to London. After a month it was clear he had left for good and the furniture and books that Joyce had lent him had to be sold to settle his accounts. She didn't mind about the furniture, but she was upset about the books, which included signed copies by George Bernard Shaw and the E. Nesbits that Noël Coward had given her. Tommy's only communication was to send a telegram on Wilton's first birthday. Betty gave little away, and whenever Joyce phoned her she was 'wonderfully cheerful, and about as expansive as an oyster'.

Tommy finally cabled to say he had a job with Metro-Goldwyn, in the team writing *Broadway Melody of 1940* starring Fred Astaire and *A Yank at Eton* starring Mickey Rooney. He left it to Betty to decide whether she stayed in London or returned to America. Only twenty-three and homesick, Betty decided to go and see her father in Florida, leaving Wilton with Joyce and his nanny at Parr's. 'I think Betty loves the baby in her own rather detached fashion,' wrote Joyce. Little opportunity for bonding had occurred between mother and son: Wilton had a full-time nanny and Betty spent her days in bed or out with friends.

Joyce thoroughly enjoyed being Wilton's surrogate mother and wrote down every new thing he could do. Her favourite trick was saying 'bye-byes' to him, whereupon he would lay his head down, shut his eyes and remain inert for a few seconds, with his bottom high in the air. 'He really is the most enchanting child and we find him so companionable and endearing,' she wrote to Nora. 'Reggie adores him and they are too attractive together.'

After two months Betty wrote to say that the marriage was over and asked Joyce to arrange for Wilton to be shipped to Florida with his nanny. Joyce wanted a child, adored Wilton and believed that two parents would be better for him than one. She desperately wanted to adopt Wilton, but Reggie took a firm line and pointed out that Wilton had two healthy parents – even if they were no longer living together. Betty may have been young, but she was Wilton's mother and they had no right to him. Joyce was distraught at being parted from her eighteen-month-old nephew.

'Wilton left on Thursday and it was one of the less pleasant moments of my life,' she wrote to Nora. 'He was particularly alluring those last few days. Very funny and sturdy and solid and smelt good. Thank goodness he's gone now before he can talk. He really is the most angelic little boy.' She still missed him a year later but did not see him again until 1946, when he was eight years old. Joyce kept in touch with Betty and they met when they were both in New York or London. 'We kept up together and Joyce was always very kind to me. Paul Phipps gave me *Science and Health* and I never looked back,' Betty said sixty years later.

Joyce settled back down to life at Parr's but when she wrote her *Observer* review for 14 August 1938, she was unaware that it was to change her career yet again. A programme called *A Guide to the Thames* had delighted her: it followed the river with snatches of conversation, real sounds and local songs, using radio in a new way with pace, humour and style. Until then it had been rather serious, and voices spoke straight at the listener, whereas this programme made the listener feel like an eavesdropper.

Joyce's childhood friend and cousin-in-law Phyllis Nicholls (née Spender-Clay) decided that Joyce had better meet Stephen Potter, the producer of the documentary. So early in November the Grenfells were invited to dinner at the Nichollses' house in Victoria.

Stephen Potter was tall and gangly with fair, tousled hair. His tie never sat right underneath his collar and a cigarette usually hung from his mouth, dropping hot ash on to his clothes or the surrounding furniture. He had written the first biography of D. H. Lawrence and a few unsuccessful novels, and had been employed as a freelance producer by the BBC since 1936, progressing from schools programmes to documentary features. With subjects such as Dr Johnson, Chaucer and cricket, he pioneered the technique of quick, spare dialogue with fast edits, giving radio a more realistic feel. Potter had a healthy disregard for bureaucracy: in response to a telegram from the BBC asking for his promised script, Potter replied: 'EAR ON THE BALL/ MUSIC OF THE SPHERES/ SONG OF THE RUBBER HEARTED/ THE RUBBER CHIEF/ TOO MUCH BOUNCE − POTTER+'

Over coffee at the Nichollses Joyce described the Women's Institute meeting she had been to a few weeks before, where the theme had been 'Suitable Gifts for Christmas or the Bazaar Stall'. As the lady in Cliveden Recreation Hall had demonstrated how to make birds from pine cones and candlesticks from old cotton reels, Cousin Alice had had to suppress her giggles and Joyce had 'nearly strangled from not laughing'. Joyce reproduced the WI demonstrator's voice and her advice for useful Christmas gifts. The Nichollses and the Potters loved it, and all agreed to meet up again soon.

A few weeks later, Joyce wrote again about Potter in the *Observer*: 'I hardly dare even whisper the good news in case it all turns out to be a beautiful dream, but it really does look as if the feature programme has swung out of its rut into a wide new spaciousness that leaves one breathless. The man behind this revolution is Stephen Potter . . . And now comes the glad news that, in January, he is to join the features department as a full-time writer and producer.'

Potter responded by inviting Joyce and Reggie to supper on Friday 13 January 1939, the evening which Joyce subsequently said changed her life.

In her two-door Ford, Joyce drove to London and picked up Reggie from his office in the City. She had spent the afternoon lying in front of the fire, drying her long hair, which she combed back into a low bun. She wore a plain black dress and a sequinned jacket. Stephen and Mary Potter lived in a small, attractive Georgian house in Chiswick Mall overlooking the Thames. Mary's semi-abstract paintings hung in pale wooden frames on the sitting-room walls. A stocky woman with a good laugh, 'Att', as her contemporaries at the Slade called her, was a member of the 'London Group'. There was little money for decoration, so she had painted the walls and furniture white and made matching curtains and covers for the two divan beds. A scarlet armchair, books and spring flowers added colour while a blazing fire warmed the room.

The Grenfells knew none of the other ten guests – artists, writers and BBC producers – but the atmosphere was relaxed and welcoming. French loaves, a cheeseboard, a big block of butter and Austrian *apfelstrudel* were laid out on top of an upright Bechstein piano. Joyce ate hers sitting on the floor next to a Swedish diplomat. The guests included Francis Meynell, the socialist publisher and poet; Herbert Farjeon, the theatre producer and editor of the Nonesuch Press Shakespeare; Farjeon's beautiful wife, Joan, and his sister Eleanor, writer of children's books.

After supper everyone was expected to do a 'turn' – a song, sketch or a dance. Mary Potter usually played the ukulele, singing long, sometimes bawdy, narrative songs. Stephen Potter did a satirical lecture on 'Eng. Lit.' full of unintelligible, intellectual phrases, based on his time as a lecturer at London University. Another Potter party trick was imitating a pompous radio programme, with Mary as the hiss and sizzle of radio atmospherics.

Joyce followed with a song by Virginia about eight-year-old Princess Margaret Rose, sung with a lisp. Then Potter said, 'You must do the Women's Institute woman.'

'Which woman?' asked Joyce. Potter reminded her of the Nichollses' party the month before.

'Oh heavens, I don't remember what I said.'

Potter was insistent and she caved in. Sitting on the floor, Joyce launched into 'gifts that are not only easy to make, but ever so easy to dispose of'. The lady lecturer spoke carefully, her consonants neatly clipped, in her dainty voice with all her vowels aslant. 'A boutonnière from empty beech-nut husk clusters' was a creative way 'to take Nature's gifts and make them even lovelier'.

The guests responded with laughter and Joyce became carried away, embroidering on the original material. By sticking torn-up wallpaper in beige tones onto old biscuit tins, one could achieve 'an unusual piece of modernistic furniture'. The 'comic turn' was a calendar made from india-rubbers held together with stout wire. 'It is our duty to beautify our surroundings.'

When the laughter had died down, Herbert Farjeon, who had been sitting quietly in the corner, approached Joyce. He had dark eyes and an El Greco face and hands: long, pale and bony. He smoked a pipe, wore tweed jackets and laughed silently, his head and shoulders shaking. His nineteen-year-old assistant stage manager, Ian Carmichael, described him as 'a loveable, underfed Old English sheepdog'. He was theatre critic on the *Tatler* and known to be the wittiest, most literate writer of satire in the business. One of his first songs was the 1920s hit *I've Danced With a Man Who Danced With a Girl Who Danced With the Prince of Wales*. Farjeon's latest revue, *Nine Sharp*, was just finishing a long run in the West End. He asked Joyce who had written her sketch.

'Nobody,' Joyce said, 'I just made it up.' Farjeon said he was interested in using it in the new revue he was planning. He asked her to write it down and invited her to his home in St John's Wood, where Joyce could meet the character actress Charlotte Leigh. Already booked for the revue, she might perform it.

On the way home, the fog was so thick that Joyce and Reggie could only travel at ten miles per hour up the Great West Road. Reggie leaned out of the driver's window while Joyce leaned out of the other. But she didn't care – she was glowing with pleasure, and the excitement of the evening kept her warm. They had been to see *Nine Sharp* twice, so to be invited to write for Farjeon's next revue was beyond her dreams.

Over the next four days Joyce wrote out and improved 'Useful and Acceptable Gifts'. She took it to the Farjeons' home where she met

Charlotte Leigh. After lunch Joyce read them the script and Farjeon sighed with relief: it was as funny as he had remembered.

'I thought Joyce's impression was brilliant,' remembered Charlotte Leigh. 'But I was even more impressed by Joyce herself. When she'd gone, Bertie and I turned to each other, and said, "Isn't she magnificent?" We talked a bit more and I said, "Yes of course I'll do it if you want me to – but, you know, it won't be like *her*!"'

'It was quickly borne in on me,' said Farjeon later, 'that Joyce Grenfell and only Joyce Grenfell was the person to do Joyce Grenfell's material as only Joyce Grenfell could, so I asked her to come into the revue.'

Joyce was reluctant: she thought of herself first as a wife, second as a writer. Making people laugh was useful for entertaining friends, but not an earner. 'Thank you so much,' she said, 'but you see I've got a job. I'm a radio critic and I'm married and I live quietly in the country. Thank you for asking but I just couldn't.'

There was no shortage of provincial concert-party and music-hall artistes longing to appear on the West End stage, but Farjeon knew exactly what sort of entertainers he wanted for his revues – with individual talent, without big reputations, adaptable and willing. Despite her lack of experience, Joyce fitted his criteria, and in those days the actors' union, Equity, did not object to newcomers appearing on the London stage.

A week later, Farjeon wrote to Joyce that he believed that in the right theatre she would be an enormous success. He tried to entice her with the thought of the applause ringing in her ears. But she was not to be moved: she said she needed to be at home for Reggie in the evening. She also needed to be near a wireless at all times to continue her *Observer* reviews.

Joyce asked the three men in her life what they thought. Her father said, 'Why not?' J. L. Garvin, the editor of the *Observer*, said in his ringing voice, 'My dear Joyce, whatever widens your horizon makes you more valuable to us.' And Reggie said, 'You'll always think you could have done it if you don't try, so you'd better try.'

There was still the problem of the wireless set, but Farjeon was not to be defeated. 'I could definitely make arrangements for a set to be installed in my office. That would be perfectly simple,' he wrote.

Next, Joyce said that she could not stay out so late. Farjeon said she could confine herself to two stand-up turns, one in each half, and she need only come into rehearsals for her own material.

At last, after three weeks of letters and phone calls, Joyce agreed to appear – but she said she could not wait for the final curtain: she must get the train home from Paddington as soon as her second sketch was over.

'The next thing I remember,' said Charlotte Leigh, 'is Bertie ringing me up and saying, "I've got her!", to which I replied: "Cheers!"'

The final problem was her stage name. She did not want her relations to know what she was doing, so 'Joyce Grenfell' would not do, and 'Joyce Phipps' whistled. She toyed with 'Jane Wilton' and then settled on 'Jane Phipps'. Two weeks into rehearsals the family all knew anyway, and Reggie suggested using her real name. The Grenfells raised their eyebrows but were far too polite to say anything. Nancy Astor made it quite clear that the theatre was not the place for a young woman of Joyce's standing and hoped she would grow out of it.

Farjeon was working against the clock to write the whole revue himself, and asked Joyce if she had more material, either monologues or group sketches. By the time rehearsals started in March 1939 she had written several more monologues: a Brown Owl; a conversation at a cocktail party; and a gawky, jolly-nice head girl – a sketch she had often done for friends. Other ideas were still in her head. She found she could only write if she imagined herself in the part. Farjeon liked the head girl, but had already written a song for Hermione Baddeley about a schoolgirl. So Joyce's second monologue was *Three Mothers*: the Understanding Mother, whose daughter wants to marry a middle-aged Portuguese conjuror; an American Mother, who is trying to teach her daughter Shelley's 'Ode to a Skylark'; and the Village Mother, whose son Ernie has swallowed a conker, 'a conker what 'e'd borrered'. Joyce had discovered the Village Mother while brushing her teeth – by putting her tongue in front of her lower teeth, her speaker became instantly more rural. Later this technique was revived for Mrs Moss, the Terrible Worrier. The American Mother was inspired by Ruth Draper's monologue *The Italian Lesson*, in which she is constantly interrupted while trying to recite Dante. This became Joyce's longest-surviving monologue – she was still performing it thirty-three years later.

'Joyce came to a company party at my parents' home,' remembered Farjeon's son Gervase, his stage manager. 'It was two days before rehearsals began and she was very nervous of the company, who had all worked together before. Joyce sat slightly apart and talked only to me, aged eighteen.' One actor asked her if she had played in the Little Theatre before. He looked shocked when she replied innocently, 'O no, I've never played anywhere before.'

A few days later Joyce wrote to Farjeon, 'I think I begin to feel some of that pernicious tingling excitement of the theatre even after that brief introduction to it on Wednesday!' However, four weeks into rehearsals some of the cast were seriously worried about Joyce's ability to pull it off. She could still dry up. 'I am no good in re-hearsals,' she admitted thirty years later.

I work hard, but I don't do the job until the audience is there – or so it was then. I was not, somehow, at all scared about it. After all, it wasn't my job. I was a writer. This was an extra – my only fear was that I might forget my words so I did them all day long, in the bath, train, bus, in shops, hairdressers, getting up and going to bed. I knew them inside-out but still I was a very bad rehearser. The company looked aghast, they were appalled. I was a complete amateur.

Cyril Richard, one of the stars, told Farjeon that if he let Joyce remain they would all be on the streets at the end of the first week. Farjeon said she must be given a chance in front of an audience; his plan was to establish her as a hit, appearing twice very conspicuously and independently. Before the show opened, he told the *Evening Standard*: 'Joyce Grenfell's work is extremely individual and I feel I am justified in taking the risk.' This worried the established cast even more – were they going to be upstaged by an amateur? One of them demanded that Joyce should not appear more than once.

The exact scripts of all public performances had to be approved by the Lord Chamberlain before the first night. Farjeon often had problems with this: the sketch *Winter in Torquay* was censored because Hermione Baddeley as hypochondriac Mrs Twiceover used the word 'constipating'. The Lord Chamberlain objected on the grounds that 'it is a very unpleasant thing and calls up very unattractive pictures and, as such, is likely to cause embarrassment . . . to allow it once would open the gate for its future use by lesser playwrights, actors and actresses. Once a word of this sort is allowed, there is a tendency for it to come into popular use.' He agreed to the substitute 'costive' – a less common word for the same condition. Farjeon's song *Even Hitler Has a Mother* was banned altogether, because no one was permitted to 'hold up a Head of State to ridicule'.

The first public performance was not the official first night but a charity preview, and Joyce felt quite relaxed. Her Christian Science practitioner Mrs Mildred Rawson had been praying for her and in the afternoon she went to the movies before eating supper at a Lyons Corner House. She did not dress up for the stage, but wore a smart grey chiffon dress by 'Rita of Berkeley Square' with a pink embroidered jacket from her mother – clothes that she might have worn offstage. Charlotte Leigh showed her how to use stage make-up and then left her to experiment. 'Eventually I found out how not to look as if I had a temperature of a hundred-and-ten. It's so easy to get carried away with a pot of rouge.'

When Joyce stepped out onto the stage, the audience was laughing within seconds. 'My goodness this is fun,' she thought. 'I felt as if I was riding a big white horse – we were in perfect rhythm, or like playing tennis. I said something and they laughed, I said another line and they laughed again. I have never felt such a sense of power before or since.' She knew she had worked hard, but had then just let it happen. She was hitherto unaware that she had perfect timing, a rare gift that Farjeon had spotted immediately. The disgruntled stars said the audience only laughed because they were Joyce's friends and relations. In the taxi home she 'smiled all over': she had never had this feeling before and she felt 'knocked for six'.

Next day was the final dress rehearsal, performed without an audience except for Virginia and Reggie sitting in the back row. Joyce dried, her mind went quite blank, and she realised that she had no professional technique to fall back on. As soon as the rehearsal was over, she offered her resignation for the end of the week. Farjeon refused it.

All London's critics were present at the first night on Friday 21 April 1939, at the Little Theatre in John Adam Street, off The Strand, when 'Joyce Grenfell' made her professional debut. At midnight they did the whole performance again for an audience of actors and theatre workers.

The revue consisted of over thirty songs and sketches satirising contemporary theatre and culture. *Chekov-Mixture*, *Magyar Malady* and *Flotsam and Gypsum* satirised the fashion for musicals set in Hungary. Laughing at folk dancers, gala-matinée organisers and the Women's Institute was permissible, but the *Sunday Times* was shocked that Farjeon poked fun at the sacred cow of Glyndebourne Opera, then only five years old.

> Where dear Mozart is ultra smart, And even more expensive . . .
> Even your grass, your velvet grass,
> Assures we are upper-class . . .
> It *must* be good, we've come so *far*,
> At so much inconvenience!

The revue ended with a song written by Joyce's first cousin, Nicholas Phipps, who had been acting and writing for the theatre for some years. He had made his stage debut at the Old Vic in 1932 and toured with Sybil Thorndike in plays by Shakespeare, Coward and Euripides. Everyone in the company received £5 per week and, with her percentage of the profit, Joyce took home £11, the equivalent of about £500 today.

Fargeon's *Little Revue* received glowing reviews. The *News Chronicle* said, 'Mr. Farjeon was born always to write the best revue in, for and at London.' James Agate of the *Sunday Times* thought 'this revue is like a race in which all the runners consist of Derby winners. My own choice would be the two contributions written, devised and acted by Joyce Grenfell. These monologues are the best thing in their kind since Miss Ruth Draper, the difference being that Miss Draper's are too long. And Miss Grenfell's too short.' 'Beyond question, Herbert Farjeon is easily our wittiest writer of revue. Miss Joyce Grenfell gave brilliant slices of type impersonation,' reported the *Daily Herald*. 'I have not heard so much loud laughter from dramatic critics for many months, if ever,' sang the *Daily Telegraph*. 'Joyce Grenfell is another joy. She hits off with gentle but deadly precision a whole series of well-meaning women.' The *Daily Mail*, *Evening News* and *Manchester Guardian* all compared Joyce to Ruth Draper.

After reading the reviews, she wrote to Farjeon:

Of course I don't believe any of it and I'm quite sure there must be some mistake – all the same I do want to thank you very very much for your all important part in it. It is exciting and I feel quite unreal and most peculiar. You have been so 'understanding' and encouraging and I do appreciate it. And those lovely flowers and the telegram – thank you for them too. As my papa said: 'Farjeon has *quality* – the real stuff' and he's right –
Yours Joyce

Perhaps the secret of her appeal lay in the respect she felt for her audience. 'Joyce used to drive us mad because she *liked* matinée audiences!' said Charlotte Leigh. 'The more experienced girls in the dressing-room always referred to the audience as "Them",' said Joyce. 'Someone asked a girl in the opening number, "What are 'They' like tonight?" It was obviously the thing for the actors always to expect "Them" to be awful! I couldn't adjust to this attitude. It seemed to me that, after all, these people had paid to come in – and surely, the chances were that they were determined to have a good time.'

Joyce also did not adjust to the 'complete lack of standards' of her colleagues in the company and regretted that they did not go to church or read books and that many were homosexual. She could not resist telling Farjeon how to run his theatre, either.

Dear Bertie, The sofas are lovely BUT do you think something could be done about the waitresses [usherettes] appropriating the sofas and chatting over their knitting? I realise they've got to have rest too, but perhaps not so essentially as we do. And do you think it would be possible to have something said about silence in the foyer? If people want to talk there are always the dressing rooms but personally I feel I'll scream if there isn't one spot where silence is the absolute rule. I'm writing this without asking the others but I know they feel the same. This note does not require an answer – only a ruling!

Despite these problems, she did enjoy going with the company to the Chelsea Theatrical Garden Party, the event she had loved as a child. She helped to make £23 with a penny-rolling stall and chatted with Noël Coward and Ivor Novello. She still thought the whole adventure was simply an extraordinary experience that would come to an end soon.

As the *Little Revue* settled into its run, Joyce and Farjeon got to know each other better. Their letters reveal a relationship akin to that between Eliza Doolittle and Dr Higgins in *Pygmalion*. Farjeon had 'created' Joyce and she had succeeded further than even he had hoped. He fell in love with her, not in a physical way but as a talented daughter, and he became quite possessive. Several theatrical agents approached her, but he warned them off.

'There is nothing I want less, theatrically speaking, than to lose you,' Farjeon wrote to her in June 1939, 'because you are a treat and have made an even greater success than I expected.' He planned to produce Joyce in matinées: 'I have a tremendous belief in you, now fortified by the opinion of everybody else. Listening to your Village Mother, it has occurred to me lately that you could do "Serious" character studies extraordinarily well too. I'd like to say what a pleasure it is personally to have you in the company quite apart from art-and-all-that – and I'm so glad you have found a friend in Charlotte [Leigh]. Ever yours – Bertie'. When they first met in January 1939 their letters began 'Dear Mr Farjeon' and 'Dear Mrs Grenfell', but by April it was 'My dear Joyce' and 'My dear Bertie'. Farjeon and his wife became regular Sunday guests at Parr's for lunch and tennis.

Joyce recorded *Useful and Acceptable Gifts* on a His Master's Voice gramophone record which sold for three shillings. When the BBC asked if they could transmit it she wrote, 'I hold an extremely low opinion of the record you wish to use – it's just too fast & so peculiarly pitched!' This was the only time that she recorded a monologue before she had stopped performing it.

Invitations to perform at charity shows and parties were coming in, and Joyce realised that if she didn't charge a fee, people would assume she was free and always available. In order to make these appearances she suggested to Farjeon that he change the running order of the revue. He gently rejected the idea, though he did agree to Joyce leaving early when she was invited to perform at a private dinner party for George VI and Queen Elizabeth. 'Great surgings of loyalty kept going up and down my spine as I looked at their two sweet little faces,' she wrote to her mother. A week later they brought the Regent of Yugoslavia to the show. Nanny Lucy, on the other hand, was not so impressed. 'Never mind, ducky,' she said, as if going on the stage was a punishment to be endured.

At the end of her three-month contract with Farjeon, Joyce worried about not seeing Reggie enough and insisted on fortnightly contracts, so that she could leave the company when she wished. 'Up till now I've had a grand time,' she wrote to Farjeon, 'but now that it's turning into harder work – novelty having worn off! – I find that my private life, which is by far the most important to me, is gradually getting sort of out of focus. I will certainly go on in the revue if you want me to. But I just couldn't sign on for three, or two or even one month. All of which is selfish and unprofessional but I do feel strongly about it and I hope you can understand.' Farjeon was planning to take his *Little Revue* to New York in the spring of 1940, when Joyce planned to visit her mother.

'What a find you were! I do hope you'll go on being happy,' he wrote in August 1939. Within weeks their outlook on the future was to change.

Within the Astor family there were several Members of Parliament and Cliveden was always buzzing with politicians. However, Joyce was not interested in politics and showed little concern when the Astors found themselves castigated in the press as pro-Nazi appeasers. Claud Cockburn, who coined the phrase 'The Cliveden Set', admitted as early as March 1938 that he had it made up – but the rumour ruined both Waldorf's and Nancy's political careers. They *were* at first more optimistic about Hitler and the Nazi Party than was Churchill, but they were not alone in hoping for peace in Europe: the Peace Ballot of 1935 collected over eleven million signatures. Once Hitler's expansionist intentions were clear, the Astors accepted the inevitability of war. When Waldorf had visited Hitler as part of a Christian Science delegation, he told him that relations could not improve between Britain and Germany until Hitler stopped persecuting the Jews. Hitler flew into a rage and had to be calmed down by his aides before the meeting could continue.

For much of 1938, war with Germany had seemed imminent: in March, Hitler invaded Austria and was threatening Czechoslovakia. Gas attacks were expected and lectures were given on gas-proofing a room with cardboard. Joyce thought she would rather sit in a wood alone or be blown up in a field than cower, masked, in a gas-filled house. Her father, still living in Chelsea, was more concerned about the possibility of having to share a lavatory bucket in the corner of the room with his housemaid.

Gas-mask distributors were surprised at the number of mothers of unregistered illegitimate children who came forward for the first time. They also noted that many Christians were reluctant to use masks that may have been tried on by Jews. The gas-mask distribution brought home the possibility of war to ordinary people, and house-wives filled their cupboards: Joyce ordered extra tinned soup and Virginia, about to marry Tony Thesiger, bought enough lavatory paper to last a decade.

By September 1938, as Chamberlain negotiated with Hitler and trenches were dug in St James's Park, the feeling of uncertainty was so potent that Joyce had been unable to settle to do anything. But she trusted Chamberlain would succeed, because 'to put yourself into an aeroplane for the first time at seventy and get hurled across Europe is pretty good. His knowledge of music endears him to me; and he knows all about birds, too. Such men have integrity, I feel.'

Chamberlain's 'Peace for our time' statement had dispersed every-one's fears and Joyce celebrated by going to a promenade concert of Beethoven's *Choral Symphony*. 'The militant-minded don't seem to realise that war cannot bring about peace,' she thought. 'The Germans won't learn through violence.' Hitler invaded Czechoslovakia the next day.

By Saturday 2 September 1939, everyone – even Joyce – knew that Chamberlain would declare war on Germany the following day. Joyce struggled through the pouring rain to the last performance of the *Little Revue*, where Beatrice Lillie made up for the tiny audience with her loud laughter. In the blacked-out train home, crowded with people escaping London, Joyce made friends with a family who were planning to walk several miles through the rain with their newborn baby and two-year-old son, to stay with relations. Joyce took the matter in hand – Reggie walked from the station while she drove them to their destination.

The next day, all theatres closed down; black-out curtains and barrage balloons went up; and homes were prepared for gas attacks by blocking the windows with brown paper or blankets. Joyce stocked up in Maidenhead with winter vests and six pairs of silk stockings. Nancy bought Joyce a new car and herself a new bicycle.

Over the next week, one and half million adults and children were evacuated from major cities to the country. Much to her surprise, Joyce was allotted two girls. Gwen Cooke was an eleven-year-old scholar from Godolphin & Latymer School in Hammersmith. She and her friends and teachers had had no idea where they were going when they boarded a train from Paddington.

'After a train journey to Windsor, I found myself at the Women's Institute in Taplow and was then taken with a schoolfriend, Margaret Wallis, to our new "home". We pulled up outside a pretty white-washed house, set in a large garden surrounded by pine trees, and a somewhat harassed lady opened the door.' Joyce explained she had to catch a train to London, but she would ask Rene to come back from her holiday.

'Mrs Grenfell dashed away and after we unpacked our suitcases we settled down to read. Not long after, we were greeted by a young man who appeared through the French windows, saying, "Hello, I'm Michael Astor. Do you mind if I help myself to a drink, then we can talk?" He was charming and stayed with us until Rene arrived. Years later I learned of Lady Astor's revulsion for alcohol.'

Gwen and Margaret adapted to their new life quite happily.

On Sundays Mrs Grenfell drove us to church in Taplow while she attended her Christian Science church. I can still recall the warm comfort of the Aga and smell of toast in the kitchen where we did our homework with Rene. She was quiet and shy but shared lots of fun and she made us feel part of the family. There was also a stout daily, Mrs Jaycock, who cleaned and made bread.

We ate with Mr and Mrs Grenfell and after dinner we gathered round the piano and learned a host of new songs. They were both unfailingly kind and warm-hearted.

Every morning girls and staff billeted around Taplow gathered at the village hall for lessons. 'In the afternoons we went blackberrying and for long walks with the dogs. Lady Astor often looked in, and our most exciting day was when she invited us to tea at Cliveden.'

Billets were paid 10s. 6d. (52p) a week for the first child and 8s. 6d. for each extra one. This hardly covered the cost of food when butter was 1s. 7d. a pound and milk was fourpence a pint. After food-rationing was introduced in January 1940, Women's Institutes, which had considered closing down, realised that they were now needed even more. The emphasis moved from 'Making Beech-nut Boutonnières' to feeding a large family on hedgerow fruit. Joyce was much exercised about the morality of obtaining more than their fair share of food. 'Mr. Hall the butcher seems to have too much meat & anxious to sell. But would it be *legal*?'

The countryside was filled with urban children wearing labels and carrying gas masks. Gwen and Margaret often visited the eighty-one orphans under five who had been billeted on Cousin Alice at Taplow Lodge. 'A clutch of cherubs clothed in coloured wool', Joyce wrote in a poem for *Punch*.

> Round heads, round eyes,
> Rose noses and rose knees
> In tottering progress two by two they walk,
> Squealing broad Bermondsey . . .

She was relieved that she had not received any 'little street arabs with wide vocabularies', and enjoyed having Margaret and Gwen to stay: 'they are both darlings, and no trouble at all', she wrote. They fitted her image of ideal girls – intelligent, well-mannered and tidy, they laughed but were not noisy. Gwen remembers that Joyce ensured they made their beds, dusted their rooms and helped Rene lay the table.

'Our idyllic life could not go on for ever – the school was scattered across two counties. With formidable persistence our headmistress persuaded the authorities to share Newbury County Girls School and after three weeks the entire school left for Newbury, our home for the next three years.' By the spring of 1940 a million evacuees had returned home, saying they would rather be killed on their own doorsteps in an air raid than die of boredom in the countryside.

The 'phoney war' from autumn 1939 to spring 1940 was a time of suspense – gas masks were carried, saucepans were collected to be melted down for arms, and conscription began. During the early part of the war, unemployment among women actually rose. Those in 'light or inessential' industries were laid off, and the Women's Land Army and the ATS could not cope with the huge numbers of women applying. Petrol-rationing led to redundant motor mechanics, who then became tractor drivers. Consequently, although thirty thousand young women volunteered to join the Land Army, by January 1940 only two thousand were employed. Joyce was relieved that her beloved Rene could stay on as housekeeper.

Despite her reservations about her country going to war, she accepted that it was the only way forward and appreciated that

Reggie was keen to join up. However, the Army did not need thirty-six-year-old men with varicose veins. With his mathematical skills, he was advised to try the War Office but they told him to stay where he was until vacancies were created by fatalities. In February 1939 he had been given a job by his stepmother's cousin, Oliver Lyttelton, later Lord Chandos, with the mining company British Non-Ferrous Metals. The job combined Reggie's accounting ability and his experience with his father's mines in Europe and Africa. Britain depended on imports from the British Empire of copper, lead, tin and zinc, and during 1938 Lord Chandos noticed that the Germans were buying abnormal amounts of copper – just as they had in the run-up to the First World War. Copper was needed to make cartridge and shell cases but no one in the government was interested in his information. So Chandos dispatched Reggie to various parts of the country to persuade copper-producing companies to enlarge their holdings. The war began with seven thousand tons of copper in stock; by the end of 1940, fifty thousand tons per month were needed.

Reggie may also have helped to secure the one ton of uranium ore that the Air Ministry imported in July 1939 for nuclear research. Until the advent of nuclear energy and arms, uranium was an unwanted by-product of other ores, chiefly mined in the Belgian Congo and left in piles in Belgium. The possibility that uranium might be used as a powerful explosive emerged in 1939, and British nuclear physicists considered it imperative to acquire the uranium in Belgium before Germany did.

In January 1940 Reggie was given a job at the Foreign Office, working long night shifts decoding telegrams. He still wanted to join the Army but first his varicose veins had to be treated. 'Reggie looked heavenly – hair all curled up from exertions (gardening) and damp,' Joyce wrote in her diary. 'I love him so, it may be disloyal and selfish but I don't want R. to be a soldier. He's doing enough at the Foreign Office. I do hope his legs don't pass.'

With the evacuation of first children and then businesses, many people believed that London would soon be empty and there would be no need for theatres. But, as Oswald Stoll wrote to *The Times* on 4 September, 'Entertainment is necessary to the morale of the people . . . It is not logical to close theatres and cinemas and to open churches to crowds.' The following day in *The Times* George Bernard

Shaw urged the immediate reopening of all places of entertainment and added, 'All actors, variety artists, musicians and entertainers of all sorts should be exempted from every form of service except their own all-important professional one.' Within three days of war being declared, Farjeon began planning to reopen the *Little Revue*, possibly in the cellars beneath the Adelphi Theatre.

'Come and work for me again when you like and when you can,' he wrote to Joyce. 'Don't wait to be asked. There is always hope for the world while there is emotion, and there will always be emotion. Happier days will come and then we shall all be able to cry. Ever yours, Bertie.'

Newspapers had to cut down on paper and report only censored news, so Joyce's *Observer* job came to an end. At first she thought she ought to work 'in some organising capacity in which my natural bossiness might at least be put to some use. It's certainly a very queer war so far. I don't feel anything very much except a passionate longing to return to normal. Maybe I am meant to be an entertainer though I can't say I feel at all funny for the moment.'

Everyone's lives had changed. Celia Johnson lived with her baby son and six of his cousins at Nettlebed and found herself driving tractors, being a local policewoman and acting in the West End. Virginia's husband Tony had joined up and she herself joined the Women's Voluntary Service, set up by her indomitable friend Baroness Reading to harness the energy of middle-class housewives. They escorted evacuee children, ran mobile canteens and distributed clothes. For many such women, this was their first experience of urban poverty and they were amazed at the stoicism of East Enders. Virginia never had to worry about money: when all her domestic staff left, she evacuated to Claridge's Hotel.

By the end of October, Farjeon was ready to reopen the *Little Revue*, this time including *Even Hitler Had a Mother*, described by the *Sunday Chronicle* as 'the banned song that all the troops are singing'. Due to the possibility of night air raids, the show began at 1.15 p.m. and ran for three shows continuously until 6 p.m. 'We'd hear people get up and go out as they do in the movies when they got to the bit where they'd come in!' said Joyce. 'It was very disconcerting, like a slap in the face.'

'Joyce Grenfell, tall fresh-looking, unsophisticated, was the sensation of the revue,' announced the *Radio Times* when the show was broadcast live. 'In her monologue The Head Girl she is heard first collecting subscriptions for a mistress who is to be married, and then chiding her colleagues for letting down the spirit of the school. Weren't two girls seen washing in the same basin at the same time? Her impression has a touch of genius.' Everyone in the cast was paid £5 a week, and after paying income tax, theatre tips and train fares, Joyce was left with £2. 7s. In November 1940, a second edition began with only two performances a day and a month later the third edition opened with early-evening performances.

'Herbert Farjeon's new revue has passed The Censor with flying colours,' said the *Daily Telegraph*. 'The author has had some difficulty with one member of the cast – Miss Joyce Grenfell. Her stage career may be called an accident. She came home one day from a village fete and gave an impersonation of the protagonists. This proved so successful that she repeated it to friends. In the end she was persuaded to put her talents to professional use. She did so with a success that made her a star overnight.'

The myth that Joyce had seen the WI lecturer the same day as she was 'discovered' imitating her at a dinner party was now in print, but in fact the original talk had been absorbed for thirteen weeks, rewritten over several more and finally performed four months later.

January 1940 was so cold that even the English Channel froze. 'Sucked an orange down Ennismore Gardens under a young moon's eye and brilliant icy stars,' wrote Joyce. She wore trousers for the first time and slept in a flannel nightgown, bed-jacket, shawl and bed-socks, with two hot-water bottles under six blankets. Audiences were so small that the show was only expected to last another week. When the pipes froze at Parr's, Joyce had the whole of Cliveden to herself for a weekend. On her thirtieth birthday she felt very melancholy – she missed her mother and Wilton terribly – but felt better after a laughter-filled lunch with Reggie and her father. Virginia wrote to her: 'I can think of no thirty years more usefully and disinterestingly spent – & I find it particularly clever of you, now that you have attained such a large measure of success, to have changed not one morsel. Perhaps it is because, unlike others, you attribute your success to God. Whatever it is, you have managed to remain consistently Joyce, and for this we love you.'

After the show on St Valentine's Day 1940, Joyce wrote in her diary: 'At theatre thought I looked queer, discovered covered with a rash – all over!' She telephoned her CS practitioner Mildred Rawson, who said she must have the rash diagnosed. In spite of a high fever, swollen glands and the rash, Joyce was sure she could go on performing. Reggie called in Dr Bankoff, a Russian Jew who lived upstairs from Pauline Spender-Clay's flat in Knightsbridge, warning him about Joyce's religious beliefs.

According to Reggie, Dr Bankoff examined her and said, 'I understand that you do not have German measles and that it is only an Idea. But your audience will see the rash all over your face and neck, and they will believe that you have German measles. This would worry them and prevent them appreciating your performance. So it would be best if you stay in bed until the rash goes.' Joyce agreed and spent the next six days in bed, phoning Mildred up all through the night. All visitors were banned and her letters were sterilised in the oven before posting. In spite of these precautions, three of Joyce's female friends and Peter Fleming also caught it. Fleming spent his sick-leave writing a best-selling comic novel about Hitler called *The Flying Visit*.

When Hermione Baddeley got tonsillitis, Joyce became the star who came down the centre of the stage for the final curtain call. She was surprised and touched when a friend told her how proud Aunt Nancy was of her – Nancy could never show it to her directly. By the end of February the theatre was sold out again, but Hermione Baddeley's tonsils were no better and the revue closed in March, after over 350 performances. Farjeon laid on a big meal for the company and they gave him a gold pencil.

'Oh dear,' Joyce wrote in her diary. 'I've *loved* the Little Revue.' She felt depressed and miserable for several weeks, even though she was very busy. The war led to a big demand for charity performances and she appeared at the Countess of Munster's Wool Fund, Jewish Services Clubs and a cocktail-cabaret at the Dorchester in aid of the Free French. She entertained 'a nice homesick crowd of international refugee students. There were Czechs, Austrians, Poles, Indians, Gold Coast gents of incredible darkness and all caught here by the war in a state of great poverty'.

Only eight months since she first set foot on a stage, Joyce decided to write a handbook for amateur drama enthusiasts. 'Oh amateurs!'

she wrote in her diary after a concert near Bedford. 'We had no compère, no stage manager – we worked like beavers to a very sticky houseful of 600 airmen and finally broke them down with Harold Lindo swinging at the piano and me singing over the mike.' Joyce applied her stage make-up on the train back to London, and arrived just in time to replace Bea Lillie in a charity show at the Strand Theatre. 'I'm always the Guest Artist in an Amateur Bill,' she wrote to Farjeon. 'They don't know when to stop and by sheer man power wear down the audiences, turn after turn. It's good practice.'

She felt a real pro when she was asked to be in the finale of the Royal Command Matinée. Joyce had difficulty learning the lines for Lady Bull, a hostess entertaining a party of refugees with a conjuror played by Leslie Howard. Out of the conjuror's hat came excerpts from plays: Michael Redgrave and Peggy Ashcroft played Romeo and Juliet, and Ralph Richardson, on leave for three days, played a scene from *Henry V*. Edith Evans and John Gielgud were 'WONDERFUL. It is fun seeing craftsmen at work, oh dear! I know so little.' After four rehearsals the cast of stars performed at the Palace Theatre and Reggie and Paul paid a guinea each to be in the audience with the King and Queen.

Joyce took part in troop shows at hospitals, gun-sites and camps around London, adding songs such as *A Nightingale Sang in Berkeley Square* to her repertoire. The Master of the King's Musick, Sir Walford Davies, showed her how to get troops singing, even if they were in bed. She hid her nervousness, and treated the patients as if they were friends. The *Daily Sketch* reported:

> In a drill hall packed with hundreds of soldiers this weekend I took part in a remarkable singing lesson. Our teacher was Miss Joyce Grenfell, who demurely announced she wished us to learn a song called 'I paid a shilling to see a tattooed lady'. She soon had a brace of generals, a covey of colonels, a monocled adjutant, and all the men singing lines like 'Somewhere on her spine is a regiment all in line, and round about her kidneys there's a bird's eye view of Sidney.'

Joyce had learned that song from an American soldier at Cliveden Hospital during the First World War.

Charlotte Leigh remembered, 'The first inkling I had that she could really reach the front rank was when we were entertaining the troops. The way she so naturally handled those audiences was incredible. They just ate her up.'

After hearing the news on 10 May 1940 that Holland and Belgium had been invaded, Nancy insisted that she and Joyce played tennis all afternoon. When invasion of Britain seemed imminent, parents had only days to decide whether to send their children overseas. Joyce's Cousin Alice sent her daughters Anne and Elizabeth, aged fifteen and fourteen, alone to American cousins. Pauline Spender-Clay took her grandchildren with their nannies to the USA, while Reggie's sister Mary Waldegrave took her five daughters to Canada and gave birth to her first son soon after arriving. No one realised that it would be up to six years before they saw Britain again. For the first time in twelve years, Joyce was relieved that she had no children.

As everyone prepared for invasion, the Prime Minister issued a leaflet entitled 'Beating the Invader'. It declared: 'STAND FIRM. Do not run away, or stop work. Do the shopping, send the children to school, do not evacuate to other areas . . . With a bit of common sense you can tell whether a soldier is really British or only pretending to be so. If in doubt, ask a policeman. Disable or hide your bicycle, destroy your maps, hide the distributor head of your tractor.'

When she went shopping in Maidenhead, Joyce took the rotor arm out of her car in case a Fifth Columnist or German parachutist stole it – fines of up to £50 were imposed for leaving a car without immobilising it. Sitting on the terrace after dinner at Cliveden, Joyce and the Duke of Devonshire spotted a flashing light on the opposite bank of the Thames. They phoned the police to alert them to this possible spy sending messages.

Many of Joyce's friends were killed, injured or captured at Dunkirk in June 1940. The fall of France meant that, despite the state of Reggie's legs, he was called up to the King's Royal Rifle Corps in Wiltshire as a second lieutenant. 'I felt sunk and had such a good cry after which I felt much worse!' said Joyce. Before Reggie left Parr's, he lent his shotguns to the local Home Guard.

Joyce experienced her first air raid in London the night before Reggie left for the Army. She was terrified as they huddled with the servants in the cellar of 4 St James's Square until the all-clear sounded at dawn. Later that morning Reggie left: 'He looks *so* attractive in his uniform and I was proud to walk with him. I didn't like it one bit. I hope he likes it – 37 is a bit old to go back to school.' To take her mind off his departure, Joyce helped with the hay-making on Cliveden Farm.

After a few days, Reggie settled into the camaraderie of the officers' mess. His regiment was based in Swindon, and he and Joyce saw more of each other than most married couples. During his leaves they pottered happily together, gardening, going on long walks, and shooting pheasants, snipe and rabbits for the larder. Despite her earlier reservations, Joyce was thrilled when Reggie gave her a regimental brooch.

'Having Reggie home is enough to make me happy. It's so cosy too & so right. The house is always warm and friendly but it blossoms when R is home & I feel sort of complete. I don't like the separation one bit. Blast Hitler.' They wrote to each other every day, though Joyce complained that Reggie's letters dealt mainly with games of bridge. Reggie pointed out that they would be less boring if she learned the game.

Shortly after more than four hundred people were killed in London in one night, seven bombs fell a few hundred yards from Joyce while she sang to troops near Beaconsfield. 'The noise wasn't too bad,' she wrote in her diary, 'one felt a rush of air past the ears and that was about all. The drive home alone wasn't very nice – *so* dark.' To her mother she wrote, 'there are few lovelier sights than search-lights on a starry night', and reassured Nora that she was able to cope, thanks to Christian Science and 'a nice solid constitution'.

Soon after the Battle of Britain, Joyce went to the Queen Victoria Hospital, East Grinstead, which specialised in treating the burns of fighter pilots. She found one of her debutante friends, Silvia Combe, working as a VAD nurse. 'She came down to sing to the men, and it cheered us all up.' Joyce was moved 'beyond words to see these great, tall, young men so disfigured, so crippled and oh, Golly, so uncom-plaining. How right he was, Winston, when he said of these boys "Never was so much owed by so many to so few".'

During the Blitz, on 16 October 1940, No. 4 St James's Square was damaged. Joyce went by train with the Cliveden domestic staff to clear it up and wrote, 'St James's Church [Piccadilly] has gone and

Leicester Square is a shambles. Blast and damn those bloody Nazis.'
She felt increasingly angry with the American government for not
joining the Allies, and Nora tried to compensate by sending nylon
stockings and food parcels. Joyce missed her terribly and when, in
September 1940, the BBC began broadcasting to North America,
she accepted every offer of work in the hopes Nora would hear her.
It also gave her the opportunity to say thank you for 'the neighbourly
gestures the *little* people are making', in the hope that the 'big people'
would hear. Nora encouraged the housewives of Tryon to knit, sew
and can vegetables, and persuaded every local farmer to cultivate an
extra acre of land for Britain. By now Tommy had moved from
Hollywood to Tryon and married local girl Donrue Leyton. When
he became a full US citizen Joyce was saddened, especially as she
believed he should be fighting for Britain.

As soon as war had been declared, Waldorf Astor had decided to build
a hospital for the Canadian Red Cross. It was finished in August 1940.
Built on the Cliveden polo fields, it resembled a small town, with
twenty wards of twenty-four beds each, operating-theatres, offices,
storerooms and its own roads. When Joyce saw it she described it as
'huge – a whole village. Beyond description. Hope it's never used.'

During the First World War, Nancy had been in charge of
Cliveden Hospital and had her own special way of treating patients –
'If you can't rouse a man, you have to insult him.' Sometimes she used
bribery, offering wounded soldiers valuable watches if they were still
alive in the morning; it often worked. This time the Canadian Red
Cross threatened to leave if Nancy interfered. She was not pleased
but gave in – she had plenty to do comforting her bombed Plymouth
constituents, where she organised afternoon dancing on the Hoe
and, aged sixty-two, did cartwheels to entertain families in the air-
raid shelters.

Nancy decided Joyce should work at the hospital, and the
Canadian authorities agreed as long as her orders came from them.
Joyce was asked to visit the two chest wards, filled not with war
wounds but infections such as tuberculosis. The wards were light and
cheerful, with french windows opening on to lawns, and beechwoods beyond. She did more than just visit the seventy men: she

wrote letters to their mothers, bought birthday cakes for them, sang to them and took the walking sick out to tea. She cycled to Burnham village to buy them soap, razors, and Valentine cards for their sweethearts. She taught the men embroidery to distract them from their pain and boredom. One man decorated a linen towel with the unpunctuated words FROM YOUR LOVING SON JESUS DIED FOR SINERS. Her favour patients included 'Scotty' from Nova Scotia, who had what he called 'Bronical Azmar'; and MacNall, a lifeguard from Florida who worked his way through Shakespeare.

The wounded and sick soldiers at Cliveden were better off than most – Joyce invited Beatrice Lillie, Clemence Dane and Celia Johnson to entertain them and they had official visits from Queen Elizabeth, the royal princesses and the Duchess of Kent. The hospital was soon full and Joyce was working flat out, looking after her wards and singing in the others.

Meanwhile Reggie's sisters Laura and Vera worked every night feeding bombed-out East Enders while Hilda Grenfell urged the London County Council to requisition the cellars of large houses for the homeless. Paul Phipps was a fire warden at St Paul's Cathedral and enjoyed exploring the stairways and galleries. One night Joyce went too and was 'deeply stirred' by seeing the vast place lit by a single hurricane lamp under the dome.

At Christmas 1940, there was no leave for Reggie, but Joyce decorated her wards with holly, silver bells and a tree. She also bought Christmas presents at Selfridge's and Woolworth's for the families of over a hundred patients and sent 175 telegrams to Canada. She was touched and surprised when the soldiers presented her with gifts of food they had saved from their Red Cross parcels.

The only problem was that the job was unpaid, and she needed to earn enough to support herself and pay Rene. There was no rent from St Leonard's Terrace, which had been commandeered to house Belgian refugees. She could have earned a wage in the theatre: Herbert Farjeon asked her to tour with the *Little Revue*, but Nancy wanted her to remain at Cliveden and even issued an ultimatum – if she gave up her hospital work and went back on the stage, Nancy would take back Parr's. Joyce was livid, but gave in to her aunt's demands. The incident prompted her to write her first sonnet, about 'giving with a touch so light':

> Let me give freely lest my giving take
> With it freedom . . .
> Beauty dies like a linnet in a cage,
> Beneath the bruising hand of patronage.

Joyce tried harder than most people to understand and get on with her Aunt Nancy. She knew that underneath the ostentatious teasing was a generous heart, but it was always difficult to know what Nancy would do next. 'She *is* touching you know,' she wrote to Nora. '*And* maddening. Like quicksilver – here one minute and way over there the next but she's so angelic and thoughtful of me that I'll never feel anything deep down but the greatest affection. Few people could do the good she does, for her gestures are wide and benefit the majority.'

– 9 –

Between September and November 1940, over thirty thousand bombs fell on London. A yellow sign saying DIVERSION was placed at the end of each bombed street, and Herbert Farjeon took this as the title of his new revue. His friends invested £50 each to raise the £1,700 capital needed. Once again, Nancy threatened to take Parr's away from Joyce if she returned to the stage; but *Diversion* was to open only for matinées, which meant she could visit her wards in the evenings.

'Rehearsals were conducted against temperamental train services, telephones that just laughed at you, and time-bombs sitting outside the very shop where props were due to come from at the eleventh hour,' reported Farjeon in the *Tatler and Bystander*.

Diversion opened on 28 October 1940, the same day Italy declared war on Greece. Apart from the Windmill Theatre's *Revudeville*, featuring nude actresses who were not permitted to move, it was the only show in London. Each performer compèred the item following their own. This did not always work – one day Joyce completely forgot Wally Crisham's name. She performed a new monologue, *Canteen*, based on volunteers she had met. 'Miss Grenfell's notion of a lady like canteeneress, is of the ilk who treat all their helpers as oxen while most coaxingly addressing them as lambs,' wrote Ivor Brown in *Punch*. 'Nobody could more deliciously suggest that leaving all the workload to others is the noblest form of self-sacrifice. Miss Grenfell, waiving to her inferiors the right of cutting a sandwich, is a very angel of abnegation.' The *Daily Sketch* reported that Joyce was 'cool and fresh as a spring morning and as withering as an east wind, contributing some devastating monologues'.

Joyce was glad to be on stage again, but felt she performed less well when friends or family were in the audience. 'There is something very exciting about making people laugh and even if Aunt Nancy does insist that it is all purely gratification and flattery, I do believe it's a good thing to do. But it's a tiresome life and quite hard.' She could not understand why critics described her as 'devastating, cruel, or sharp-edged' when she felt she was simply 'an instrument for joy to play through. I'm on the side of the people I'm doing, or I couldn't do them.'

Edith Evans, who had first inspired Joyce to love Shakespeare, showed her how to reach the furthest corners of Wyndham's Theatre without shouting. When Joyce learned Evans was a Christian Scientist, she invited her to Parr's, where she enjoyed watching Nancy and Edith Evans trade famous friends such as George Bernard Shaw and T. E. Lawrence.

Joyce often had to stand all the way to London on the train and after shopping for her soldiers at Selfridge's, eat a hurried lunch in her dressing-room before curtain-up. When the Reading-to-Paddington railway line was bombed she had to hitch-hike up to London. She was somewhat alarmed by the man who clutched her gloved hand while driving and asked, 'What's a little lady like you doing going up to London on a Saturday?'

Once home she visited her wards again, where her patients were thrilled to know a celebrity and asked her to sign her photo in the *Daily Sketch*. By the time she had got home from the hospital, bathed and eaten supper prepared by Rene, she was 'fit for nothing except the Times crossword puzzle'.

Audiences were good, and in addition to the £10 weekly wage Joyce earned 4 per cent of the takings, which could amount to an extra £15. If an air-raid warning went off, the show continued as long as there was an audience – but it was usually over before the first air-raid sirens sounded. Wyndham's was never hit, but Herbert Farjeon and his son Gervase spent many nights sleeping in the cellar rather than risking the journey home during a raid.

The show was often sold out and Joyce began getting her own fan mail: 'You looked so lovely and entertained us so cleverly. Please may I be a little sentimental and tell you so? You have provided a delightful memory to take back to duty from a dear and hard hit London. It would be dull to sign this letter with any name except A Sapper on Leave.'

She was also beginning to be recognised in public, but she did not like it. 'There was a woman on the train who obviously recognised me, for some perverse reason I was furious about this – it's all very well to be a public face behind the footlights but away from them one ought to be invisible. I read Punch held high in front of my face but it was a sadly thin war-time edition with few pages and didn't last me long.'

There was no Christmas leave for Reggie but Joyce did get time to perform to his company in between the theatre and rehearsals for *Diversion No. 2*. She also broadcast to America, sending Christmas greetings to her mother and Elliot Coleman over the air. Joyce noted in her diary, '1940 was a beastly public year but for me personally it has had lots of happiness. I count my blessings.'

Diversion No. 2 had the best of the first edition, and some new material. During the forty-five-minute train journey from Paddington to Taplow the sound of the train wheels aided Joyce's concentration and she wrote a monologue called *Local Library*, inspired by the Boot's Library in Maidenhead. Graham Greene in the *Spectator* noted that, 'like a high explosive bomb, Miss Grenfell leaves no institution she touches quite the same'. *Punch* said, 'Miss Grenfell dispenses Gems of Literature with the special brand of benign and bright-eyed idiocy which once she employed in her first exquisite address to the women of the parish.'

Joining the chorus was nineteen-year-old Dirk Bogarde, then called Derek Bogaerde, who, like Peter Ustinov, also nineteen, was waiting to be called up. 'The first rehearsal on the stage at Wyndham's was pretty frightening,' Bogarde wrote. 'All in our Best, Edith Evans magisterial in mink, Dorothy Dickson in fox and an orchid, and our Director, Wally Crisham, elegant in pale blue silk. The six "Chorus" sat on one side of the stage, the Elite on the other. We were all perfectly friendly and integrated, but everyone knew their places, and a feeling of discipline, position, and West End reigned quietly.' The final rehearsal ended as bombs fell outside, hitting the Hippodrome theatre opposite. The cast crouched in the stalls and after a while crept outside.

'We left the theatre to enter an inferno in Charing Cross Road,' continued Bogarde. 'The whole world seemed to be on fire, the sky crimson, dust and smoke like a thick fog, the glass canopy round the theatre shattered into inch long splinters, rubble, broken branches and fire hoses every where. The Hippodrome was burning fiercely, people cursing, coughing and running, wires looped across the street and everywhere belching heat and smoke.' The night of 29 December 1940 turned out to be the worst of all the incendiary raids, when sixteen of Christopher Wren's churches were destroyed and St Paul's Cathedral was surrounded by fire. When Joyce visited it she was amazed 'at the beauty revealed by the new space surrounding the church'.

Joyce escaped unhurt when, a few nights later, a large bomb fell near by when she was on stage. 'The blast blew the tabs [curtains] around me & I had to fight my way out. And later, when buzz bombs came we felt them blast quite often & I was miserably afraid. They were *far* worse than the blitz, more sinister.'

Diversion No. 2 opened on New Year's Day 1941, and the critics were thrilled with the quality of the performers. The *Daily Herald* said: 'this would be the brightest show in town even in normal times. Today it is an oasis of pungency in a theatre-starved city, and its 25 items are as satisfying as they are varied.' Stephen Potter wrote in his diary: 'The best, in order, was one, Ustinov doing the pansy producer; two, Joyce Grenfell doing the library girl (Canteen not quite so good), her wide all-clear smile being on the side of the characters she does. She gave me a brilliant recognition from the wings.'

Joyce was lying in her bath when she heard John Gielgud say on the radio, 'Brilliant people like Ruth Draper and Joyce Grenfell are the true exponents of make-believe kind of theatre.' She claimed to be so surprised that she nearly went down the plughole and was 'pink with pleasure long after I'd cooled down from the bath'.

Virginia wrote some songs for Joyce, including *My Bonny Lies Over the Mm-mm*, satirising the censorship of place names, and Nicholas Phipps wrote a musical sketch called 'Exit to Music'. Vida Hope, a stout young woman, sang *Nude on the Dole* by Farjeon, about being sacked for moving during a nude show. In 'Producing King Lear' Peter Ustinov gave impressions of theatre directors tackling Shakespeare: the Continental, the Cockney Communist and the Semi-Precious. He also played his own creation, 'Madame Liselotte Beethoven-Finck', an ageing Austro-German *lieder* singer who sang Schubert songs unknown even to Schubert.

Ustinov and Bogarde's small dressing-room became the place to eat picnics, drink tea and talk to a stream of visitors in a variety of languages. 'Up in the dressing-room between numbers in the show,' observed Bogarde

> Ustinov would sit writing a play. I think it was his first. And there was Joyce Grenfell, who was his acolyte, lying on the floor in blue velvet, taking the pages from him while he was playing Russian music on the gramophone. He used to hand her the sheets and she'd take them saying, 'Oh, they're divine . . . too wonderful,' and nurse them as if they were the Holy Grail or the Turin Shroud, and Peter would put another record on.

Ustinov showed his tragi-comedy *House of Regrets* to Farjeon, and it subsequently had a successful run. After he was called up, he made films with Lieutenant-Colonel David Niven, directed by Major Carol Reed, under the auspices of the Directorate of Army Psychiatry. He was admitted to hospital when the strain of combining film-making and the Army caused his gall bladder to seize up. 'Joyce and I had one unforgettable encounter off the stage in 1942,' he recalled. 'She came to do "her bit" and sing to the troops at a military hospital in Shenley, Buckinghamshire. All went well until, in the middle of her act, she caught the eye of an acquaintance in one of the beds. That acquaintance was me. She forgot her lines, melody and all. This meeting enabled me to smuggle vital messages to the world outside and did wonders for my reputation within the hospital.'

During the run of *Diversion*, Joyce made her first appearance in a film, *Letter From England*, directed by Carol Reed. Celia Johnson, also in her first film part, starred as Mrs Taylor, a London housewife and air-raid warden whose two small children had been evacuated to New York. Joyce played Mrs Rogers, their American foster-mother, whose accent slipped between American and smart English as she read out Mrs Taylor's letters to her children. *Letter From Home* was a propaganda film to show Americans how the British were coping with air raids, egg shortages, queues, and putting out incendiary bombs with stirrup pumps. Carol Reed's economical, bold style used humour to contrast with stiff-upper-lipped Britons continuing their 'normal' lives. Celia stayed with Joyce during the two-week filming and together they enjoyed crosswords, poetry, and belching after meals. They spent one whole evening talking in the style of Jane Austen, with speech impediments.

After *Diversion No. 2* closed in May 1941, it ran for a week in Oxford's New Theatre. Rather than stay in the city, Joyce took Edith Evans and Dorothy Dickson to stay with her cousin Nancy Tree at her Georgian mansion, Ditchley Park, which Paul Phipps had renovated. When they arrived they learned that Winston Churchill and his entourage had left just a few hours earlier. Since becoming Prime Minister in May 1940, Churchill had moved around to avoid an attack from the air; Chequers was considered too dangerous on clear nights and Churchill had asked Ronald Tree if he could stay at Ditchley 'when the moon was high'. Tree agreed to complete confidentiality and, when Churchill first arrived in an armoured car, even Nancy did not know who her guest was.

Hardly anybody knew of Nancy's role as a political hostess, but now Joyce was trusted with this secret and could only hint in a letter to Nora, 'I can't explain what I mean but her home is now often the scene of much important entertaining and it is funny to think of somehow. Your sister [Nancy] doesn't know about it and that's even funnier!! Bother the censor but I can't say more.'

In later life Joyce said that the Second World War was her university. One unexpected part of her curriculum was classical music performed in London's National Gallery.

The pianist Myra Hess realised that, with black-outs and lack of transport, no one could go out in the evening, so she wanted to put on classical concerts at lunchtime. The National Gallery had been closed and emptied of all its pictures and Kenneth Clark, the director, suggested using it. 'I gave the first recital on October 10 1939,' Myra Hess recalled. 'I thought perhaps forty or fifty of my friends would turn up. At ten minutes to one Kenneth came and said, "There are a thousand people waiting outside on the pavement." Most of them had to sit on the floor.' After that there were nearly two thousand lunchtime concerts, held every weekday over six years for anyone working near Trafalgar Square.

Joyce had known Myra since they had met at a Gloucestershire house party for the Three Choirs Festival in 1937. One afternoon as

Myra played a Bach gigue, Sir Walford Davies, aged sixty-eight, had leaped to his feet and led Joyce in a spontaneous dance in and out of the furniture. This progressed to a conga-line of all the house guests, around the hall and up the staircase, with Myra bouncing on the piano stool as she played. 'When it was over we all collapsed into our chairs in laughter – one of those unrehearsed, delightful nonsenses,' Joyce remembered. 'It was one of the most enjoyable moments of spontaneous exuberance I ever experienced.'

The National Gallery concerts attracted all the finest musicians in London, who gave the audience a wide repertoire of solo and chamber music. Joyce adored Dvořák played by Malcolm Sargent and the Kitchen Quartet, and Bach's Ricerare played by Howard Fergusson was 'so beautiful that it bowled me over. One can hear Bach in these times and be helped with his sane clarity and confidence. Holland surrendered last night.' The music frequently moved Joyce to tears – while Harold Craxton was playing the Moonlight Sonata she 'was much too moved. I saw Wales and all the lovely times we had there. Great waves of homesickness swept over me and I was very shaken.'

Thirty years later Joyce wrote to Benjamin Britten:

> During the restlessness and muddle one was able to refresh one's sense of Truth in the unchanging certainty of music. I remember feeling this in the war when I worked for Myra at the Nat Gall. There was a day at the time of Dunkirk when the future had no face & someone played Mozart – a quintet – & I had a sort of revelation of the intactness of that which is true. More and more I realised that real substance is something you can't touch or see or feel.

Joyce went to the National Gallery almost every day for over a year, and became a close friend of Myra. Joyce would do anything for her – fetching her meals, helping her choose new clothes or collecting her from the station. In exchange, Myra invited Joyce to frequent tea parties and any vestiges of anti-Semitism that Joyce may have had as a young woman left her. 'I wonder what makes people anti-Semitic?' she wrote in the new diary which Myra gave her.

She basked in the reflected glory of knowing Myra. Queen

Elizabeth was planning to have her portrait painted by Augustus John and asked her brother David Bowes-Lyon, who asked his wife Rachel Spender-Clay, who asked her cousin-in-law Joyce Grenfell if she would ask her friend Myra Hess to play the piano while she was being painted. Myra agreed and eight weeks later Joyce was with her when Buckingham Palace phoned to arrange the date. 'Rather fun to make that sort of history,' Joyce wrote. The following week 'Myra rang to say playing for the Queen a great success and she never had such a happy day.'

Joyce volunteered to help Irene, Lady Gater, who organised cheap and nutritious lunches. She took great pride in inventing sandwiches, which became famous for their original use of rationed food – honey and raisin, cream cheese and walnuts, ham and beetroot chutney. She found spreading honey on brown bread 'surprisingly hard work' but was rewarded by being allowed to take refreshments to the artists' room. An added delight was standing over the grille in the floor to catch the warm air. 'It is such a comforting experience on a cold day,' she wrote.

The highlight for Joyce was New Year's Day 1940, when over a thousand people came to listen to Schumann's *Carnaval* played by eight famous pianists in turn. This was followed by Haydn's *Toy Symphony* conducted by Kenneth Clark, with Myra Hess and Irene Scharrer as cuckoos, and Benno Moiseiwitsch and Isolde Menges playing quails. Joyce was immensely flattered to be invited to play the nightingale on a water whistle: an exacting part of sixteen bars in one breath.

After the performance Myra laid on tea at her home in Hampstead and Howard Fergusson played his new piano sonata. Over the next few months Joyce heard it twelve times, and each time it was 'even more lovely than the first time. So big and so wide in scope, but brought right down to essentials. The slow movement is nostalgic and at the same time full of promise. It had me in pieces.' It inspired her to write a sonnet called 'On Hearing Myra Hess Playing HF's Sonata', which was published in *Punch*.

For the hundredth National Gallery concert Myra played Mozart, and Joyce spread 250 pieces of bread and butter single-handed. Not long after this, Myra was created a dame.

★

Both the practicalities and the thought of the war depressed Joyce when she was tired and alone. Then she would remember how lucky she was compared to many of her contemporaries, such as Reggie's sister Frances, whose husband Patrick Campbell-Preston was a prisoner of war in Colditz Castle, and friends who were already widowed. At least Reggie was in Britain and she saw him occasionally. On Joyce's thirty-first birthday Reggie arrived at Parr's on a motorbike, bringing a cake made by the regimental cook and a still-bleeding rabbit he had shot for her. He was umpiring a mock battle between the King's Royal Rifles and the nearby Cookham Home Guard, using tennis balls in lieu of hand grenades. During leave at Easter 1941, Reggie had learned that he had been promoted to captain and would be the Garrison Adjutant. Humming happily, he dug up the herbaceous borders and replaced the flowers with cabbages, while Joyce completed the khaki scarf she had been knitting him for two years. She also missed Virginia, who had moved to Bristol and was driving trucks around the West Country for the WVS. After an afternoon lying under a truck getting engine oil in her permed hair, Virginia said she found it 'hard to be a mechanic *and* a lady'.

By the end of 1941 all women under thirty without children were called up to replace men in factories or services to support the military. Joyce was unsure of the Christian Science ruling on war but registered along with all the women born in 1910, hoping that her Red Cross hospital work would count. Mildred Rawson told Joyce that this was not a Christian war and only when the organised churches were disbanded and the Old Testament discarded would the world ever improve. Joyce thought it was certainly a Human Error but whether Christian Scientists should join in was not clear. She and Virginia spent many hours discussing this and finally agreed that they would participate in the war effort, but drew the line at working in a munitions factory. Neither of them felt that their views should influence the actions of their non-Christian Science husbands.

Joyce was distraught when Rene was called up in August 1941. 'My beloved maid, secretary and friend stood between me and the world. I didn't have to bother at all about ration books, meals, or how the house ran. It just did so on oiled wheels.' Rene joined the WAAF as a batwoman to a female officer, and Joyce wrote a poem for *Punch* called 'Tribute to a Treasure':

Her very presence blessed this place
She never got a message wrong,
She cooked and cleaned, she sewed, she swept;
She almost never over-slept . . .
She sang along the years,
Five happy years of carefree days!

Joyce's observations of upper-class people struggling to run large houses with geriatric butlers and arthritic maids were turned into her monologue *Situation Vacant*. A lady seeking a housekeeper pleads with a domestic employment agency to put her on the waiting list for the waiting list. 'All I want is some clean, happy person who can cook just a little and answer the telephone and not get called up. Of course it makes it nicer if she happens to be honest and sober at the same time, doesn't it? A place called Practical Peasant Agency have offered me an Unrestricted Croat of sixty-five. But you see she's used to titled people.'

Joyce was lucky to find Mrs Proctor, a thirty-seven-year-old widow with two daughters who was 'A tiny bit woolly minded but spotlessly clean and an excellent cook. Also very cheerful.' Shirley, aged six, had pink cheeks and an irrepressible giggle and always called Joyce 'the Lidy', while eleven-year-old Truda had 'a worried face and a sense of responsibility'. Mrs Proctor and the girls went away every weekend, and for the first time Joyce had to lay the fires and keep the Aga going.

She was not so keen on the officers billeted on her. One was 'small, dark and had eyes too close together'; another 'went on leave as soon as he arrived'; and a third was unmemorable 'except that the top of his head was too flat'. They changed regularly, and left full ash-trays and wet towels. Worst of all, their batmen marched through the house in hob-nailed boots to wake them at dawn. 'I do think the male animal, without his spirituality, is a nasty messy thing.' The idea of sharing her house with other *women* was even worse and she never told her Canadian Red Cross colleagues when a room fell empty. Her ideal billet was a commissioned male officer who did not smoke and ate all his meals out.

The bombing of Pearl Harbor in December 1941 finally brought the USA into the war and, much to Joyce's relief, Tommy joined the

Army as a lieutenant in Georgia. Reggie, meanwhile, had been promoted to major and moved to Cheltenham, and for the second year running had no leave at Christmas. He came home for one night after hitching a lift on a regimental lorry going to Smithfield Market. On the return journey he sat in a deck-chair in the back of the lorry, surrounded by live, crated turkeys.

After Christmas Reggie was sent on a bomb-disposal course in Southampton, during heavy raids on the south coast. When he phoned Joyce, she was 'glad to hear his voice. After eleven years of marriage I can truly say that the mere sight of his face or the sound of his voice do something to my heart. I love him very much indeed.' A few days later, 'a darling letter from Reg today in which he deplores our separation and looks forward to the time when we are together again forever. Me too.' He was then posted to Yorkshire, where he was wounded: during a snooker game in the officer's mess, the ball broke his nose.

In the spring of 1942 Herbert Farjeon asked Joyce to join him in a new revue called *Light and Shade*. Once again Nancy Astor was, as Virginia called it, 'indulging in that blackmail stunt peculiar to her' and insisted that Joyce remain at Cliveden Hospital. By now Joyce's work had expanded to include three wards and being liaison officer between the British and Canadian Red Cross Societies. She wanted to be in the show, but decided she should concentrate on Cliveden Hospital, troop concerts and occasional radio broadcasts.

Light and Shade opened at the Ambassador's Theatre in August 1942 and was a dismal failure, partly because the best parts had been censored, including a Farjeon song called *Englishmen Never Make Love by Day But at Night They are Quite Alright*. The young actor Frith Banbury was in the cast. 'The main item was a nativity play,' he remembers.

It was terribly serious and beautiful, mostly written by Eleanor Farjoen. I played an ass. The nativity play put the revue right down the drain The censor cut so many lines from it that it made very little sense. By modern standards it was a pure scene, but sixty years ago it was considered indecent to represent the nativity as a drama. We knew it would be a disaster and we were heading for the cliffs, but Bertie wanted everything his way. The trouble was everything was done by the Farjeon family – Bertie; his brother, Harry; Eleanor, his sister; clothes by Jocelyn. It was all a bit too homespun. Max Adrian, Betty Ann Davies and Vida Hope weren't really amateur, it just had that feel.

The show also missed the talent of Walter Leigh, composer of previous revues, who had just been killed in action in Libya.

One critic wrote that he came out of the theatre looking for a hearse to take him home. Joyce went to the first night with Reggie and Virginia. They found the show 'rather lovely but too sad, with not enough edge'. Eleanor Farjeon's writing was too sweet and needed Herbert's sharp wit. Joyce wrote Farjeon a long letter with suggestions for improvements and he pleaded with Joyce to come into the show and rescue it. Somewhat reluctantly she risked Nancy's wrath, cancelled eight hospital concerts and agreed to help.

Several more sketches were cut and two weeks later Joyce appeared with two new monologues, *Situation Vacant* and *Cardboard Figures* – which was never heard of again. She also sang two songs, one written by Virginia with music by the young pianist Joseph Cooper. As with previous revues, Joyce did not join the choruses and some of the cast resented her apparent aloofness. 'What used to irritate me was Joyce's amateurishness,' recalled Banbury.

The curtain was about to go up at a matinée at the Ambassador's. Betty-Ann Davies and myself started the show. Suddenly onto the stage bustles Joyce. She said, 'I must just see who is in front,' and peeped through the curtain, and then, 'I like to know who's in front, don't you?' and Betty said, 'No I don't (bloody amateur).'

I always thought it amazing that Joyce was so like the people she took off, but she didn't see it in herself. Bertie could see there was an extraordinary talent lurking there. Joyce had this eagle eye for the silliness of human behaviour.

The new playbills were slipped with 'Guest Artist: Joyce Grenfell' in type the same size as for the rest of the company. The producers wanted bigger type, some of the cast wanted it smaller and one leading lady threatened to leave if Joyce's name was not moved lower. Farjeon was torn between keeping his cast and saving the show. The slips were moved down to the bottom of the bills, where they were hardly noticed, and *Light and Shade* wobbled on for only four more weeks. It was to be Farjeon's last revue – he died suddenly at the age of fifty-nine in May 1945 while he was working on a show for television. 'He was the greatest single influence in revue during the past 20 years,' wrote Max Adrian in *The Times*.

A s soon as war was declared, the government had decided that there was no time for fun or frivolity, and radio should be as dull as possible. George Bernard Shaw described this as 'a master stroke of unimaginative stupidity'. They soon realised their mistake and the BBC Forces Programme opened in January 1940 with dance music and comedy for the troops, while the Home Service broadcast *Music While You Work*, *Let Us Be Gay* and *Worker's Playtime* to keep the morale of the nation high. 'London goes on with its radio programmes as if nothing had happened,' commented a German diplomat, 'people singing in shelters; reports from a cricket match; nice and clever people making their talks; there is more dance music than before.'

Joyce had been trying to get on the radio since 1936 but once she had appeared on stage, the BBC was asking her to be on the radio, rather than the other way round. A few days before the *Little Revue* opened in 1939 she sang on *Dance Band* for a fee of eight guineas and a third-class train fare to Bristol. A month later the producer Leslie Perowne invited her to present her favourite records by women and she was soon regularly presenting 'gramophone recitals' – early versions of *Desert Island Discs* – choosing her own records and talking about them. Other radio appearances, in which she sang popular songs and performed her own monologues, included *Cocktails, Kippers and Capers*, *Moonlight and Splash* and *Henry Hall's Guest Night*. Some of the monologues Joyce first performed on the radio during the war went on to become classics in her stage revues, such as *Headgirl* and *Local Library*. Others, such as *Shopping – East-side New York*, *Living Space* – a cockney hall porter's wife – and *Woolgathering*, about a knitting-bee, were never heard of again, whilst a Japanese lady performing a tea ceremony was dropped after the bombing of Pearl Harbor.

After live stage performances, Joyce's favourite medium was the radio. 'It's a one-to-one medium, and uses the imagination,' she said. 'The audience does 75% of the work – I make a suggestion but it's up to them to imagine the person or the situation.' When Joyce began on the radio, she would only broadcast live, as she believed her monologues lost something by being recorded; then she realised that if she still imagined the audience sitting at home when she recorded them, the effect was the same. She had learned quickly the difference between a packed theatre and the intimacy of a radio at home.

A farmer commented during audience research, 'Of all radio comediennes Joyce Grenfell enchants me most completely. I constantly wish we could have more, much more, of her. She is so particularly suited to radio because of her amazing power of representing an entire scene or personality in a few apparently quite simple words. One can't see how it's done, one only knows it is done – sheer verbal magic.'

There were few women on the radio in the 1940s, but the BBC archives show that Joyce was always in demand: she was asked to appear about twice as often as she had time for. When too busy, she apologised in writing: 'I feel a pig – guilt-ridden too. I'm a conscientious type and wouldn't let you down unless I felt I just had to.' Joyce's initial lack of experience was made up for by her enthusiasm and efficiency and throughout her career producers were impressed by the speed with which she sent them scripts – usually within a few days.

Many of Joyce's fan letters began 'I have never written a fan letter before but . . .' and were addressed simply to 'Joyce Grenfell, BBC, London'. One of her radio fans regularly sent her parcels of fresh eggs from Dorset. When Joyce agreed to meet him in a West End restaurant she found a very small, shy man, who had stood for four hours on the train. She was so touched that she accompanied him to the cinema, before he caught his train home. She treated all her fans with respect – she was flattered by their interest in her, and knew that without them she had no career.

In October 1941 Val Gielgud, Head of Drama, commissioned her to write a twenty-minute programme, to be produced by Stephen Potter. Within three days she had composed the first ever one-woman show, in which she played seven different characters. It was broadcast live in the evening, when up to three million listeners usually tuned in.

The BBC's Director of Variety was annoyed that Joyce had apparently defected to Drama. Potter apologised, excusing himself on the grounds that 'first she is doing sketches of rather more serious type than usual, and secondly I always try, rather unconvincingly, to maintain that I discovered J.G., as I got her to say her pieces before Herbert Farjeon. Please, therefore, forgive this temporary muscling in on your territory.'

At the end of 1942 Potter invited her to lunch at the Savoy Grill to ask her to co-write a new radio series called *How*, based on typical situations such as applying for a job, learning to speak French or 'blowing your own trumpet'. With its subtle social satire and gentle mockery of etiquette, combined with Potter's mastery of the radio medium and Joyce's characters, *How* pushed the frontiers of radio forward a decade. Between 1942 and 1955 Joyce and Potter wrote twenty-nine different *How* programmes, developing many of their ideas which were to appear later in Joyce's monologues and Potter's books. As the *Observer* commented, 'Like most people who do things with the greatest of ease, Potter and Grenfell evidently spent hours erecting and testing their flying trapeze.' The *Daily Worker* complained that it was upper-class, and Potter was rankled when the *Listener* said it was a cross between *Punch* and Chekhov. All experiences were put to use: after moving house they wrote *How to Move House*, and when Potter wanted to go to America he persuaded the BBC that he needed to research *How to Cross the Atlantic First Class*.

Creatively they sparked off each other, developing their own method of script-writing by creating characters and improvising lines of dialogue. 'He was really a brilliant improviser,' Joyce said. 'When we were working on *How to Woo* he was in turn Young and Ardent, Polished and Sinister, and Inarticulate and Helpless, while I was the appropriate girls.' There were no tape recorders available, so everything they said was taken down in shorthand and typed out for editing.

When Potter's office or Joyce's kitchen dampened their creativity, they took picnics to Regent's Park or Kew Gardens and scribbled their ideas in notebooks. Their working styles were quite different – Joyce liked to get things done early and out of the way, whilst Potter could never get started until the last minute. This was tough on his secretary, Betty Johnstone, and often meant that scripts were only ready shortly before transmission – and more changes were often made in the studio. They had to be careful what was finally transmitted – good taste and decency governed the BBC, which had banned all jokes about lavatories, effeminacy, honeymoons, fig leaves, ladies' underwear and animal habits. Extreme care had to be taken with prenatal influences (such as 'his mother saw a monster'), lodgers and commercial travellers. The surviving scripts are covered in scribbles, rewrites and Joyce's doodles.

Roy Plomley was one of the eight members of the How Repertory Company and wrote: 'Potter allocated to each member anything up to a dozen voices, and left him to do his professional best with them. He cheered us on with lots of encouragement, and chuckled with pleasure as scenes took on pace and came alive.' Being transmitted live, all mistakes were included and the sound of the pages being turned was audible. Only four recordings of *How* still exist because sound effects were taken from gramophone records, which were not permitted to be re-recorded. This meant that even if *How* programmes were scheduled to be repeated, they had to be made new each time, allowing for yet more revisions. Potter noted in his diary after the first day's production of *How to Apply for a Job*: 'The great Joyce, untroubled and unhurried, was as funny rehearsing as she is doing the stuff.'

During the first minute of each programme, listeners heard 'How to do' something, and the next twenty minutes was 'How *not* to do it'. In *How to Give a Party* the guests include Joyce as Fern Brixton, lover of beauty and folk music. Talking to a poet – 'I imagine you feel things pretty deeply' – she speaks in a voice which in the notes is 'clear, low and "analysed"'. Joyce as the hostess gushes, 'Freddie will do his Hitler turn – he's so funny,' and to a composer: 'I strongly disapprove of people inviting famous musicians to their houses and then asking them to play, but it would be wonderful if you would.' When he proceeds to play jazz, she says, 'Mr Martin, will you play something we can all sing?'

How to Deal With Christmas begins with plans being made during the summer holidays. Celia Johnson says, 'I'd rather have an El Greco Christmas card than Father Christmas in a silver jet plane,' to which her friend Joyce replies, 'I especially don't like bunches of anemones in black bowls reflected in polished tables.' Joyce also plays Mrs Welt-Hennies, who buys 'divine little diamond rabbits at Waverley's to wear in your lapel which couldn't be gayer or more ridiculous'. Uncle Freddie's contribution to the family Christmas is 'an enormous packet of lard'.

'Working with Joyce intensifies my talent for social satire,' wrote Potter in his diary. 'It also intensifies a weakness for superficiality and I am tied to being rather caustic.' 'They sparkled when they planned the programmes together,' said his son Julian. 'But at the same time Stephen seems to have regarded Joyce as a moral mentor, keeping a rein on his lack of self-discipline.' Joyce forgave Potter for his unpunctuality, untidiness, chain-smoking and drinking because they made each other laugh.

One day Potter found he had invited both Joyce and Celia Johnson to L'Apéritif – so, to appreciate fully the company of both women, he ate two lunches, one after the other. On another day, Potter and Joyce were lunching together at the Savoy Grill when he was called to the phone. When he finished, he walked straight out of the restaurant. Joyce had to haul him back inside, in gales of laughter at his absent-mindedness. Another day he told Joyce he had planned to bring her some flowers, but he had no money and had forgotten which florist he had an account with. 'He is most loveable in some ways and quite hopeless,' she wrote in her diary. 'It is a lucky thing we have never been at all attracted to each other.'

In early 1942 Joyce was invited to a theatrical party held by the playwright Clemence Dane, alias Winifred Ashton, in her flat over a florist in Covent Garden. A large and enthusiastic woman, she became a close friend of Joyce's for the next thirty-five years. Also there was Richard Addinsell, who had recently composed the Warsaw Concerto for the film *Dangerous Moonlight*. Dick, as he was known, was very shy, and was playing Gershwin and Irving Berlin songs quietly on a piano in the corner. Joyce told him they were her favourites and he invited her to join in. Ignoring the rest of the party, they sang together for the whole evening. Dick's playing complemented Joyce's singing perfectly. He liked her voice and asked her if he could write her a song. A few days later he sent her the melody and within a few hours she had written a draft of their first song, *There Is Nothing New to Tell You*, inspired by the letters between her and Reggie. After being broadcast on the radio it was recorded on wax at the HMV studios in Abbey Road and became an instant hit.

They soon established a musical rapport and developed a method whereby Dick composed a tune on the piano and played it to Joyce over the phone. Sometimes Dick gave Joyce a melody and she wrote words to fit it, and sometimes it was the other way round. Joyce felt that a song should have a carefully worked shape, with a beginning, middle and end, that even an unmusical listener could respond to. After several phone calls and different versions, Dick arranged each song for orchestra. He had a superb mastery of harmonised chords and simple, lilting melodies and the 'ballads' they wrote together were romantic, with an enchanting 1940s freshness.

I'm Going to See You Today celebrated the prospect of reunion and became Joyce's signature tune; it was broadcast three times in one day, sung by Gracie Fields. Joyce wrote from her own experiences and often found that others shared them. One fan wrote that she heard the song on the day her baby was coming home from hospital, and a clipper on the buses in Lancashire told Joyce: 'I start my day by singing it and it's surprising how it helps a day along.' *My Heart Is as Light as Air* told of receiving a longed-for letter; *Turn Back the Clock* was an end-of-leave song and wistfully looked towards an uncertain future. Many of their songs, such as *When You Go* and *Someday*, were about lovers parting – a common preoccupation. They wrote one called *They're a Lovely Bunch of Boys* for Tommy Trinder, the cockney comedian, but then decided to let George Formby have it for his next film. Their songs were sold both as records and as sheet music, featuring Joyce on the cover.

Dick was constantly ill with 'nerves' and 'low blood pressure'. When his housekeeper left, Joyce rushed to clean his flat in Bloomsbury and cheer him up. She bought his rations at Fortnum's and called in Clemence Dane to cook for him. Joyce coped by writing a 'Hymn to the Hoover':

> Oh Blessed Household Hoover,
> Our humble thanks to thee,

For thine electric presence.
Oh Praise thee, Mighty Monster,
Thou whale that swallows all.

She was longing to teach him the benefits of Christian Science, but she decided to wait until he was well. She grew very fond of him, despite his neurotic narcissism and hypochondria. Joyce was amused when people thought they were lovers, but in her innocence it didn't occur to her that he was homosexual. 'He's very sweet and long and gangling and sort of un-sexed,' she wrote to her mother. 'Very gentle and sensitive but not a beau in any way.' Joyce found homosexuality difficult to comprehend, even with people she knew well. In 1931 her first cousin Bobbie Shaw, having already resigned from the Guards, was prosecuted for 'gross indecency' and spent four months in Wormwood Scrubs. It nearly killed him but he emerged determined to be 'cured' of what even he thought of as a 'horrible disease'. Homosexuality was not just illegal until 1967, but considered perverse, evil and incomprehensible. These attitudes help to explain why Joyce preferred to ignore it and did not approve of men who were publicly homosexual.

'Joyce liked good-looking, well-dressed men,' remembers Dick's doctor, Patrick Woodcock. 'Gay men were her ideal friends – she could flirt with them quite safely. She liked the idea of romance, but without any possibility of sex.' She became very fond of Dick's boyfriend, the Jacqmar couturier Victor Stiebel, who during the war designed army-camouflage and Utility clothes.

Joyce was now singing on the radio regularly, accompanied by Geraldo and his dance orchestra. Group Captain Derek Conder, stationed in Yorkshire, wrote:

Some months ago, I was sitting alone in my billet, feeling very fed up, and half listening, when a voice suddenly started singing *Turn Back the Clock*. I am not usually given to sentiment, but the singer really did seem to mean what she was singing. Last Saturday, I suddenly heard the same voice begin to sing the same song. Flying downstairs, much to the amazement of my landlady, I switched the set on louder, and sat entranced. My point is this, if that voice has that effect on me after several months, that

voice has surely got something plus, and I hope the owner real-
ises it, and is doing something about it.

What Joyce did was to become a singer with the Entertainment
National Service Association (ENSA). A few weeks after *Light and
Shade* closed in the autumn of 1942, she was officially 'called up'. She
was afraid she would be given a job in munitions, so when she was
designated to work with ENSA she was thrilled. Nancy wanted to
persuade the officials to allow her to continue working at Cliveden
Hospital but after two demanding years there, Joyce was looking
forward to a change. Her aunt had already threatened never to speak
to her again and now Nancy changed tactics: instead of Fury, she
tried Deep Disappointment. Bolstered by Virginia, Joyce retaliated
with Plain Silence.

Theatre producer Basil Dean had put on the first ENSA concert
for troops just one week after the outbreak of war. Within three
weeks, fifteen concert parties were on the road and by 1943 there
were 3,750 ENSA performances taking place somewhere in the
world every week.

Based in the Theatre Royal, Drury Lane, this semi-public organisation soon became a target for criticism. The actress Diana Gould
wanted to erect a sign outside its office: ABANDON HOPE, ALL YE WHO
ENSA HERE. In theory the Navy, Army and Air Force were responsible for the organisation of entertainers, both at home and abroad; in
practice, they were much too busy, and consequently ENSA gained a
reputation for inefficiency and poor communication – though it did
not always live up to the nickname Every Night Something Awful.
By the time the London Blitz began, ENSA was providing entertainment of every size and description, from symphony orchestras, plays
and concert parties to stand-up comics and tap-dancers. Shows were
given in garrison theatres, messes, tents and the open air. ENSA
artists followed the troops wherever they went, through the North
African deserts, on the Italian beaches and on to Berlin and Japan.
Dean produced the best-quality performers that he could find but
was still attacked for not sending more orchestras and productions of
Shakespeare to far-flung parts of the British Empire. Maurice Jackson
worked with Dean and explained that 'Throughout his career he was
intolerant of anything and anyone who did not measure up to his

high standards. Of course he was a dictator, but, within my know-ledge, he did no graft, he was not corrupt, and certainly he was not inefficient or wasteful.' Dean's personal unpopularity did not deter performers from coping with gruelling conditions in order to enter-tain the forces and civilian workers in all theatres of the war. The worse the conditions, the warmer the reception they received. Everyone in the theatre was involved, from famous stars to young hopefuls. Whatever their status, they were all paid a standard wage of £10 a week, exclusive of billeting and rations.

In the autumn of 1942 Walter Legge, head of ENSA music, sent Joyce to Northern Ireland for an eight-week tour with the Music You Love Company. These 'rather refained second-rate' musicians played 'gems from the classics', such as *Your Tiny Hand is Frozen*. The bottle-blonde middle-aged soprano from Lancashire was built like a house and was sensitive about her size. This was not helped when Joyce absent-mindedly said to the audience as she introduced her, 'And now, I'll just move the chair to make room for our soprano.'

Joyce was startled that the Welsh tenor, the violinist and the Jewish baritone all wore corduroy trousers in public. Gwen Byrne, the solo pianist, was well dressed in tweeds and the only one whom Joyce could relate to, though her Roman Catholicism made her slightly suspect. Joyce felt she had nothing in common with the other members of the company – the men treated the job without any sense of service or feeling, and the women's only interest was in window-shopping and competing with descriptions of clothes, real or imagined. They did not describe colours, only 'shades' of 'powder', 'lavender', 'wine' and 'dove'. This was the first occasion in her life that Joyce worked away from home with people of a different social class, and she was amazed that the women longed to live in semi-detached homes in suburbs, with fringed lamps and china Pierrot dolls.

Joyce's role was to perform monologues, sing songs and compère everyone else, which meant bobbing in and out of the wings. She was also their self-appointed head prefect and they thought she was far too grand, which was hardly surprising considering that on her days off she visited people like her godmother Peg, the Countess of Antrim, at Glenarm Castle. Although she didn't like them either, she tried hard to *love* them, which possibly annoyed them even more. The manager of the company and she rarely spoke after she told him he was rude and inefficient.

The singers also squabbled among themselves – Handel's 'Largo' was a great bone of contention. It was a sure-fire hit with the audiences because it was familiar, and they clapped in happy recognition. Unfortunately it had been arranged as a solo for either tenor, or baritone, or contralto, or the 'cello. The Music You Love Company had all four – and they all wanted to perform it. After nightly arguments, they finally agreed to a rota.

Joyce observed all this closely and wrote half a play about an ENSA troupe on tour. But either the material was too close to her or she felt uncomfortable about being judgemental, for she never finished it.

Their itinerary was gruelling, with two concerts a day, and each venue was a fifty-mile drive from their base. In her poem 'Groans About Touring in Northern Ireland' she described the 'glow worm stove that yields no heat' and 'little dressing rooms of tin, with inconvenient Sani-Bin'. Where there were no dressing-rooms, blankets were suspended on ropes to protect the women's modesty. The audience could be up to seven hundred soldiers, and she had to be on her guard for unintended innuendo. Before she set off, Celia Johnson told her about an ENSA pantomime at a large naval base: the Fairy Queen, who was neither young nor pretty, began with, 'I am the Fairy Queen. This is my magic wand. What shall I do with my magic wand?' A quick-witted officer had stood up and shouted, 'The first man to answer that question goes straight back to the ship.'

The company performed in camps, village halls and hospitals to British and American troops. The Americans were mainly from small towns in the Midwest and believed that 'classical' music meant songs from musicals. Joyce's monologues were received with puzzled disbelief. They sat in silence, as if they were being read a bedtime story.

Joyce was not used to the communal life of a travelling company. She refused to share a room and some nights escaped the ENSA billets by paying for a hotel room – a habit that made her even less popular with the others. Even in the hotels she found no hot water, thin walls and hard beds: one mattress had 'the personality of a granite-hard spinster in a Victorian Novel'. She forced herself to eat at least one meal a day with the company, and managed to show restraint when she met a black beetle in her porridge. It was also hard work emotionally: she felt ignored by the rest of the company and looked-down-upon by her audiences for being part of ENSA. She had arrived full of good intentions of raising morale, but was finally tempted to view the tour as her colleagues did – just a job. She turned often to Christian Science and reminded herself that it really didn't matter and would all be the same in a hundred years. She was delighted to find in Belfast a thriving Christian Science church, where the First Reader wore a draped Greek-style ballgown and the Second Reader was in a tailcoat.

When stuck anywhere for an afternoon, she took the first bus she saw and bought a ticket to the end and back so that she could be alone for a while. She found Northern Ireland charmingly unspoiled with its small farms and friendly people. On one bus she overheard the conductor ask a passenger, 'And how is Mrs McCarthy?', to which he replied, 'Ah, she's doin' her best.'

Even though she knew that Dick would hate it all, she asked him to join the tour for the last three weeks. She was relieved to have someone on her own wavelength to talk to and giggle with. Rather than being impressed that the famous pianist and composer was joining them, the rest of the company were furious. The Warsaw Concerto was not 'real music' and, even worse, the audiences loved it. There were now three pianists, all vying to outplay each other. Joyce and Dick's rendition of songs by Gershwin and Rogers & Hart went down well with the audience but the rest of the company complained they were 'unnecessary'. Even Gwen lost her temper and swore at Joyce. She had a point: the original purpose had been to perform classical music, and now Joyce and Dick were upstaging them with modern, popular songs. Joyce claimed that, if music was good, it *was* classical, whenever it was composed.

On the final day of the tour Joyce and Dick celebrated by being rowed across Carlingford Lough to a village in Eire. In the village pub, they sang and played for the publican's wife, the Customs officer and three American technicians. They then stayed behind in Belfast after the others had gone and performed for the American Red Cross, where they could set their own programme and be free to excel. They travelled south to Dublin, where there was no black-out and no food-rationing, and the Germans mixed easily with the Irish

– an activity that she found difficult to cope with. On their way home they stopped in Edinburgh to see Noël Coward in *Present Laughter* and *Blithe Spirit*. The actress Judy Campbell was in the company and recalled, 'I was rather in love with Noël, but far too young to notice that he wasn't interested in women. We were on tour in Inverness-shire, in January, with deep snow. The theatre was freezing. We were standing in the wings when Noël slid his hands inside my bra. "At last," I thought, "he loves me." Then he said, "Thank you so much, that's the first time my hands have been warm all day." ' After dining with Coward and his company, Joyce decided that after all she did enjoy the company of theatricals – but only successful ones.

– 11 –

Back home from Ireland Joyce realised that it was no longer practical to continue living at Parr's – her work was now mainly in London and stricter petrol-rationing made commuting impossible. Somewhat reluctantly, she handed the cottage over to her Cousin Alice and rented the drawing-room of a house near Harrod's which had been converted into a bed-sit. It had a bed that let down from the wall and a cellar for air raids. Within a fortnight Reggie was posted from York to the War Office so they needed somewhere bigger, but their house in Chelsea was still not available. Joyce trudged the streets looking for a slightly larger home: there were plenty of mansions to let in Kensington and Mayfair requiring several servants to run them, but no small flats for two. Pauline Spender-Clay invited them to move into the spare room in her flat in Knightsbridge and Reggie insisted on paying her £1 a week to cover their food and washing.

There was a restaurant underneath the flat, but they usually ate at the Café Royal, Chez Victoire, Claridge's, Quaglino's, the Savoy Grill or Simpson's. The price of all meals was restricted by the food-rationing law, regardless of the venue. At the Dorchester, customers paid only 3s. 6d. for fish and 5s. for 'stuffed quail in puff pastry with mushroom sauce'. Smart places levied an extra charge of 7s. 6d. for dancing. Joyce and Reggie often went to Hatchett's, where Stéphane Grapelli played French swing violin. During lunch there, the comedian Ed Gray from the Crazy Gang gave Joyce a signed US dollar bill, which she kept in her wallet throughout the war. One night in The Ivy they ate 'rabbit brilliantly disguised as Chicken à la King – the rabbits are raised on the roof in Grosvenor Square'. 'Roof rabbit' was a wartime euphemism for domestic cat and maybe Joyce was taken in by it. Their ration books informed them at which shops they were to buy their meat, sugar and dripping. One page advised: 'Do nothing with this page until told what to do.'

Air raids continued over London during 1943, and Joyce and Reggie took their turn at night fire-watching in the street. They had to remain on duty from 7 p.m. to 7 a.m. and were issued with stirrup pumps and buckets. Whenever there was a crisis in the war, Nora threatened to volunteer for the British Red Cross. Although Joyce had not seen her mother for five years and had established a workable relationship by writing to her every week, this was the last thing she needed. On 26 February she telegraphed Nora: LIFE GOES ON NORMALLY SO PLEASE STOP WORRYING WE ARE ABSOLUTELY ALRIGHT PLENTY OF FOOD AND ONE WARM ROOM LOVE JOYCE.

Joyce's reputation on the stage led to more film parts, and though none was more than a few minutes long all were strong, eccentric characters. In *This Demi-Paradise*, one of the first Ealing Comedies, she played Mrs Pawson, the village organiser, and the teenager George Cole played an office clerk. This propaganda film was made to show Anglo-Soviet co-operation after the USSR and Britain became allies in 1942. Laurence Olivier, as engineer Ivan Cuvnichov, invented his own accent rather than attempt a genuine Russian one. After running a canteen, Mrs Pawson, dressed as Nell Gwyn, organises a march of Polish soldiers and Free French while Cuvnichov announces: 'We must all stay pals after this war is over.'

While the Sun Shines, also made in 1943, showed Britons getting on with their new American allies. The handsome young Earl of Harpenden is about to marry the daughter of the Duke of Ayre and Stirling. Joyce, in a hat covered in cherries, played a twittering upper-class woman called Daphne who spills the beans to the duke's daughter that her fiancé has a floozy. After an American lieutenant acrobat intervenes at the Albany, Piccadilly, the rich earl marries the impoverished duke's daughter.

The Lamp Still Burns was made with the Ministry of Health to recruit nurses. Rosamund John played Hilary Clarke, who gives up her career as a successful architect to become a nurse. Joyce played Dr Joan Barrett MD MRCP, who gives a technical lecture on blood transfusions and then, with supreme confidence in white coat and stethoscope, saves the life of an injured factory worker. The handsome factory owner, played by Stewart Granger, donates £11,000 to the pre-National Health Service hospital, and gets the nurse. As a Christian Scientist, Joyce's conscience was tested by this part but at this stage her ambition to appear on the screen overrode her antipathy to medicine.

Noël Coward was at first rather dismissive of Joyce's talents, but by 1943 acknowledged that she had become a professional and asked her to be in his film *This Happy Breed*. He wanted her to caricature a Christian Scientist, but her conscience would not allow it, so Coward told her that the part was really a member of the 'Temple of Spiritual Radiation'. She took a screen test but the role went to the more experienced actress Joyce Carey. She then auditioned for a part as a Nazi but failed to get that too.

By now Joyce's professional life encompassed not only ENSA concerts and radio broadcasts, but also records and films, which all required contracts. Celia Johnson recommended the theatrical agent Aubrey Blackburn at Christopher Mann Agency in Park Lane. After a brief meeting, he became Joyce's agent for all her work and remained so until he died thirty-one years later. He gave her his full support, always ensuring she received the highest fees possible. Within a week he secured her a part in a new comedy play called *Junior Miss*, set in New York. Joyce was to play the American mother of a twelve-year-old schoolgirl and learned her part quickly. But the rehearsals were harder work than she had imagined and the producer, Marcel Varnel, didn't like her. Reggie watched a rehearsal and later that day warned her that she should pull out before failure ruined her reputation. Amidst many tears she finally agreed, and after less than a week, her career as a straight stage actress was over. For a few days she felt depressed and humiliated, but six months later wrote a poem describing her relief at her timely escape. She never accepted a part in a play again, saying that she could only entertain looking straight at an audience, as she did not know how to act 'sideways'.

Joyce's income from radio improved when Blackburn noticed that the BBC had only been paying her performance fees and had ignored the fact that she also wrote her own scripts. Reggie, too, encouraged Joyce to insist on the best deals. It was not greed for money that made her demand high fees, but more a desire to be valued and taken seriously. When the producer of *Saturday Afternoon* invited Joyce to perform 'a little of your act', she was so irritated that she asked him if he wanted her to include sea-lions or a performing pony. The BBC archives contain over twenty-five files bulging with letters, memos and contracts relating to Joyce, and their contents demonstrate the high value she put on her work. Within less than a year of first broadcasting she had asked for a higher fee, and by the end of 1943 she was receiving twenty guineas per appearance – far more than most people. She objected every time the BBC omitted to pay her a repeat fee or underpaid after verbal agreements. For the 1943 variety show *Starlight* – 'the cream of vaudeville' – fees were adjusted according to the BBC's definition of 'star' and, after considerable debate, the Contracts Department agreed that Joyce qualified.

By mid-1943 all women up to forty-five years old had to work thirty hours a week at factories, shops or farms. Joyce was luckier than most in her designated war work – although hard, it was never monotonous. After her experience in Northern Ireland she planned the concerts herself, doing more than 120 all over the country, in YWCA, Jewish Services and Land Army clubs; for prisoners of war, sailors, American bomber officers and searchlight batteries. When a concert went well she described it as 'horses'. She often compared herself to a circus horse, which, once it sniffs the sawdust in the ring, is away. As the year progressed, more concerts were 'horses' and fewer 'claphand cripples', a phrase that Virginia and Joyce shared to describe awful occasions.

In August 1943 she reluctantly agreed to tour the north of England with another ENSA concert party. This time, Joyce got on better with the six singers and instrumentalists, managed by a retired major from the Welsh Fusiliers. Once again she stayed in hotels, and she was glad she could afford it when the musicians reported they had been given one crab-apple each for dessert. In the Park Hotel, Preston, she spied 'three black satins in a large glass cage called "Recep": two smilers and a fierce grouch' – the role model for the hotel receptionist she played ten years later in *Genevieve*. For three weeks, Joyce compèred and sang every day in hospitals and convalescent homes, in Chester, Clitheroe, Liverpool and Manchester. Her patience was sorely tested by Leon, 'the Fiddling Funster', who wore a clothes hanger in his purple velvet smoking jacket, one sock and plus-fours while he performed joke fiddle pieces. Leon felt that he and Joyce had a lot in common – he too wrote lyrics and monologues and tried to persuade Joyce to perform them. She tactfully pointed out that he would do them better. What Joyce really disliked about Leon was that he was conducting a torrid public affair with Hilda, the Junoesque contralto.

In October Noël Coward returned from a tour of the Middle East and talked on the radio about its forgotten troop camps and lonely gun-sites. Joyce immediately wanted to go out there. Two weeks later Basil Dean officially asked her and Dick Addinsell to go. 'You'll find it much harder work than the stage,' Dean warned. Joyce thought she could cope: she had learned that concert parties were not for her and was much happier as a 'troubadour', performing for small audiences who could not get to theatres.

Dick was keen, but his health was not up to it. Joyce was disappointed but not deterred, and started to look for a suitable accompanist. She had used many over the past three years and only one or two had met her exacting standards. They had to be able to adapt their playing to the situation, pick up new songs quickly, have no qualms about the type of music *and* be prepared to cope with tough working and living conditions. They also had to allow Joyce to be the star – all of her accompanists were shy, retiring types. Reggie's aunt, Lady Evelyn Jones, came to the rescue, reminding Joyce of three musical siblings who lived near her in Norfolk. The oldest was Viola Tunnard, a classical pianist who had studied at the Royal College of Music. They had a rehearsal together and Joyce declared that she liked her. At twenty-six, Viola was seven years younger than Joyce, old enough to be able to cope with a tough assignment and young enough for Joyce to be the older sister. Joyce liked her for her 'drawable face, with dark hair, alabaster skin and beguiling, shy smile'.

Joyce and Viola's first concert together, for the nurses at the Elizabeth Garrett Anderson Hospital, was a bit shaky but Joyce was confident it would improve. 'She is quiet and competent', she wrote to her mother, 'and, praise be, speaks the King's English – which does, let's face it, make a difference! Good sense of humour and quiet, intelligent and nice, she has a true gift and has a lot of sensitivity. She is very shy and almost too humble but her playing is heavenly and everyone loves it.'

Preparations for the tour took over a month, with frequent visits to Drury Lane for inoculations, uniforms, tickets and form-filling – one

1. Joyce Irene Phipps, aged three in Canada, contemplating the imminent arrival of a brother.

2. Joyce's grandmother, Mrs Wilton Phipps, painted by John Singer Sargent in 1884.

3. Joyce's mother, Nora Langhorne, with her nanny, Aunt Liza Pie, in Virginia, 1891.

4. The Langhorne family home, Mirador, in Virginia, built in 1825 and renovated in 1895.

5. Tommy Phipps, aged twelve, and his sister Joyce, aged fifteen, ready for the summer term at boarding school, 1925.

6. Tommy, aged fifteen, at Eton College.

7. Joyce and her father, Paul Phipps, at Cliveden, Buckinghamshire, in 1936.

8. Joyce, soon after 'coming out' in 1928, with Nora, posing for Cecil Beaton.

9. The Astors' country home, Cliveden, unchanged since 1893.

10. Cousins at Cliveden, April 1939. *Standing:* Bill Astor, Michael Astor, Reggie, Uncle Bob Brand, his son Jim and Jakie Astor. *Sitting:* Joyce, Aunt Nancy Astor, Dinah and Virginia Brand, and Uncle Waldorf Astor.

11. Mr and Mrs Reginald Grenfell emerge from St Margaret's, Westminster, on a windy day in December 1929.

12. Reggie and Joyce opening a chrome mine named after Katie Grenfell near Skopje, Yugoslavia, in November 1934.

13. The Grenfell family all dressed up for their sister Katie's wedding in July 1935. Vera, Frances, Harry, Reggie and Laura outside Nannau in Wales, with Joyce behind the camera.

14. Joyce about to plunge into the River Thames at Cliveden. Taken by Reggie in July 1935.

15. Virginia Graham and Joyce on top of the Empire State Building, October 1935, just before Joyce met Elliot Coleman.

16. Elliot Coleman in North Carolina, date unknown.

17. Entertaining a party in Connecticut, October 1934. Nora on tennis racquet and Joyce playing the piano dressed as English schoolgirls, with Bill Astor between them. Behind them are David Niven, Tommy Phipps, Frank Parker and Lefty Flynn.

18. Reggie at the wheel of the old Wolseley in front of the Grenfells' new home, Parr's, Cliveden, in June 1936.

19. Nancy Astor, on the right, opening Britain's first state nursery school, purpose-built in Slough, on 25 October 1937, accompanied by her niece Joyce (not seen). The headteacher, Mary Davies, holds the hand of Gordon Crompton, the original 'George'.

20. August bank holiday at Parr's, 1938. Comfort Hart-Davis, Mary Grenfell, Celia Johnson just back from China with her husband Peter Fleming, and Virginia Graham. Behind them are Rupert Hart-Davis and Reggie. Joyce took the photo.

21. Who's for tennis? Stephen Potter, Reggie, Mary Potter and Herbert and Joan Farjeon at Parr's, soon after Farjeon's *Little Revue* opened, May 1939.

22. The American monologuist and family friend, Ruth Draper, in 1938.

23. Joyce in her first revue, April 1939. *Above:* Understanding Mother and Village Mother. *Below:* American Mother and *Useful and Acceptable Gifts.*

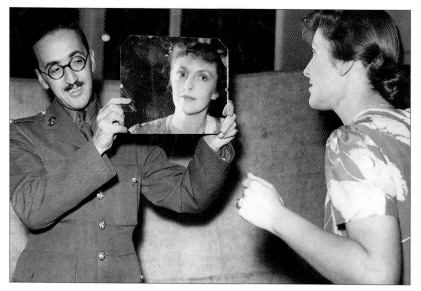

24. Harold Lindo, architect and amateur pianist, and Joyce backstage at a troop concert in September 1940. Joyce is wearing the same frock as she wore when photographed by Cecil Beaton in 1928. The frock was a present from her cousin Nancy Tree.

25. Ward 11 of the Canadian Red Cross Hospital built on the polo field at Cliveden in 1940. Photo taken by their social welfare officer, Joyce.

26. Transmitting a 'Transatlantic Quiz' from the underground Criterion Theatre, Piccadilly, at 2 a.m. on 16 April 1941. The team, which included Joyce (behind the microphone), Harriet Cohen, Beatrice Lillie (in stripes), Carroll Gibbons and producer Cecil Madden, slept in bunks in the theatre.

27. Joyce, Myra Hess and Howard Fergusson discuss his piano sonata, first performed on New Year's Day 1940 at the National Gallery.

28. Joyce and Viola Tunnard on tour for ENSA in Persia, 1944.

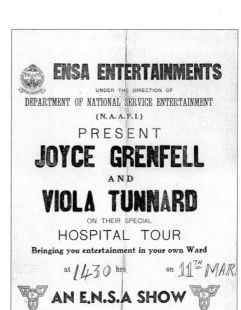

29. The poster put up in hospitals in North Africa, the Middle East and India for Joyce and Viola, 1944–5.

30. British troops enjoying some
female company: Viola and Joyce in
Iraq, 1944.

31. Prince Aly Khan and
Rita Hayworth in 1949 just before
they married.

immigration form even required details of Joyce's beard. After her experience with American and British troops, she and Viola rehearsed all the cheerful, rhythmic songs they could find: Carley Robinson sent sheet music from America. Every single item of printed material they wanted to take – songs, monologues, even the Bible – had to be checked by the censors and was not returned until after they left England.

Joyce and Viola were on standby to leave from the middle of December and Joyce appreciated every last day she was with Reggie. They expected to fly out to North Africa, and had reduced their luggage to forty-four pounds each. Joyce chose a new silk dress designed by Victor Stiebel; an old lace frock which never needed ironing; White Lilac perfume; an inflatable cushion; an old fur coat from Aunt Pauline; Reggie's spotted silk dressing-gown; and copies of *Howard's End* and *Orlando*.

After several weeks' waiting, with many false starts, Joyce and Viola were told they would be going by sea. They finally left England on 13 January 1944 – exactly five years to the day since Joyce had been 'discovered' by Herbert Farjeon. Since then she had appeared in three revues, one of which had failed, she had written six monologues and learned several popular songs that could be accompanied by a single piano. For security reasons they could not say where the train, let alone the boat, was going. They set off, with no company to support them, to entertain hardened troops all over the Middle East. No one in ENSA had briefed them – they couldn't, because nobody else had undertaken such a task on their own.

– 12 –

Second Lieutenants Grenfell and Tunnard embarked at Liverpool on troopship *D19*, a converted P&O liner previously called *SS Strathmore*. This was only the third convoy to be heading for the Mediterranean and the risk of air attack during the two-week journey was high. The previous convoy had been dive-bombed by twenty-seven German planes in the Strait of Gibraltar, missing the *D19* by only feet and sinking three other ships, one of which was carrying ENSA artists. Half an orchestra was picked up by a British destroyer, still clutching their instruments, and that night they gave a concert to their rescuers.

The captain of the *D19* warned everyone that keeping a diary contravened military regulations. Ignoring this order, Joyce began a detailed account which continued for all her overseas ENSA work. The enemy would have been hard put to make use of her descriptions of conversations, clothes and meals.

In addition to troops, the ship carried members of the Free French and Red Cross. Other passengers included WVS workers and diplomats' wives, who enjoyed 'gallumphing in rhythmless cavorts' as Viola pounded dance reels on a piano with no middle C. Also beginning an ENSA tour were 'The Two Leslies' – short, blond Sarony and tall, thin Holmes – an act of smutty songs and jokes. The audience of sailors loved them, and Joyce wondered whether she should have set off on this adventure. She had learned that neither her monologues nor her songs mixed with conjuring tricks or dirty jokes. For her act to work, she had to create her own intimate atmosphere. She reminded herself that this was a job in which she must forgo prestige, though in fact throughout the next five months she struggled to maintain her composure when she felt unappreciated.

The ship arrived in Algiers on 25 January 1944, seven months since the German Army had been driven out of North Africa. Joyce and Viola put up in a dormitory in the depressing ENSA hostel, which had no running water. They collapsed in giggles when they saw that the 'sun room' had frosted windows hiding the sea. The peace and spring weather proved a tonic after winter in Britain – lemon trees and geraniums glowed against an aquamarine Mediterranean.

Joyce and Viola had met only a few times before they set off from London. Viola had been well educated by her clerical father, and Joyce was willing to learn a lot from her: about musical structure and how to listen to it, and about the ancient ruins they visited in Algeria, Sicily and Naples. They both appreciated the clear blue skies, young wheat, flowering citrus trees and 'spaniel coloured lambs with petal shaped ears'. The local fruit market too was a delight to their war-rationed eyes. Better still was an invitation from Reggie's old friend Roger Makins, assistant to Harold Macmillan, then Minister Resident for Allied Forces in Algeria, to stay at the minister's residency, Villa Desjoyeux. Macmillan was somewhat surprised when he returned the next day from Naples. 'Back in Algiers we found two women in our house – Joyce Grenfell and Miss Tunnard. They are singing to hospitals and so on, and they appear to be more comfortable in our house than in the hotel,' he recorded. He had hitherto been careful to make the villa an all-male preserve, billeting his female typists elsewhere and employing Grenadier Guards as batmen. Joyce had imagined that Macmillan would be dull, and was surprised to find him charming and witty, 'an endearing small-boy type'.

Joyce and Viola enjoyed eating the fresh food served by handsome young soldiers and the comforts of the residency. There was a grand piano for Viola to play, and plenty of hot water in the huge bath. What they didn't know was that the food was from the black market; coal to heat the water was obtained only after Macmillan befriended an admiral; and the linen and cutlery had been salvaged from a P&O liner bombed in Algiers Docks.

Joyce did not seem unduly surprised by the number of old acquaintances that she met. Halsey Colchester, a friend of Richard Addinsell, was in the SAS on the Algerian coast. He drove 350 miles across the desert in a jeep to present Joyce with a huge bunch of mimosa and invited her to supper in the SAS camp. Joyce accepted, and after a long day's work in three hospitals, she and Viola drove without headlights to the camp, hidden up a mountain near Philipville. The Italian prisoners of war cursed as they carried the 'Mini-piano' from the truck down a dark, slippery slope to a Nissen hut, decorated with battleship paint and made cosy with a cork-bark fire.

Joyce and Viola also dined with Duff Cooper, British Representative to the Free French. Lady Diana Cooper's fame as a social beauty and actress had bedazzled Joyce, but she, too, turned out to be friendly. Whereas Macmillan lived on what he called 'the pewter standard', the Coopers had established a 'silver standard', with fine wines and bone china.

As the 10th of February approached, Joyce and Macmillan discovered they shared a birthday. Makins organised a picnic in the Forêt de Bainein and they walked through sun-dappled pines to a clearing of fresh green grass. 'It was a lovely day,' he recorded, 'and we picked great quantities of wild flowers – iris, jonquils, crocus and scilla. It is terrible to reflect on all the follies and mistakes of so many years – so much attempted, so little achieved.' It was to be another thirteen years before he became British Prime Minister.

Despite their differences in temperament, Joyce and Viola's shared experiences gradually drew them together. After several days in the Algerian desert, they let off steam by laughing about the embroidered flannel dressing-gowns which the nurses had lent them to cross the muddy yard between their dormitory and the outside lavatories. Unlike Joyce, Viola neither needed nor sought applause and would often disappear as soon as a concert ended. Both women proved tough in the difficult physical and emotional circumstances, but they coped in different ways. There were times when they exasperated each other, especially when Joyce's Pollyanna brightness clashed with Viola's 'black dog moods'.

Joyce and Viola were driven around by a surly French-Algerian called Grassin whom they nicknamed 'Le Joli Garçon'. Returning to Algiers one evening along a mountain road, they found the hairpin bends could only be negotiated by backing to and fro, above a sheer drop. Le Joli Garçon put the truck into forward instead of reverse gear and they shot towards the precipice, stopping only inches from certain death. For some miles, they were shocked into silence. Eventually he said with a Gallic shrug, '*Et c'est tout fini dans un instant*' – 'It's all over in a moment.'

Both women were exhausted by their demanding social life combined with hospital work, though Joyce soon decided it was worthwhile. Their assignment was to play in places where it wasn't practical to send a whole show. Entering a hospital ward, they spoke to half the patients each, finding out where they came from. Then followed thirty minutes of songs, while the nurses continued giving injections or changing dressings. Viola played either the Mini-piano provided by ENSA or the resident pianos, which were usually hopeless. This was a strain for any musician but especially for one with such high standards. She carried her own tuning-key but some pianos went out of tune before the end of the concert. One seemed to be strung with woollen strings; the pedals of another fell off at the first touch; and a blue-painted instrument made such frightening noises that they had to muffle it with a sock.

Their repertoire now included cockney songs such as *Any Old Iron*, *Old Kent Road* and *Lily of Laguna*, though Joyce continued to resist *Ave Maria* – she said she had the wrong sort of voice. She also found it impossible to sing songs like *Some Day* and *All My Tomorrows* to men with no futures. In one ward a young man asked Joyce to sing a song about a mother. 'The nearest I could do was a lullaby. It taught me a lesson – don't be so damned grand. Learn all the songs of all types,' she said.

During one show, two soldiers led in a friend who had recently been blinded. They kept looking at him to see if he might join in but he just stood there smoking. Halfway through he dropped his cigarette and started to sing too. Joyce had to summon all her self-control to continue, especially when she saw the tears in his friends' eyes.

At the end of each concert the audience were invited to perform: a cockney with his leg strung up on a pulley did an impression of Popeye by taking out his teeth; a jockey sang *Blaydon Races*; and in one ward the nurses sang a duet to roars of applause, and then returned to giving blood transfusions. Their ship had been torpedoed on the way to Algeria but they laughed it off as all in a day's work.

Where the piano was good enough, Viola finished off with the Warsaw Concerto, followed by 'God Save the King' – Joyce was surprised how many of the British soldiers did not know the words. In addition to driving east across North Africa, they did three or four shows a day and, if there was time, talked to the patients and wrote letters for the very sick ones. She was, she discovered, 'a useful piece of blotting paper' to homesick men. At thirty-four she could be mother, sister or girlfriend to her audience: both young enough to be attractive and old enough to laugh off innuendos. When introduced by an over-enthusiastic ENSA officer as 'Miss Joyce Grenfell and Miss Viola Tunnard who have come out especially to entertain you in your beds', she relished it as much as the men did.

Joyce learned not to take advantage of an audience who couldn't get up and leave. She also realised that those who read newspapers or looked the other way were rarely malevolent, but more often embarrassed. The 'smart-Alec' who made rude comments in a stage whisper was often the one who thanked her most warmly at the end: 'See you in Piccadilly by Eros at the Peace Parade!' What pleased her most was being asked when she was coming back. 'Take all the orchids, all the telegrams, all the press notices, and give me that, accompanied by that absolutely genuine eagerness of the British soldier away from home!' she wrote.

The hospitals held up to 2,500 patients each and the wards could have anything from six to sixty beds in them. They had no names, only numbers, but each was quite different. Hospital No. 94 had been an orphanage, No. 95 a boys' school; No. 96 was a series of Nissen huts in the docks, No. 97 a row of brown marquees; and No. 99 was a TB sanatorium in the mountains. Among the patients there was not only a Welsh hymn singer and an Irish tenor, but also a tap-dancer. While Joyce sang *There Is Nothing New to Tell You*, a rainbow formed over the plain below and she noticed several soldiers wiping away tears.

Joyce soon found that any more than sixteen men could not hear her performing monologues. There were acoustic problems with singing, too: canvas walls absorbed sound and monasteries echoed like public swimming-pools. In a tented ward of sixty beds she eventually found the solution was to get everyone singing as loudly they could.

The atmosphere of each hospital was set by the matron in charge. Each had made her own small corner of England, with rugs, ornaments and calendars. Joyce placed them in the 'outskirts of Tunbridge Wells', 'Barker's of Ken High St.' or 'D. H. Evans'. Their rooms often had a 'wee doggie' atmosphere, as if a Yorkshire terrier should have been there. A few were unfriendly, probably exhausted by their work. They and their nurses had coped with unimaginable conditions: being attacked by Stukas as they rescued injured men; dressing wounds by touch in the dark; and witnessing colleagues being killed. There was nothing they could do for many of their patients but smile. However hard she tried, Joyce was never going to be part of this – she had not been at the front line and, although tough, her life was not in danger. Yet despite promising herself not to expect special treatment, she was annoyed if they were not invited to eat with the staff. Even in the desert she believed that good manners should prevail.

Some of the patients were convalescing from the North African battles the year before; others were more recent injuries from the fighting in Italy. Joyce found these troops were different from the ones she had met in Britain – they had experienced the horrors of battle. There was either a meditative quietness about them or a cheerful resignation to their fate. They were all homesick and many knew that they would never make it. For the badly injured, the show was reduced to encompass only the immediate three or four beds. In one hospital Joyce spoke to a man who was so ill that he could barely move his head. She had to hold on hard when he not only cracked a joke but also joined in the singing. He died a few hours later.

In less than three weeks in Algeria, Joyce and Viola performed thirty-nine concerts of an hour each. The transport, accommodation and venue fell to ENSA officers, who varied in their efficiency. Joyce expected to find posters displayed, a playable piano for Viola, transport and an audience. When these were not forthcoming, Viola would suggest that the time had come to be 'altesian' – from the French *altesse*, as in 'Your Highness'– and Joyce would make clear her displeasure by becoming taller and more distant. It was hard work, however, and the lack of a stage manager left less energy for the performance.

Reading the daily Christian Science lesson gave her the inner strength needed to cope with this tough world. Her conscience was constantly pricked by the conflict between her natural desire to be the centre of attention and her religious views on humility. On bad days she remembered her mother's advice: 'You are always enveloped in God's love and wisdom. Be still and know that you are in God.'

From Algiers, Le Joli Garçon drove them to Tunis. They had to cross a high plateau, where the truck broke down in a blizzard. As Le Joli Garçon mended the truck, a line of wild Arab ponies galloped out of the swirling snow, crossed the road and disappeared again: 'One of those magic moments,' commented Joyce.

They drove for 290 miles in one day through the battlefields and saw abandoned tanks and cemeteries reaching to the horizon. The huge health-education billboards warning of infectious diseases shocked Joyce. Malaria, dysentery and typhus were rife and anyone driving into Tunis was warned THERE IS VD HERE – LOOK OUT! Venereal diseases were a major problem because, unlike the German Army which had state-run mobile brothels, British and American soldiers were expected to either abstain or make their own arrangements. In Naples, there was so little food that women offered themselves to soldiers in exchange for a tin of bully-beef for their children. Consequently, by the end of 1943 hospitals in Naples had as many VD patients as war-wounded.

After a week of performing in the hospitals around Tunis, Joyce and Viola had their first flight in an aeroplane, a DC3. They took it in turns to sit in tin seats beside the Australian pilot as they flew only three hundred feet above the waves to Malta.

Joyce liked Malta – it reminded her of childhood picture books of flower stalls, peasants in national costume and tasselled horses pulling dainty carriages. They went to a Sunday service at the English Cathedral, where the elderly priest stepped out of the procession to thank Joyce for making him laugh in the *Little Revue* in 1939. They were taken to visit a White Russian princess, who insisted that in Italy they buy worm medicines for her adored terrier. Joyce would have no more bought medicines for a dog than for a human but Viola agreed to try.

ENSA women were expected to be flirty, drinking girls, parts neither Joyce nor Viola were prepared to play. 'The sodden male is an uncharming thing,' Joyce wrote after one evening in a mess. 'I'm not much good, islanded in sobriety, while merriment goes on in a beery sea around me.' They did enjoy dancing, and wherever it was available they were overwhelmed by queues of men wanting to foxtrot with them. Each man believed that in Joyce he had at last found a woman who understood him. She was kind, firm, and careful to give no encouragement.

Reggie's stepmother was touring YWCA hostels and had written from Baghdad suggesting they extend their tour to 'Paiforce', the area in Persia and Iraq where British troops were stationed to protect RAF bases, oil pipelines and the Aid-to-Russia route from the Persian Gulf to Azerbaijan. It was a non-combatant zone, so the troops were bored and felt left behind; some of them had been there for four or five years and few ENSA entertainers ever got that far. Noël Coward had already refused a request to go there and had warned Joyce that the climate was hell, there was sandfly fever and malaria, and the trip would be the 'acme of arid discomfort'. Joyce was tempted, but also keen to get home to London. She finally made up her mind when she and Viola were waiting at Malta Airport to leave for Sicily and out of a small plane emerged Walter Crisham and Hermione Baddeley, her colleagues from Farjeon revues. After delighted greetings, Crisham said they had been asked to go to Baghdad but 'We couldn't face it, darling.' When Hermione Baddeley exclaimed, 'My dear, Baghdad is *The End*,' Joyce and Viola decided immediately – they would go.

In Sicily, they did thirteen shows in five days, plus going to the opera, visiting the ancient Greek theatre at Syracuse and being taken to a cocktail party in Prince Borghese's sumptuous palace, where he kissed Joyce's hand too often for her liking. The colonel in one hospital told Joyce that 'All the patients played to the day before were more cheerful, had slept better and *were* better.'

The next stop was Bari on the Adriatic coast of Italy, where it was very cold, ENSA had lost all the posters advertising their show and the piano was 'beyond praying for'. There were many Canadians in southern Italy and Joyce bumped into both doctors and patients from Cliveden Hospital, and was thrilled to find that Hospital No. 5 was run by a staff nurse from Cliveden. She welcomed them with lunch in her tent which, like all the wards, was erected on the side of a muddy hill.

The Allied forces were pushing their way north up Italy and casualties were high - over three hundred thousand young men were killed or injured during the two-year campaign. In Bari they did four shows in the amputation wards of No. 3 New Zealand Hospital, which was coping with casualties from the battle for Monte Cassino. Joyce saw 'bed after bed filled with mutilated men, heads, faces, bodies. It's the most inhuman, ghastly, bloody, hellish thing in the world. I couldn't think or work or even feel in the end. It was quite numbing. All the time we were playing there were sisters doing dressing, patients feeding from tubes, orderlies bringing people in from the theatres and newly arrived from the line. About half the room was too ill to listen or care: the others lay and took it in with their eyes, it was no fun to see the suffering going on in there. I struggled to get a clear mind.' Other wards had shell-shocked men, or men being held down for treatment.

Joyce was moved by the tenderness with which the convalescent men looked after the newly injured. Many amputations were performed simply because there was no time or resources to save the limb. Joyce secretly wondered whether it wasn't better for them to be killed outright than to suffer so much, so far from home, only to lose their youthful good looks and energy. She and Viola agreed that with men struggling just to stay alive their presence didn't really help – they were of more value to convalescent men, who were getting bored and homesick. Joyce was getting very tired, but felt carried through by the 'buoyant, spiritual selfless feeling' of the people she met – both the wounded and their carers.

Next stop was Naples, where Allied aerial bombing had wrecked the city. As the Germans had retreated they had mined the sewers and electricity sub-stations. As if this wasn't enough, Mount Vesuvius was erupting. As Joyce and Viola flew into Naples, the plane had to keep below the thick grey cloud which spread out to sea for up to a hundred miles. From the roof of their hotel they could see the volcano spewing fire and huge 'cauliflower clouds' of ash which it belched several thousand feet up into the sky. When the wind blew inland, everything was covered in grey ash, making the countryside of olive trees and fields look like a black and white photograph. At night the volcano sounded like bombs and shook the doors and windows. Several villages and hospitals were evacuated and the roads were closed to non-essential traffic so that civilians could move fast if they needed to.

One evening an American driver called Tchaikovsky took Joyce and Viola across country to within a mile of Vesuvius. They watched a continuous firework display of red light and hurtling fire and the wall of red-hot molten lava move down the mountain only a quarter of a mile from them. 'The whole sight was evil but rather beautiful like an old picture painted on glass,' Joyce wrote. That night a whole village was engulfed.

Viola's younger brother Peter was a captain in the Scots Guards who two months earlier had landed behind the German lines at Anzio, just south of Rome. Casualties had been very high, the family had not heard from him and Viola had been having nightmares about his safety. She hoped that she might get some news now that she was in Italy. Out of the blue, he left a phone message at the ENSA office in Naples – he had been wounded, and was now convalescing. To Viola's delight, they met up, though she was shocked by the change in him. At first he hardly spoke, but after three days escorting them around Naples he began to thaw and started to laugh. Joyce envied their close relationship, which she had never had with her brother.

Once again they bumped into Roger Makins, accompanying Macmillan on an official visit. He invited them to Macmillan's villa overlooking the Bay of Naples. After lunch they watched Vesuvius erupt and heard gunfire in the distance while Macmillan read aloud from Boswell's *Life of Johnson*.

Joyce wrote daily to Reggie, and his replies took from three to six weeks to reach her. Three letters she received from Reggie at once in Malta had all pleaded with her to come home as soon as possible. But everyone in ENSA agreed that a tour of Paiforce would be invaluable and they began to work out an itinerary. Joyce and Viola prepared to fly to Cairo, where they could get some summer clothes for the Middle East. From Italy they flew via Malta to pick up injured soldiers, who travelled strung up on hammock-stretchers. During a refuelling stop in the desert of El Adem in Libya, a khamsin – an oppressive desert wind – blew up and they were grounded until the next day.

The colonel at the airfield commandeered a car to take Joyce and Viola sightseeing. They were in the centre of the battlefield where thousands had lost their lives only fifteen months before. Shacks were built from petrol tins, and millions more were scattered everywhere. Abandoned German and Allied vehicles were rusting in the flat, brown desert. On the way to Tobruk they stopped at a vast cemetery of regulation white crosses, many of them unnamed. Joyce was discomfited by the lines of graves, especially the ornate marble tombs that some families had had erected. She felt that it would be better to leave the graves unmarked, let the desert take over, and allow the memories of the loved ones to speak for themselves. It may have been this experience that influenced her to ask for no physical memorial for herself.

In Tobruk Joyce and Viola wandered round the ghost town of shattered buildings and barbed wire, guarded by a few British troops. There was little water or food, no entertainment, and the men were at risk from malaria, dysentery and landmines.

Back at the airfield, an audience of seven hundred men had been gathered from the surrounding camps for a concert under the stars. The airstrip's transit mess was transformed into a women's dormitory with colourful blankets and they were joined by a Free French woman pilot, whose biplane had also been caught by the khamsin. During the night, the storm ripped the roofs from the officers' quarters and the aeroplane hangar, and three hundred tents were blown away. Joyce was grateful for her fur coat and her mother's hot-water bottle.

IN CAIRO JOYCE'S status changed from ENSA singer to being the niece of the British High Commissioner, Miles Lampson, Lord Killearn. His first wife had been Rachel Phipps, Joyce's father's sister, who had died of meningitis. After a distinguished diplomatic career in Siberia, Tokyo and Peking, Lampson had been appointed Britain's first ambassador to Egypt in 1937. King Farouk was not amused when he was described as 'the British Ambassador to Egypt and for all practical purposes its actual ruler'. When the German Army was closing in on Cairo in 1943, and everyone was scrabbling for trains to Palestine, he ordered the embassy railings to be repainted, while indoors his staff were busy shredding diplomatic papers. He was rewarded with a peerage and the post changed to high commissioner. Although technically his home became a 'residency', it was still referred to as 'the embassy'.

Lord Killearn enjoyed the pastimes of an English gentleman. When Joyce's cousins Gavin Astor and Michael Tree were passing through Cairo with the Household Cavalry, they were invited on his weekly duck shoot in the Nile Delta. The Earl of Uxbridge (now the Marquess of Anglesey) was with them: 'We sped in Rolls Royces to the duck killing grounds *lined* by policemen. All the cartridges belonged to Lord Killearn and they were handed out to us on arrival. The number of them returned at the shoot's end and the corpses of the ducks showed how many cartridges were employed per duck. I recollect my very poor performance with my gun. Very cruel!' That day, Anglesey shot twenty-seven duck to Killearn's 140, out of a total bag of 553.

When Joyce had first left Britain, her father had written to Killearn to say she might pass through Cairo, so she had been expected for some time. His staff kept him informed of all the comings and goings and only a few days after receiving Paul's letter he heard that Mrs Grenfell had booked into a hostel. Killearn immediately invited her to stay at the embassy. When he entered the dining-room to greet his niece he was astonished to discover that it was Joyce's sixty-year-old mother-in-law, Hilda. He recorded in his diary: 'When, in the course of lunch, Mrs Grenfell said she might have to stay here a week to do her work, we were still more taken aback. However, she is a charming person. A comic mix-up.' After inspecting YWCA hostels in Egypt, Hilda Grenfell continued on her tour of the Middle East, Australia and America.

Two months later Killearn's intelligence was more accurate and he knew exactly when Joyce and Viola would arrive at Cairo aerodrome, thirty miles from the city. Judging by the tone of his diary, he was looking forward to meeting his niece, whom he had not seen for over five years. 'Then a message came that Joyce Grenfell has at last arrived in Cairo and a few minutes later I went out and met her in the hall. She looks extremely well but naturally was feeling somewhat travel stained.'

Monday – Naples; Tuesday – Malta; Wednesday – Tobruk; Thursday – Cairo: Joyce was whirling from the speed of air travel. The British Embassy was the perfect place for a few days' respite: it was run on 'the gold standard', with Egyptian domestic servants in red and gold livery and Chinese furniture and Persian carpets collected on Killearn's travels. A flight of stairs led up to the large house, surrounded by wide colonnaded verandahs. Field Marshal Smuts had recently given Killearn a new swimming-pool, surrounded by rustling palm trees, and the spacious garden was an oasis from the hurly-burly of the city. Joyce was delighted to collapse into the luxury of it all and Viola had a good piano to play. After army rations of tinned bully-beef, strong sweet tea and hard-tack, Joyce was amazed by the abundance of good food – fresh fruit, butter, cream and chocolate. They ate breakfast on the verandah outside their bedrooms overlooking the Nile. Miss Tee, the housekeeper, whisked away their clothes to be washed and pressed. The Killearns still changed for dinner and Joyce longed for some decent clothes – her dresses were now worn out and her fur coat was full of Vesuvian ash and Saharan sand. After long deep baths and rinsing her hair in fresh limes, Joyce wrote her diary lying on a *chaise longue* by the window, sipping fresh orange juice. They had missed epidemics of malaria and smallpox in Egypt by a few weeks and the weather was perfect – ninety degrees with a slight breeze.

Exhausted by constant entertaining, Killearn's second wife, Jacqueline, had gone to recuperate in Alexandria. He was delighted to show the two young women around Cairo in his official car, with Union Jacks flying and an armed guard standing on the running-board. An escort of motorbikes cleared the streets ahead. Noël Coward caught the atmosphere of an evening in Cairo: 'The air was soft and hot; expensive cars whizzed by; the crowded pavements of the city were ablaze with light and there was the usual cacophony of street noises; shouts and yells, motor horns, klaxons and thudding noise in the background as though lots of people were banging invisible tin trays.' They went to the Opera House, decorated with ornate plaster-work, and sat in a box to watch a play by Emlyn Williams's company.

Killearn cancelled his Friday duck-shooting and took Joyce and Viola to Gezira Sports Club, with its magnificent polo fields, cricket pitch, croquet lawns and tennis courts. That day, Killearn had several runners at the racecourse. As they entered his private box the British national anthem was played by the brass band. Noël Coward reported that:

> The whole procedure was a model of courteous autocracy and would have curdled the lifeblood of the Daily Worker. All the fripperies of pre-war luxury living are still in existence here; rich people, idle people, cocktail-parties, dinner parties, jewels and evening dress. There is a perpetual undercurrent of social and political feuds. Enjoyable of course for a brief visit, but it felt rather old-fashioned and almost lacking in taste.

For once, Joyce agreed with Coward and tried not to think about the begging children, powerful smells of spices and open sewers.

After two days in Cairo, Joyce and Viola were informed they could fly to Baghdad early the next morning. They were just beginning to recuperate and so Killearn pulled some strings to postpone the next leg of the journey. 'Quite a successful wangle but actually fully justified on the facts,' he boasted in his diary. That evening he took them to L'Auberge des Pyramides, a glittering open-air nightclub near the Sphinx. As Killearn entered, everybody bowed and they were led to the best table. On the way back they went to a party given by Alphonse Alexan, the handsome son of an ancient Egyptian Copt family. Among the other guests was Princess Joan Khan, daughter of Lord Churston, whom Joyce had known as a debutante, now married to Prince Aly Khan, son of the Aga Khan. Joyce agreed to sing with the band. 'Definitely good,' wrote Killearn in his diary.

The next day Joyce went with her twenty-five-year-old cousin Graham Lampson, an officer in the Scots Guards, to a party in a Greek-owned house, which she found 'very Park Lane'. An American swing band played and after quick-stepping with Graham's colleagues Joyce accepted a dance with Prince Aly. He was shorter than her and slightly plump, but he danced beautifully. Long after midnight, he drove her back to the embassy in his sports car, so fast that Joyce could only shut her eyes and pray. He collected fast cars: in 1938 he bought a Delahaye sports car for £11,000 – the equivalent now of over half a million pounds.

On their last evening in Cairo, Joyce, Viola, Graham and Killearn attended a large party in honour of Princess Shevekiar, an immensely rich woman who had been married five times, including to the first King of Egypt. Joyce was later annoyed that she had not realised quite how royal the princess was, and had not curtseyed to her. As soon as Crown Prince Paul of Greece arrived – two hours late – an American band struck up dance music and Prince Aly whisked Joyce onto the dance floor. That night she wrote in her diary that she danced with him 'for most of the evening, ending cheek to cheek in the most intime way'. Two years later, when she had her diary typed out, she deleted all mention of Prince Aly's presence that evening.

The following morning Joyce and Viola left for Baghdad. Until now they had managed not to wear ENSA's military-style uniform, known as 'Basil Dress', and had even been issued with a 'permit for plain clothes', partly because they felt that they had more value as two ordinary women representing home and civilian life. They were told that in Paiforce they would have to wear uniform, especially when travelling, in case they were arrested as spies. A Cairo tailor made them each a suit, which looked to Joyce as if they had been cut out with a knife and fork. Although they fitted passably well, Joyce found the khaki colour hideous and she refused to wear the peaked cap.

They flew to Baghdad in a biplane with open windows, sitting on wooden boards. Stewart Perowne, the press attaché at the British Embassy, met them. He was an old friend – his father, the Bishop of Worcester, had married Joyce and Reggie and his brother, Leslie, was a BBC producer. Perowne told them there were few injured soldiers, but all of them were homesick. A few ENSA concert parties had got this far, but their quality had been so poor that even the entertainment-starved troops had booed them off the stage.

The *Iraq Times* reported that in Baghdad Hospital Joyce and Viola 'enchanted their audience with a performance of rare charm and brilliance. Viola Tunnard is an essential part in the whole intricate and colourful pattern and has an uncanny knack of making even a NAAFI piano produce music.' The newspaper *Trunk Call* was delighted too:

> Typical of her [Joyce's] experience in the Command was the show at Lancer Camp Baghdad. It is a huge theatre and several hundred troops turned up to see what it was all about. For the first five minutes they were not sure, but gradually the charm of this unusual entertainment began to get them. Joyce and her indispensable half-section, Viola Tunnard, kept the house enthralled, laughing one minute, near to tears the next.
>
> Viola Tunnard is just the right accompanist for this kind of work. The other night a well-meaning but over enthusiastic fatigue party dropped the piano and Viola had practically to rebuild it. She was quite unperturbed when the upper register failed to respond to treatment. 'Oh well', she said, 'I just won't have to play up that end.' No member of the audience was any the wiser.

ENSA looked after them well and for the train journey north to Kirkuk they were issued with blankets, pillows and even an ice-box packed with orange juice. Another train took them east from Kirkuk to the Iraqi Petroleum Company refinery near Khanakin. In the middle of the desert, it was laid out with bungalows which reminded Joyce of Hampstead Garden Suburb. At their first show Viola played the piano on the back of a truck and Joyce sang to seventy men sitting on petrol tins. The next show was for 150 officers and oil executives

sitting indoors and Joyce treated herself to performing several monologues before Viola played Chopin, Bach and Rachmaninov on a
decent piano.

They then sat in the back of a truck for 115 miles south across the
desert with an armed escort to Kut on the River Tigris. When the
sun shone they were covered in dust, and when it rained they were
cold and muddy.

Joyce had lost so much weight that her dresses were now hanging
off her and her stage dress had more darning than original lace.
Concerts were the usual hard work – at one, the rattling windows
were beaten by sand and half the audience were Italian prisoners of
war and Palestinians, none of whom spoke English. Usually the local
Arabs were not invited in, but always crowded round the windows.
Viola's pianos were no better – some had no top notes, others were
missing the ivory. Some days she was so worried about her brother
Peter that she barely spoke.

Then, in RAF Basra, almost in the Gulf of Persia, 550 men in a
large hall responded so well that Joyce felt in complete control. She
and Viola were as one, and the show was not just 'horses' but
'Windsor-greys-Pegasi-winged-Arabs and Derby-winners all in one'.
The ENSA officer was so impressed that he suggested that Joyce
should perform in music halls.

An hour's drive away from Basra was Shuaibah, their last stop.
Noël Coward recorded that 'the heat rose up from the ground and
enveloped and pressed down from the airless sky, it shimmered visibly
all around like the fumes from a burning brazier. Shuaibah consists of
Nissen huts, hangars and sand. There is nothing else whatever except,
of course, aeroplanes to go in the hangars and several thousand men
to gasp the hours away.'

Their very last evening was almost a disaster. The Royal Army
Ordnance Corps had been issued with beer *before* the concert and
had thrown themselves into a punch-up with Iraqi Other Ranks.
Once they were separated, and the Iraqis evicted from the hall, Joyce
and Viola began. Joyce sensed their belligerent mood and did her best
to quell their wolf-whistles and catcalls with the most sentimental
songs she knew. Viola was just as distressed and they performed for
only half an hour before escaping to the officers' mess. To compensate the officers, they did another show just for them in a Nissen hut.

'We rarely saw any women at all, let alone to entertain us,' remembered Alfred Turner, aged twenty-one, of the Royal Signal Corps. 'It was very, very hot and I was on night-guard duty. I suppose I had a touch of the Shuaibah blues: I had been there nearly three years and I'd just been in hospital with malaria. I marched around the hut and then peeked inside. Miss Grenfell had a long face and was singing "Miss Otis Regrets". I was very impressed that a real "lady" had come out to us.'

They had performed 155 concerts in nine weeks: an average of three per day. The rewards of the job had given Joyce extra energy to keep going longer than anyone expected, but now all she wanted was a good rest. 'Home will be mighty nice and unpacking bliss,' she wrote on her way back to Cairo.

Cairo, when they returned in April 1944, was even hotter than before – 104°F in the shade. Joyce had told her uncle that they planned to return in three weeks' time and once again he had asked them to stay. However, the British Embassy was full and Killearn had already turned away several other potential guests, including the King of Greece. He was also trying to cope with the imminent arrival of the Governor of Nyasaland – 'Rather a dull dog' – the Maharaja of Kapurthala and the Maharaja of Jaipur. 'There seems to be an unfortunate fate of muddledom about all these comings and goings of distinguished visitors. I find this inefficiency quite intolerable,' he spluttered to his diary.

Joyce was squeezed in; Viola stayed at the Metropolitan Hotel nearby and came for meals. They expected a flight back home within a day or two, but plans for the Allied invasion of Europe were being completed and all passenger flights to and from Britain were cancelled. With no idea when they would leave, they could not even plan more concerts. Joyce was resigned to making herself useful at embassy meals where distinguished guests such as British generals, exiled royalty, African prime ministers and Egyptian politicians had to be entertained. Joyce's mood matched that of Cairo – the city was winding down as the war moved from North Africa to Europe. Even Killearn found that Cairo had become 'flat and bored, definitely drab and dull'.

The morning after her return to Cairo, an embassy servant came to Joyce's room and handed her a huge bunch of flowers – six dozen roses, delphiniums and carnations. Tucked inside was a card from Prince Aly Khan, welcoming her back and hoping they would meet soon. She was not sure whether to be flattered, or insulted to be added to the list of women with whom Prince Aly flirted. On the three occasions that she had met him on her previous visit, she had got the message – he was 'a charming bounder'.

At the outbreak of the war the Khans had been living with their two young sons in France near their stud at Deauville. Although he was a British subject, the Indian government expected Prince Aly to serve as Director of Intelligence in Delhi, running agents throughout southern Asia. Instead, he joined the French Foreign Legion in Syria, where he planned to mobilise a Bedouin cavalry force to fight on the Western Front. After this dream had collapsed, Prince Aly and Princess Joan moved from Beirut to Cairo and their two sons were sent to Kenya.

Prince Aly was the son of Aga Sultan Sir Mohammed Shah Khan III, the spiritual leader of several million Ismaili Muslims and former President of the League of Nations. He was directly descended from the prophet Mohammed, while Aly's Italian mother had been a dancer at the Monte Carlo Casino. Prince Aly's main interests were horses, cars and women, and at thirty-three he was a deep disappointment to his father. Three months earlier he had tried to impress the Aga Khan by persuading an Indian dignitary to recommend his promotion from major to lieutenant-colonel, claiming it would encourage Ismaili Muslims in Africa and India to support Britain. Anthony Eden, then Foreign Secretary, had telegraphed Killearn for his opinion: he knew that the prince and princess often attended his parties. Killearn had replied in a coded telegram that promoting Prince Aly might be politically expedient, but 'in Cairo it would be a bit of a joke. We all of us here know our Aly pretty well and personally I like him. I also think he was pretty plucky joining the Foreign Legion. But as I am sure you also know, all Aly's characteristics are not so praiseworthy.'

Two months later this proved to be even more true. While Joyce and Viola were in Cairo for the first time, Prince Aly had provoked an international scandal which could have brought the Aga Khan's religion into dispute and would certainly have rocked Indian politics, sending ripples to Whitehall. He had been conducting an affair with a married woman, and her husband was out for his blood. William Rees was a British car salesman, director of the Universal Motor Company in Alexandria. He had forgiven the infidelities of his wife once, but when he discovered her and Prince Aly together again, he sued for divorce in the Supreme Court in Alexandria. Rees wanted the marriage dissolved, custody of their eleven-year-old daughter, and costs with damages of £20,000 to be borne by the co-respondent.

Just twelve hours after Prince Aly had danced cheek-to-cheek with Joyce, he was carpeted by Killearn. The prince had asked for a meeting with him, hoping for advice on how to suppress the affair and save his reputation. Killearn pretended that the affair was news, though in fact he had known about it for some time and had already warned Eden in case the Foreign Office became involved. The High Commissioner told the prince that he should have thought about the implications before getting involved with a married woman. Prince Aly claimed to be sorry, and even wept as Killearn tore into him. Whether true or crocodile tears, he was not used to the humiliation of being first threatened with a writ for adultery and then reprimanded by the British High Commissioner.

'I left him in no doubt that he had been a consummate ass and that I was very doubtful if I could do much to help him,' wrote Killearn in his diary. He warned Prince Aly that the results of his action on both Indian politics and religion might be serious and he would have to consult at the highest level in Whitehall and Delhi. Prince Aly left the embassy with his head held low. By the time he got home, the writ had been served on him by the British Consul General. That evening Killearn telegraphed to Eden asking him if they should bring pressure on the courts to suppress the story.

A week later Killearn met Princess Joan at a party and they discussed the affair. She had put up with her husband's escapades for years and told Killearn that Aly had been quite impossible for some time, squandering his money and 'expressing foolish sentiments about the British'. Killearn thought 'the whole affair was unspeakably sordid and stupid'.

The very next day Rees agreed to settle out of court. Presumably his wife had repented when she realised that she would lose both her daughter and her lover, and that they could live happily on

£20,000 – £550,000 in today's money. The case was withdrawn from the courts and remained classified information until the Foreign Office files were opened in 1995.

Only three days after this, Joyce returned from Baghdad and became the prince's next target. What better revenge than to aim for the niece of the man who was not only the most important in Cairo, but had also recently humiliated him? Prince Aly may have also known that Killearn had rejected his promotion to lieutenant-colonel. What better way to cock a snook at Killearn than seducing his niece, right under his nose? What more exciting challenge for a gambler than to send messages and flowers, knowing that they would all go through the ADC's office – which reported directly to the high commissioner?

This was no accident of chemistry between two people: Prince Aly had been planning it even before Joyce came back to Cairo. For several days he had been ringing the embassy to find out when she was expected. The morning after she arrived, he ordered the huge bunch of flowers to greet her.

'Being weighed by the pound has never flattered me,' Joyce wrote in her diary. 'I like the little man and am amused by his fierce oriental goings on.' She had no intention of being seduced, so decided to ignore his invitations. But he persevered, phoning every few hours with nonchalant invitations to go dancing, 'just for an hour or so'.

Prince Aly's bodyguard, Emrys Williams, described him: 'A well built man with an athletic figure, he had black hair and dark express-ive eyes with pale creamy skin. He had the winning smile of a child and when he spoke made me think of a dog wagging its tail.' He expected to get his own way – his staff were on twenty-four-hour duty to give in to his every whim – and in only a day he succeeded in persuading Joyce to join him for tea.

They met at Groppi's, an intimate outdoor café, with a garden of flowering creepers and strings of coloured lights. Prince Aly asked Joyce out to dinner, and she felt too tired to refuse. She had never been pursued like this before – her love for Reggie had grown by stealth, not passionate seduction. Prince Aly represented everything that she disapproved of – a non-Christian, gambling, spoiled, self-centred man who thought nothing of cuckolding his wife. 'Everything he believes, does and stands for is foreign to my nature,' she wrote. However, he also had charm, wit and culture. He owned paintings by Degas, Renoir and Utrillo; he read books and played the piano. She had been away from Reggie for over four months, working hard in difficult conditions. She felt disorientated by the sudden change from extreme hardship to luxury and her defences were low.

'His technique is perfect,' she wrote in her diary. 'The simple humility and the nonchalance. I spent an entire evening dancing with Aly and the fox-trot has quite a different meaning under his guidance.' Little did she know that he was also experienced in the eastern art of *Imsak* love-making, in which the woman's satisfaction comes first and the man can control himself indefinitely.

Princess Joan was not only in Cairo when this pursuit began, but attended some of the same parties. When the Khans were invited to the embassy, there was dancing after dinner on the verandah. Prince Aly persisted with his campaign, and Joyce began to crumble – she disapproved of herself and tried to resist behaving like her mother, but she also loved it. 'I feel far off and unreal and half of me, the worser half, loves it,' she confided in her diary. She told him there was no hope, but he pleaded with her that this was the Real Thing. The following morning yet more dozens of red roses were delivered to her at the embassy. She was still amused by it all and planned to tell Reggie all about it when she got home. She was missing him 'more and more as a lasting enduring darling and real person'.

The Killearns threw a party at the embassy for their son Graham, with dancing to a band in the big drawing-room. Joyce admitted that the atmosphere was seductive – delicious food, excellent music, palm trees silhouetted in the moonlight, the smell of night-scented flowers, and a charming man paying her exquisite attention. She was not used to it and it felt more like being in a play than reality. Prince Aly had the 'silk skill of a perfect conjuror'. Writing her diary before falling into bed at 4 a.m., she tried to convince herself that it was merely an interesting academic exercise that had nothing to do with her, and that she was not the slightest bit emotionally involved.

The following morning, Sunday, she went to a church of Christ, Scientist for the first time in four months. She was sure the lesson had been chosen for her – 'Do not indulge.' There was still no progress in finding a plane home and she was getting desperate. She recalled her mother telling her that one couldn't move on from a problem until it was resolved. She wrote Prince Aly a note saying that they must not meet again: she realised she was getting in deeper than she wanted and that people would start to notice. She kept telling herself that she was not in love, while manifesting all the usual symptoms such as lack of appetite and thinking of nothing else.

After a further week she was getting visibly thinner, felt even further from reality and was feeling 'ashamed of my feebleness'. There was no definite news about travel, so she could only wait. Her resolution not to see Prince Aly was broken immediately and they met every day. She blamed her inability to resist him on exhaustion and loneliness, and she was probably right. It was too hot and her life felt suddenly empty. Prince Aly filled this void with dancing, parties, driving in his fast car, bunches of flowers and unlimited fresh orange juice. Whatever his earlier motives, he seemed to have become smitten too, or so he told her.

Ten days after Joyce arrived, Princess Joan left for Kenya to see her sons and went to the embassy to say goodbye to Lord Killearn. He was relieved to hear from her that the threatened divorce and court case had melted away. Now Prince Aly had more freedom to pursue his quarry, and still Killearn had noticed nothing.

Viola could see what was going on and was amused, though also protective of Joyce. She too was having fun, going to parties and dancing with ADCs. For all their differences, the two women were now very close. Viola was too shy to express her feelings of friendship out loud, but she wrote a poem for Joyce and slipped it into her hairpin box. She cheered up when she heard from Italy that Peter was in hospital with scarlet fever – at least he was safe from the front line.

Although the weather had cooled to an unseasonable eighty-five degrees, Prince Aly's ardour did not. As his attention increased, Joyce could feel her resistance weakening. 'The whole thing is quite under my skin and I ache for all I have lost after five weeks groping and bewilderment.' She became even more desperate to leave Cairo and tried to persuade Killearn to pull strings on her behalf. He pointed out that even if she had been the wife of a governor rather than a mere second lieutenant, flights were still restricted. He continued to take Joyce to glittering dances at the Auberge nightclub and to dine with rich Cairenes. One family had a *dahabiya* moored on the Nile near the embassy and had lashed two barges together as a floating dance floor. Wherever Joyce went, Prince Aly always appeared, but Lord Killearn's eyes were too firmly fixed on the baccarat table to notice. If he had suspected anything, he would have been furious, and would certainly have mentioned it in his very detailed diary and not described his niece as 'charming and talented'.

Eventually Joyce appealed to the Americans for a flight home and within days was granted two tickets to England. On their last night together, she and Prince Aly were alone on a terrace overlooking the city. From his pocket he produced a selection of gold and diamond jewellery for her to choose from. 'I can't,' she protested. 'You must,' he insisted, 'as a token of our time together.' Joyce chose what she hoped were the least valuable – flower-shaped emerald earrings with diamond dewdrops.

Nora had once told Joyce, 'If what you have been calling love is free from anxiety, then that is love.' Whatever Joyce felt for Prince Aly, it was certainly full of anxiety, whereas when she thought of Reggie all anxiety fled. She told one friend that this had been her first experience of 'sexual love', by which she meant physical desire. During this period she wrote a love poem to Reggie:

> You are secure within my love,
> Unquestioned and unquestioning,
> Unchanging like the certain nursery days,
> In all your ways.

It is as if she had to remind herself that she still loved him and that he would love her, whatever happened. Even so, she felt that she had lost something.

Early on the morning of 17 May 1944, Prince Aly and an ADC took Joyce and Viola to the airport, where they boarded a Fortress passenger plane with fitted cabins and upholstered seats. Despite this unusual comfort, Joyce felt wretched: she had never worked harder, met more people, travelled so far, lived in such difficult conditions, nor had her emotions so thoroughly churned up.

Arriving back in London, Joyce felt miserable, lost and cold. Her first reaction was 'Can't say I am in the least glad to be back. Which is bloody of me but there it is.' Reggie and her family were there, but she couldn't relate to them. She collapsed in a state bordering on a nervous breakdown as she wrenched her heart away from Cairo. She never wore the diamond earrings, and eventually sold them at Philip's. She had never wanted to belong to the ranks of Prince Aly's romances, who included Zsa Zsa Gabor, Judy Garland and Grace Kelly. As far as we know, he never contacted Joyce again, and it was not long before he began chasing Rita Hayworth. Joyce did note in her diary when they divorced in 1951.

If Reggie suspected something had happened, he never asked and Joyce never told. She believed strongly that some things were better not confessed between a husband and wife; that revelations could be an unloving self-indulgence. 'You take it off your chest and put it on somebody else's,' she said twenty years later. 'There are ways of asking forgiveness without indulging in the confession. I have a respect for reticence. Relationships between people are extremely delicate. The great test of whether you love somebody is "Do you really care more for what happens to them than what happens to you?"'

'Joyce told me that she had "loved the preliminaries" but was not sold on the grande finale,' said her friend Carley Robinson. Joyce told at least three of her close women friends about Prince Aly Khan, swearing each to secrecy. She told two other close friends that she had gone further than she wished and it had been very difficult to stop feeling guilty. How far this was, we shall never know. But we do know she had a low sin threshold and felt guilty at the slightest error, even temptation.

Many of her subsequent monologues were on the theme of adultery or its temptations. *Dear François* is a letter-song about a woman with a seventeen-year-old daughter who, between the lines, is the child of a French man with whom she had an affair during the war. The singer writes to him every year on her birthday, but never sends the letter and has told no one the truth. In *The Past is Present*, a grandmother from Virginia is waiting at Waterloo Station to meet Henry Bassett-Palmer, the handsome Oxford man with whom she fell in love forty years before. It had been a four-day affair, followed by a year of letters, and she tries to blame her husband for not being there to protect her, though she knows she is responsible for her own actions. She, too, has told no one about it. In *Life Story*, the wife of a famous Swedish pianist tells his biographer that he had 'a hospitable heart' but that this isn't the end of a marriage. She wanted the biographer to know just one thing: 'My husband always, always came home, to *me*.'

Twenty years after Cairo, Joyce wrote a monologue about an old woman in Virginia who reads of the death of a schoolteacher called Lally Tullet. This brings back memories of a hot summer fifty-five years before. She suspects that Lally and her husband had been together, but she stops him confessing with the words: 'Don't you say anything that's going to make it impossible for me and you to get right back where we are now.' It was the only time Joyce ever wrote a monologue in one sitting, and she said it was her favourite. All she wanted to do now, in May 1944, was to get right back where she had been six months before.

– 14 –

W HEN JOYCE RETURNED from Cairo, Reggie was her constant and loving linchpin as she struggled with lethargy and low moods. He was now a major based in Oxford, responsible for posting officers to the Far East. Friends in London helped her recover by taking her out to lunch at The Ivy and dinner at the Ritz. She resumed her broadcasting and began writing sketches and songs. From now on, her poems were restricted to her notebooks and she rarely sought publication for them.

After four months she felt fully recovered and agreed to undertake a short tour of the Middle East and India with Viola. By now Reggie was re-established in Joyce's heart, but he was expecting to be sent to liberated Europe any day, so she felt less bad about leaving him.

Bearing a certificate stating that their journey was 'of national importance', Joyce and Viola set off by plane on 27 September 1944. Little did they know that their tour would last six months and cover eight countries, including much of the Indian subcontinent. Their first stop turned out to be Cairo, where Joyce was relieved to learn that Prince Aly Khan had left for Paris three weeks before, to liaise between the French and British Armies. The Killearns were away too, so they stayed with Lord Moyne, the Minister Resident and father of her friend Bryan Guinness.

For once, ENSA had organised their itinerary carefully, remembering that they wanted to go to places off the beaten track. An eight-seater bus carried their Mini-piano and was big enough to hang their stage dresses in. The next fifty days were spent travelling to and fro across the desert and performing two or three shows a day, to troops guarding the oil pipeline which ran from central Iraq to the Mediterranean, and at radio sites and transit camps in Lebanon, Jordan, Syria, Iraq and Persia. One evening they drove cross-country around boulders to a secret training-camp near Haifa, where they performed on a makeshift stage lit by jeep headlights. The audience of four hundred soldiers sat on the ground or on giant cable-spools, and the next morning set off across the sea to liberate Crete.

Back on the road, camels tried to outrun the bus and the surface was so rough that the piano's insides slipped sideways one day and another day it broke free of its mooring and the front fell off. Viola's attempt to mend it with string and a penknife failed to improve the constant buzz. The piano's tone was also enlivened by scorpions, mice and large beetles. On the smooth road from Beirut to Damascus, Viola sat on a suitcase and played Bach, Handel and her own arrangements of nursery rhymes. Unlike Le Joli Garçon their driver, Corporal Sid Weatherill, drove with confidence, concentration and the comfort of his passengers in mind. He went to every show, laughed at all the jokes and analysed the audience afterwards. Joyce dreamed of employing him after the war as her driver-handyman, and wondered to herself whether his wife could cook.

Joyce's voice was familiar to many in the audiences from her work on the radio. During the summer in London she had told a BBC producer, Norman Collins, that she found the troops overseas preferred old-fashioned, sentimental songs such as *Night Like a Rose* and *Mother o' Mine*. 'She is perfectly ready to capsize her professional reputation over here by being heard singing this kind of thing for forces overseas,' Collins wrote in a BBC memo. As a result, she sang on the Forces Programme's *Palestine Half-Hour*, *Middle East Merry-Go-Round* and *Here's Wishing You Well Again*. Glenn Miller thought her songs the one thing worth hearing. The listeners had no idea that these programmes were made in full evening dress. On one occasion, Joyce annoyed the producer when she appeared in day clothes to transmit to troops overseas.

Captain Rogers from 'somewhere in the Middle East' wrote:

When you started to sing on our old wireless, there was a most amazing change in the atmosphere – it was electrifying. Fellows struggled up from semi-somnolent positions, and listened more intently, even the most ardent of Vera Lynn fans. I was utterly charmed, your singing sounded so delightfully fresh and unaffected, altogether different from the usual run. The effect of your voice on me as I was then, decidedly dirty and travel-stained, weary and out of sorts with everyone and everything, was indescribable.

Cecil Madden ran the BBC Empire Entertainment Unit from the underground Criterion Theatre in Piccadilly. He warned broadcasters not to make jokes about wives fraternising with Americans or the Free French, and if a bomb fell during a broadcast they were not to mention it, 'assuming that you are still in one piece'. To escape the V-bombs, performers were invited to sleep at the theatre: Vera Lynn used the orchestra pit while Joyce preferred the bunk beds at the back of the stalls. Nobody told her about the resident rat.

The *Dez Weekly News* in Syria reported that Joyce 'visited every unit, no matter how long it took her to get there, or how small . . . sang to audiences of two signal men whose nearest neighbour was 200 miles away, gave informal shows, chatted to the men, and went to hospitals in some of the hottest places'. Joyce was amazed herself at the reserves of energy that emerged even after three or four concerts. When the hard work took its toll in Damascus, Bryan Guinness pulled her out of 'a little death' with some energetic tangos in a nightclub.

Trunk Call reported Joyce was pleased to be back in Paiforce: 'I hope you got the messages I sent you all on the wireless. When people at home ask me what Paiforce is like I tell them that the scenery is a little gritty. I gather that Iran has more ups and downs. I am lost in admiration for the way you all stick it out here – grumbling a bit which is good for the soul, but remaining the nicest audiences that we've found.'

The road south from Tehran was known to have bandits, so they travelled in a convoy of armed police jeeps. Joyce and Viola went with Sid Weatherill in a station wagon while a lorry driven by an Indian in goggles carried their piano and an English lady missionary. Over the 175 miles of rutted road through snow-topped mountains, each jeep broke down in turn. Weatherill repaired them and then, after dark, Joyce saw in the headlights their own back wheel overtake them and roll into the ditch. The station wagon ploughed slowly into the opposite ditch. Weatherill and a policeman were left to guard it with one Tommy gun and enough cigarettes to last the night.

The road from Malayer to Andameshk in Iran was 220 miles of hairpin bends, blind corners and deep gorges, and news of their progress travelled ahead of them in Morse code. It was the start of the aid route from the Persian Gulf to the Soviet Union a thousand miles to the north, and Weatherill told Joyce to shut her eyes as convoys of up to forty trucks bore down on them from the opposite direction. They stopped at nine signal posts, where Joyce sang against backdrops of naked pin-up girls, sometimes with pictures of Princess Elizabeth smiling in her party frock among them.

From the head of the Persian Gulf, Joyce and Viola flew to Bahrain, where they performed outdoors to the Royal Navy, the RAF, American oil workers and Indian sailors. There was a howling wind which blew Viola's music off the piano and carried Joyce's voice away from the audience. With 25th December approaching, they added Bing Crosby's *White Christmas* and *Good King Wenceslas* to the communal singing.

On arrival in Bombay they were allocated a bearer, Ghulam Mahid from Bhutan, who looked after them for fourteen weeks on their travels around India, carrying their luggage, making their beds and washing their clothes. His first job was to dispose of a two-inch cockroach which they had failed to drown in the lavatory. He warned them to look in their shoes every morning for snakes and he saw off beggars with protective zeal.

ENSA in India was run by the actor Jack Hawkins, which stretched his sanity to the limits. Headquarters in Drury Lane expected him to provide 'blanket coverage' of entertainment but had no idea of the huge size of the country. The few acts that were sent out were usually appalling. One company arrived with velvet jester costumes which were so hot that they had to be cut out of their tights after their first, and only, show. Joyce enjoyed an evening of theatre gossip with Hawkins, who persuaded them to stay for at least three months. He issued Joyce and Viola with a piano and a letter stating, 'These artists are most willing workers but please see that their good nature is not imposed upon.'

The Middle East had been a whistle-stop tour of over thirty places in fifty days. Here they decided to spend more time, in fewer places. From Bombay they went by train to a hospital at Poona, where they did four shows a day, competing with flocks of noisy birds: 'TB officers at noon; surgicals at 2; neuros at 3 and TB Other Ranks at 6.30.' They simultaneously entertained two isolation wards, on opposite balconies, positioning themselves a safe fifty yards away, while competing with crows, parrots, rumbling ox-carts, low-flying planes and a postman with large boots.

Gunner Frank Darns, aged twenty-two, met Joyce first in Secunderabad Hospital and then a few weeks later in Ranchi. 'Before they began their show,' he remembers, 'Joyce Grenfell asked everyone in the ward where they came from. When I said "Lincolnshire", Viola came to talk to me. I told her my father was a barber in Spalding and when she returned home she went to tell him that we had met. It was a great relief for the family as I had been away for over two years.'

A week before her fifteenth wedding anniversary Joyce sent Reggie a telegram, and on the day wondered what country he was now in. She felt she was 'in the centre of a thick and impenetrable cloud of cotton wool' as she tried to sing to a hundred men with polio and then to a ward full of jaundiced men in 'deepest mud-like glooms'. The penicillin ward was also rather miserable – the new drug was only used on very sick men and required painful three-hourly injections. In surgical wards, laughter often led to considerable pain, but the men said they didn't mind. In one hospital the matron casually asked as she led them towards a tent, 'You don't mind smallpox, do you?' They stood in the doorway to sing and found the audience one of their best. Observing the effect that she had on patients, Joyce wondered if she should devote her life to healing the sick as a Christian Science practitioner.

Staying in the British Residency at Hyderabad, Joyce and Viola were alarmed that whenever they walked within sight of the gates, the Sikh guards presented arms. They were flattered by this gesture of protection, but did not know the etiquette. They thought they ought to salute, but felt it didn't really go with a cotton frock and no hat. Joyce chose to murmur, 'Good-afternoon,' while Viola said, 'Thank you most awfully.'

In Secunderabad they stayed with an RAF major whose wife had organised a dance in her garden. Staying in homes was pleasant, but being shown off to friends was the last thing they needed at the end of a hot, busy day. Their hosts went away for Christmas, leaving Joyce and Viola alone with the servants. 'Few luxuries compare to staying with people and having them go away,' Joyce noted. She woke on Christmas morning to find that Viola had filled a pair of striped socks with small presents from the bazaar and had composed Joyce a piano piece. Viola got a new frock, cami-knickers and a poem. Ghulam gave them each a coconut and a garland of flowers. They had managed to avoid all social invitations that day and in the afternoon visited patients in hospital.

Joyce was missing Reggie and grateful for Viola's friendship. They had reached 'that comfortable state of sympathy when silences are often more articulate than speech'. Viola also knew how to be silly, a characteristic that Joyce valued highly in a friend. She still disappeared inside herself on occasion but Joyce felt less compelled to jolly her out of it.

On New Year's Day 1945 they took a night sleeper to Bangalore where they met up with the Red, White and Blue ENSA concert party, who were at loggerheads with one another. The show was bad, the comedian drunk, the violinist had a fever and a dancer had been caught with two soldiers in her room. More to their taste was the Good Music Company, Italian ex-prisoners of war now employed by ENSA, who treated Joyce and Viola to a private concert. Viola was in such ecstasy over their Beethoven quartet that she lay on her back under a table. Joyce too was so overcome with pleasure that she 'almost forgot to breathe'.

The Indian Army gave them 'the highest possible rail travel priority' for the journey from Bangalore to Madras. From the window Joyce saw 'Endless naked children, more bullocks sitting in more ponds up to their nostrils, and more brass pots on the heads of more willowy women.' She did not like India: she was unmoved by the scenery, upset by the poverty and shocked by the bullying that domestic servants suffered from their British employers. The tributary of the holy Ganges reminded her of the Regent's Canal behind Paddington Station. She could not understand Hinduism and found the painted figures of gods hideous.

Joyce wanted to get to know Indians but no one she met ever socialised with them, although in Secunderabad she and Viola were taken to visit the local nawab, Salur Jung. They were horrified by his palace, which contained room after room of mosaics, jewelled daggers, Victorian paintings and Viennese chandeliers. The Nawab showed them countless drawers filled with emeralds, rubies, ropes of pearls and gold. When they were already reeling from these sights, ten bearers carried in chests of cigarette boxes, fob watches and diamond-encrusted trinkets. Viola was appalled by the rusting Bechstein grand piano, regularly tuned but never played. The Nawab had his own army and police force, and 'ministers' in co-respondent shoes lurked in the courtyard. In contrast, the streets outside were full of deformed beggars, malnourished children and naked holy men.

Madras was very 'hot and depressing' and they reduced the number of concerts to two a day. Viola was sick of playing terrible pianos and believed she had lost the ability to play. As the tour progressed, Joyce would sometimes be suddenly overcome by exhaustion in the middle of a show and had to work hard to pull herself together.

The magazine *Entertainment Calcutta* reported that Joyce did not expect applause – but usually got it. 'She "drifts" into a ward and gradually men find there is a show going on. She tells them, if they don't feel like listening and would rather turn over and sleep, they can do so. After the show she talks to the patients, never spending less than an hour and a half.'

In Dacca they stayed with Miss Hodson, Theosophist vegetarian, and her brother, the local police chief. Known to everyone as Aunt Margaret, Miss Hodson was the willing, put-upon maiden aunt who never complained. Her brother was an overgrown Boy Scout who leaned on her but never considered her feelings. Aunt Margaret inspired the song *The Three Brothers* that Joyce wrote in 1954: 'I was allowed to wait on them,/To be their slave complete,/I was allowed to work for them,/And life for me was sweet.' It is one of Joyce's most poignant songs: between the lines she knows that she is being used, but we never really discover whether she minds.

Joyce often raised a laugh by inviting the men to shut their eyes and pretend she was Rita Hayworth while she sang. In Comilla, East Bengal, she remembered just in time that many of the men had recently lost their sight. The British, Africans, Indians and Ghurkas of the 14th Army were suffering not only from severe wounds but also jungle sores, dysentery and malaria. It was unbearably hot, even at night, and the hurricane lamps attracted huge flying beetles which became entangled in the nurses' hair as they did their rounds.

Later that year Joyce received a letter from a soldier still in India:

Looking through a 'Blighty' paper this afternoon, I saw your photograph. It brought to my mind a tent serving as a Hospital Ward in Comilla. I'd seen other artistes, but none so friendly, so intimate, so sincere as you, & you really brought us a breath of England. You might have been performing before a first night audience at the Picadilly – the energy & sincerity you put into your songs. You will live in my memory as a grand person.
Sincerely, Sgt. Fred Walmsley.

Second Lieutenant Robin Nicholson was recovering from jaundice at Comilla Hospital and sixty years later remembers clearly Joyce performing in his ward:

Much of it related to girls' boarding-schools. One girl had had her bicycle stolen – 'foul play was written on every spoke'. Another had been abducted by a French man: 'Loss of honour was a wrench, but think how it improved her French.' The inmates of our ward were officers of a very diverse background and one wondered how she would go down. One need not have worried; with her informal manner, she had the whole ward relaxed and cheerful in no time.

Back in Calcutta, they collected a huge pile of mail. A telegram from Noël Coward read: DEAR JOYCE DEFINITELY PLANNING REVUE TO OPEN MAY OR JUNE WOULD LIKE YOU HOME AS SOON AS POSSIBLE CABLE ME EARLIEST TIME YOU CAN BE HERE ALL LOVE. Joyce replied that she would be back at the end of March and hoped that would be soon enough. Inside, she felt alarmed by her lack of inspiration for new material.

After their three months of hard work, Joyce and Viola had a week's leave and took a night train from Calcutta to a bungalow in the foothills of the Himalayas. They woke to see snow-topped Kinchinjunga, almost as high as Everest, glowing pink above the clouds. It was very cold, so they took turns to bathe in a tin tub in front of the fire while listening to Beethoven on the gramophone. They visited a Tibetan monastery with 'incredible gods and a giant

old Lama with poor feet and a belch like a thunderclap'. Wild rhododendrons were coming into flower, distant Tibetan bells sounded and
the air was so thin that when, despite being on leave, they performed
at a nearby convalescent home, Joyce had to take a breath between
each note.

Sergeant Evans from Coventry was recovering from malaria and
heard a friend ask, 'Where is she going from here?' He shouted back,
'She is on her way to climb Mount Everest.'

In four months Joyce and Viola had covered India from Bombay,
Hyderabad, Mysore, Madras, Bihar and Sikkim to Bengal and Assam.
Joyce was almost sad to see the last of the piano which had accompan-
ied them by train, truck and river-boat for over four thousand miles.

In Delhi for their final week they were back in the lap of luxury,
staying with the Viceroy, Lord Wavell, in Lutyens's Government
House with its 350 indoor servants. Cecil Beaton, an old friend of
Nora's, was also there and commented that Joyce had 'the lovely pale
flower looks of a delicate Edwardian beauty that are rarely seen today,
a tragic expression worn as a gesture'. The 'tragic expression' was
more likely exhaustion. She also met other old friends – Harold
Lindo, her first concert pianist, and Peter Fleming, who had been
feeding the Japanese false intelligence.

Ghulam pleaded with Joyce to take him to England but she didn't
think his negative attitude towards anyone who was not Bhutanese
would be appreciated in London. Two years later he turned up in
Camden, as the bearer of an army officer. Joyce invited him to tea
and he told her that he was cooking, cleaning and child-minding for
sixteen hours a day and paid £1 a week. After a few months he went
home again, disappointed that the British were giving India back to
the Indians.

The journey back to England in a BOAC flying-boat took five
days. Viola intended to return to classical music and Joyce would start
rehearsing Coward's revue. She was dreading London, where she had
no home. However, Reggie was on leave and there to greet her with
his comforting smile. 'Being home is very busy and complicated and
I'm spinning, spinning and I want not to,' she wrote in her diary.
When Reggie went back to Belgium she stayed with Virginia, who
helped her through the inevitable anti-climax.

Joyce had left England in January 1944 as a talented ENSA

amateur. Now, fifteen months and fourteen countries later, she could rightly call herself an experienced professional, and the entry in her passport read 'Writer-Entertainer'.

'The war was the most rewarding time of my life,' she said later. 'It was my college, my university, my training ground, my experimental laboratory. I've never worked so hard or noticed it less. I did an average of three shows of an hour each, every day, sometimes more. Now when I go on tour anywhere in the British Commonwealth I find men and nurses I met in those days and we talk with nostalgia of Poona or Comilla. Egoistically speaking I had a lovely war.'

– 15 –

Virginia helped Joyce to 'iron out' with expeditions to Kew Gardens and weekends in the country. Joyce was in Wales when peace was declared on 8 May 1945. She immediately took a crowded train to London, where she met Celia Johnson, and together they sallied forth, starting with a drink at Clemence Dane's in Covent Garden. 'We found Gladys Calthrop, Dick Addinsell and Victor Stiebel,' Celia Johnson wrote:

> So the six of us set out, C. Dane sailing like a ship in full sail and along the Strand we went. The National Gallery floated away above a mass of cheerful people, and Nelson on his column was lit by several arcs. We walked up to the palace with thousands of others. The crowd was as nice a crowd as you could wish to find, cheerful, weary and extremely good-humoured. We sang and shouted 'We want the King', and talked to one and all and cheered the King and Queen when they came out. There were searchlights doing a sort of ballet and fireworks coming from Wellington barracks and it was all fun and dandy and a bit emotional too. We started back home fortified by the sight of three sailors paddling in the fountains – one walking about, waist deep, reading a paper, one fishing solemnly with a long stick and the third was being the fish. They were very sweet, rather serious, and perfectly silent, encouraged by the crowd and managing to remain remarkably dignified. We trudged home, Victor, Joyce and I past a brilliant Dorchester and with our feet several sizes larger than when we started.

A few days later Joyce sang in the 'Victory Edition' of the variety radio show *Monday Night at Eight* and joined Arthur Askey and

Kenneth Horne in the Victory Concert in 'Much Binding-in-the-Marsh'. Despite all that ENSA had contributed to the war effort, the organisation was not invited to participate in the Victory Parade through London in August.

Joyce's cousins had all taken part in the war, and some of them had lost their lives. Michael Astor had been with the Third Army in France; David Astor had been in the Marines and with the Free French; Jakie Astor had commanded a squadron in the SAS; and their half-brother Bobbie Shaw had been a canteen waiter in Trafalgar Square. Jim Brand, a tank commander in the Coldstream Guards, was killed in Germany and Peter Brooks trained pilots for the American Air Force, but after succumbing to drink committed suicide, like his brother Winkie. Bill Astor was now an MP; David was on his way to editing the *Observer*; Wiss, now Lady Willoughby de Eresby, was raising a family; and Bobbie was learning shorthand and typing. In the post-war years Joyce saw less of her family, preferring to deepen her friendships instead. Reggie's family had also done their bit: Reggie's brother Harry was badly wounded in Burma and both his feet had to be amputated. Vera had run youth clubs in the East End, Laura worked for the WVS in the day and as an air-raid warden at night, and his three married sisters were raising families.

Many women found that their new skills in mechanical engineering were now redundant, or their jobs were wanted by returning men. Joyce was lucky: entertainment was a career that she could continue to develop. At thirty-five and after sixteen years of marriage, she had given up thoughts of ever becoming a mother; and although she still had dreams that she was pregnant when she was well past forty, she decided to achieve the highest standard possible as an entertainer. Rehearsals for Noël Coward's new revue *Sigh No More* began in June 1945.

Unlike Herbert Farjeon, who was always charming and open to ideas, Noël was a tough, autocratic director and felt free to change the show without consulting the company. Joyce offered several new monologues, but only one survived to the first night. *Travelling Broadens the Mind* was inspired by several ENSA performers, including one singer in Northern Ireland overheard saying, 'I'm a terrible thinker. I can't help thinking.' Joyce's humourless creation tells a reporter how she sang *Ave Maria* six hundred times to 'our boys' in fifteen countries. She was dressed in a white gown, 'very simple, very draped', and accompanied by her friend Doreen on the gypsy accordion.

During the first rehearsal Noël asked Joyce to sing his song about a schoolgirl joyfully recounting the family's domestic disasters such as Aunt Isabel's shingles, Granny's varicose veins and Ernie's boils. It had been popular with the troops and he had cleaned it up for London. Joyce read the lyrics and said, peering over the footlights, 'My public won't like it.'

'*What* public?' shouted Noël from the stalls.

Joyce recognised in him a spitefulness she had known in Aunt Nancy, a desire to attack where it hurt most. The actress Judy Campbell commented, 'The difference between them was that Noël was an actor who wanted to be an aristocrat. Joyce was the opposite – an aristocrat who wanted to be an actor. Both pulled it off quite well, really.' Noël eventually persuaded Joyce to sing *That Is the End of the News* in a schoolgirl voice, dressed in a gymslip, no make-up and black cotton stockings.

During the dress rehearsal Beatrice Lillie's protégé, seventeen-year-old James Grant Tyler, appeared in the chorus wearing tights. Noël halted the rehearsal. 'Stop! What do you think you are doing?' he screamed, pointing at a mystified Tylor. 'Your tights! You look as though you are wearing an entire Rockingham tea set down there!'

The only song by Joyce and Dick that made it into the show was *Oh, Mr du Maurier*, about a fashionable young woman in the 1890s who, though much admired by poets and painters, wanted only to be noticed by George du Maurier, the *Punch* cartoonist. For the first time Joyce was given a real stage costume: a white satin and chiffon dress, designed by Gladys Calthrop, worn with long black gloves. She had lost so much weight during the war that her hips had to be padded to obtain sufficient curve. Noël directed her with stylised precision in the use of a fan. Two days before the show opened in Manchester, he wrote in his diary, 'I am horribly worried about Dick and Joyce's material. It is all pretty amateurish and gets nowhere.' He secretly hoped that by the time the company reached London, Joyce could be dropped altogether.

On tour, Joyce suffered from the same isolation she had experienced with the ENSA concert parties. Marooned in a strange place without her favourite people, she found it difficult to mix with the company during the day and went to bed early after the show. Noël either raged or praised, and the cast never knew whose turn it would be next for a rocket. She cheered up when Viola, touring the north with 'yet another ensemble of unblended musicians', visited for the day and they went for a long walk in the country. Stephen Potter came too and after the show they listened in her room to a programme they had made called *How to Go to the Ballet*.

Sigh No More opened at the Piccadilly Theatre in August 1945. It was one of the first shows to open in London after victory, and the audience dressed up for the first night in all their pre-war glitter. Noël Coward wrote in his diary: 'Notices good for box-office but patronising for me. Joyce and Graham [Payn], as predicted, made the outstanding hits and have really got away with it.' Over lunch he told Joyce that he had never met such an uncanny theatre sense. Even at the back of the stalls, he told her, he could hear every word that she spoke, perfectly. She positively purred when he said her strengths came from the vitality and gaiety of her American side, controlled and disciplined by her English side.

The critics however felt that *Sigh No More* lacked Noël's usual kick. The *New York Times* pointed out that 'You cannot dress up pre-war jokes in their peacetime feathers without seeming out of date.' Noël wrote in his diary, 'I don't know what the modern post-war world is coming to but it certainly isn't coming to *Sigh No More*.' He stopped coming himself and Joyce and Cyril Ritchard, an established American star, took the show into their own hands and restored some of the numbers he had cut. They succeeded in turning it round and Noël, to his credit, bore no grudge. Joyce received plenty of encouragement. The *Sunday Pictorial* offered her their Week's Bouquet: 'To Joyce Grenfell for stealing the show from Noël Coward, the hearts of the audience and the gift of inducing people to laugh with her, from the gods.' 'Miss Grenfell is in her best form,' wrote *The Times*, 'doing quite perfectly the kind of thing she has often done before but securing for it that effect of surprise which perfection never loses. In *Travelling Broadens the Mind* she proves once again that a ninny may circle the globe and remain a ninny.' The *Jewish Chronicle* wrote that Joyce's 'goo-goo eyes and naïve simplicity bring out the full biting satire of the Ensa girl'. Harold Hobson in the

Christian Science Monitor thought that 'No other item meets with such applause as "This is the End of the News". But is it more a tribute to Mr Coward, who wrote the words, or to Miss Grenfell, who recites them?' The *Daily Telegraph* agreed: 'Her grimly gay schoolgirl, her fluffy-minded actress and her du Maurier young lady are firmly and delicately done without a false touch anywhere.' J. C. Trewin in *Punch* noted that 'her ear for the shades of accent is as accurate as that of Shaw's Higgins. She is devastating both as the too-sweet singer of Tulse Hill and as the terrible schoolgirl, who obeys orders to sigh no more, lift up your heart, keep your chin up, and come smiling through.' Many critics noted that Joyce had learned the art of holding a large audience. She was already dreaming of doing a revue on her own one day.

In July, while they were still on tour, Churchill's government had lost the general election in a landslide victory to Labour. Waldorf Astor knew that Nancy had lost touch with her pre-war majority of ten thousand in Plymouth and stopped her from standing in the election, an act for which she never forgave him. For several years she hardly spoke to him and they only made up shortly before he died in 1952.

Joyce was pleased with the new government. 'The more I see of people brought up in the easy way the more I lean towards socialism,' she wrote to her mother. 'I needn't worry; we're hurtling in so called – or comparatively – easy stages towards it. Things will never, can never, *mustn't* ever be the same, as they were before the war.' After meeting so many soldiers abroad, she hoped they would return to a fairer country, with better conditions for their families. Shortly after the election, while she was in Liverpool, the Americans dropped atomic bombs on Japan and a week later Prime Minister Clem Attlee announced the end of the war. The days of large house parties, of tennis and lemonade on sunny afternoons, would never return. Her song *I Wouldn't Go Back to the World I Knew* reflects her feelings:

> I only see the skies as permanently blue,
> All the people I loved as young as handsome too,
> It's haunted now and dead,
> A different wind is blowing, and who knows what's ahead?

Meanwhile, she was making history within the BBC. On Boxing Day 1945, when Aubrey Blackburn was on holiday, she was furious when *Variety Show* was rebroadcast on the Light Entertainment Programme, without her permission. Her main objection was on artistic grounds – she had recorded the programme on the Home Service in June for troops in Asia, and she did not think it suitable for families in Britain on Boxing Day. She pointed out that the BBC had broken their contract on two grounds: firstly, they had only paid for the right to broadcast on the Home Service, and secondly, retransmission rights were only granted for the duration of the war and up to three months after it ended. No one had challenged the BBC over these issues before. Confidential memos flew between departments, reminding each other that they must settle this quickly in case other performers also complained. They decided to redefine the 'Home Service' as any broadcast made in Britain, even if it was then broadcast overseas. As to retransmission within three months of the end of the war, they decided that the end of the war had 'not yet been legally defined'. They finally paid Joyce an additional fee, but would not agree to inform her if her material was repeated and never informed her when the war officially ended.

While she was performing in London, Joyce lived in a room in Old Church Street, Chelsea, but with Reggie due to be demobbed, it was time to make a proper home. They considered their house in St Leonard's Terrace but decided that it was too large. They let it out and were rather indignant when the tenants asked if they could demolish the servants' quarters. When they went to look, they realised that what had seemed modern twenty years before was now small, dark and damp, and they readily agreed. By the time Reggie returned from Belgium in November 1945, Joyce had found a maisonette to rent over Mr Kent's toy and sweet shop in King's Road, conveniently next to a number 19 bus stop. It was up three flights of stairs and had a tiny living-room, a small bedroom and a damp bathroom along a dark corridor. Up more stairs were a kitchen/dining-room, another bedroom and two lavatories. At first they saw it as a temporary home but after a year they decided that they would not find anything better in the area. Both Joyce and Reggie had grown up in Chelsea and it was where they wanted to stay. They persuaded the landlord to remove his furniture and replaced it with their own, which had been in storage since they left Parr's. They bought a new sink and their first refrigerator, from Harrods. New curtains came from Peter Jones and wallpaper was specially designed by Colefax & Fowler, the interior design company just set up by Cousin Nancy Tree. The narrow stairs were papered in candy stripes and adorned with photos of all their friends. Joyce usually saw her visitors off from the top. 'Do let yourself out,' she would say, 'but don't bang the door. Mr Kent says it makes the sweets fall off the shelves.' Having made an attractive and comfortable home, they lived there for the next ten years.

In spite of its small size, Joyce decided she needed a daily cleaner. She advertised on a sixpenny postcard in the newsagent's window and got eight replies. The first to arrive was a plump, smiling woman who, after climbing the stairs, said, 'In case you have a prejudice, I must tell you I am German.' Disarmed, Joyce said she didn't mind. Whatever her prejudices, she didn't approve of herself for having them, and she certainly wasn't going to admit them to a German. Anna Gavrieldes was married to a Cypriot tailor and, knowing that no Briton could pronounce her name, she advised Joyce to call her Mrs Gabe. Joyce employed her on the spot and for eighteen years she was the Grenfells' much-loved cook and housekeeper, coming six mornings a week. 'Mrs Gabe did a very slow, very thorough, very talkative, dust round my room,' wrote Joyce in 1947. 'I like her so much but did wish she'd finish.' After her husband died, she married Reg Brimm of Edgware but readily accepted that to Joyce and Reggie she would remain 'Mrs Gabe'.

Reggie, meanwhile, was employed working out a new health insurance scheme, which was to turn into the National Health Service. He was then appointed financial director of his cousin Harold Grenfell's copper mine at Messina, in the Transvaal. Reggie went to South Africa twice a year and it was to become a regular escape for Joyce from British winters.

Sigh No More ran for over two hundred performances, ending in February 1946. Joyce had only had three days' holiday in the past nine months and desperately wanted to visit her mother, but all the Atlantic ships were booked for months ahead except for VIPs or those on business of national importance. After several weeks, she managed to get a flight, via Ireland and Labrador.

Joyce had not seen Nora for nine eventful years, though they had kept in close touch with weekly letters. After the drab greyness of London, North Carolina in the spring was just the tonic she needed. Nora greeted her with new clothes, perfume and magazines. Nancy Astor and her maid Rosina Harrison had just visited, and had told Nora that Joyce was very thin. So Nora fed her up with fresh straw-berries and cream from Daisy, Lefty's jersey cow. 'It's a perfect place to do nothing, for there is so much of nothing to do,' Joyce wrote to Virginia. She was pleased to find Lefty 'unchanged and in top form'. After supper all three sang together under the stars, the air pungent with gardenias and jasmine. Tommy, now demobbed and writing short stories, came to stay with nine-year-old Wilton. Joyce hardly recognised him, and found that her maternal ache had truly subsided. She never met Tommy's second wife Donrue, who left him when he was with the US Army during the liberation of Europe.

Later Joyce went to New York and met up with Dick Addinsell. After seeing a revue on Broadway, Joyce reckoned she could do better, so they visited agents and Stephen Fry, the BBC's man in New York. Four of their songs were accepted by Chapell-Harms for pub-lication and there was talk of further work.

To add to the excitement, Reggie sent Joyce a telegram telling her in crossword-puzzle code that the King wished to give her a 'three-quarter robe' – an OBE – for her work in hospitals and troop camps. There were too many honours conferred after the war for everyone to attend an investiture at Buckingham Palace, so eighteen months later the medal arrived by post. Sadly, Viola received no official tribute for her work.

In New York, Joyce was intoxicated by the shops, especially the hats 'covered in entire flower beds'. She rationed herself to only three and sent Virginia a modern 'pull-on' corset. She dined with Elliot Coleman, now the first professor of creative writing at Johns Hopkins University, Baltimore. In 1940 he had dedicated his epic poem *An American in Augustland* to Joyce. She loved it, although it was also 'obscure, too ambitious and confusing for most readers'; Reggie reckoned it was 'pretentious poppycock'. She had dreaded seeing Elliot but was pleased that they now had 'the very nicest warmest undifficult affection – it is lovely when it ends quietly in real friendship.'

Joyce introduced him to her old schoolfriend Carley Robinson and they became close friends. 'Elliott was a poet, a good one, and a fine teacher,' she wrote. 'He attracted many well known writers such as Stephen Spender, WH Auden and Dylan Thomas and he had over a dozen books of poetry published. He was essentially homosexual, with occasional straight leanings. There was a wispy quality to him. My father was afraid that I would marry him and used to say "Oh darling he's a cripple" and in many ways he was, though not physically.' Elliot never married, and whenever Joyce performed in America he would turn up at the stage door and pull gently at her heart strings.

ONCE THE WAR was over, the BBC reorganised its schedules. The Forces Programme became Light Entertainment, broadcasting popular music and comedy, while the Home Service continued with current affairs, drama and features. Plans were soon under way for a Third Programme, for 'selective listeners'. The head, George Barnes, declared, 'We shall make no effort to appeal to everyone all the time, nor shall we be all things to all men.' Hopes were high among the intelligentsia. Edward Sackville-West commented, 'The Third programme may well become the greatest educative and civilizing force England has known since the secularization of the theatre in the sixteenth century.'

Three weeks before the opening on 29 September 1946, Joyce and Stephen Potter were asked to write 'something light' to contrast with the rest of the first night's offering – the première of Britten's Festival Overture, Bach's Goldberg Variations, and talks by Field-Marshal Smuts, Max Beerbohm and Sir William Haley, the BBC Director General. Spaces between programmes were to be filled with readings from Henry James. Joyce and Stephen wrote and produced *How to Listen (or how not to, how they used to and how you must)* in ten days. It began with the whistles and crackles of an untuned wireless and a 'producer' giving instructions. Radio was satirised with 'Professor Crump' studying the social manifestations of radio culture, and a serious literary discussion about the memorial erected to Thomas Cobbleigh, the Dartmoor poet, in Ipswich. In search of 'the Perfect Listener', Roy Plomley then eavesdropped on licence holders all over the country. Joyce was the first woman to be heard on the Third Programme, playing nine parts including Special Effects (Domestic), 'Jean Gledding, ATS of Bexley Heath' and a smart girl in Mayfair with a radio set in a cocktail cabinet with a 'supersonic incessor switch and Hypertonic two-way mega-cycle baffles'. Mrs Moss (the Terrible Worrier) made her first appearance, remarking to Mrs George, 'It's getting chilly, turn up the wireless.' 'The Perfect Listener' was eventually found, who checked the *Radio Times*, tuned in carefully and wanted to listen to the whole of Shakespeare, with no music or sound effects.

The next morning the *News Chronicle* said: 'True to the Third programme's policy of ignoring time, "How to Listen" *under* ran by seven minutes. Poetry readings and spontaneous discussions were mocked with cruel justice.' The *New Statesman* commented: 'How To Listen was above all a lesson in oral discrimination and was therefore exactly in place at the beginning of a new programme and it rollocked along with a lack of solemnity that augurs well for the general tone of the whole venture.' The *Daily Express* called the Third Programme 'the timeless wonder', whereas Evelyn Waugh wrote, 'I have listened attentively to all programmes and nothing will confirm me more in my resolution to emigrate.' *How to Listen* was remade four times, the last time in 1962 for the fortieth anniversary of BBC, when it was chosen for *Pick of the Week*. On the fiftieth anniversary of the Third Programme, in 1996, *How to Listen* was incorporated into a radio play about its creation.

The winter of 1946–7 was the coldest on record – icebergs were seen off the Norfolk coast and by February national coal reserves were down to six days' worth. To save energy, the Third Programme was suspended for two weeks and Stephen Potter had nothing to do, so he wrote a book about his philosophy of sport. Joyce suggested sending it to Rupert Hart-Davis, who had recently established a new publishing house. *Gamesmanship, The Art of Winning Games Without Actually Cheating* was an instant best-seller, and with Ronald Searle's *St Trinian's* and *Parkinson's Law*, it set the tone for humorous books in the 1950s. While many of Joyce's monologue characters came out of her collaboration with Stephen, much of his humour also came from sparring with her. For example, they wrote 'The Art of Writership' together for the first Cheltenham Literary Festival in 1949, which later appeared in Potter's book *Lifemanship*.

When Joyce was asked by the BBC to act in educational radio programmes, the scripts were so dull that she vowed that in future she would only broadcast her own work. Almost immediately she was asked to devise, write and perform a fortnightly programme of songs and monologues called *A Note With Music*. Joyce found that going straight from speaking to singing made her feel 'quite panicky. I never seem to be able to do a really deep lung-filling breath.' Shirley's Girl Friend first appeared here, with her face powder by 'Dawn O'May – Chiffon Mist Facial Gauze', her green plastic mac, her mauve angora wool gloves and her paper bag of fondants.

When a second series was made in 1949, George Benson, the actor from the *Little Revue*, was in it.

> It was a joy to see how Joyce's style and performance had deep-ened. Radio highlighted her talent – because her subjects are always people whom everyone, however dimly, can see in the mind's eye. Mrs Bosanquet, the earnest American journalist oppressed by the conviction that her husband and child were sapping her vitality. Miss Fern Brixton in her hand-woven, blue-green tweed, with her love of folk culture. Mrs. Martin, quite nice when not on a bus – but will ask friends at the top of her voice questions like 'How's the psycho-analysing going?'

Joyce received around fifty fan letters after each broadcast, often asking for copies of her script. Although she had no secretary, they were always answered within a few days. A BBC audience research report put her 'Appreciation Index' at the same level as Gracie Fields' and Al Read's. However, not all listeners liked her: one man com-pared her humour to 'a Church concert, where you have to smile', and another sent an anonymous postcard which simply asked, 'Who told you you could sing?'

The programme that got most talked about was *We Beg to Differ*, which ran from 1946 to 1954 featuring a panel of four women and two men discussing 'light-hearted problems of a domestic nature designed to bring out the opposing male and female attitudes'. Actresses Gladys Young, Kay Hammond, Charmian Innes and Joyce took on Kay's husband John Clements and the cantankerous Gilbert Harding or the equally opinionated Radio Doctor, Charles Hill. The chair, Roy Plomley, chose questions from the listeners' postbag of up to 120 letters a day. Addressing the question 'Are men justified to resent working under women?', Joyce thought that women would rather work for men because then they could get their own way. C. N. F. of Kent wanted to know, 'Should girls be trained for a career or for marriage?' Kay Hammond reckoned that men expected women to be everything – mothers, nurses and accountants. Joyce believed that all girls should be trained in domestic skills and regretted having to teach herself to cook late in life. She was happy for labour to be divided along gender lines as long as women were paid equally. Gilbert Harding claimed that men could do anything they chose better than women. Asked, 'Are men frightened of witty women?', John Clements replied, 'Very few men have the chance to find out – there are so few witty women about.' A woman from Chester wrote to say that her husband was horrified that she had taken up smoking a pipe. Joyce replied, 'All smoking is unbecoming, there is nothing nastier than smoke and ash dripping everywhere.'

'*We Beg to Differ*' was something quite out of the ordinary run of radio shows,' said Joyce. 'At first, it was intended to be funny, but as the thing developed, it became more serious. After all, it is rather dull to be funny for ever, don't you think?'

By 1951 *We Beg to Differ* was so popular on the radio that it was simultaneously made for television. The same teams sat behind counters but the discussions never took off. Joyce hated it and even Gilbert Harding lost the urge to be belligerent. Things improved when the young Ian Carmichael took over as producer and designed a new set to resemble the library at Woburn Abbey. Everyone relaxed but only two weeks later it returned solely to the radio.

Joyce continued to cause anxiety within the BBC Contracts Department. When she negotiated another rise they were terrified that Gilbert Harding would discover that he was paid half her fee. When the panel was barred from appearing on commercial radio, Joyce, although she had no intention of doing so, refused to sign the new contract on principle. After a spate of letters, memos and phone calls, she won and the BBC accepted a verbal undertaking that she would not broadcast on Radio Luxembourg.

When the show was finally taken off the air in 1954, many fans wrote in to complain, including Miss Gladys Southwell of Wisbech, who never accepted invitations on Monday nights. 'I was disappointed that it lasted for only half an hour. This is my first letter to the BBC but when those ghastly "Archers" go on for ever – and the Goon Show ad libs – I feel rather strongly about it.'

At the start of 1947 Noël Coward asked Joyce to record fourteen of his songs with Graham Payn for HMV. Joyce liked only a few, but 'those bloody little duets' did pay for new wallpaper in her flat. She disapproved of Graham Payn's sideburns and blue homburg hat, but thought 'there is something very sweet about him though it's ebbing fast under the Master's influence'. She kept Noël at a professional distance, and he responded with theatrical adoration. 'Dearest Joyce, I thought your recording of my beautiful numbers quite enchanting. I am always a push-over for the way you sing – it is the sort of singing I particularly like & that is the way my music should be done, so kindly do a great deal more to oblige. Yours with love and kisses, Noël.'

Socially, there were two theatrical camps in London – Noël Coward's followers were Gladys Calthrop, and his lovers Graham Payn and Cole Lesley; while round Clemence Dane gathered Victor Stiebel, Richard Addinsell and a fascinated Joyce, who dragged along her obedient Reggie. She noticed he was often the only 'normal' man. Noël Coward would invite them to his parties at the last minute. Victor and Dick then refused out of pique and Joyce wondered whether she should too, but usually could not resist the lure of his famous guests. When Dick entertained his friends, Noël was never invited. After his death, Joyce described him as 'never likeable, too self absorbed, beady, snobby and aggressive. I'm glad I wasn't part of the inner ring. All its members danced to the Master's tune, knew he was a beast but were somehow caught and became devoted. Undoubtedly because he made them laugh. He was very clever, adroit, talented and excellent company but he was sinister and a beast.'

Also in Clemence Dane's circle were the actor Laurier Lister and his partner, the Irish actor Max Adrian. In January 1947 Laurier asked Joyce to work with him on a new revue to be called *Tuppence Coloured*, after the Victorian toy paper theatres. He had only directed poetry-readings before but Joyce was impressed by his enthusiasm and believed that she could make up for his lack of experience with what she had learned with Farjeon and on ENSA tours. Binkie Beaumont of H.M.Tennent Ltd had agreed to back it, and the plays he produced rarely failed.

Tuppence Coloured would be 'an intimate and slightly high-brow revue', on the lines of Farjeon's but with a variety of contributors – 'a contemporary anthology of writers and composers'. Laurier and Joyce drew up a shortlist: Osbert Sitwell, Stephen Potter, Benjamin Britten, William Walton, John Piper, Richard Addinsell and Rowland Emett. Laurier also knew John Betjeman, who suggested using his poem 'Sylvia Paddington' as a monologue in the revue. 'She is,' he wrote, 'a lady who speaks in a rosy soft voice. She will probably wear homespun and a necklace of painted cotton reels.' The idea struck Joyce as too like her own Fern Brixton and she politely turned Betjeman down.

Benjamin Britten had never met Joyce, but he accepted her invitation on a postcard with an Edwardian poem, 'Sister of Mine':

> Other folks have sisters
> But never have I known
> Of anybody's sister
> I'd rather call my own.

Over tea in King's Road, he agreed to contribute a ballad and told her he hoped to write a whole show with her one day. A few weeks later Joyce saw his opera *Albert Herring* at Glyndebourne and wrote of the thirty-four-year-old composer: 'I suspect him of being a genius and probably the biggest thing in creative music of our era.' When it arrived, *Sweet Polly Oliver* required fifteen instruments and had to be rearranged by Geoffrey Wright for the two pianos and percussion.

Stephen Potter wanted to collaborate rather than contribute, though he confessed in his diary that it was partly a lack of ideas and partly because nobody noticed who *wrote* in a revue. Sitwell, Emett and Addinsell all contributed, but in the end Joyce and her cousin Nicholas Phipps wrote most of the material.

Joyce was inspired to write *Artist's Room* after observing Myra Hess's fans. She played four enthusiasts with differently priced tickets waiting to talk to a pianist. The lady with the most expensive seat comments, 'Beethoven does go on so, doesn't he, bless his heart. Just when he's finished, the entire thing starts again.' A cockney woman with complimentary tickets worries that the performer 'must be tired after all those notes'. The young deb from the balcony asks, 'Doesn't Ogden do it quicker?' and a woman from the unreserved seats simply adds, '*Thanks* most awfully.'

While out shopping for Laurier's lunch, Joyce had the idea of *Odyssey*, about a rich American woman who has survived two weeks of 'a perfectly typical British life' in the Dorchester Hotel. She tells her friends in New York how ghastly London is under the post-war Labour government: she had to queue for a bus and was advised not to visit Scotland because there were no grouse left to shoot.

Joyce's diary records that it was while listening to Peter Pears singing in Chelsea Town Hall that the idea came to her for *The Countess of Coteley*. In 1910 an aristocratic woman sings about the life awaiting her in 1947: typing for the WVS; reading the *New Statesman*; changing her book at Boot's; and living with no servants in a stately home which is now owned by the National Trust.

Joyce topped the bill, supported by the singer Elisabeth Welch and Max Adrian, who had recently played Puck in John Gielgud's production of *A Midsummer Night's Dream*. Max kept them all laughing with his razor-sharp wit and unlikely tales about his chickens, all named after actresses. They were joined by Daphne Oxenford, whose monologue at the audition had aroused Joyce's jealousy, but who soon became a lifelong friend. Together they performed *Nice Song*, by Nicholas Phipps and Geoffrey Wright, dressed in 'green net gloves of beautiful horror' as Miss Bulstrode and Mrs Moltis, who meet on early-closing day to exchange news of young doctors falling in love with nurses. *Echo Song*, in which Joyce was unable to locate the sound of her own voice, took two weeks to write and involved learning to sing and dance at the same time. She wore a shapeless embroidered dress and, for the only time in her life, her long hair was loose on stage.

Now that she was in control, Joyce felt more at ease with the company. Where hitherto she had volunteered advice, now she was asked for it. However, when the show opened in Cheltenham in mid-July, she was not convinced it would work. There was a heatwave, the lighting rehearsal lasted until dawn, Max Adrian fainted during the dress rehearsal and everyone squabbled. Cecil Beaton had declined to design the costumes so Gladys Calthrop, whom Joyce did not trust, 'hard as nails and as dangerous as a snake', had been brought in and Joyce was sure she was spying for Coward. At the dress rehearsal it transpired that all the clothes were the same dull, autumnal colours. 'Nothing was going right,' remembered Elisabeth Welch, 'the costumes weren't ready, it was a mess. There was gloom and absolute despair from everyone. But Joyce always had this joy and hope, and it rubbed off onto the rest of us.'

In fact, she had serious reservations and she was not alone. The morning after the first night, Clemence Dane, Virginia, Dick, Victor and Reggie descended on her hotel room and told her that it was not just bad, it was terrible. Laurier was a creative man but he lacked the strength of character required to change orders, sack actors and tighten up the revue. 'Laurier was a curious man,' remembers Geoffrey Wright. 'He was rather prim and buttoned up. We didn't like him much because he was unknowable. He had this dear little smile, which hid everything. But Joyce always forgave him because he was a Christian Scientist.'

Binkie Beaumont was asked to send someone with 'a new eye and a firm hand', and he dispatched Nicholas Phipps, who wrote some more songs and cut several numbers, including a song for Elisabeth Welch by the twenty-two-year-old director Peter Brook.

When the show reached Leicester a week later it was still woolly, and there were rows and jealousies among the players. Calthrop was 'very acid and in poisonous form' but Joyce's dresser, Ida Ladbrooke from Brixton, kept her amused with malapropisms. She had a 'dasmak' tablecloth, bought Joyce a box of 'Le Clairs' for tea, was 'not one to quiver over details' and told Joyce that 'as a subject you often prop up'. Ida said she didn't fancy Laurier's job because of 'all that responsibility holding the candle at both ends'.

The heatwave continued in Bournemouth, and Elisabeth Welch fainted during the finale. In Brighton Joyce and Dick argued about *The Countess of Coteley*, the sets did not arrive until late afternoon and the lighting was not ready until moments before curtain-up. Dick resented being upstaged by Laurier, whom he considered a second-rate amateur. The day before the revue opened at the Lyric Theatre, Hammersmith, he retired to bed with 'spasms of the muscles'. Once admitted to the London Clinic and visited by all his friends, he mended rapidly.

At the first night in London, Reggie hated the first half and Virginia still hated it all. The reviews, however, were favourable, especially for Max Adrian and Elisabeth Welch, and tickets were selling. *Vogue* described Joyce as 'all teeth and limbs, with the plunging enthusiasm of a healthy schoolgirl; hung about with a homespun shift and relentless white bloomers, she emits the wild open notes of an Indian love-call. Her weapons, a fleeting expression, an observation as sweetly precise and deadly as a new razor-blade.' Stephen Potter noticed her ability to make herself look 'super-attractive and then in the next scene appears as ghastly hoyden in white, looking exactly like a Thurber worm.' He wondered if she knew how funny she looked trying to do a 'hot style' of dancing. She knew perfectly well.

By October, the audiences 'yelled their delight' and up to two hundred people a night were turned away, so the revue moved to the Globe in Shaftesbury Avenue. Oscar and Dorothy Hammerstein came to see it, and took Joyce to lunch at L'Apéritif. Hammerstein asked her to write and perform a whole revue for Broadway, and said he would back it. There was no money in revues, he told her, but for her he was willing to throw it away. 'Or how about a musical about the Countess of Coteley?' he suggested. Joyce was flattered and somewhat overawed and thought him a 'huge kindly bear'. However, she said she didn't want to go to New York just yet.

In spite of its wobbly start, *Tuppence Coloured* ran for a year and then had a sell-out tour in Scotland. While there, Joyce was thrilled to be invited to dine at Holyroodhouse with the King and Queen. Completely unprepared, she wore her stage frock, borrowed a fox-fur cape from the pianist and her dresser ran her up a silver lamé bag. It was an 'intimate' dinner for twelve, and included Princess Margaret, the King's equerry Peter Townsend, and his private secretary, Edward Ford, who was soon to marry Joyce's first cousin Virginia Brand. She was only too pleased to perform three monologues after dinner.

Reggie looked after Joyce well when she was working. The strain of seven performances a week sometimes caused her to wake up with a fever or a 'bowler hat' headache. Sundays brought a respite when, after church and lunch with her father, she would sit beside Reggie, listening to the radio and doing a tapestry together. Reggie cooked the dinner: he was a dab hand with a beef joint in the pressure cooker. It was one of the rare moments when she could be persuaded to stop organising. At other times she not only knew the correct rules for games, she also knew the correct tunes for hymns and the correct way to make toffee. 'Sometimes,' she confessed, 'the only way to resist the temptation to take over and organise everything is to go out of the room and nibble a biscuit.' She told her radio listeners to 'let your husband think he has made the decisions and then he will be happy'. The irony was that Reggie played the same game with her – and to greater effect.

Joyce's busy social life was confined to lunchtimes, when she could be found at L'Apéritif, Le Caprice or The Ivy, with Dick or Victor, though rarely both together. When she met up with Celia Johnson and Virginia Graham, the three women told 'surprisingly dirty stories as if we were old men in a club'.

As for family, Nora and Lefty had wanted to come over for the opening of *Tuppence Coloured* but, although Joyce longed to see her mother, she dreaded the emotional complications this might create between her parents. Paul was only sixty-eight but his health was poor: he had arthritic hands, was going deaf, demanded a lot of attention and said he had not enjoyed life for years. Joyce feared he might have to move in with them, but managed to find Christian Science ladies to care for him.

The Flynns made it to London in time to see Joyce in the show in 1948. At fifty-eight, Nora was still chic and flirtatious. Her pleated skirt, white blouse and beret still attracted men and she found old friends among the taxi drivers. One man remembered her from fifteen years earlier and both wept with joy. As usual, she showered everyone with presents and left Joyce to pick up the bills.

After *Tuppence Coloured* closed, Joyce and Viola did occasional concerts for disabled troops and prisoners of war, during which she tried out new sketches, such as 'Nursery School' and 'Shirley's Girl Friend'. When they did one in Mundesley, north Norfolk, for the new Arts Council, their payment was three dozen fresh eggs.

When in town, Joyce and Viola saw each other at least once a week. Viola was working as rehearsal pianist on *Billy Budd* at Covent

Garden and for a period she coached Joyce in singing for an hour a day. Of all Joyce's teachers, she was the most caring and professional in her approach, though she thought of Joyce's songs as 'froth music' compared to her work with Britten and the Ballet Rambert. They shared laughter and tears over meals in Viola's studio basement, and Viola had her own key to Joyce's flat and would curl up on the sofa whenever she felt lonely. In Glasgow Joyce received a telegram saying, FORGIVE SILENCE. LOST MY VOICE BUT IT'S COMING BACK. SO ARE YOU. HURRAH. VOLE.

– 17 –

As her fortieth birthday passed, Joyce kept herself busy with radio work and writing and recording songs but she longed for the applause of a live audience. In January 1951 Laurier Lister asked her to join his next revue, *Penny Plain*. He was hoping H. M. Tennent would back it again, but they were already backing another revue, starring Graham Payn, with songs by Noël Coward. A few days later Joyce was asked to join this revue, but she was already committed to Laurier. Dick Addinsell was committed to no one and offered new songs to both Lister and Beaumont, in order to see who would pay more.

The effort of finding contributors for *Tuppence Coloured* had been more trouble than it was worth and Joyce knuckled down to writing new material. As usual it proved difficult to get started and she found herself reading not only the personal columns of *The Times* but all four leaders as well. Eventually the monologue *Thought for Today* flowed onto the paper, about a woman in Belsize Park who believed the world's problems could be solved by taking off one's shoes and allowing the 'Earth Ray Thought Forces' to influence the mind. Joyce worried that people might be upset by a satire on religion but Virginia reassured her she was not too near the bone. *Life and Literature* pictured a keen young reader talking to an 'important' author about his new novel. Joyce had written it for a party that John Gielgud gave at the Royal Shakespeare Company in 1950, but its origins went back to 1939 when Stephen Potter had improvised the author and Joyce spontaneously became the ardent admirer. Dick and Nicholas Phipps wrote *A Moment With Tennyson* for Joyce, a delightful skit on Maud, who *won't* go into the garden, wouldn't *dream* of coming into the garden, and is 'much too old, for a strangle-hold'.

Laurier had recently discovered the song-writing partnership of

Michael Flanders and Donald Swann. They wrote five songs for *Penny Plain* and Swann supplied the music to Joyce's lyrics for *Joyful Noise*, a pastiche of a Haydn oratorio with Miss Clissold, Miss Truss and Ivy Trembley from Wembley, who 'sometimes sing in **FFF** and sometimes *ppp*'. It was inspired by her recent appearance in the Boulting brothers' *The Magic Box*, the film industry's contribution to the Festival of Britain, in which every British actor of note appeared. Joyce and Oda Sloboskya were surrounded by the BBC Choir and between takes Joyce led them in songs by Ivor Novello.

Joyce and Virginia wrote a song called *Calypso* for Elisabeth Welch celebrating the Festival of Britain, and one for Max Adrian about an actor scared of his understudy and another about a philosophical fly on a slice of salmon. June Whitfield, then twenty-six years old, whom Joyce described as 'plain but has personality and a very good voice', was taken on for the chorus. '*Penny Plain* was fairly early in my career,' she remembers, 'and I learned a great deal from watching and listening to them all, especially Joyce, Max and Elisabeth.'

During rehearsals, Joyce worried again about Laurier's qualities as a director: 'He is so nice and so depressing, he saps all vitality.' However, everyone was in a good mood at the opening in Southsea in May 1951. Joyce bought each of the twenty-two members of the company a four-penny plastic pan pipe from Woolworth's.

While on the seven-week tour prior to the West End run, Joyce edited all her material, sometimes cutting a line a day. 'The tauter a number, the more power it has,' was her rule. Elisabeth Welch still needed a solo and the American film composer Hugh Martin came to the rescue with a number called *Patisserie*. During rehearsals Joyce asked his opinion of her singing. 'After watching the rehearsals I told her it was all marvellous,' he remembers. 'She asked, "But did I sing well?" "Well, yes," I said, "you always sing adorably. Sometimes you do go a little flat, just under the note. But don't worry about it, that's fine, Edith Piaf always sings flat." Joyce wanted to be perfect. She got a tape recorder and recorded her voice and worked on it until she wasn't flat. After that I never heard her sing even a mite out of tune.' Hugh Martin thought June Whitfield sounded like Judy Garland and wanted Joyce to write a musical for her. But there was never enough time and June left to join *South Pacific*.

When the show reached Oxford, Joyce was invited by students to the 'Torpid' boat races, where the winning oarsmen of Brasenose were dressed as St Trinian's schoolgirls, three years before the first film inspired by Ronald Searle's *Punch* cartoons appeared.

At the first night in Glasgow, a drunken stagehand talked loudly all through Joyce's monologue and the set did not come down from the flies. When the stage curtain would not open either, she managed an impromptu song in front while the chorus waited behind. In Bournemouth, Max overheard a woman say of *Thought for the Day*, 'Not much point to it, is there?' and her friend reply, 'No, but she is very fascinating.' 'Oh yes, fascinating, but wasting her time.'

When *Penny Plain* finally reached London in mid-summer, Joyce was glad to be back, despite the heat. St Martin's Theatre, though small and intimate, was falling apart. The fly-ropes were broken, there was dry rot, and much of the lifting-gear was too old to use. There were thirty-two steps down from Joyce's dressing-room to the stage and since she had nine complete changes of costume, she ran down *and* up 448 steps during every performance.

The first night went well for Joyce, especially as in the audience were Betty Phipps and Wilton, now fifteen and 'attractive, tall, slim and charming like his father'. However, the critics hated the revue and advance ticket sales were sluggish. Joyce's worries about Laurier resurfaced and she wished she had 'a real director with new ideas, pace and discipline'. Reggie said that the show was still too slow, and advised Joyce never to work with Laurier again.

After the second night's performance, things worsened when Laurier burst into Joyce's dressing-room and collapsed in tears. With no established backers, he had already persuaded Michael Flanders to invest £1,600. Now £700 was needed immediately to pay the rent. The producers had known for weeks but had failed to raise the funds. Unless the money could be raised by noon the next day the show would have to close.

Joyce sent for Reggie and after a midnight meeting with Laurier, he told her to invest her savings in the show. The next morning he took £700 in cash from her account. At the theatre he discovered the rent was still £29 short, and ran back to the bank with only minutes to spare before it closed for the weekend. After a further meeting with the revue's producers, Reggie realised that the show would still collapse unless they invested another £2,000. He agreed to put up the money on condition he took control of the accounts. Virginia also invested £500 and gave Joyce an open cheque should it be needed. A week later Joyce put in another £1,300, and her eventual investment came to nearly £5,000, the equivalent today of over £80,000. She confessed in her diary her amazement that she had saved this much from her songs and radio work: her growing reputation had meant that she was able to demand high fees. In 1951, the normal payment for being the guest on *Desert Island Discs* was twenty-five guineas, but Aubrey Blackburn had already established with the BBC that she never worked for less than thirty. In 1957 BBC Accounts noticed that some editions of *Call the Tune* cost more than others. The answer lay with Joyce: whereas Constance Cummings received fifteen guineas, Joyce had successfully negotiated forty for the same programme.

Reggie remained Joyce's financial manager and backer for the rest of her career, a role that suited them both. 'Reggie is kind and thoughtful without any effort, all those things I have to struggle to be,' wrote Joyce. He had always wanted to run a business, and now he was presented with an opportunity that would benefit them both, in a world that he enjoyed, with the woman he loved. His childhood of uncertain prosperity had made him unwilling to take dangerous risks and he only spent or invested what was already saved.

Whenever the opportunity arose he watched rehearsals, beaming with pleasure. He was a calming influence, not only on Joyce but on the whole cast. 'Dear Reggie,' Elisabeth Welch said at the time, 'he's like a long glass of cold water on a very hot day.' He was also Joyce's strongest critic: no song or monologue was performed without his approval and much of her work was never heard beyond their living-room.

Soon after the show opened, Joyce received a letter from fifteen-year-old Annabel Murray-White of Surrey, saying her parents were celebrating their wedding anniversary with a trip to *Penny Plain*. Annabel asked if a signed programme could be given to them and enclosed a postal order for three shillings with the suggestion that any change be given to the blind. To enable the usherette to recognise her parents, Annabel would give her mother a flower to wear. Joyce replied that this had been arranged and was pleased to receive a box of chocolates from the three Murray-White girls. She did not tell them that she had also arranged for their mother to be presented with a bunch of carnations. The whole evening had been planned in secret, as Mrs Murray-White wrote to Joyce afterwards:

In the morning I was given a box of chocolates with a return railway ticket to Charing Cross attached. My husband was given an itinerary with a table booked at Simpson's for dinner, and a ten-shilling postal order to cover the cost of taxis! Attached were our theatre tickets. We do not give them much pocket money so it must have taken them weeks to save up. The part that has pleased them most is the way you entered into the scheme in such a generous way. When I told them about it this morning they were speechless!

Joyce was so impressed by the girls' initiative that she sent them all tickets for the next Saturday matinée.

Anxious to attract publicity for the show, Joyce and Reggie went to an Astor party where they chatted to Princess Margaret. She said she would like to see *Penny Plain* and Reggie promised to arrange complimentary tickets. Joyce was thrilled and invited the princess and her lady-in-waiting to dine at their flat afterwards. When Mrs Gabe was told, she was so excited that she offered to lend her best tablecloth and then spent her day off practising curtseys. She only had two days in which to clean every article in the flat, including the insides of the cupboards, while Joyce planned the royal menu – vegetable soup followed by cold mutton chops, mashed potatoes and lettuce, and for dessert, Reggie's favourite – whipped blackcurrant jelly. Joyce decided that Princess Margaret, who was twenty-one, would enjoy company of her own age, so two young men were invited to make up the party. On the day, the piano was tuned, an electrician mended the bathroom light and two carpenters rebuilt the lavatory surround. Reggie was sent to Peter Jones to buy new champagne glasses and pink lampshades for the stairs. Joyce wished that she could somehow prevent her neighbours from frying onions that evening. She also worried that the princess's arrival would coincide with the nightly exodus from the Gaumont cinema opposite.

Joyce was convinced she had told nobody what was happening, but when they arrived from the theatre in a hired car, Mr Kent and his family were in the sweetshop window and all her neighbours were standing at the bus stop, pretending to be a queue. Princess Margaret pecked at the chops and they talked about radio programmes and listened to the gramophone till after midnight. The next morning Joyce thought it was in very bad taste that the newspapers ran stories about the princess going to supper over a sweetshop.

Following this excitement, a Buckingham Palace aide phoned to ask for tickets for the King and Queen. It was to be the first public outing made by King George since an operation to remove his lung. Before it occurred to her that this really should be kept a secret, Joyce had already told Mrs Gabe, Viola, and Dick as he was leaving for a flight to New York. There was a real danger that he would tell Nora, who would tell a friend, who would tell the American press. In a panic, she telegraphed New York, 'THURSDAY EVENING IS TOP SECRET.'

Without telling them why, Reggie gave tickets to Ted the butcher, Mr Kent and Mr and Mrs Gabe, but on the evening there was one of the worst pea-soup fogs of the year and the King did not venture out. However, the Queen and Princess Margaret sat in the front row, with Peggy Ashcroft and Diana Churchill behind them. It was 'a glorious evening with laughter ringing from every nook and cranny and the royal party leading it'. All the women in the cast had their hair done specially and the company assembled on the stage during the interval to be introduced. After this Joyce said the name should be changed to *Penny Royal*.

Penny Plain limped along throughout the summer and autumn. Some weeks it made a profit and then a spell of good weather would put them back in the red, so that Joyce prayed for grey days to bring in the punters. Reggie did his best: one evening he filled two rows with members of his family. Company morale wasn't helped by news that Graham Payn's rival *Lyric Revue* was selling out in Hammersmith. At Christmas *Penny Plain* too sold out for a week, before sales slumped again. It finally closed the following summer after a provincial tour of twelve weeks. The producers then declared themselves bankrupt and the backers, including Michael Flanders, Virginia and the Grenfells, lost their investments. Reggie vowed never to let this happen again and formed a company called 'JG Productions Ltd', of which he was a director, to control all Joyce's future work, on stage, television, film and radio.

For the latter, Joyce and Stephen Potter made two further *How* programmes. For the BBC's twenty-fifth anniversary in 1951, they wrote *How Not to Broadcast*, which sent up many of the BBC's dearest institutions. Joyce read a *Listen With Mother* story about a Big Red Bus and they pilloried Richard Dimbleby's outside broadcasts: 'This is me, John, John Vaughan Dimbleby, on one of the last trams, one of the last romantic trams, to the Balham High Road, ten twisting miles of it. By the way, this tram is B 136241. You get the sense of traffic, of movement, of buses. We'll wave to the driver. No, he didn't wave back. Over to you, Tooting.'

Desert Island Discs, which Roy Plomley had presented since 1941, was another target: 'If you were at the top of the Eiffel Tower for ever which favourite pictures would you take? If you were stranded on a desert island with an unlimited supply of gramophone needles, which record would you take? Let us hear the choice of a Famous Actress.' Joyce, who had actually been on the programme a month earlier, answered in a lush voice, 'I would like to have one particular piece of music which has always meant a great deal to me, because of its inspiring vitality and lifting magic.'

Stephen Potter's marriage was falling apart but as he cried in Joyce's arms she felt little sympathy for him. They had been making *How* programmes together for eight years and she was by now irritated with his pacing and ash-flicking. When Stephen and Mary were divorced in 1955, Joyce wrote to Mary: 'I have told Stephen exactly what I think in the most basic English. We are starting on a possible "How" and he begins to work once more. And high time too.'

Another collaborator of the period was Norman Newell, who began producing all Joyce's records for EMI at Abbey Road Studios in 1951. 'As a recording artist she was extraordinary,' he remembers. 'We only ever did one take and it was perfect. She was so professional – always punctual, friendly to everyone. When you came away you were a better person.'

One day in 1952 they were having tea together between a matinée and an evening performance of *Penny Plain*. Newell recalls:

> Joyce began to sing this tune. It had no words, but a very catchy melody. 'What's that?' I asked. 'Oh, it's just a silly little tune that my mother and I used to sing together. She called it

"Narcissus".' I asked her to sing more. By the time she finished I was on the floor laughing, it was so funny. 'You must record it with a man,' I said. 'There's a new young man who I've seen at the music hall called Norman Wisdom.' The next time he was at Abbey Road, I made sure that Joyce was there too and I invited him to drop into a studio to meet Joyce. Norrie Paramor non-chalantly played 'Narcissus' on the piano and Joyce hummed along. Norman picked up the melody and Joyce encouraged him and joined in with a harmony. It worked and I said, 'I like that, let's record it.' Paramor made an orchestral arrangement and a week later we met up again.

The recording gives the impression that Wisdom and Joyce are improvising, and they slowly dissolve into helpless laughter.

Wisdom always believed that this is what happened. 'We impro-vised as we went,' he recalls. 'For the recording session we had a palm-court orchestra and we were behind a glass screen – the orches-tra had no idea what we were singing. They thought it was a serious duet. When it was played back they all fell about.'

For the the B-side, Addinsell and Paramor composed a duet called *I Don't Arf Love Yer* with Joyce and Wisdom as cockney buskers. When Joyce and Viola went on a six-week tour of British troops in Libya and Egypt the following winter, they found both the songs were so well known that there was always a soldier in the audience prepared to leap onto the stage and take Wisdom's part. When he appeared on *Desert Island Discs* in August 2000, *Narcissus* was among his eight records.

Nora came over from New York for the summer of 1951 and stayed in a flat in Belgravia, paid for by Nancy. During her previous visit in 1948, Joyce had decided that her mother needed something to occupy her and suggested she write her life story. Back in North Carolina, Nora found a young man called Chuck to help her and, though she was older than his mother, she soon fell for him. Lefty decided that he couldn't compete and went to live with a married woman with three children in Newport. By the time Nora arrived in London in June 1951, she was divorced from Lefty and he had married his fifth and final wife. Nora was still pining for Chuck and the book was only half written. She desperately wanted her daughter's attention and affection, but Joyce found it hard to respond. She loved her mother in a dutiful way but still felt let down by her and thought that Nora's sins were finally catching up with her.

Meanwhile, Paul Phipps's health had continued to deteriorate. He was doubly incontinent at night, frequently confused and could barely walk. Joyce was ashamed by her irritation at his inability to function. 'It is as if he has already gone, for the poor old log of a man we have to hoist about isn't him anymore.' Mrs Brookes, the Christian Scientist who cared for him, was kind, but he only really cheered up if Joyce sat with him after lunch for a *Listen With Mother* story read by Daphne Oxenford.

Faced with Nora's weeping, Paul's incontinence and seven performances a week, Joyce wrote in her diary, 'I now see that real artists *must* be orphans, or else heartless brutes.' To keep her mother occupied, Joyce persuaded her to sing the American slave songs which Aunt Liza Pie had taught her. Viola transcribed the melodies while Joyce wrote down the words, and two weeks later she took them to Columbia, who agreed to record them. Joyce subsequently performed over a dozen 'Songs My Mother Taught Me' on the radio and on stage, with musical arrangements by Viola.

Towards the end of Nora's stay, Joyce suggested that she might remarry Paul and make his last years comfortable. Nora pointed out that she had no spark left for him and she could only marry for love. Later that night Joyce wrote, 'I feel like a boiled owl and wish I was an orphan.' Her mother returned to a lonely life in New York, without a husband or even servants to talk to.

The following year Paul suffered a small stroke, after which he seemed to lose the will to live. He died peacefully at home in Chelsea in 1953, aged seventy-three. Joyce felt 'infinitely sad. Grey and mild. Egotistical abysmal *self*-sadness. I can see all is well & this mirage is about nothing but golly I do feel *sad*.' Nora came over for the funeral, which added to Joyce's melancholy. She inherited the John Singer Sargent portrait of her Phipps grandmother and hung it in pride of place in her sitting-room.

– 18 –

JOYCE WAS ALWAYS grateful for the audience that her films brought her, even though she found hanging around a set so tiring. Never one to waste time, she always took with her a book, writing-paper and sewing, though usually ended up chatting or singing duets with members of the crew. In 1947 the Central Office of Information commissioned her and Stephen Potter to write the film *Design for Women*. Joyce played Miss Arty and was appalled at her appearance. 'I looked so awful in it,' she wrote to her mother, 'that I'm glad you won't see it in America! I play it with my jaw out & I really look terrible.' When they saw it, Joyce and Stephen insisted on removing their names from the credits, and *Design for Women* has since disappeared.

Miss Arty was the first of Joyce's 'gallumpher' roles, similar in spirit to the gawky Fern Brixton first heard on the radio. She was soon the obvious choice of directors for such roles and often wished she had not been typecast. In 1949 she played Miss Daisy Horsefall-Hughes, a folk-song and dance enthusiast, in Eric Linklater's *Poet's Pub*. She wore a hand-woven cloak over a Liberty lawn frock with chunky necklaces and never stopped talking about poetry and folklore. During filming she danced with such zeal that she bounced out of shot and had to be asked to leap lower. 'Splendid news,' Miss Horsefall-Hughes tells the bank manager: 'the vicar's got mumps so you'll have to be Essex.' She organises a pageant in which, dressed as Queen Elizabeth, she 'rode a huge white horse, for hours & hours and was stiff for days afterwards'.

That year she also played the willowy, lantern-jawed Mrs Pargiter, who kept a dress shop in *A Run For Your Money*, starring Alec Guinness. When the wicked and beautiful Moira Lister lures a Welsh miner into a shop to try on a chiffon *décolleté* frock called Desire Under the Elms, Mrs Pargiter is at hand to say, 'I'm all for French fitting, aren't you?'

Alice in Wonderland took three years to make and was one of the most innovative movies of the 1950s, a musical using puppets. As the Dormouse, Joyce spoke in a sleepy, husky voice, and sang 'Twinkle Twinkle Little Bat'. She also dubbed the voice of the Duchess. 'I nearly blew up doing her false voice, an awful strain and I felt I might never speak again. All of it chest notes of great power and hideosity.' Filmed by Claude Renoir, grandson of Pierre-Auguste Renoir, in surreal Festival of Britain-style sets, this was a successful attempt to recreate *Alice* on film, but when Walt Disney's cartoon came out in 1951 his studio prevented its distribution and it vanished.

Many people remember *The Happiest Days of Your Life*, made in 1950, as a St Trinian's film because it was set in a boarding-school and starred Alistair Sim and Margaret Rutherford as the headteachers. Joyce played the enthusiastic but vulnerable hockey mistress Miss Gossage – 'Call me Sausage.' Remembering her own schooldays, Joyce added the scene where she writes with her finger in dust on the stairs, and resurrected hockey skills in what she called 'the queen of all gallumphers'. *Laughter in Paradise*, a year later, was a comedy with a message – that we should all be ourselves, unconstrained by others. Joyce played a stuck-up army officer who walks like a carthorse and she found the film 'slow, dull and pedestrian. It goes on and on in spurts. I thought I was awful.'

In *The Pickwick Papers* of 1952 Joyce played a social climber, Mrs Leo Hunter of The Den, Eatanswill. She hosted a fancy-dress literary breakfast dressed as Britannia, and recited Dickens's 'Ode to an Expiring Frog':

> 'Can I view thee panting, lying
> On thy stomach, without sighing;
> Can I unmoved see thee dying
> On a log,
> Expiring frog!'

Most of her film roles were of the gawky kind. 'Jolly hockey sticks does get boring,' she said. The roles attracted tactless comments from the public: she would be greeted in the street with, 'You aren't half as ugly as I thought you were' or 'Glad to see you've had your teeth fixed.' She acted fourteen such parts before her first glamorous part, as the Edwardian Duchess of Cromarty in *The Million Pound Note*, made in 1953 and starring Gregory Peck. She wore period costumes over a figure-enhancing corset and kept her jaw firmly in. For once Nora could be proud of her daughter and told her friends to watch it. It was also the first of several occasions that she rewrote her part. 'The script was so deadly, that I asked Ronald Neame if I might paraphrase it. Bit by bit I worked on it till I had reasonable things to say. The writer had no sense of character at all and had clearly never even *SEEN* a Duchess or heard one either.'

She returned to gallumphers the following year, as Sergeant Ruby Gates in the St Trinian's series inspired by Ronald Searle. *The Belles of St Trinian's* was directed by Frank Lauder and the screenplay by Sydney Gilliat, who had co-written *A Yank at Oxford* with Joyce's brother Tommy in 1937. Alistair Sim starred as both the bookmaker Clarence Fritton and his sister Millicent, headmistress of the school whose name brought terror to adults and wild joy to children. Joyce was now forty-four and Gilliat added a cruel twist to her sexual innocence. Ruby had been engaged for fourteen years to Superintendent Sammy Kemp-Bird, played by Lloyd Lamble, who persuaded her to join the school disguised as the new gym mistress Chloe Crawley.

'Chloe Crawley's a terrible name. They'll call me Creepy Crawley,' she said. 'Oh well, I'll have to polish up my hockey stick before I bally off.' Once again, Joyce's hockey skills were tested, especially as one goalpost was smaller than the other. At least twice the girls knock Crawley out cold as she uncovers a plot to rig the Gold Cup. George Cole played Flash Harry, the start of his career as a cheeky criminal. 'Joyce was heaven to work with,' he remembers. 'The only thing I hated about her was the fact that she finished the *Times* crossword each day while I was still on the third clue.'

Blue Murder at St Trinian's followed in 1957, with Flash Harry planning to sell the most attractive St Trinian's girl to Europe's leading bachelor, Prince Bruno. Ruby joins the school trip to Rome, disguised as Ursula Bluette, an interpreter. In Paris she becomes romantically entangled with the scheming bus driver, played by Terry Thomas. Despite some energetic tango-dancing, she faithfully returns to the unwilling superintendent.

The Pure Hell of St Trinian's, made in 1960, opened with the school burning down. Ruby was so long-suffering a fiancée, so bad at her job and so like a resourceful Girl Guide, one wondered how the now fifty-year-old Joyce would ever escape the role. Although hardly sexy, Ruby nevertheless attracts undesirable types. A cruise ship taking St Trinian's to Greece is hijacked and Ruby ends up in Arabia (a sand quarry near Woking, where filming was interrupted by thunderstorms) with a devious Cecil Parker and George Cole. Rescuing the girls from an emir's palace, Ruby has to carry a piece of Hoover on her head in a line of swaying houris. When Ruby finally walks up the aisle after a sixteen-year engagement, Sammy is called to another fire at St Trinian's. 'This film will need the abandoning of all critical standards to be enjoyed,' Joyce wrote to Virginia. 'But I rather think it is funny on a sort of wild level.'

Despite its surreal plot, it contains several contemporary literary references: the smallest schoolgirl is called 'Lolita Chatterley Peyton Place Brighton' and the British Consul in Arabia is also the Hotpoint washing-machine representative – shades of Graham Greene's recently published *Our Man in Havana*. 'Actually,' Joyce said some years later, '*St Trinian's* were jolly bad films, but there were some very funny moments – not, alas!, contributed by me. I have nothing to do but look surprised and shocked, and that soon palls.'

Looking back, George Cole felt that 'They did have wonderful casts and were great fun to make. *The Belles of St Trinian's* was the best. It had a real understanding of farce. But it was all there, in Ronald Searle's cartoons, including my part of Flash Harry.' After making three St Trinian's films Joyce decided that she had had enough. Although they offered her more money, she turned them all down.

'Joyce was a natural,' remembered Roy Boulting, who directed her in *Happy Is the Bride*. 'She hardly needed any directing. The script was written with her in mind and if there was anything she didn't like she would change it. Her characterisation of any role never lost contact with truth. If only all actors were as good as that. One of her strengths was that she kept within her abilities – she never stretched herself beyond that.'

The film starred Irene Handl, Joyce's old friend Athene Seyler, and Ian Carmichael, who described it as 'a little domestic trifle of timeless charm'. Joyce was the bride's aunt, who plays the church organ during the wedding. Nobody had thought to provide music and Joyce had to improvise the Wedding March from Wagner's *Lohengrin*.

'I would say she was the greatest character comedienne of our time,' said Boulting.

No one else has conveyed the middle-class woman in her various roles and attitudes as well as Joyce did. Her search for perfection enabled her to take what was no more than a stock 'funny character' and invest it with a startling extension, which never went beyond reality. The variety of her characters was enormous, but you could believe every one of them. She brought laughter and joy to audiences everywhere. Innately modest, she was ever generous to her fellow-performers and, in turn, loved by them. There are few who live as she did: embodying the spirit of goodness.

Not many movie fans wrote to her, but Charles A. Kennedy, who reviewed competitors' movies for 20th Century Fox, wrote from America:

The secret to my job was to watch the audience. If only you could've seen the looks on their faces. There was actually a form of love between you on the screen and all the faces looking up there. It happened every time, over and over from small neighborhood places to gigantic cinema palaces. If you've ever been to San Francisco you know how sophisticated that city can be. They pretend no celebrity can faze them. Joyce Grenfell is one of the very few personalities that makes them forget. One manager let me stand behind the screen – you can see through you know – and by the faces I could tell when you came on even before a word was spoken.

I travel a lot – you would be surprised how much – everywhere you are so deeply loved. I think more than any other living person in entertainment.

★

After *Penny Plain* ended in the summer of 1952, Joyce decided she had had enough of traditional revue. 'I prefer being solo,' she said. 'I don't know what to do with other actors – I only know how to have imaginary actors around me. Can you imagine anything more luxurious than not having to say anything you don't want to? And be the only one on stage?' She had been secretly hoping to mount her own show since 1940 and by the end of 1953 she had written sufficient new monologues and songs to begin serious planning.

Laurier Lister wanted to direct her and she overrode Reggie's warnings and agreed. Appearing on her own, she would clearly have far greater control. Anyway, Joyce's choice was limited: there were few directors with the experience necessary for an intimate revue who were also compatible with her. They needed to adore her sufficiently to put up with her bossiness, and have the skills to tighten her work where necessary. They also had to decide who else to use between Joyce's monologues and songs. Singers or comedians would compete with Joyce's work, whereas dancers would complement it. By alternating Joyce's sketches and songs with dancing, she would have time to change her costumes and appear as a different character. Wendy Toye, who had choreographed *Sigh No More*, suggested three young but experienced stage dancers. Irving Davies had also been in *Sigh No More*; Paddy Stone had been with the Royal Ballet; and Beryl Kaye had danced on Broadway. Their style as Three's Company was unusual, strong and sophisticated.

Dick agreed to write the music but they still needed a musical director to lead the band of seven musicians from the piano. Joyce asked Viola but she was busy at Ballet Rambert and anyway wanted to focus on classical music. Donald Swann suggested William Blezard, who had won prizes in piano and composition at the Royal College of Music and had arranged the music for several films. 'The first time I met Joyce was six p.m. on 18 December 1953, at the home of Dick Addinsell,' he remembers. They hit it off at once and started a partnership which continued for twenty years.

Dick's partner Victor Stiebel had been designing stylish and elegant day-clothes for Joyce for some years. She chose his designs for eight costumes using masses of silk, netting and corsetry in fuchsia pink, lime and ultramarine, one of which ended up in the Victoria & Albert Museum. 'Victor has dressed me up, so that even my best friends do not know me,' Joyce wrote to Leonard Gershe. 'Victor made her elegant by emphasising her lovely top half – elegant shoulders and shapely bosom – with low necklines and three-quarter-length sleeves,' remembers Patrick Woodcock. 'Her body rather let her down from below the waist so he covered up her large legs and hips with soft gathers and masses of petticoats. Victor knew exactly how to make her beautiful and chose fabulous coloured silks.' The stage gowns were designed with an extra gusset under the arm, like a conductor's jacket, so that she could throw her arms in the air without the dress ripping. *Housewife* magazine featured a paper pattern of one of Victor's designs for Joyce – a draped jersey top over a full, New Look skirt.

Joyce's new songs included *Mrs Mendlicote*, who stood beside a fluted column in a satin Edwardian gown, singing about her famous At Homes in Belgravia. People drifted in and out, but where was her husband? 'He has gone, and gone for ever.' Her new monologues included *Writer of Children's Books*, who is unmistakably Enid Blyton. In 1947 Joyce had been to a Foyle's literary luncheon at which Blyton spoke. 'Pure grist to the mill,' Joyce said afterwards. 'Egotism at full flower and totally humourless but with a wide eye to business.' It was one of Joyce's cruellest and most accurate portraits, and she dropped it not long after.

Flanders and Swann wrote a song for the show about the months of the year, ending with 'Freezing wet December, then . . . Back to bloody January again', but Joyce could not bring herself to swear on stage. Irving Davies overheard her wondering what to use instead: 'It's no good asking Michael, because he'll only suggest I sing "and back to *fucking* January".'

As usual, the show began with a provincial tour of two months. Joyce's seventeen costume changes were reduced to thirteen. The scenery, props and costumes were few compared to most productions, but they still had to charter a transport plane to get to Dublin. Paddy Stone danced a solo as a giant spider. It finished with him hanging on a rope which was pulled up into the flies, where he could alight on a gangway. In Glasgow the stagehands forgot to pull, so he climbed the rope until he was out of view of the audience. Joyce came on to sing *Mrs Mendlicote* but above her she could hear Paddy swearing like a trooper as he struggled to hang on. Afterwards, she told him firmly that if he was stuck up a rope again, he should please keep his voice down.

'She was lovely to work with, but steely inside,' recalled Beryl Kaye.

She could be like a bossy nanny. For instance, she always insisted on everyone arriving early at the theatre. She liked to think of herself as very law-abiding, but once behind the wheel of a car she completely changed character. She hated being overtaken by men: she speeded up if she saw one behind her. If a pedestrian crossed the road she would say, 'I can kill them if I like, when they're not on a zebra crossing. But I won't today.'

Audiences were unpredictable. In Folkestone they made less than £200 in a week, whereas in Dublin a week later they took £246 in one night. When the show opened in Cambridge it was called simply *Requests the Pleasure*. 'Several of her relations wondered whether she was wise,' recalled her cousin Simon Phipps, then chaplain at Trinity College. 'Would she really be able to sustain a whole show on her own? But it was wonderful and all our fears were allayed. When she got to *Shirley's Girl Friend* and the beetroot salad, the whole house was in uproar. After the show she came into the restaurant, and everyone stood up and applauded.' By the time the show reached London it had become *Joyce Grenfell Requests the Pleasure*.

Nora, recovered from her divorce and looking gorgeous and chic, came over from America for the first night at the Fortune Theatre, off Drury Lane, in June 1954. Joyce considered this the most important night so far in her career. Even so, she was surprised and delighted to receive telegrams from John Gielgud, Gladys Cooper and sixty-seven other well-wishers.

The reviews were ecstatic. *The Times* said, 'This experiment comes off delightfully. Between the four performers they carry through what might be described as a revue with a touch so light, easy and amusing that at no time are we tempted to sigh for even one more performer.' Harold Hobson said it was 'an entertainment which, in wit, humour, grace and pathos, is like nothing else in London', and A. E. Wilson of the *Star* concluded that Joyce 'has such infinite variety that she is equal to a multitude of players'. The reviewers were all impressed that Joyce had written her own material. T. C. Worsley of the *New Statesman* commented, 'she can sketch in a whole social background with the smallest crooking of her arm or backward bend of her waist'. The dancers were, according to Ivor Brown in the *Observer*, 'in turns graceful and grotesque, acrobatic and bizarre', and the *Daily Mail* wrote of 'the three supercharged dancers who spring on to the stage whenever her back is turned'.

Even Joyce's relations had to concede she had succeeded, though Nancy Tree couldn't resist a cousinly jibe:

> I cannot tell you the pride I felt in your really staggering accomplishment – I could almost feel Nora's jiggles of pleasure. When you were a schoolgirl they used to say 'You've no idea what real humour Joyce has'. Certainly Paul had a most subtle and delicious sense of it, and Nora with her keen ear had genius. They both seem to have come out in you. You looked lovely and so young. Somehow your face has fined down – several people have remarked how beautiful you have become. The colours of your clothes and the hat are perfection. I did feel Steeble [*sic*] should change the blue neck line – some how it is Too Gothic. This goes with much love and deep & real congratulations,
> Affec, Nancy.

For the first time Joyce had introduced a serious song – *The Three Brothers* – inspired by Aunt Margaret in India, and she had not been sure whether it would work. When she entered wearing a straw hat and a carrying a gardening-basket, the audience were at first confused – they expected to be made to laugh. To her relief, the audience fell for the pathos of the elderly spinster who has devoted her life to her three brothers, 'all of them handsome and good at games'. Harry Andrews, husband of Rebecca West, wrote to her: 'My wife said to me: "You didn't expect to enjoy yourself as much as that, did you?" Your humour enables you to express tragedy. The character sketch of the unmarried sister was deeply moving. Anyone who like myself has spoken sagely and a little pompously of the importance of our system of primogeniture in building up the Indian Empire must have felt shamed.'

Requests the Pleasure ran until September at the Fortune and then transferred across Covent Garden to St Martin's until the end of January 1955, before a further tour of ten cities around Scotland and England. It was a punishing schedule made worse by bad news from America.

For some months Nora had been in considerable stomach pain and when she returned to New York she had sought the help of her

Christian Science practitioner. In April 1955 Nancy Astor found Nora alone in New York, suffering from intestinal cancer with no support: her CS practitioner had abandoned her when he learned she had been treated by a doctor. Nancy took Nora back to Tryon and employed a nurse to look after her. She then telephoned Joyce and told her to cancel the tour and go to America immediately, saying that 'the stage manager would understand'. Joyce was torn, but decided she could not cancel – too many other people's livelihoods depended on her. Somehow she got through the final month in Liverpool, Oxford, Streatham and Golder's Green, and a week later she flew to North Carolina.

She arrived to find Nora weak, frightened and in pain. Her doctor said there was no hope, so Joyce used Christian Science to help her mother overcome her fear and co-operated with the doctor, who prescribed painkillers. They had a happy final five weeks together. Joyce's irritation melted away and she was able to give her mother the undivided attention she needed. At long last, Joyce resigned herself to loving Nora for who she was and gave up any hope that she could be changed for the better. Parting was very painful. 'When I die,' Nora said, 'promise me you won't grieve. You know I'll be all right. Go to the movies and know I'll be glad you've gone.' She died ten days after Joyce arrived home in Chelsea.

'She was such a good mother, and I do miss her,' Joyce wrote to Rene. 'It is much less fun without her but I'm sure she is now free and complete. It is only us here who seem bereft.' It dawned on her that Nora would never see another spring, 'But then I realized that spring is part of eternity because it happens every year and she is now in eternity and that thought healed me of grieving.'

Despite her inability to pay bills, Nora left money to both Joyce and Tommy, the remains of Chillie Langhorne's trust. Buck Langhorne's daughter, Phyllis Draper, said of Nora, 'She was the most loved member of the entire family, without any doubt. Young, old, everybody, you couldn't help love Aunt Nora. She was the funniest woman that ever lived.'

On leaving Tryon, Joyce had been to New York to audition for Broadway. 'If the moment is right, if the management is suitable, if the Lord wills it, I will play in America come what may,' she wrote to Leonard Gershe. 'I am only a mite apprehensive, but it's no good being cowardly, and I dare say I will take the plunge.'

The producers made it clear that backing Joyce on Broadway was a big risk as nobody in New York had heard of her as a revue artist: her slim reputation rested entirely on small parts in films.

At the beginning of September 1955 Joyce, together with Three's Company and Dick, embarked at Southampton on the RMS *Mauritania* bound for New York. The American Musicians' Union had insisted that their own members should replace William Blezard and the orchestra. Among the passengers was Myra Hess, who invited Joyce into her first-class state-room for games of Scrabble. One evening she offered to play for Joyce on her Steinway and Joyce sang a group of pastiche encores composed by Dick.

'There was a noble Elgarian one, a French *bergerette* and others,' remembered Joyce. 'But the one Myra liked playing best was a florid vehicle for a show mezzo-soprano who is reluctant to stop. It has a splendidly pretentious introduction of cascading octaves and passionate chords and we had a good time doing it, encoring ourselves several times over and adding quality, so we thought, with every rendering.'

Joyce was met in New York by Tommy and his wife Mary Cheeseboro, whom he had married in 1949. Two-year-old niece Sally greeted her as 'Puppy', a comforting sign of recognition. Myra Hess introduced Joyce to the Laurelton, a small, old-fashioned hotel at the back of the Carnegie Hall. From her bedroom she could see dancing-classes in the studios above the auditorium, and a silent singer with his mouth wide open. She made friends with all the staff, including Gaston, who ran the newspaper stand. When he greeted Joyce with 'God is out there enjoying you too,' she was delighted to learn that he was a Christian Scientist, keeping the works of Mary Baker Eddy behind his cigarette shelf.

Three weeks of rehearsals were required for the new orchestra, conducted by George Bauer, an experienced musical director on Broadway. Reggie, Max Adrian and Victor Stiebel arrived in time for the first night at the Bijou Theatre on 45th Street, west of Broadway, on 9 October 1955. Cecil Beaton and Princess Margaret sent telegrams; Noël Coward and Oscar Hammerstein sent flowers. Virginia's telegram read: BIJOU GOOD OR BIJOU BAD WE LOVE YOU.

Many people had warned Joyce that she would not be understood in North America, but they had reckoned without her adaptability. She only had to find herself in a new country for a few days and she could pick up not only the mannerisms of the people but the angle from which they looked at life. She adapted her performance to her American audiences, and they loved it. The ENSA entertainer in *Travel Broadens the Mind* became an American and all references to the war were removed. When Shirley's Girl Friend asked, 'May I divest you of your plastic mac?' she changed 'mac' but found 'raincoat' didn't carry quite the same punch. In *Thought for Today* the suburban housewife whose life is influenced by Earth Ray Thought Forces became a wealthy New Yorker with homes on Long Island, Manhattan and Maine and employer of 'the only White Russian butler in New York – moody *and* depressed'. The audiences were thrilled that her American accents were completely convincing, and identifiable as to region. They especially loved the 'Songs My Mother Taught Me'.

Three's Company loved performing on Broadway. 'We had a gay old time,' recalled Irving Davies. 'It was such fun because all the stars came backstage after each show, whether they knew Joyce or not.'

'The 1955–56 season was decidedly one of the most flourishing of the past ten or more years on Broadway,' wrote Daniel Blum in *Theater World Annual. Requests the Pleasure* had to compete with *The Diary of Anne Frank*, *The Pajama Game*, Enid Bagnold's *The Chalk Garden*, 'the stimulating though puzzling' *Waiting for Godot* and 'the riotous box office bonanza' *My Fair Lady*.

It was hard work performing eight monologues and six songs in eight shows a week. When Ed Sullivan, the television impresario, came backstage and asked her to appear on his Sunday-night show she replied, 'No thank you, I really have to rest on Sundays,' just as she had to Alistair Cooke. The producers were aghast. She had refused the highest accolade she could have been offered. An estimated fifty million people watched the show in the USA and Canada, and the publicity would be immeasurable. With some reluctance, she agreed to appear the following week.

Sullivan collected together an unusual mixture of big names and acts from the circus and music hall, which he compèred with an air of disinterest. The show was so popular that the audience had to be moved through in relays, even during rehearsals. Joyce performed *The Nursery School* after Edith Piaf had sung *If the Stars Would Only Cry* and Al Hibbler followed with *Unchained Melody*. Three's Company had a blues dance. Irving was told not to grind his hips but he replied that if they didn't like it they could always focus on his face. Between each item 'dramatically new' Mercury Lincoln cars with chrome 'quadralite grilles' and 'power lubrication' were advertised.

Reggie came to stay for a month to sort out the finances. Walking home after he had left, Joyce reflected that she had just earned $3,000, was considered Big on Broadway, had been invited to three different dinner parties, and yet chose to return to her hotel, where she would make herself a cup of hot chocolate on a primus stove in the bathroom.

When Patrick Alexander of the *Daily Sketch* had asked her for the secret of her successful 'showbiz' marriage, Joyce replied that the marriage always came first. 'When I made my first stage appearance, we had been married ten years. The theatre was, and still is, a sideline.' Her recipe included give and take 'but I've an awful feeling Reggie does most of the giving. Don't play golf, and *don't* give way to a morbid desire to thrash *everything* out. Probing old wounds and raking over cold ashes can do more harm than good.' When she wrote 'An Ideal Husband' for the *News Chronicle* she added:

It is a definite advantage if he is clean, can cook, and is generally good about the house. I am in favour of solvency, an equable temperament, enthusiasm and an interest in life. I would like him to play tennis well enough, to wear white shirts, be liked by my friends and to be a great deal cleverer than I am. I think intuition is enough for a wife, but it is just as well if one of the pair has a brain. My Ideal Husband would not be a politician in any party and he would never be at home for lunch, except at weekends. Luckily for me, I am nicely suited.

American union rules meant that, even with a cast of only four, a company of forty had to run the show, including fifteen stagehands. This meant that, to break even, almost every performance had to be sold out. Joyce wrote to Leonard Gershe:

Well, our 'season' at the Bijou was of a brevity that caught me quite unaware! We never had a losing week and we were building, but I suppose the thought of those sagging weeks before Christmas scared the management. Anyway they put up the notice on Friday after Thanksgiving. Next day the violinist came to me and said the band would like to take cuts if that would help. They were joined on Monday by the stage crew. Such things, I gather, are utterly unheard of in the history of Broadway! Well, the management huddled and agreed to carry on. Then it was discovered that the theatre was already let, so we closed Dec 3rd. We ended on a tremendous crest – such audiences! They piled in and each was more wonderful than the other. The last three performances were like the first night. Glorious.

There had been a plan to take the show up the East Coast but it would have cost $18,000 a week and there was no guarantee of an audience outside New York, so the dancers returned home. Joyce stayed on for another Ed Sullivan show, spending Christmas with Tommy and his family in New York. She had a 'holiday' going to the theatre and small dinner parties, and turned down an invitation to dine with the Duke of Windsor in favour of going to a jazz club in Greenwich Village.

– 19 –

Of all Joyce's interests and pastimes, her friends were the most important to her. A few days after the opening of *Requests the Pleasure* in 1954 in London, the assistant electrician in the company introduced himself to her. Oliver Bernard was a twenty-nine-year-old aspiring writer, the eldest son of Dora, who had known Joyce when she was a soloist at the Church of Christ, Scientist. After she was widowed, Dora supported her four children by singing for ENSA as 'Fedora Roselli' but once the war was over, finding work as an entertainer proved more difficult. Jeffrey Bernard, her youngest son, was thirteen and had already been expelled from two prep schools. He was sent to Pangbourne Nautical College in 1946, where Joyce agreed to pay his fees. During the school holidays, his older brothers Bruce and Oliver introduced Jeffrey to the joys of Soho and after two years at Pangbourne his only success was in organising sweepstakes. Joyce's contribution to Jeffrey's education did him little good – by 1954 he had worked as a labourer and a boxer, deserted from the Tank Regiment, and was on probation for shoplifting. He was later more successful writing for the *Spectator*, except when he was 'unwell'.

For three months in 1954 Oliver Bernard not only saw Joyce at the theatre but also wrote to her almost every day, describing the books he read and the poetry he was working on. He chose not to mention his life in Soho, where he had been a rent-boy and later a member of the Communist Party. Joyce asked him to call her 'Aunt', but within a week it was 'Joyce' and he signed his letters 'Bless your little white woolly boots, love from Oliver'. For several weeks he mooned around, hinting at love in his letters, and Joyce was alarmed to think that she was the object of his admiration. She was greatly relieved when she learned it was the dancer Beryl Kaye. At first Beryl showed no interest, so Joyce tried to cheer him up by asking him to type out her poems.

'I wasn't expecting anything in return,' he remembered, 'but she gave me twenty large white five-pound notes; and when I had tooth-ache, she took me to her dentist.' She also gave him Reggie's old jackets, and invited him to tea when the *Spectator* rejected his articles. In return Oliver lent her books such as Dostoevsky's *The Idiot* and Salinger's *The Catcher in the Rye* and poems by his drinking compan-ion, Dylan Thomas. They commented on each other's poetry and one Sunday Joyce took him to tea with Water de la Mare, where she sang *Oh, Mr du Maurier*, and de la Mare replied with a song of Maurice Chevalier's.

Oliver was surprised at Joyce's interest in him, because, as he told her, he was only a donkey whereas she was a horse. This was not as rude as it sounds, for in her song *The Music's Message* the singer calls herself 'a great white horse'. When he decided to go and teach English in Corsica, Joyce ended a poem to him with 'From your old Friend the Horse.'

Before he left, Oliver lent Joyce his dictionary and she gave him a new pullover. They continued to write regularly, and Joyce sent him the Sunday newspapers, books and records. When he came home he wrote advertising copy and translated Rimbaud. He had no need for Joyce now, and their letters petered out.

Near the end of the run of *Requests the Pleasure*, Joyce made another young friend, Cass Allen, who later became a successful character actress. Cass was brought up over her mother's sweetshop in Shepherd's Bush and at fifteen was already a presenter on *The Younger Generation*, a teenage radio programme. 'At school I impersonated Joyce in St Trinian's *ad nauseam*. My ambition was to have a one-woman show of my own, so in 1955 I went to interview Joyce for *The Younger Generation* at St Martin's Theatre. She was delightful and fun.' Joyce was impressed by Cass and wrote to Virginia: 'She has a real talent for mimicry and observation and can talk exactly like me for one! Horrifying.'

'I was a very small fifteen-year-old and Joyce was so huge!' remem-bers Cass.

That became a joke and she used to bend down to greet me even when I grew a bit. Joyce introduced me to people like Pat Dixon, the producer of *The Goon Show*, which led to light-entertainment radio work. She was always encouraging me, making me write material. She said, 'You must practise, practise, practise.' She commented on my writing and I started selling sketches and lyrics.

After I left school I was asked to do voice-overs for television commercials. Joyce didn't really approve, but she rather loftily gave her blessing. One was a cartoon for a soft drink with an offer of a wobbly ball. During rehearsals I tried various voices, including a Joyce-voice, which they said would not be used. To my horror it was. The following week I got a letter from her saying, 'People have been asking me if I've done a voice-over for a beach ball commercial. You know I wouldn't ever work for ITV. It must be you.' I was so embarrassed that when I replied I couldn't mention it, and Joyce never referred to it. But she knew, and I knew she knew, and I never used her voice again. A few months later, someone impersonated another famous actor's voice in a commercial and was sued. I realised then how generous Joyce had been in not pursuing this.

We became good friends and I became her 'courtesy niece', and she was my 'courtesy aunt'. I had to call her 'JG'. 'And I shall call you Courtesy,' she said. Sometimes we would impersonate each other. She'd say, 'You be me and I'll be you.'

Cass provided a ready supply of young friends who were livelier than the usual BBC studio audiences. Joyce had complained they were too old, not the people she envisaged listening to her at home. 'Can't you find a more hip audience?' she asked. 'Joyce would phone and ask how many free tickets I'd like for her shows, and then invite us all round afterwards,' said Cass.

When she was at the Haymarket I went to a matinée and Athene Seyler was in the dressing room. Joyce asked her what she thought of her new sketches and Athene said, 'Well, Joycie, I think you could have dug a little deeper.' Joyce didn't like me hearing an adverse comment and I was dispatched with some haste!

We wrote nearly every week. She came to visit my mother at the sweetshop and I often went to her home. Time was allotted to you. If you were invited to tea you got one hour, then she would stand up and say, 'Now I must turn you out, dear girl.' Once after coffee, I was invited to stay for lunch. I explained I was now a vegetarian and she said, 'It's cucumber soup made with chicken bone stock. Eat up. It won't kill you.' I had no option but to do what I was told, even though I was nearly thirty!

★

George Henry Clews was sprawled on the pavement outside South Kensington Station when Joyce first met him in 1956. Passers-by were walking round him, but despite her antipathy to drunks, Joyce stopped; she found that he was not drunk, but hungry and suffering from low blood sugar. He was nearly eighty and his pension would not buy enough food to last a week. She sat him on a low wall and learned that he had once been a master tailor, working all over America, but when he returned to Britain his relations had all died. Joyce gave him £2 and her address. A week later she received a letter detailing how he had spent the money: not only on food but also a second-hand raincoat, trousers, shirt and boots.

They were soon meeting regularly. Mr Clews lived in a men's hostel in Camden Town but he refused to meet her there, nor would he bring his cough up to her flat. Joyce offered to take him for drives in her Ford Zephyr, but he said he was too deaf. However, she was allowed to pick him up from the number 74 bus stop and then they sat in her car outside Regent's Park and shouted at each other. It was some time before he discovered Joyce was famous, but it did not alter his attitude. He was very particular about the food she provided: his lack of teeth meant he could only cope with soup or two-day-old white, crustless sandwiches. He loved reciting long, passionate Wild West poems. Joyce wanted to improve his clothes, but he was a difficult man to please. 'Dear Mrs. J Grenfell,' he wrote. 'I enjoyed our little talk and hope I did please you. I am very pleased to know that you are a God fearing woman – that accounts for you looking so young & charming. I don't want any pyjamas or nightshirt – I always sleep in my underpants & shirt. I count the days to seeing you again.'

Joyce thought she would save him the trouble of ironing and gave him a drip-dry shirt and some ties. Knowing how much he disliked gifts, she removed all the packaging and pins and stuffed the shirt into a paper bag. He was not impressed and wrote:

I received the ties & appreciate very much your generosity & followed your suggestion to give to someone if I did not wish to keep them. I gave one to an old man who gave me a tie several weeks ago. Mrs. Grenfell, I hope you won't be offended when I say that I cannot follow the 4 directions concerning the shirt – it would be impossible – I wish you could change it for a common cotton shirt. Goodness! Did you read the directions? I am very sorry you spent so much for a shirt that would be impossible for me to use. I hope I shall never lose such a wonderful friendship. I have no complaints at present. Wishing you, and those you love, always, GH Clews.

When, two years later, he 'came over queer' in a teashop, Mr Clews told the police that he had no family, and only one friend – Mrs R. Grenfell. The police telephoned her and she rushed to the hospital, where he insisted on leaping off the stretcher and going back to his hostel. His cough turned out to be tuberculosis and he spent a few months in Colindale Hospital, ruling the men's ward in a striped bobble hat, a present from Joyce to keep out the draughts. After he died, the superintendent of the hostel told Joyce Mr Clews's version of their friendship. He said he had been a professional singer in South Africa when he had met Joyce backstage. He then caught malaria and lost his singing voice, but being fellow-artists they had remained close friends. Whether he had really been a master tailor, she never discovered.

Her greatest and longest-lasting friend was of course Virginia Graham. They were the same age, shape and social class, neither had children and both were happily married to men who also got on well. They both viewed life with optimism, bolstered by their shared faith in Christian Science. Every morning at 7.20 Joyce phoned Virginia to discuss their news. Ten minutes later their respective housekeepers brought them breakfast in bed. When apart, they wrote every day, sometimes twice. But their correspondence reveals little of all that they did together: lunches, theatres, CS meetings and holidays. 'Virginia and I are more like sisters. That wonderful thing when you don't have to edit the conversation and you're on the same beam without any holds barred. You don't have to blurt out, you just know you are thinking the same.'

Joyce never told Reggie about Elliot Coleman or Prince Aly, because 'my antennae tell me that that those whom one truly loves should be spared burdens', but she and Virginia had a friendship which withstood all confidences.

'To me, Joyce has always been the old reliable,' said Virginia. 'Exactly the same since I first knew her. She is both good and funny. This is a very rare combination and a very good thing for a friend to be. Even in her extreme youth, when she took people off – which she did a great deal – it was always without a trace of malice. I don't know how to put it, but she gives you that sort of "safe" feeling.'

For over twenty years, Joyce's 'Magic Circle', as she called her favourite friends, remained almost the same: Virginia and Tony Thesiger, Victor Stiebel and Dick Addinsell, Athene Seyler and Beau Hannen. Athene first met Joyce through Nora. 'There was this little girl – no, she was never very little – aged about fourteen or fifteen – singing some lovely American Negro songs with her mother. In all the years I knew her, I never saw one flicker of doubt in her face, I can't remember Joyce ever saying, "I *think* I might, or I often *wonder if* . . ." No, never, she was sure of everything.' Joyce's friends loved her regardless of her faults.

Patrick Woodcock was the GP to Reggie, Tony and many of Joyce's friends such as Victor Stiebel, Noël Coward and Clemence Dane. 'The Magic Circle were a bit like hot-house flowers at Kew,' he remembers: 'they looked wonderful through the window, but if you opened the door and let anyone else in, they withered from the cold. They could be very bitchy about other people, but never in front of Joyce. Even her closest friends knew that there were things you just could not say to her. Joyce was easy to mock but nobody ever did it in front of her.'

Joyce found it difficult to be spontaneously funny unless she was relaxing with very close friends such as Virginia or Dick. She probably had no idea that he was unfaithful to Victor but his hardness made it increasingly difficult for her to like him and eventually even Joyce became fed up with his egotism and hypochondria. Although he earned substantial royalties from over sixty films, revues and musicals, he never supported Victor. When Victor retired, Virginia bought him a flat near hers in Hyde Park Gardens and, together with the Grenfells, supported him. They never told anyone, and never complained about his extravagance, though they did laugh when he worried about money, having apparently forgotten where it was coming from.

The Magic Circle became smaller after Victor died from multiple sclerosis in 1976, and then a year later Dick died of pneumonia. Having been so close to him during the war, Joyce was sad that she did not miss him.

Beyond the Magic Circle were friends she saw less often or in particular places – Leonard Gershe in California; John Betjeman at poetry recitals; and the Potters in Aldeburgh. 'I can't list my friends in order,' she said, 'but they are all of great worth to me. Some friends do not mix with others, but that's all right. It is good when friends like friends but it isn't important except to one's sense of tidiness.' Friends, relations and colleagues were well compartmentalised and many did not meet until Reggie introduced them to each other after her death.

If friends were in trouble, she was a good listener and had the ability to make each distressed person feel their problem was important. Many a husband or wife poured out their marital troubles to her and left feeling encouraged to get the marriage back on the rails. She was deeply disappointed if they were unable to ride through difficult times and resorted to divorce.

Whoever Joyce met, she gave them her full attention so that they often felt they were her best friend after only a short meeting. This meant that if they met again, the person assumed that Joyce remembered them. She didn't want to hurt their feelings, so she would say, 'Yes, of course I remember you, but I've forgotten your name.' 'Wilson.' 'No, not your surname, I remember that, your first name.' (Or vice versa.) Fans and Christian Scientists might be invited to tea, but were more usually blessed with a bright conversation backstage or after church.

Sometimes she gave more. When sixteen-year-old Julia Fitch wrote to Joyce about the courage of her widowed mother, whose chronic back injury meant she could only stand or lie, Joyce turned up unheralded on their Eastbourne doorstep for a chat. She kept in touch and the next time she performed in Eastbourne she arranged for Lillian to watch the show from a bed in the wings of the Congress Theatre.

Among Joyce's more unlikely friends were Laurens and Ingaret van der Post. Reggie had met Laurens in South Africa and couldn't understand why his opinions on the environment, Africa and psychology were sought by people like the Prince of Wales and Margaret Thatcher. But, like them, Joyce fell for his charm and they met often in London and Aldeburgh. Reggie was right to be suspicious: J. D. F. Jones's recent biography has shown that Laurens was indeed a fraud: he was never, as he claimed, personal representative to Lord Mountbatten, had no commission in the South African Army and did not help to broker the transfer of Rhodesia to Zimbabwe. His 'explorations' in Botswana and Malawi were not those of a lonely and intrepid explorer and he knew little about indigenous Africans yet he wrote five books, made a television series and gave a lifetime of lectures as an expert on 'Bushmen'.

Neither Laurens nor Joyce liked to sit and listen – both preferred to hold centre stage in a conversation. There was much discussion during the 1970s about Rhodesia and although neither Laurens nor Joyce had any real understanding about the situation there, they had strong views and were united in their opposition to economic and cultural sanctions as a solution for change. Their views on a multi-racial South Africa were liberal for the 1950s but paternalistic by the 1970s. Joyce was less keen on Ingaret, a Jungian analyst, as she disapproved of both psychoanalysis and spiritualism. She would have been horrified if she had known, as many of his friends did, that Laurens had been conducting an extra-marital affair for many years and often had flings with young women. Reggie only ever expressed opinions in private and was always unfailingly polite to Laurens, and indeed to everyone.

After Reggie had left for his office each morning, Joyce would settle down to writing monologues, talks or letters, but after a few hours on her own she needed company. Almost every day somebody was invited to a meal, or she met friends in a restaurant. If her close friends were away, then others would do. She had discovered during her ENSA war work that she could find something interesting, even likeable, in most people. 'You can get on with anybody, even if you don't like them,' she said. 'You can find something good in absolutely everybody – whatever they are like. There's a lovely line I heard in North Carolina about an old man – "He never met a stranger." If you never meet a stranger, then nobody is ever dull. The most interesting and richly contented people I have met all had one thing in common: a never-ending sense of discovery and wonder.'

Joyce loved eating and thought she was a good cook, though her range of recipes was limited. She only began to teach herself to cook after the war, making her very first, rather soggy, cake at the age of thirty-seven after she tripped on the stairs and broke the week's ration of eggs. A week later she embarked on her first pastry, for jam tarts – but did not know that the jam has to be added *after* cooking, so they were rather chewy. During food-rationing, Joyce invented recipes such as sliced potatoes, onion and ham cooked in condensed milk.

Her housekeeper did most of the cooking. When Mrs Gabe remarried and retired in 1964, her sister-in-law, Mrs Agos, took over and stayed for over twenty years. Joyce liked meals to be cooked in advance and her favourites were mutton chops, beef casserole or cold chicken in curry sauce. She usually made the salads – apples and celery, and cucumber soaked in milk, were two favourites. She loved her electric blender and was very proud of her soups, such as spinach and bacon. Her ambition was to write a book of soup recipes and she frequently described food in her letters. 'We just ate a delicious ome-lette and two pieces of toast, followed by my special grapes in orange juice,' or 'R and I consumed two sausage rolls and a glass of water.' She shared recipes with friends, sometimes with drawings to show how, for example, to pat a hamburger into the right shape. Joyce liked quite bland food and never ate oysters, curries, tripe or crystal-lised ginger.

Joyce was terrified of boredom, which was to her an active sin. 'Anyone who has time to be bored, unless they are ill, deserves spank-ing,' she wrote in 1951. 'I don't know what it is to be bored. Even if I find myself next to somebody who is boring, I play a game where I give them marks out of ten for how boring they can be.' She never gave herself the time to risk boredom. On trains she always talked to her fellow-passengers. Walks in the countryside were filled with flower identification and counting the number of bird species seen. While listening to the radio she made tapestry cushions and when watching television she would sketch the people on the screen. Even her spiritual life was active – reading Mary Baker Eddy and the Bible and 'working on' problems through prayer. At the end of each day, she filled her diary with the day's events, words tightly crammed to the bottom of the page – empty spaces implied she had not kept busy.

Even Joyce's extraordinary output of letters may have been to prevent boredom. Her friendship with Virginia would have survived perfectly well without writing such detailed letters, which included the colour of the curtains, the weather and what everyone was wearing. Virginia did point out that Joyce never commented on *her* letters but only related what she herself was up to. She would write over a dozen letters in bed before breakfast and never went out without paper, stamps and envelopes in her handbag.

She did not forget her family. Every week she visited Reggie's mother Hilda until she died at the age of eighty-six, and she kept an eye on her Aunt Pamela Phipps, who lived across the square. Many relations have commented how Joyce made sure that the family kept in touch, always going to weddings or staying with them for week-ends. But it was no accident that the Grenfells had no spare room – Joyce liked to see friends and family for meals and feared that if they had a spare room they would be inundated with overnight visitors. Occasionally when Reggie was away she invited Christian Scientists to stay, but only very quiet ones.

Holidays and weekends away were taken in hotels or with friends, rarely on their own in empty houses. They appreciated having friends living in beautiful places and every year went to the Lake District, to the Hart-Davises in the Yorkshire Dales, and to Suffolk. After their retirement they considered buying a house in the country and looked at some around Aldeburgh, but decided that not owning a house gave them more freedom and the chance to spend time with friends. Joyce was not impressed if they were taken out to dinner: 'It is the hosts we want to see, not their pals.'

As she grew older, Joyce preferred the company of ordinary people, possibly because she liked to be the centre of attention. She often commented how boring she found many famous people. A few, such as Cleo Laine and Johnny Dankworth, met her criteria of 'loving kindness, humour and integrity'.

The Dankworths ran a centre in their Buckinghamshire village where music of all kinds was taught and performed. Joyce was a keen supporter of the Wavendon Allmusic Plan and did several concerts for them. Every summer they held a fête and one year Cleo Laine had just pinned prices to a pile of old clothes when the front door opened.

A bright and cheerful voice called out, 'Coooeee!! Anyone at home? I'm here!!' Joyce Grenfell had arrived to lend a hand. When she saw my marked prices, she realised that here was someone who didn't know what a charity garden fête was about, and she immediately set about re-pricing everything. I was quite happy for Joyce to be a bossy-boots, and to let her preside over the hugely successful sale in the tent. If things were not moving she gave the crowd a shove, with a jolly pep talk in the style of St Trinians.

One of Joyce's more unusual friendships was with Katharine Moore, who lived in Kent. They wrote to each other regularly from 1957 and decided early on in their pen-friendship not to meet but to have an 'invisible friendship'.

'It is a unique relationship, and somehow being confined to paper makes it free-er,' wrote Katharine to Joyce. 'It is rather amusing that I could be quite near to you or see you at a concert and you wouldn't know it was me. I like that, it makes me feel invisible, which I always thought would be great fun.'

'I saw Joyce on stage several times,' she remembered, 'and I could have met her at any time backstage or at her home, but I decided that I wanted to keep the relationship clear and simple, untarnished by who we were in the outside world. When we wrote to each other we were free to be Katharine and Joyce.' As a result, they trusted each other completely and told each other things they didn't even share with their closest friends. For example, at Aldeburgh in 1965 Joyce confessed to feeling jealous of someone else's skills. She wrote how surprised she was and that she didn't like it because she expected to be able to control her feelings.

Katharine had received the education that Joyce always wished for. During the First World War she had been a Suffragette and in 1921 was one of the first women to graduate from Oxford University. After Oxford, she did social work in the East End and then taught

English literature and wrote books of criticism and short stories. Joyce was flattered to be able to discuss these with Katharine and delighted when asked to write the introduction to Katharine's book on women theologians, *She for God*. She frequently quoted from Katharine's anthology *The Spirit of Tolerance* and was especially fond of William Blake's 'The man who never alters his opinion is like standing water and breeds reptiles of the mind.'

'We share a taste for the eternal pleasures of reading, seasons, music, sounds and sights,' wrote Joyce in her autobiography, 'and people who pleasantly surprise us by their diversity. We seem to agree on some fundamental ideas and are interested in each other's lives.' Like Joyce, Katharine was happily married and, as a Quaker, had a strong religious faith. When her husband died suddenly, Joyce wrote with sympathy and compassion by return of post. 'I felt her warmth, which came through even though we were only pen friends.' The last time that Katharine wrote to Joyce, in September 1979, she decided that Joyce should know what she looked like, and she included a photo of herself.

With her firm Christian beliefs and no children of her own, Joyce was a popular choice as a godmother. She chose her godchildren carefully: she had to know the parents well enough to feel there was already a bond and she did not want so many that she lost count. Charlotte Leigh's daughter, Nancy Seymour, was her first (in 1941), followed by Celia Johnson's second daughter, Lucy. Daphne Oxenford's first daughter, Sophie Marshall, was the same age as Joyce's niece Sally, so Joyce often bought two of the same garment, such as a good winter coat. Christmas presents were always sensible – woollen tights, jerseys from Marks & Spencer (so they could be changed if the wrong size) or book tokens. When giving a radio talk to an imaginary god-daughter, who happened to be the same shape and personality as herself, she warned her not to play tennis in shorts. 'It may frighten your opponent into losing but that is taking an unfair advantage'.

On at least one occasion, Joyce took on a whole family as her friends. She first met the writer Verily Anderson when she was performing in *Penny Plain* in 1951. Verily interviewed her at St Martin's Theatre for the Girls' Friendly Society's magazine. 'Such a nice plump young woman [of thirty-six] with three young children and a fourth impending. She's a vicar's daughter and very refreshingly simple and nice,' Joyce wrote in her diary. The 'fourth impending' was Janie, the author of this book, born six months later. In 1957 Verily's husband died, leaving her to cope with four daughters and a son, aged three to fourteen. She supported the family by writing but during the big freeze of 1962 she fell ill. 'I was in hospital in Chelsea and Joyce would come in non-visiting hours. In those days not everybody had television so she wasn't so frequently recognised. The other patients asked me, "Why do you think it is that when your friend comes in we all feel better?"'

When Verily asked Joyce she said, 'Oh, it's not me, personally I can do nothing. But spiritually, perhaps one can convey some of one's own sense of what is real. You are a spiritual idea in the Mind of God and nothing can ever touch or harm this perfect concept. You are safe in the continuity of good, which is God.'

'Then she told me about being a Christian Scientist,' said Verily, 'She had never mentioned it before, and she didn't press it, she lived it. I not only felt better but I got better too.'

Joyce wrote to Katharine Moore:

> We are running a sort of 'meals on wheels' from here for a friend, widowed and mother of five, who is in hospital. My housekeeper, who is an expansive loving character, has embraced the situation and makes large casseroles ready for reheating and they are delivered at intervals. The idea was to spend January and February writing new material but the Lord has found other uses for my time and quite genuinely I'm very grateful to be free enough to be a bit useful.

Eddie, Alex and I were still at school; Marian, the oldest, was an art student; and Rachel, aged nineteen, was writing a book and looking after her younger siblings.

'Joyce dropped in like an unexpected angel,' remembers Rachel.

Unlike most people in London that winter, she didn't say, 'Isn't the weather awful? When will it end? Your poor mother looks worse.' She popped on a pair of pink rubber gloves and gave our kitchen bin a quick wipe-out. 'You'll find, Rachel, that a little drop of Jeyes every day keeps it nice.' The casseroles she left steaming on our doorstep was our introduction to Hungarian goulash with red pickled cabbage. Joyce managed to point out, without actually saying so, that we weren't homeless, frozen or dying but were in fact quite a healthy, happy family.

Joyce always arrived at our house looking elegant, in a Chanel-style suit with a silk blouse tied in a bow. When she bent down to kiss you, she smelled fresh and soapy and never had that cloying, over-powdered and perfumed smell that children dread. Her skin was as soft as kid gloves. The only clue to her theatrical background was her eyeliner, unusual in a woman her age. Her silky hair was also unique – short and curly on top, with a neat bun at the back. She once told me that when it was loose she could sit on it. I longed for the pins to fall out so I could see it tumble down her back.

Carley Robinson was over from America at the time. 'Joyce let slip that she had been housekeeping for a family of several children whose mother had had to go to hospital. She skimmed over this story in a way that indicated she had not meant me to know.' When Verily wrote about that winter in her book *Scrambled Eggs for Christmas*, Joyce insisted on being renamed 'Kate'.

Once my mother recovered, Joyce provided a car to help her research her next book, a history of her ancestors in Norfolk. We really needed to move to Norfolk, but there was no money, so Joyce suggested that if Verily found a suitable house she and Reggie would buy it. We moved into Sally Bean's, a flint cottage near Cromer, at Easter 1967. We children were not supposed to know who had bought it, but when Joyce and Reggie drove up to see us the next day, we knew it must be them. Why else would they come all the way from London just for tea? They brought curtains, and clothes that we could remake into new outfits. But first, when nobody was around, my sister Alex and I had to try on the Victor Stiebel stage gowns, with their stiff petticoats and yards of silk in the gathered skirts. Alex put on a lime-green one, and I took the magenta pink and stuffed the boned corset with socks. We climbed up into a flowering laburnum tree in the garden and marvelled at the clashing of the vulgar colours. The next day they were converted into sofa covers and mini-skirts.

Other additions to our new home included the pair of bookshelves that Nancy Astor had bought for Parr's in 1936.

Three weeks after I married in 1971, my mother also acquired a new husband, the architect Paul Paget. Joyce was the maid of honour at their wedding in St Bartholomew the Great, Smithfield, and Paul's neighbour and friend John Betjeman was best man. The bride wore a white spotted dress from Joyce's wardrobe. Joyce was taller and thinner than Verily but, as she said, 'Your width takes up the length.'

A few months later Joyce had a turn-out of drawers and sent me a Harrods box of 'treasures' – scraps from her couture clothes, gold-edged table napkins, lace hankies and velvet ribbons. It was the perfect present and I recycled much of it back to Joyce as patchwork cushions. The cheques my mother received for car repairs and gas bills, which came out of Joyce's earnings from films, radio and television, were invaluable at the time, but it was the frocks and curtains that have lived on.

Like many Britons, Joyce thought of the Royal Family as friends; but, unlike most citizens, she actually met them. Reggie's niece and his sister both worked for the Royal Family and Joyce was torn between protecting their privacy and wanting to share with friends the gossip they told her. In 1960 she was thrilled to be invited to *the* wedding of the year, between Princess Margaret and Anthony Armstrong-Jones in Westminster Abbey. She had a green chiffon outfit designed by Victor Stiebel, who had also made the princess's going-away outfit.

In 1972 Joyce and Reggie were staying in Virginia's flat in the home of their childhood friend, Rachel Bowes-Lyon, in Hertfordshire. The Queen Mother had spent her childhood there and came for a weekend. 'She is easy and friendly but it meant a lot of conversation as opposed to just talking,' commented Joyce. A week later they were bidden to lunch at Clarence House with Noël Coward, Celia Johnson, Princess Margaret and Princess Alexandra. The Queen Mother, in lilac silk organza, welcomed them, early as ever. 'I do hope you don't mind a picnic,' she said. The picnic table was laid with damask linen, Crown Derby china and carnations, under two giant plane trees. Three courses were served by red-coated footmen, overseen by butlers in black.

– 20 –

Opposite the Grenfells' flat in the King's Road was a pub, the Nelson. Joyce couldn't bear the shouting and fighting that spilled out of it: she found all drunkenness 'inexcusable and boring'. By 1956 she was also feeling ashamed of bringing friends up the three flights of narrow stairs to a flat over a sweetshop. They had already disposed of St Leonard's Terrace, so she and Reggie started to look for somewhere else to live. It had to be easy to manage, within walking distance of King's Road and either on the ground floor or equipped with a lift. The Borough Surveyor of Chelsea had been a friend of Paul's and suggested Elm Park Gardens, off Fulham Road, where the council was converting large Victorian houses into modern flats. Since her childhood, Joyce had hated this yellow-brick square with its uninteresting, high, flat walls. Inside, however, the conversions were ideal for their purposes and they took out a long lease on a top-floor flat. Joyce described it to her Aunt Nancy: 'The outside is hideous but inside it is exactly what we want – on two floors, central heating, lift and very quiet.' Her cousin Elizabeth Winn organised the decoration and Reggie arranged for Harrods to move their piano to the attic of their new home. Joyce wrote to Daphne Oxenford in January 1957: 'We are mad about our lovely new nest – oh the peace, oh the warmth, oh the *prettiness*.'

As a child, I remember a visit to the Grenfells as both daunting and exciting. You rang the street doorbell and a lilting voice said, 'Come in' out of a grille. You pushed the heavy front door open into a plain corridor leading to a tiny lift. Reggie would come down in it, and then run up the three flights of stairs to meet you at the top. Joyce would be standing outside her front door to welcome you in. The artist John Ward remembers, 'She always had a warm welcome – she didn't step back, she stepped forward to greet you.'

Off the passage to the left was the sitting-room – bright with Regency-striped wallpaper and large windows overlooking the tennis courts and plane trees of the square. Under the black-framed window was her grandmother's two-tiered round table, covered in tiny vases of flowers.

On the right was a sideboard with the latest copies of the *Listener*, the *New Yorker* and *The Times*, and above them the Sargent portrait of Joyce's grandmother. Two large, pale sofas lined the walls and at the end of the room was a fireplace with bookshelves on either side. On the floor were *gros point* tapestry rugs designed and made by Joyce. Next door was the dining-room, just large enough to seat a dozen, and opposite was a small kitchen with a window box. The walls leading to Joyce's bedroom were covered in photos of herself with theatre colleagues. Beside her bed was a phone with a special gadget for hooking it over the shoulder, so that she could have long talks with Virginia. In 1954 Joyce had described her idea of comfort in *Housewife* magazine: warmth, plenty of hot water all the year round, no draughts, no overhead lighting; and pictures, but no books or magazines, in the bathroom. This new bathroom was bright spring green, with blue and white towelling curtains and bird prints. Up a narrow staircase was a second, smaller bathroom, used as a laundry, and beside that was Joyce's study, decorated in an early American wallpaper of small roses and leaves, with a green carpet and built-in cupboards for her music, scripts and accumulated letters. Against one wall was the upright piano and in the corner a rocking-chair, sometimes used as a stage prop. From her large desk, Joyce could see the top of a plane tree and plenty of sky. At long last she had a room of her own, where she could leave her typewriter and papers undisturbed. Reggie's bedroom was next door. From now on they slept in separate rooms unless staying with friends because Joyce said that he snored. He hadn't expected this arrangement, but he put up with it.

Elm Park Gardens was a home intended to last, and moving there was a final acceptance of the Grenfells' childless state. Although it made her sad, Joyce felt she would not have been a very good mother: she was too inflexible about her very high standards. Parenthood would probably have rubbed off those traits, but then it would also have made her into a different person. At fifty, she wrote to Katharine Moore, 'Not having children was a sadness when we were young, then one got used to it, now I am almost grateful for there have been many compensations: our particular companionship over and above love, and that as well; and the need to canalise the various little talents that I'd played with as a child. I must say I would like to have grand children.' Among the press cuttings she saved was an article from *The Times* of 1958 about the joys of looking after a small grand-daughter.

'I envy those who live without clutter,' wrote Joyce, 'whose living rooms are spacious without books under the table, or pile ups of magazines, not yet read; end tables busy with letters for answering; photographs waiting to go into albums and more books due for reading, kept handy.' Joyce always employed a housekeeper, so she didn't in fact have to worry much about clutter, and the new flat was always neat and tidy. Many people were surprised that the Grenfells did not have a larger home, but Joyce was relieved not to have inherited a large house or castle. 'I'm too selfish to struggle with dry-rot,' she said. 'I want a warm, self-contained flat with an electric fire, and the presence of my husband of whom I am very fond. I don't want any possessions. I have some pretty things, but they aren't that important.'

As soon as they were settled in, Joyce began work planning her first truly solo show. Laurier Lister directed *Joyce Grenfell at Home*, which toured North America before opening at the Lyric, Hammersmith, in September 1957. Eighteen years since her 'overnight success' in the *Little Revue*, Joyce could now hold an audience entranced for a whole evening.

'My word, my word,' Mary Potter wrote.

I have been meaning to write to you for days. I think you are truly wonderful. I had far more enjoyment from your evening than any from Ruth Draper. With her I had a feeling of *one* person, but with you I was left remembering everybody you made. Such is your art, that I still feel a little uncomfortable in being stuck up at the top of the Big Wheel with Shirls' Girlfriend and the Teddy boy! I felt as if you had given me a lot of lovely presents.

Nine years earlier, during the run of *Tuppence Coloured*, Stewart Perowne saw Ruth Draper going to see Joyce in her dressing-room at the Lyric and commented, 'I have witnessed the Changing of the Guard.' Now, Ruth Draper had just died in New York, on the penultimate day of 1956. Joyce had grown up watching her performances and there were striking similarities between their careers. Both women performed in private drawing-rooms for many years before appearing on stage, and both preferred to hold the stage alone. Both made their audiences use their imaginations rather than have theatre sets. Both had stamina and ambition, though Draper's force of personality was often stronger than Joyce's. Both based their characters on observation but never impersonated actual people. Joyce's *Lally Tullet* owes something to Draper's *On a Porch in a Maine Coast Village*. But whereas Draper's German Governess constantly harangues her young charges, one of whom has a guinea pig in his pocket, the Nursery School Teacher appeals to her children's better nature. Many people commented that Draper's work was like a large oil painting compared to Joyce's detailed watercolours. Draper's monologues were much longer than Joyce's, lasting up to fifty minutes each. She often portrayed several characters in one sketch and summoned up another dozen but there was little warmth in her characters. Her portraits were impressive in their accuracy but, unlike Joyce's, were rarely likeable.

To publicise her show, Joyce needed new photographs. Noël Coward recommended Tony Armstrong-Jones, later married to Princess Margaret, who was beginning to make a name for himself. Joyce found him 'amusing and Bohemian. Always late for everything but spontaneous and creative.'

'Joyce was unique to work with,' he recalls.

> I was young and inexperienced and she went out of her way to let me take lots of photos. She didn't mind how long we took to get it right. She was a real professional, and never hurried me. She was very adaptable – could be beautiful one minute and then pull funny faces the next. She wasn't afraid to look silly. She never complained when during the development of the photos I distorted her face to make it even longer.

The photos were a success and appeared in *Queen*, *Harper's Bazaar*, the *Tatler* and *Everybody's Weekly*. In 1939 *The Sketch* had dedicated a page to photos of Joyce in various poses of absurdity, and eighteen years later it repeated the compliment with a page of Armstrong-Jones's more bizarre portraits of her.

Joyce Grenfell at Home established the pattern of solo performance with piano accompaniment that continued unchanged until her retirement. With no sets, no dancers and no orchestra, the simple format was adaptable, cheap and reliable: perfect for maintaining the exacting standards she set herself. William Blezard was an ideal accompanist: talented yet self-effacing, he never tried to upstage her. She often had to fight to get him credit and complained if his name was not on the posters or he was omitted from reviews. As Dick produced less and less, so William took his place and by 1965 was composing all Joyce's music. She repaid him not only with generous fees and bonuses but also an annual trip to Aldeburgh Music Festival with his wife Joan. His only failing was his hair – it was too long for Joyce's taste and she sent him off to Reggie's barber, Mr Trumper.

Like Reggie, William was a patient man and he learned to cope with Joyce's idiosyncrasies.

She was always very punctual – she would insist that we met at the airport or railway station hours before it was necessary. I knew I would always be met with a happy mood when I got into the theatre for our warm-up. Except for one occasion when we were playing Manchester Opera House, and I thought we were to start at eight. I strolled along to the theatre with fifteen minutes to go, and, to my horror, I heard the orchestra playing the overture without me! The show had started at seven-thirty. I dashed into the pit just in time to bring the overture to a close. Joyce glanced down at me, and raised one eyebrow. Afterwards all she said was, 'You'll never do that again, Bill.' I didn't.

During the 1960s we went three times to Australia, twice to New Zealand and the United States and Canada, and once to Singapore, Hong Kong, and Switzerland. Everything went marvelously because Joyce was so well organised and worked everything out to the last detail. She called herself 'Planny Anny'.

William could play any tune by ear and arrange in any key.

As a break from rehearsing her songs, we used to improvise. We were especially good at fake Debussy and Joyce had a good line in mock-Schubert. Joyce said there was no greater pleasure than improvising a song, gliding from one key to another. Her voice was very sweet, with a large range. It tended to be a bit flat if she didn't concentrate. The odd thing was that if she was acting, say, an opera singer, she could manage higher notes than if she was singing 'straight'.

Joyce's favourite song was *Stately as a Galleon* – based on her experience that there were never enough gentlemen at parties. As she grew older, she stopped performing action songs because they made her so out of breath. One of the first to go was *What Shall I Wear?* in which, as a large fairy, she leaped on and off tussocks of grass while she dressed herself in cobwebs, bumblebee buttons, foxglove gloves and velvet moss. She pretended to be out of breath by the end to cover the fact that she really was.

By 1960, when Harold Holt Ltd arranged a British tour of *Meet Joyce Grenfell*, Joyce realised that she needed her own stage manager – someone who could set up the stage, do the lighting, look after her costumes and drive a van. Diana Lyddon, who had been the first assistant stage manager on *The Mousetrap*, heard about it through the grapevine and applied for the job. Joyce liked her immensely: ten years younger than Joyce, she replaced Viola as the female colleague who could give her admiration and not steal the limelight.

'We both went through life assuming that if things were well planned then they would go right,' remembers Diana. 'And if things went wrong, then they could be sorted out without a fuss.' Their first job together was a short tour of the Midlands. Diana had an old Bedford van in which she carried the lighting equipment, props and a rack for the stage dresses.

The Victor Stiebel dresses were so big they took up half the van! In her early solo tours she had less confidence and kept on changing frocks throughout each show. I had to iron them all before the show, as well as set up the lighting. Eventually the Bedford died and I needed a new car, and Joyce paid for half of it. She said it was part of her business expenses. She was the most awful back-seat driver – sometimes I got the feeling she was at the wheel and not me! She drove even Reggie mad. Mind you, it was even worse being driven by her. She drove a car as if she was still learning. It was easier when she sat in the back doing the *Times* crossword.

Diana had assumed that Harold Holt Ltd was the backer and at first found it difficult asking Joyce for expenses. 'But of course Joyce paid up readily and after that Reggie gave me a large float.'

They started by doing a show in a different town every night but it was too much for everyone, and on future tours they took a day's break in between. Joyce travelled with photographs of her loved ones and a portable radio, and arranged local wild flowers in the tooth-mug. After lunch she was very strict about going to bed, not to sleep but to lie on her back, going through her words for that evening.

Joyce and Diana met at the venue at six to go through the lighting cues. Diana kept a careful record of the order of every show and the timing of every sketch and song, the lighting arrangements, the quality of the piano, the frocks worn, the temperature of the auditorium and the size and response of the audience. The duration of a show varied by ten minutes, depending on the length of the applause. Joyce used the information when returning to the same place, so that, although some numbers might be repeated, new ones were always introduced and the order changed.

Diana saw Joyce's approach become simpler over the thirteen years they worked together.

In her early career she had special costumes for each sketch and sometimes quite elaborate props. But gradually she realised that, as with radio, the audience didn't need props and costumes – her voice would take them to the character. But it was also her facial expression and body language that portrayed the character. With apparent ease, she persuaded her audience to suspend disbelief and join her in a nursery school, a high-rise flat or a mansion.

Watching her monologues on video without the sound, you can still tell which sketch it is from her facial expression.

'They still thought of her as an amateur because she *appeared* so effortless. What they didn't know was the amount of effort and rehearsing that went into each performance. They really thought that she just wandered onto the stage and told a few stories.'

Victor Stiebel continued to design her stage dresses up to 1963, by which time couture clothing was no longer fashionable and he was suffering multiple sclerosis. His friends bought from him simply to keep him going: in March of that year, Virginia not only ordered several suits she did not want, but also paid the wages of his employees until the business was closed down. Victor passed his remaining customers on to the designer Clive Evans, who recalls:

Miss Grenfell had a very clear idea of exactly what she wanted. The dresses had a close-fitting bodice with a face-framing collar, which she turned up or down according to the character she was performing. If she was playing a frumpy person, she would pull on an old felt hat, alter her body shape and the new character was instantly achieved.

Her figure was what the French call a 'belle poitrine': a neat, small waist, above fuller hips. She had a typically 'English' complexion and colouring and wore very little make-up. Her hair was always up, a soft, undyed brown with a trace of silver. She had large, expressive blue eyes and a long neck, which gave her an aristocratic style and beauty.

Joyce was one of the first entertainers to use a radio microphone, and her dresses were made with special pockets for the chunky batteries. But it amplified the rustle of her frocks, so the fabric had to be chosen carefully and in some places it picked up the police or the local radio station.

'Once we went to choose fabrics at Liberty's,' said Clive Evans.

I was about to launch a new collection and Miss Grenfell sensed that I had a lot on my mind. In the lift she turned to me and said, 'Whenever you are feeling in a flap, just remember that *you* are quite still, like a rock, and that it is *everyone else* who is rushing around you.' I still use that wisdom. I'm sure Miss Grenfell followed her own advice, as she always appeared calm and unhurried. She was friendly and interested in other people, but there was a certain barrier which discouraged over-familiarity. One felt she would not suffer fools gladly. She always took the trouble to send postcards of appreciation to Mrs Pryce, our fitter, and Doreen who made the clothes, so of course they were devoted to her.

The Haymarket Theatre had a rule that only the name of a show and never the actors could be up in lights on the front and sides of the portico. In 1962 Reggie suggested they call the show they were mounting there simply *Joyce Grenfell*, and thus she became the first performer whose name illuminated Haymarket from Piccadilly to Pall Mall.

I was ten when I was taken to see Joyce at the Haymarket. I knew her as an old family friend, and had no idea she was famous until I looked down from the circle and saw the packed theatre and heard the applause as she walked onto the stage. It seemed enormous and quite empty, but she filled it with imaginary people. Backstage in her large dressing-room she was surrounded by huge bunches of red gladioli. I expected to find her reclining on a *chaise longue*, but she stood to greet us and remained standing throughout our visit. Joyce felt a sense of let-down if no one came round after a show, but she liked to get home to bed early: standing was one of her 'tricks' to make sure nobody stayed too long. If she was on tour, she went straight back to her hotel, had a bath and then ate a picnic in bed of cheese, chocolate, apple and cake. She was a good sleeper and rarely had nightmares.

Joyce loved being in the limelight and at first she appeared in any film offered. The early 1950s had been the heyday of British film-making, but as the offers started to be limited to *Carry On* films, she turned them all down. When, in 1963, she was asked to Hollywood to make *The Americanisation of Emily*, starring Julie Andrews and James Coburn, she agreed. She was in Australia at the time, so she flew home via California, inviting herself to stay with film script-writer Leonard Gershe in Beverly Hills. Joyce was amazed by Leonard's heated swimming-pool and that his garage door and colour television were operated with 'a small device in the hands – no wires!'. She told Leonard about a play she had seen on Broadway which contained too much swearing and sex for her taste.

'But real life is like that, you have to accept it,' said Gershe.

'Diarrhoea is real life,' she replied. 'But I don't pay thirty dollars to go and see diarrhoea.'

A week of rehearsals was followed by two weeks of filming. *The Americanisation of Emily* was set in wartime England and Joyce played Julie Andrews's tweedy mother, Mrs Barham, who is so shocked by the deaths of her son and son-in-law that she pretends nothing has happened. Compared to her own more subtle attitude to death, Joyce found this 'bitter and savage – about false standards of heroism'. She thought the story strong, but was not impressed by the scriptwriter's idea of a British woman, so she rewrote her lines.

The Hollywood designers did not meet her standards either. The set of an upper-middle-class London home in 1944 would not do. 'Straight Balham *circa* 1925,' declared Joyce. There wasn't time to rebuild it, but they did remove the lace doilies, fairground china statuettes and aspidistra. She was somewhat alarmed by the familiarity of the film crew, especially when the chief cameramen put his arm around her. She watched Julie Andrews and James Garner doing a love scene in bed and couldn't imagine how they managed it in front of so many people. She got on well with Julie Andrews, whom she had met before in New York, and between takes they sat on a sofa singing close harmonies.

Arthur Hiller, the director, recalls working with her. 'Unlike many actors, Joyce was a pleasure to direct. She wanted me to go over her emotions with her so that she would do justice to this three-dimensional character, particularly in one terrific scene where she comes to face the reality of war and death as against the glory.'

Joyce had to cry real tears and found the process of dramatic acting harrowing and exhausting, but she was pleased to play a character with some depth instead of the usual ninnies. By the end of November her scenes were filmed. Leonard remembers the last day of her stay only too well:

After breakfast, Joyce started packing. I sat in her room, chatting and giggling with her as she folded her clothing. It was about eleven o'clock in the morning when the phone rang. It was the actor Clifton Webb, sounding hysterical.

'Are you watching television?' he kept asking. I asked why he thought I'd be watching television in the morning. 'The President has been shot!' he screamed. Joyce and I watched in horror as Walter Cronkite announced that Kennedy had just died. Now, Patricia Lawford, Kennedy's sister, and her husband, Peter, were close friends of mine and lived near by. I wanted to be with them, but was this the appropriate thing to do? There was no precedent for this.

He tried phoning, but the number was always engaged. Joyce went on with her packing, saying nothing.

Finally, she told me, 'Leonard, go out there.' I explained there might be secret-service men everywhere. I couldn't just drop in. 'You must go to Pat,' said Joyce, 'You can leave your name. At least she will know that you wanted to see her.' Reluctantly, I drove out to Santa Monica. The street had been roped off but when I gave the cop my name, he said, 'Yes, you're expected.' Expected! If it had not been for Joyce, I would never have gone and they would have minded. This was just one of life's little messages that Joyce taught me.

By the mid-1960s she turned down nearly all the films offered. To the disappointment of her American agent, Lionel Larner, she rejected, among others, *My Beautiful Career*, Norman Jewison's *The Russians Are Coming* and *The Age of Consent* starring James Mason. She disliked acting other people's scripts and feeling out of control. The last of her twenty-five films was *The Yellow Rolls-Royce*, made in 1964 and starring Omar Sharif and Ingrid Bergman. By a strange coincidence, some of the scenes were shot at Cliveden, and Joyce played a Virginian lady called Hortense Astor. She had one good line: 'Why are those Arabs looking at you like that?' Bergman asked. Joyce, her straight-backed travelling companion, replied in a Southern drawl, 'Lust.'

– 21 –

O<small>F JOYCE'S MANY</small> qualities, the most striking was her extraordinary gift for observation of people: their voices, characters and facial expressions. Her imagination was fired by this and, as she freely admitted, she wrote only from her own experience: Women's Institute meetings, the National Gallery canteen, the ferry boats of Sydney. Joyce composed and wrote over a hundred different personalities. All but one of these were white and female, and nearly all were middle-aged – whether she was twenty-nine or fifty-nine when she wrote them. Every single one had spirit, including her only male character, a black South African. She never despised her characters, because they were an element of herself: 'I know an awful lot about those silly women I do. All those people are me,' she said. 'My close friends say, "You sound just like one of your own monologues." That reduces one to size.' At fifty-seven she wrote *Unsuitable*, a song about a 'hat and gloves and pearls type' woman who had a slight problem: 'I go jazzy when I hear the beat, I swing and sway in a groovy way.' Joyce was portraying herself – a well-dressed woman on the outside, with a love for dancing and rhythm on the inside.

'Apart from physical disabilities, anyone is fair game. Whether rich or poor, fat or thin, refined or vulgar, educated or uneducated, silly or sensible. But you have to have compassion with your satire. I hope it comes out with an affectionate bite. I've never done anybody I hated.' What amused her were snobbery, lack of humour and pomposity. The women in *Opera Interval*, *Learn to Loosen* and *Artist's Room* are all very idiotic, but Joyce sympathised with their weaknesses, and then painted them with the detailed care of a miniaturist.

'One of the miracles of Joyce's talent,' wrote Virginia, 'is that she is able to laugh at the human predicament without being unkind. A walking observatory-cum-radar-station – no one within a radius of five miles is safe from her ear and eye – she is aware that there is a lot that is ridiculous, indeed unattractive, in her fellow-men, but because she is able to look at them from the heart, her caricatures are never cruel.'

'I entertain because I love it,' said Joyce, 'and it takes me all over the world and I get paid for doing what comes naturally. It's not meant to be patronising, nor superior. People all talk differently, and think differently, and that's what is so fascinating. It is this *differentness*, whether cockney or county or colonial, that is so enjoyable. It's not that some people are worth less for being different.'

Many of her characters and stories began with a chance remark overheard. Joyce collected eavesdroppings like other people collect stamps. 'An overheard that rings the bell arrives whole and unexpected, without a lead-in or a follow-on to blur its crystalline perfection,' she wrote. In a shop she heard a woman tell her friend, 'He never noticed anything funny about her, except she liked to play the piano nude.'

The telephone was a wonderful invention for use in monologues – as in a real overheard telephone conversation, the audience can only guess what is said on the other end, sometimes incorrectly. She loved dropping into a conversation between strangers, being left wondering for ever what it was about, such as 'I said to her, Gladys, you'll never hold with a string of beads.' Joyce had rules about eavesdropping – she never let on that she was doing it, and never listened to people she knew in case she heard something she shouldn't.

'Watching people is like birdwatching – you have to do it skilfully and quietly, and not be seen doing it,' she said. Buses were a rich source, and she often stayed on far longer than she had planned. One day on her way from Chelsea to Piccadilly she travelled all the way to Bloomsbury in order to hear more about the life of Toulouse-Lautrec. The woman in front's misunderstanding of his life ended with, 'He came from a lovely family. Such a pity.'

While on a bus in Glasgow in 1951, Joyce overheard two women.
'Has Mary's come yet?'
'Aye.'
'What's she crying it?'
'Hazel.'

'Hazel? What a shame. There's a saint for every day of the bloody month and she has to call it after a nut.'

Joyce took infinite pains to make her work sound as if it was achieved with no effort. The first stage of a new monologue was finding a new character, and then her geographical location. Joyce would talk to herself in a new voice around her flat until the voice took over and said the sort of things that the character would say. 'I never write anything down until the voice is there. I have to know the person so well that I know exactly what their bedroom looks like,' she said. She also had to know the kind of house they lived in, how it was decorated and the style of their dressing-table. She did not talk about a new monologue 'until it has its own legs and can walk'. Even in her diary she only wrote, 'thought of a new idea in church today, not sure if it will work'. She never suffered from writer's block once she realised that 'You can't come to the end of ideas, they're eternal. They're everywhere! They're around, in the air, spinning, to be gathered! You've just got to be open to them. The sky's the limit and you've got the world by its tail.'

Once the character was created, she began to write a story about her. Many drafts later, she would try it out first on Reggie and then on a few close friends. If they reacted well, she would carry on writing and editing until the monologue was a tightly constructed short play. Her longest monologue was less than nine minutes and her shortest was under two. The audience only heard a few minutes of this person's life, but they knew that the rest existed. One of the strengths of her work is not what she put in, but what she left out – the audience knew what she meant, felt pleased for working it out themselves, and often thought they were the *only* person to get the joke. 'They are gems of accurate observation and an uncanny ear that is happily a little tart. There is an air about her English pieces as if Jane Austen were looking admiringly over her shoulder,' wrote Margot Strickland.

Joyce had the ability to be objective about her writing and was never afraid to reject sections or even whole ideas. 'If you were invited to lunch she offered you a drink,' remembers Diana Lyddon.

But she couldn't tell the difference between sherry and whisky and sometimes you got a wine glass full of whisky. After lunch she'd try out something new. Once she asked me about a piece, and I didn't know how to say, 'It's not good enough.' So I said, 'For someone who's written *Lally Tullet* this isn't up to their usual standard.' Joyce cut it immediately. When Bill Blezard heard *Life Story*, about the musician's wife, he suggested she try it in a foreign accent, and it suddenly came alive. When she did *First Flight*, I knew immediately it was a humdinger.

One day she invited Patrick Woodcock to lunch. 'She didn't stop talking throughout lunch, about nothing in particular,' he remembers, 'and I couldn't think why she had asked me. After lunch she said, "Now, I want to try a new monologue out on you." She did, I laughed in all the right places, and then I was shown out. From the moment I arrived until I left I didn't utter a word. It wasn't me she wanted to see, she just needed an audience to bounce off.'

Joyce's monologues sounded so easy to write that they inspired many people to have a go themselves. A Mrs Morgan wrote her a story about a lady at the hairdresser, and then about a Turkish bath. One fan sent her a song which began, 'Woolly boots for baby Jesus'. They rarely sent stamped, addressed envelopes and were often in indecipherable longhand. Joyce always vowed to be tougher in future but couldn't help thanking them politely and suggesting that they perform the work themselves.

Professional writers also wanted to write for her, including Frank Muir, Walter de la Mare and John Betjeman. Sometimes they just had an idea, and expected her to write the script while crediting them. Often their ideas were ones she had already had – drama critic Kenneth Tynan suggested a sketch about a domestic employment agency, eleven years after she had written *Situation Vacant*. They all got the same answer: 'It's very kind of you to think of me, but no thank you, I only perform my own material.'

Only once did Joyce ever sit down and write a monologue straight off. One Saturday in 1965 while Reggie watched sport on television, Joyce took her notebook into the dining-room and began talking to herself in her mother's Virginian accent. Without planning it, out came the story of an old woman in Virginia. 'Lally Tullet,' she wrote, 'is the only thing I've ever written complete and almost entirely untouched in one fell swoop, as it were. I always have to chip and polish and cut and re-write, but this one came whole and surprised me no end! I suppose it comes out of my deep subconscious – the voice and sentence structures, I mean. My mama came from Virginia and used to tell us stories in the vernacular.' The first time she performed *Lally Tullet* in America was at the University of William and Mary in Virginia. The sketch opens with an old Virginian lady saying, 'Lord have mercy, Charlotte, guess who's dead?' To Joyce's amazement, the audience rose to applaud her: the accent was dead on.

Joyce thought improvisation on stage was self-indulgent and rarely worked: an entertainer should be well rehearsed, even if the audiences believed it was spontaneous. Occasionally a new remark might be added, but only to a very well-rehearsed sketch. When she wrote Shirley's Girl Friend describing her meeting with Mr Lewis – "'E said, "'As anyone ever told you you've got provocative eyes?" I saw 'is cuff go in the beet salad but I didn't say anything' – she thought the 'provocative eyes' was the punchline and the 'cuff in the beet salad' was an irrelevant detail. She was surprised to find that it was the cuffs and not the eyes that got the bigger laugh.

Joyce was always nervous before she went on stage but her experience in the war had given her the confidence to entertain in any venue. Faced with five hundred difficult soldiers in Egypt in 1952, she said a prayer and then swept onto the stage and 'just *loved* them into liking me'. Even if they hadn't planned to be loved by Joyce, the Tank Regiment found themselves under her spell.

'Joyce gave the impression of a talented amateur "backing into the limelight",' commented Sheridan Morley,

while really it was all planned hard work. On one level her monologues are charming, but deeper there is a novelist's ability to pin a character down. She was more a psychoanalyst than a satirist. On the surface was this nice Home Counties genteel lady, but underneath there was an outsider, a poor relation who dreads being ignored or patronised. There was an underlying anger in Joyce, a revenge for a world that didn't take women seriously. She was very gracious, but she put the knife in with such extraordinary charm you didn't feel it going in. I think she was much darker than she let on. All her best things were about being lonely: women with deep holes in their hearts.

'When I am doing the people I do in my sketches I really do feel as if I am them,' she said on *Woman's Hour*. 'It is rather like having an ear for music, or red hair – I mean it's no one's fault, I can just do it. Now, I happen to be tall, with a long face, and yet by certain sounds I can create the impression of being small and square. I do have to concentrate and rethink everything absolutely fresh each time. I can't say I recreate it, because that process was done in the early stages. But I do find that I have to re*think* it.'

An actor usually only has one character to sustain for the whole evening, and has the other actors to remind them what to say next. Joyce had only herself to cue from, and had to make a complete change of personality with every sketch. During each show there was a staggering variety in mood: from the laughter of Shirley's Girl Friend to the Nursery School, switching to compassion for the woman with an invalid father and back to the Dutch lady enjoying a cocktail party: 'I sink so nice to say hello and goodbye quick, and to have little sings for eating is so gay.'

Joyce's range of accents was wide. 'Remembering Joyce Grenfell, we sympathise with the chameleon defeated by a tartan scarf,' wrote J. C. Trewin. She could do four different American accents, and her London accents went from broad cockney to 'shopgirl refained', 'just off the suburbs', through Pont Street and into Belgravia. She could only do an Irish accent when she was in Ireland, however. In Manchester in 1954 for *Requests the Pleasure*, she prepared a last-night speech and a local stagehand helped her practise it in Mancunian. At the curtain call, Joyce stepped forward to thank the audience. Instead of the carefully rehearsed piece, out came pure Glaswegian. After that she always made thank-you speeches in her own accent.

In 1961 *Beyond the Fringe* killed traditional revue and, to some, Joyce's work looked dated and too unpolitical. For Joyce, politics was a private subject, like sex or going to the lavatory. While much of the humour of the 1960s was dominated by the atom bomb and world annihilation, Joyce remained optimistic and her characters were concerned with everyday problems such as how to dispose of a dead rabbit or where to find a good spot for a picnic. She adapted her material to the times, but she did not change her style. When Shirley's Girl Friend went to the pantomime in 1964, the orchestra at Cinderella's ball had been replaced by a pop group called The

32. Joyce posing for Victor Stiebel while on holiday in Switzerland in June 1947 with Reggie, Laurier Lister and Max Adrian.

33. Joyce singing
'Oh, Mr du Maurier'
in Noël Coward's revue,
Sigh No More, in 1945.

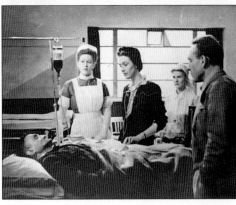

34. Joyce as Dr Barrett in the
1943 film *The Lamp Still Burns*
with Rosamund John
as the nurse.

35. Richard Addinsell and Joyce in New York to meet music publishers, May 1946.

36. Stephen Potter and Joyce improvising a *How* radio programme in the Grenfells' King's Road kitchen, 1948.

37. Nora, Joyce, Wilton Phipps, aged eight, and Tommy at Little Orchard, North Carolina, in 1946.

38. Joyce and her niece Sally Phipps at Little Orchard in 1955, just before Nora died there.

39. Joyce and Tommy, Lang, Mary and Sally Phipps on Long Island, 1963.

40. Daphne Oxenford and Joyce performing *Rainbow Nights* on television in 1956.

41. Joyce writing in her attic study at Elm Park
Gardens in 1957.

42. Joyce telling a story to a nursery school in Oldham, Lancashire, in 1952.

43. George Henry Clews presents Joyce with a bouquet after she opened the fête at Colindale Hospital, Hendon, in 1958.

44. Joyce playing Sergeant Ruby Gates, disguised as Chloe Crawley the gym mistress, in *The Belles of St Trinian's* in 1954, with Alistair Sim as Millicent Fritton, the headmistress.

45. Sergeant Ruby Gates in disguise as translator Ursula Bluette, in *Blue Murder at St Trinian's*, 1957.

46. Athene Seyler and Joyce rehearsing for *Happy is the Bride*, 1957.

47. Film director Roy Boulting between takes of *Happy is the Bride*, listening to Joyce improvising a wedding march on the organ.

48. Reggie and Joyce on holiday, *c.* 1960.

49. Joyce and her new Ford Corsair in Cumbria, *c.* 1965.

50. William Blezard composing a new song for Joyce in a dressing-room, 1967.

51. William playing Chopin during a concert in 1972.

52. Stage
manager Diana
Lyddon ironing
Joyce's frock
while on tour in
America, 1967.

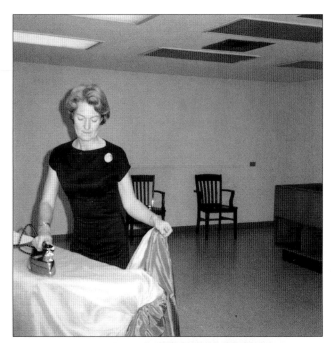

53. Joyce in her
kitchen at Elm
Park Gardens,
c. 1970.

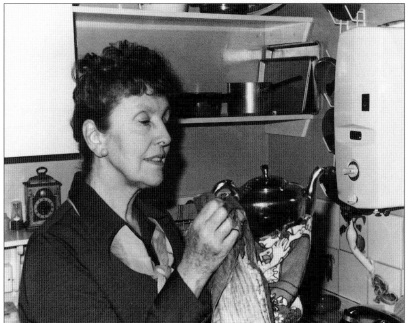

54. Rene Easden serves Joyce tea at Parr's in 1941.

55. Mrs Gabe cleaning silver in the dining-room at Elm Park Gardens, painted by John Ward in 1963.

56. Mrs Agos in the sitting-room in 1979, painted by John Ward.

57. 'The Magic Circle' celebrating Christmas, 1961. Reggie, Dick Addinsell, Virginia Graham, Victor Stiebel and Joyce, taken by Tony Thesiger.

58. The Anderson family spend Christmas Day with the Grenfells, 1962. *Clockwise from left*: Janie in her new frock, Rachel, Clive James, Marian, Joyce, Eddie and Alex.

59. Benjamin Britten, Joyce and Peter Pears at the Red House, Aldeburgh, in June 1964.

60. Verily Anderson, wearing Joyce's frock and shoes, marries Paul Paget in August 1971. Her daughters Rachel, Alex and Marian are behind.

61. Joyce's favourite *Face the Music* team, in 1976. Presenter Joseph Cooper and producer Walter Todds standing, Robin Ray, Joyce and David Attenborough sitting.

62. Joyce signing her auto-biography for Joan and Bert Axell at the Cowans' bookshop in Aldeburgh, watched by Reggie, 10 November 1979.

63. The Grenfells assembled for Joyce and Reggie's golden wedding party in Virginia's flat on 17 November 1979, thirteen days before Joyce died. *From the left:* Reggie, Vera, Joyce, Mary, Frances, Laura, Katie and Harry Grenfell.

64. Joyce pointing across her favourite valley, Loweswater in Cumbria, 1963.

Filthies. Joyce used the advice that Henry James gave to Ruth Draper: 'My dear child, you have woven your own very beautiful Persian carpet, now stand on it!'

Vaudeville and music hall were on the wane, but Joyce maintained their tradition of the performer talking to the audience. Even on the television, viewers felt she was in their sitting-room with them. 'There has to be a relationship between me and the audience as one unit – not me and them.' Joyce learned from her ENSA concerts that unless a performer respects the audience, there is no contact. 'You have to meet people in a level place – if you look down, you can't meet them.' Joyce remained firmly in touch with her audience of mainly middle-aged British women. Her sketches were often subtle cries from a woman's heart and, whatever social class they portrayed, all of her characters were courageous – whether the Countess of Coteley, who has to learn to type, or a widow meeting her daughter-in-law for the first time.

Most of her fans were women, and men tended to go to see her shows with their wives. They were often bitten, but not all. Rene's husband Leslie Humphrey admired Joyce as a person, but not as an entertainer. 'She was a wonderful woman, she had no side to her. But I didn't like her shows – they weren't funny at all.' But when she performed in California she found that 'The non-marryers flock to the stage door!' She had never expected to become a gay icon.

Reviewers who criticised Joyce's use of rural or working-class accents, or said she was classist, failed to notice that out of over one hundred monologues and songs, over two-thirds were about middle-class women. When she did imitate working women, it was not to mock them but to empathise with them. 'I'm always sad when people think I am being malicious or even a trifle unkind,' she said. Joyce pointed out that she was making fun of herself. 'Remember the canteen woman in "Diversion"? That was largely me,' she said to the *Daily Mail* in 1945. 'If I satirise upper-class people some critics say I'm not beastly enough,' she told the *Evening Standard* in 1962. 'If I do a working class character I'm patronising. They've got me both ways.'

Joyce was often asked which, out of the sixty or more characters she had invented for her monologues, were her three favourites. Her third-favourite character was the Nursery School Teacher, though Joyce did get rather bored of her. 'Let's face it,' she said, 'she's a dull girl. As a character she isn't very interesting – it's the children who are.' Joyce's Nursery School Teacher never loses her temper: she would like to, but she knows she must stay in control. Listeners know just how she feels and identify with the simmering self-control necessary when coping with small children. Joyce had observed in herself and others the false high tone that adults adopt when speaking to small children. And as the children's behaviour deteriorates, the tone becomes brighter and falser.

In her autobiography Joyce wrote, 'I had never been inside a nursery school when I wrote the first sketch' – she must have forgotten her work in Slough Nursery School before the war. Joyce's nursery school first appeared on the radio in 1943. *How to Talk to Children* captured the changing philosophies of child-rearing from the eighteenth century, through the prudery of Victorians to 'The Modern Approach of Freedom of Expression'. The 'New Teaching' voice was heard in a nursery-school teacher. During the flower-fairy dance, the mutinous Sidney made his world début wishing to be a horse, or a carrot, and eventually settling for a dancing holly leaf. By 1946, in *How to Deal With Christmas*, Sidney was making paperchains and getting glue in his hair. Sidney's teacher discovered that he didn't like Peter Rabbit but wanted a book on machine guns, and reminded him to 'Pay attention. No, dear, *don't* do that.' 'George', who later became famous for being asked not to do that, had been in the original script, but was cut before transmission. Sidney and his friends were four years old in 1943 and have never grown any older. Apart from doing something he ought not to have, George wasn't much of a character. It was Sidney the anarchist who had all the fun.

Joyce was too busy to accept all the invitations she received to visit nursery schools, but in 1951 she presented the prizes at the Park Wall Infant School in King's Road. After handing out class prizes of a scooter, books and a hamster, she was given a blotter, a Plasticine ashtray and a painted paper hat, which she wore all day.

Joyce always kept her monologues up to date. By the late 1950s Wendy had become Shirleen, and Norman had become Elvis. In 1966 the hamsters in the nursery school were called after the fashion model

Twiggy and Harold Wilson, the Prime Minister; by 1973 Twiggy had turned into Paddington, the teddy bear from Peru, while Harold Wilson still raised a laugh. Sidney was no longer in an imaginary train but in a space rocket, machine-gunning the class; and he no longer wanted to be a dancing holly leaf but a dancing super-jet. His teacher was still exasperated by his 'aggressive personality problem'.

'I'm rather stuck with the lady from the nursery school – I've scraped the bottom of the barrel now with her. It's very out of date,' she said in 1976. 'I had a very serious letter from someone who taught in a nursery school who said that if I'd had proper training I wouldn't treat the children like that.'

Whatever Joyce thought, her fans continued to love the Nursery School Teacher. Twenty years after her death, more people remember her for 'George, don't do that' than for any other character she developed.

Joyce's second-favourite character was Mrs Moss the Terrible Worrier who, in 1967, won a dead rabbit in a raffle and didn't want to 'do' it – 'You'd be surprised what goes on under that fur' – so posted it through the open window of a car. Mrs Moss couldn't put it in the dustbin because 'the dustman only comes once week – they please themselves nowadays you know'. After Joyce performed this on television her local dustmen told the caretaker of her flats they wouldn't take her bins any more unless she retracted that line. Luckily for her, the bins were communal.

Mrs Moss had also first appeared on the radio in 1943 in a *How* programme. Joyce discovered her while cleaning her teeth: she noticed that if she put her tongue in front of her lower teeth, a whole new person appeared. Although Mrs Moss was poor and working-class, there was still a bit of her in Joyce – they were both worriers, while also feeling their material needs were fully met. Mrs Moss could not leave her potted plant, and didn't want any Christmas presents because she already had two hot-water bottles. She owned a quilted satin hot-water-bottle cover but it was too nice to use: she preferred her old cardigan with the buttons cut off. Joyce, too, preferred old furniture to new and hated unnecessary spending or conspicuous consumption.

Mrs Moss's final appearance was in 1971, in one of the very last monologues that Joyce wrote and the only one with a political message. She had been moved from a slum in 'Mulgarth Street' to a modern high-rise flat and was bewildered by the loss of neighbours. Joyce felt that planners and politicians should think about the consequences of so-called 'improvements'. 'Where's it all gone to, all that friendliness?' Mrs Moss asks plaintively.

Joyce's number-one favourite character was the vice-chancellor's wife at an Oxbridge university. Her voice was also discovered while Joyce was cleaning her teeth but this time she curled up her top lip. A new face appeared and Joyce found that it talked with a slight lisp and, like her father, an inability to pronounce the letter R. At first Joyce thought she was a bishop's wife but she soon turned into a vice-chancellor's wife who assumed that everyone else had read as many books and was as lofty in their ideals as her. When a male friend described the Vice-Chancellor's Wife as a 'phoney intellectual', Joyce took great exception. 'My Eng. Lit. lady isn't the least *phoney*!' she wrote. 'She's a *real* egg-head & assumes whoever she is with to be one too. She isn't showing off, she's being herself. I am quite distressed! On her behalf – not mine. Phoney indeed. I bet *he* hasn't got Loxley Hall by heart!'

Her character was based on Hester Alington, the mother-in-law of Sir Alec Douglas-Home, a Lyttelton cousin of Reggie and the wife of the Dean of Durham. Joyce often stayed with the Alingtons when she was on concert tours during the war. Hester Alington used an interesting vocabulary – she apologised for 'the regrettable absence of essential stationery in the visitors' bathroom'. After a benefit concert in aid of the Save the Children Fund she said, 'My dear Joyce, we have not yet touched on the sordid topic of *coin*.' Joyce enjoyed this unusual use of language and often copied it. When she discovered that Verily Anderson's large feet were exactly the same size as her own, she said, 'How incredibly fortunate that our pedal extremities are so agreeably twin-spaced.'

In many ways the nameless Vice-Chancellor's Wife was Joyce – articulate, concerned about the world, interested in people, emanating light and radiance. She was also the woman Joyce wanted to be – learned, intellectual, unflappable and totally Holy. She admired the Vice-Chancellor's Wife so much that she wrote three monologues for her, always wearing an elderly cardigan, in an imaginary study with Gothic windows and a pair of crossed oars over the door.

In *Eng. Lit. I – Interview*, written in 1965, an unseen young man comes to interview the Vice-Chancellor's Wife for a television programme, but she asks all the questions. She finally agrees to go on the programme, and turns the tables with 'Mr Wimble, what would happen if I were to come on to your programme and I were to be very cruel to *you*?' This was inspired by Wynford Hicks, a twenty-two-year-old Oxford graduate with ambitions to become a journalist, who had been sent by Granada Television to interview Joyce in 1964, about a programme on critics and criticism.

'I was the rawest recruit you could imagine,' remembers Hicks.

I was delighted to meet a famous woman but I hadn't a clue about interviewing as a professional skill. I remember Joyce Grenfell's famous voice and listening to it as she talked seriously about the issues involved in TV and criticism. I arrived with a dozen stock questions and once they were answered, Joyce kept me talking about myself. She was rather serious over tea – I never remember laughing, only being told how I could improve myself, work harder, be nicer to my mother.

After the interview Joyce scribbled her perceptions of this young man into an exercise book. She had gathered a lot of information about Hicks – his political views, his schooling and his family background. She noted that he had 'dark red hair and large feet', ate all the biscuits, smoked French cigarettes and wore a leather jerkin. Joyce described him as a 'Marxist-anarchist', but to Hicks these were two quite separate philosophies and he professed to being the latter but not the former. Joyce thought they were the same thing, and imagined a modern anarchist would live 'in a garden city with plain wood furniture and mobiles and a rubber plant'. She felt that he was suspicious of her but he remembers only awe at meeting a famous woman. Hicks's ambition to become a journalist was fulfilled, and thirty-five years later he is still wearing a leather jacket, though he is no longer an anarchist.

Eng Lit II – An Event, written in 1967, also has a young man, but his personality is less clear – John the nephew is simply a foil to his aunt's thoughts about appearing on television on a panel discussion of 'Elementary Sex in Schools' with two opposing politicians and an egg-head scientist. Joyce herself had not enjoyed appearing on *Any Questions?* with 'old pros grinding their predictable axes' and confessed to know little about Barbara Castle or cod.

Wynford Hicks also inspired *Eng. Lit. III*, in 1968, in which a student wearing a leather jerkin appears from behind the sofa, flicks his ash on the carpet and lies full-length on the sofa. He wants the Vice-Chancellor's Wife to ban his 'fairly disagreeably destructive' anarchist magazine, in order to boost its poor sales. She is almost convinced of 'the charm of anarchy' until she wonders, '*Who* is to be responsible for the plumbing?' Unconvinced by his politics, she invites him to supper to meet the Vice-Chancellor.

The other inspiration for the *Eng. Lit.* monologues was the writer Clive James, whom Joyce had first met as an earnest student in Sydney. He sent her his articles and poems and then turned up in London. In a letter to Katharine Moore in 1962 she described her 'young Australian poet friend starving in Tuffnell Park' as 'far out, against everything like respect, sanctity, Royalty and wealth'. An impoverished, socialist poet, he was nurtured with hot meals, Reggie's old shoes and useful introductions. After an aimless couple of years, he got into Cambridge University and when he looked especially hungry Joyce gave him the odd cheque. He spent many hours sitting on her sofa testing out his political ideas, such as the abolition of money and equal pay for chorus girls, doctors and tycoons. Joyce discovered that from among his anti-establishment views she could tease his belief for Good, which she pointed out was the main attribute of God.

– 22 –

WHEN JOYCE WORKED in America – as she did seven times between 1955 and 1970 – Reggie went too whenever possible, staying for at least a week in order to set up the accounts. He took crossing the Atlantic by liner very seriously, exercising in the gym, playing deck-tennis, doing the ship's crossword puzzle and going to all the movies. Joyce was torn between wanting a quiet rest and a feeling of duty to join in the fun and games.

'I do feel totally English,' Joyce told the BBC World Service, 'but when I talk about my mother I go into a Virginian voice. When I'm in America I feel very, very English, but when in England I have an American allegiance. I have the best of all worlds – I can see the faults and blessings of both sides of the sea.'

One of the blessings on the American side was Tommy and Mary Phipps. Joyce adored her sister-in-law, a fashion model with whom she shared a love of clothes and interior decor. Mary was the sister that Joyce never had and she hoped, through her, to become closer to her brother. Joyce and Tommy both knew how to charm, but their relationship was never easy. Tommy had inherited his mother's passion and spontaneity and he found Joyce irritatingly domesticated, reliable and safe. 'Joyce had a full life,' Tommy said after she died, 'but it was a life with no passion. She never took risks.' The incompatibility that had dogged Paul and Nora was re-enacted in their children.

Tommy had written over fifty plays for television, and in 1957 his play *The Four Winds* was produced on Broadway. Unfortunately it faced competition from *West Side Story* and folded after three weeks. His second stage play closed a few days before it was due to move from Chicago to New York. His career as a writer never recovered after the television industry moved to California and the family struggled along on Tommy's business ventures and Mary's earnings.

When Joyce went to New York for a five-week tour in 1956, she arrived in time for the birth of a brother for little Sally – Thomas Langhorne, known as Lang. She decided that, with two small children, Mary now needed an English nanny, and undertook to find her one. Constance Hardy, then aged fifty-two, was interviewed in London. 'Mrs Grenfell decided that I was just the person for the job. I flew out to New York to take charge of Sally and baby Lang. I spent seven happy years with the Phipps and I still regard it as my second home. Mrs Grenfell came over frequently to visit. She had a very warm personality, considerate and very determined, and a wonderful way of making one feel special.' Joyce approved of the discipline that nannies instilled in their small charges, 'One of the causes of distress and maladjustment today comes from no early discipline I think,' she wrote to Constance in 1963.

On every visit Joyce took presents, such as velvet-collared tweed coats for the children, and secretly put money into Mary's bank account. Lang recalls how

Joyce's presence in our house came to me through sound. Her voice was the clarion announcing her arrival and I would look up startled from my Lego project or homework. She may have been reacting to something new in our house, the colour of a room, or a picture and I would hear, 'Oh Tommy, it is *beautiful*!' The sound was an instrument played by the most expressive and joyous of musicians. After she'd left, the human voices around me had all the life of noisy cars passing along the street outside.

Sally and Lang called her 'Tante', because Constance's predecessor had been French. 'Joyce inhabited "Tante" because it is more sprightly than "aunt",' recalls Lang. 'On the other hand she *was* "aunt-ish" in her bossiness and primness. A definite air of disapproval hovered between us when I was growing up and being an American boy. There is a photograph of Joyce and me in the woods somewhere on Long Island. I have a toy rifle and as I aim it at some imaginary buck, Tante has a "George, don't do that" expression on her face, stiff and admonitory.' But Joyce loved Lang and was sad that her work did not allow her more time to share his interests.

As the children grew up, she contributed to their school fees and took an active interest in their progress. One day Sally overheard the teacher in the next class saying, 'George, don't do that.' 'She had no idea I was Joyce's niece and you can imagine her amazement when I told her Joyce was shortly going to visit.' She turned up with Tommy during a literature lesson, which happened to be on F. Scott Fitzgerald. When the teacher heard that they had known him, he asked for their memories. 'Joyce finished by saying she rather thought her Mum had had a bit of a fling with Fitzgerald and Tommy said it was absolute rubbish!'

Sally was the nearest that Joyce came to having a daughter. Their relationship was not always easy, partly because they were so similar. Sally inherited her aunt's looks and her strength of character, but Joyce could not understand why she should *choose* to leave her clothes on the floor, or argue with her parents so loudly. She expected teenagers to behave as she had, and, like so many of her generation, was surprised and hurt when they didn't.

On 28 October 1956 Joyce appeared again on *The Ed Sullivan Show* and sang *The Countess of Coteley* in a white satin gown and a tiara. Joyce replaced the references to the Women's Institute, Boot's and Women's Voluntary Service with '. . . at first it will seem queer,/When the bus conductor calls her "ducks",/the grocer calls her "dear".'

The following act was a twenty-one-year-old rock and roll singer, of whom she had never heard, called Elvis Presley. He arrived at the studio in a white Thunderbird, which quickly became covered in lipstick kisses. His teddy-boy haircut quiffed back, he sang with his hands in his pockets and wobbled his knees to *Love Me Tender*, and *Baby It's You I Want*. He was obviously not used to appearing on television and kept shading his eyes to see the audience, who were drowning him out with their screams. Joyce decided he was 'a pasty-faced roly-poly boy and a good singer of his hill-Billy songs'. Elvis didn't know what to make of her and called her both 'ma'am' and 'honey'.

Joyce then set off with George Bauer and her 'efficient, calm and helpful' stage manager Connie Alderson on a five-week tour of twenty-eight concerts in twenty-four cities. Their itinerary took them from deep winter in Boston to summer in Florida and spring in

California. The stage requirements stipulated a Steinway grand piano, flesh-pink lights (*not* amber), and a 'qualified woman' to iron the frocks. 'Spotlights should be focused to give the stage a warm, overall light. The piano MUST be properly tuned on the day of performance.' Even those theatres that held two thousand were sold out and an audience of three hundred was considered small.

When Joyce was invited to perform on Broadway in 1958 she had not expected to find Nancy Astor on board the *Queen Mary*. Now seventy-nine, her will was as strong as ever. She refused to do boat drill and had decided to go on a diet, but couldn't find one that featured caviare. She said that Joyce's talents weren't a patch on her mother's. Joyce agreed but added that if Nora had been asked to go on stage she would never have turned up for the second night. Nancy died in 1964, aged eighty-five, luckily unaware of the Profumo scandal that had surrounded Cliveden. Joyce noticed it, but was relieved that the press made no link between her and her cousin Bill Astor or his tenant Stephen Ward.

In the 1960s her American agent Lionel Larner arranged for her to appear on several television programmes such as the David Frost, Ed Sullivan and Dick Cavett shows. 'Just being in Joyce's presence was like being bathed in sunlight,' Larner remembers. 'Everyone always felt better and behaved better when they were with her. Over here in the 1950s and 60s an English accent was unusual, and a lady of Joyce's quality was very special.'

In 1963 Joyce and William Blezard flew to New York to record a television show called *The Festival of Performing Arts*. 'For the rehearsals every single piano was out of tune. I tried three,' William remembers. Joyce sang her encores at the beginning of the performance: 'I'm not taking any risks that you might not want an encore, so here they are now.' She performed a monologue about Lady Wibberly, showing off her stately home on television: 'There's nothing pleasanter on a cold winter's day than standing over the hot air of the grating' – just as Joyce had at the National Gallery during the war.

Joyce's voice was her instrument and throat infections were an occupational hazard, but she was always determined to carry on. She could turn the microphone up for her monologues, but singing was more difficult. William transposed her music down by as many as five keys at the onset of an infection and then gradually moved it up again as her voice returned to normal. His skill was such that if, during a performance, he realised Joyce would not hit a high note, he could transpose a song there and then. This had its risks. In North Carolina, the sound of a movie camera in the audience distracted Joyce and she missed a verse. 'I had to hang on desperately to the newly transposed tune,' remembers William. 'At the end of the song, a few well-chosen words from Joyce prevented any further distractions from the audience. When Joyce was ill and needed all her energy just to get through the show, I found it difficult to muster a state of excitement too. I needed her buzz to get me into the mood for my own solo spots.'

In Winnipeg in 1970, Joyce had to speak the whole show in a *basso profundo*. She was determined to use Christian Science to get through, even when her voice disappeared entirely. The management pointed out that her contract stipulated that she had to see a doctor and grudgingly she complied with his prescription of antibiotics.

When John Gielgud heard that Joyce was visiting California he wrote to her:

I want to urge you to take a day to go to Disneyland. I would never have gone if Christopher Isherwood, of all people, hadn't persuaded me. It's rather a long drive, but I assure you it is *divine*. Nothing is over plugged and the 'rides' are marvellous: Peter Pan especially and the Snow White with shrinking witches and slamming doors. And I believe there is a new one in a submarine. All madly ingenious and amusing. I know you would love it. One is inclined to be put off by the whole idea until one sees for oneself how brilliantly it is done.

In 1966 Joyce and Leonard Gershe took Geilgud's advice. 'Disneyland is quite remarkably well done and somehow awful too,' she wrote to Virginia. She was impressed by its cleanliness but found the speaking robot birds 'quite obscene'. The 'remarkably plastic' animated Africans were horrifying, but she was 'amused at the total lack of taste, or humour of any quality: as a feat of ingenuity and electrical wonder it is astonishing. But *awful*!'

In 1967 she went on an eight-week tour of American universities with William Blezard and Diana Lyddon. 'I was supremely fortunate to work with Joyce at the height of her powers as a person and an artist,' remembers Diana.

> Setting up in a new theatre every day was hectic. I hated ironing the frocks, in case I burned them; there were so many yards to them. Then Bill would stride in and say, 'Bloody awful piano again.' Apart from pianos, the theatres were very well equipped, but my assistants, though keen, were untrained. There was so little theatre in America. They were theorists who thought they knew it all but had never actually done it.
>
> Joyce was bossy but I'm jolly glad she was. I needed all the help I could get. There was so much luggage and organisation and tipping and everything. The marvellous thing about her was that she never stepped on my toes. She never said anything that made me feel that she had superior knowledge. Sometimes I only had an hour to set everything up, and establish a radio frequency for her mike which would not pick up the local station.

Joyce often gave interviews to these stations, which inspired her monologue *Time to Waste*. A sprightly interviewer asks so many questions of her guest that between advertisements for cookies and local hairdressers, there is no time for the answers.

'In each college Joyce led a seminar on the art of communication,' Diana remembers. 'After that she usually took us out to eat somewhere really good, where we laughed and laughed. She felt a divided loyalty about finding the Americans funny and being three-quarters American herself.' Diana noticed that although she talked a lot about her parents, Joyce never mentioned their divorce. 'It was only when we were on tour in America in 1970 that I learned from her mother's friends in Virginia about Lefty.'

As well as setting up the shows, Diana also drove Joyce and William to and from airports. On their 1967 tour they went to Los Angeles, Oklahoma, St Louis, Toronto, Montreal, Michigan, Williamsburg and Baltimore. Though Joyce never drank, she knew that at the end of a day Diana and William deserved one. 'Once we were in a "dry" state and she said, "Take the car across the frontier and get yourselves a drink."'

At a Roman Catholic college in Pennsylvania, attendance was

compulsory, which produced a 'somewhat muted' response but in California it was better. 'I must just boast,' Joyce wrote to Verily. 'I had something I've never had before in my life at the vast University of California, when the students gave me a *standing ovation*. I'd read of this, but there it was, happening, they surged down the aisles towards the stage as well as standing to applaud right where they were!'

As Joyce grew older she liked American cities less and less. 'New York is my idea of hell,' she wrote to me in 1969. 'It's so noisy and dirty and frustrating: heartless too. But I love the country in America.' She felt more at home in Australia: 'There is a sort of familiarity in the humour there that is pleasing.'

When Joyce was first invited to perform in Australia in 1959 she was doubtful – it was a long way to go, nobody would have heard of her and Reggie couldn't go too. By 1976 she had been five times and Australia had become one of her favourite countries and Australians among her best friends.

The tiny Philip Street Theatre in Sydney, with only 360 seats, became Joyce's favourite theatre, despite the noise of gunfire and galloping cowboys penetrating the auditorium from the adjoining cinema. Thanks to the films she had been in, she could walk out onto the stage and meet with affection and recognition. Joyce found that, as in America, she had to slow her speech very slightly, until the audience got the hang of it.

'I am trying to speak Australian,' Joyce wrote to Beryl Hobson of the BBC. 'It's very elusive and subtle and just when I think I've got it I lapse into cockney, but I'm being coached by taxi drivers, hairdressers and friends.' She could soon imitate a passable Australian accent, but was never confident enough to use it in public until a taxi driver advised her: 'Down't owpen yer maouth, and always lean on sometin'.'

The second half of the show began with an overture played by Bill from behind the closed curtain. Just before the curtain went up, he and Joyce swapped places, and Joyce took over the final bars of the piece, giving the impression that she had played it all. The audience applauded, obviously impressed, but Joyce could not bear to cheat, so always confessed, 'Actually I had help from my friend here.'

Both William and Joyce missed their spouses and did their best to cheer each other up. Every Sunday after supper they played Scrabble, though he only beat Joyce once, by one point. William sometimes found her hard work. 'She's so galvantically worked up all the time,' he wrote to his wife, 'that one has to jump in and say one's piece if one is to say it at all. I'm getting better at it. She is terrifically visually minded and is looking pretty good, and seems to dress better than she used to.' He also missed his small son Paul, and when he told Joyce he was composing a song for Paul's second birthday, she offered to write the lyrics.

At the end of each show, the audience stood for the Queen. 'I must tell Joyce not to sing the National Anthem just off stage in my ear,' William wrote to his wife. 'I've been silently suffering for weeks now and play the piece worse every night.'

The theatre rented William a flat in King's Cross and Joyce another on Potts Point, near Sydney Harbour. The brown 1930s furniture and decor were hideous but the view from the eighth floor was a fabulous panorama, from Sydney Bridge to the rocky Heads leading to the Pacific. Whenever she felt homesick, Joyce just looked at the view and felt better.

A few days after the show opened in July 1959, the theatre's board of directors complained that they had not been given the best seats. The theatre manager, William Orr, refused to apologise and was sacked. When Joyce arrived that evening, she was told that the staff, loyal to Orr, were on strike and the show had been cancelled. She tactfully took no sides and went home. After emergency meetings were held between the board and Orr, he was reinstated. The next day Joyce was enraged to read the *Sydney Morning Herald* headline COMEDIENNE WALKS OUT OF THEATRE. Normally she ignored inaccurate press, but felt that this implied she was an irresponsible foot-stamper. She was also afraid that the story might get back to the British press and harm her reputation at home. Press statements were released, retractions were made and sales of tickets increased further. Joyce did eight solo shows a week of two hours and ten minutes each for fourteen weeks, and the theatre was sold out for every single performance. It was her longest run anywhere, and by the end she was exhausted.

While in Sydney, Joyce remet the beautiful twenty-four-year-old Irish singer and harpist Mary O'Hara, introduced to her to a few years before by John Gielgud. Joyce had given Mary tips on what to wear on television and an introduction to Ed Sullivan in New York. She appeared on his St Patrick's Day programme but it had not been a success – Mary was seated beside a giant cardboard shamrock and an Irish wolfhound, and just before the end-credits Sullivan pushed her in front of the camera. The programme ended during the first verse of 'Danny Boy'.

Mary was now on an eight-week tour of New South Wales to raise money for Catholic hospitals and Joyce invited her to stay in the spare room in her rooftop flat. 'No complaints except that I really like it best when I'm here on my own. Selfish to the core, that's me,' she wrote to Virginia. Joyce enjoyed cooking for Mary and even said to her, 'I've worked it out – you could have been our daughter.' Although Joyce was somewhat prejudiced against Roman Catholics, she liked Mary and admired her strong Christian faith. Joyce was amused that, when they both set off for their different churches on Sunday morning, Mary took her tennis racquet with her, hoping for a game with the priest.

They were together on the third anniversary of Mary's marriage to the American poet Richard Selig, who had died the year before. Mary confided to Joyce what she had told only her closest friends – that she now planned to become a nun, in a closed order. Joyce was horrified, and urged her to think carefully. Mary's mind was already made up and almost three years later she entered a contemplative community of the Benedictine Order in England.

In Sydney in 1959, Mary and Joyce talked about how difficult it was performing to audiences who did not pay full attention. 'If the audience annoy you, just keep on loving them,' advised Joyce. She told Mary about a performance she had witnessed by Ruth Draper: the packed theatre was enjoying her monologues, but there was one man in the circle who laughed longer and louder than anyone else. When the rest of the audience tittered, he guffawed. When they stopped laughing, he carried on. Halfway through a monologue, when he had laughed again at an inappropriate moment, Ruth Draper stopped and, looking straight at the circle, said, 'It wasn't *that* funny.' He shut up after that, but so did the rest of the audience. They were all intimidated, and she had lost them. After seeing that, Joyce vowed never to let anyone in an audience get to her. However, it was in Sydney when the audience *did* get to Joyce – but she handled it so skilfully that they loved her more for it and not less. Clive James, then a student at Sydney University, recalled the incident:

Australian audiences are very fond of eating chocolates after the interval. Each chocolate was wrapped in individual crinkled brown paper. With the whole audience eating their chocolates it sounded like an electrical storm. Joyce stood this for one evening. The second evening the curtain went up on Act Two and the chocolate storm started. Joyce walked up to the foot-light and said, 'Now look. If you stop eating the chocolates now and save them for later you can enjoy the show. But if you really want to eat your chocolates now then I'll have to go home.'

There was a stunned silence. They'd never been spoken to like this before. But they obeyed, and put the tops back on their chocolate boxes. The press next day tried to make a thing out of Joyce's queenly intransigence, but the public loved her for it. After that she was a truly enormous hit in Australia. She became an institution.

Joyce had tackled the chocolate-wrapper problem with care – she suppressed her annoyance and did not interrupt her own show. She did not accuse any single member of the audience, and nor did she demand obedience: she gave the audience a choice, expressing no particular interest in their decision.

One of the secrets of Joyce's appeal in Australia was her impeccable English upper-class manners. Clive James belonged to a Journalists Club, which invited Joyce to lunch. They were amazed when she came, and even more impressed by a trick that she had learned from her Phipps grandmother – how to eat a pear without making a mess. 'We'd never seen a Great Lady in action before,' recalled Clive James. 'During dessert she ate this pear with a spoon from the inside. We'd never seen anything like it: I looked down the table and there were 20 young men watching, jaws ajar. We all thought, This is *class*. At the centre of her work, even when she was imitating the cockney washer-woman, she was really a Grand Lady with complete self-assurance. That's what wowed the audience.'

A week after she opened in Sydney, Joyce received a shocking tele-gram from Tommy Phipps: her twenty-year-old nephew, Wilton, had died in an accident on Lake Michigan. He and some friends were in a rowing-boat when a freak storm whipped up and blew them beyond reach; by the time they were found, three of them had died of hypothermia. Joyce wrote to Virginia that she had 'turned quickly to God and the sense of disaster left and instead I remembered that in God's eyes life is continuous and whole'. She had seen him the previous summer and found him 'young, maddening, endearing, affectionate in the end, and I really loved him. He was not part of my close circle so it would be false to make too much of the sense of loss.' In her long daily letters to Virginia, she only mentioned the fatal accident once. Maybe she had already mourned him before, when he left Britain as a baby in 1939. It had been so painful for her that she seems to have closed a door to feelings about Wilton, the nearest she had to a son. She pulled out her Christian Science and rode it through.

When Joyce and William returned to Sydney in 1963 the Philip Street Theatre had been pulled down, and she toured the whole country, including Tasmania. She was especially pleased that, when she picked up the phone to call Reggie in London, the overseas operator recognised her and welcomed her back. On this and the following trip in 1966, she had a flat on Darling Point where she could watch the boats, 'like little white butterflies', on Sydney Harbour. For the last night she and William wrote a song called *Ferry Boats of Sydney*, 'in darkness like harmonicas at sea'.

Joyce and William had to cope with all kinds of unexpected interruptions during their shows. In Auckland they had to compete with a band of bagpipes playing in a nearby hall. In Melbourne, a hailstorm on the metal roof of the theatre was so loud that they could not even hear each other. 'We had just begun "Learn to Loosen",' remembers William:

Joyce stopped the song and immediately swung into 'Oh what a lover-ly Evening' from Oklahoma. The whole audience joined in for two verses and just as we got to 'Everything's going my way' the hail stopped suddenly, as if someone had pulled a switch, and the show proceeded without further hindrance. A friend in the audience thought it was so slick that it must have been pre-arranged. It wasn't. How do you pre-arrange a hailstorm?

After the tour finished, Joyce wrote to William, 'I feel a lovely sense of having been stretched just far enough so that there is something left for the future. Some of those gruelling US tours left the elastic entirely used up and really weren't that much fun. But this last one has been a "beaut".' 'In Adelaide one evening,' William remembers, 'Joyce inadvertently said "shit" during the dog sketch. She had suppressed giggles for the rest of the half.'

At the end of this visit to Australia, Reggie joined Joyce in New Zealand. His youngest sister Laura was wife of the Governor General, Bernard Fergusson. William had been nervous about staying at Government House but he soon found that they were relaxed and easy hosts, and after dinner he revealed some of his hidden musical talents. He could play two tunes at once, one in each hand; jazz sitting in a lotus position on the floor; and Chopin's Minute Waltz while lying *under* the piano. He also played a Victorian descriptive piece called 'The Battle March of Delhi' with captions such as 'General Wilson's arrival', 'Cannon! Mortar!' and 'Flight of the Mutineers' which had the party in such hysterics that Joyce insisted he include it in her programme. When the mood was right, Joyce and William improvised songs in mock foreign languages in the style of Schubert, Debussy and Roger Quilter.

'New Zealand is pretty if you like Scotland, Switzerland or Norway,' she wrote to Katharine Moore. The 'dark rock, grey water, gorse-bushy' similarity to Scotland filled Joyce with gloom. She liked birds, especially blackbirds, 'to sing in English accents'.

At the end of this tour she was asked to return home via New York to appear in the new musical of Noël Coward's *Blithe Spirit*, composed by her old friend Hugh Martin. She declined on the grounds that she could not act, only entertain. And anyway she had a holiday planned. She had reached the stage in her career where she no longer needed to take everything that was offered.

On hearing that she was off to Australia again in 1969, John Betjeman wrote to Joyce, 'My goodness you are lucky to be going to Australia, it is bathed in eternal sunshine for me, and I have never met an Australian I didn't like. Do go and see Barry Humphreys [*sic*] at the Fortune Theatre, it will be a nice foretaste of Australia for Reggie. I think Barry is a genius and not a satirist any more than you or I are, he likes the things he imitates.'

They were met at Sydney Airport by television cameras and a press conference. The journalists wanted to know what Joyce thought of the 'permissive society' they were hearing so much about in London. 'Would you appear nude on the stage?' they asked. At fifty-nine it was easy to say no, but instead she said, 'I have never found it necessary to undress in order to communicate.'

It had been a tough decision to go. Virginia's husband, Tony Thesiger, had been suffering from Alzheimer's for nearly ten years and by the time Joyce and Reggie left London in July 1969, he could no longer feed himself or speak. Virginia never appeared to resent this and clung to her faith in Christian Science. A month after Joyce arrived in Australia, Tony got pneumonia and died within a few days, aged sixty-three. Just as when Nora was dying, Joyce was torn between supporting her friend and keeping to her professional contract. With the help of Christian Science, professionalism won.

Joyce's 1969 tour broke all her previous records for tickets sold in Adelaide, Melbourne and Sydney. The *Hobart Mercury* was amazed that a West End star graced them with her presence at the Theatre Royal, which was packed for four nights. Wherever she went, there were up to fifty people waiting at the stage door, and fans invited her to join their family barbecues and local football matches. One schoolgirl wrote that she was playing Miss Gossage in the school production of *The Happiest Days of Your Life*. They had been rehearsing for six weeks and 'We are now just improving our character interpretation and expression. Our director is a woodwork teacher, which is very handy for the scenery.'

Reggie enjoyed accompanying Joyce to Australia and New Zealand because it gave him the opportunity to see unusual birds. During their 1969 visit, after he had identified fifty-two different species in one day, they were taken to see a rare white-cheeked honey-eater. For three weeks this normally reclusive bird becomes courageous and collects wool from koala bears' ears for its nest. They held out bits of string, which the bird took from Reggie, but it would not come near Joyce. As the party moved back towards the car, Joyce had a call of nature and slipped away behind a bush. The honey-eater followed her – it liked her blue skirt and while she squatted it picked off bits of tweed for its nest.

Each of Joyce's five visits to Australia was better than the last. She made lots of friends, and Sydney was her favourite city. 'If I was young I would come and live here. No question if it,' she wrote. 'It is so brash and big and exciting & finding its own voice & painting & writing and yelling & growing up. And the bird life is the best in the world. This continent gives me a feeling of prehistoric agelessness more even than anywhere, including Africa.'

– 23 –

As FINANCIAL DIRECTOR of Messina Copper Mines, Reggie went to South Africa twice a year. The main offices were in London and the two mines were in the northern Transvaal, a few miles from the Limpopo River, the border of Southern Rhodesia, now Zimbabwe. When Reggie went to South Africa on his own, Joyce always missed him. 'It's very hard and it gets worse as time goes by,' she said in 1954. Thirteen years later, 'Nothing is as much fun when we are apart, even though our tasks are different, it is the fact of being able to tell each other what we've done, to be able to sit in silent companionship and speak a word or two without context but perfectly understood. He has the nicest nature in the world.' In 1974 Joyce said, 'I hate it when he goes. I love him more every day.' Reggie showed his love by ensuring there was enough soap powder, lavatory paper and radio batteries to last until his return, and ordered flowers to be delivered every week.

Joyce would probably never have gone to South Africa out of choice, but in 1953 she went there for the first of many times with Reggie. Altogether, she accompanied him eleven times, usually in February. As 'Mrs Reginald Grenfell' she was simply the director's wife; few people had heard of Joyce Grenfell, the film and radio star. There was no television in South Africa until 1975, and even before the cultural boycott by Britain, the Nationalist government discouraged anything British, so only American and Spaghetti Western films were shown. Joyce enjoyed being 'invisible' so much that when a woman approached her in Johannesburg and said, 'You aren't Joyce Grenfell, are you?' she replied, 'No, I'm not,' and walked on.

Visits to Messina were a holiday for Joyce in weather she could only dream of in London. She read or wrote under a grape-covered arbour, ate meals outdoors, watched exotic birds and swam in the private pool. The chairman's bungalow was comfortable, with plenty of well-trained domestic staff who were, according to Joyce, 'not visibly in the least ground down'. She went a thousand feet down a mineshaft and walked along tunnels into the two-hundred-foot-high caverns where the copper ore was shovelled by hand.

As the wife of the financial director, she was expected to take part in the social life of Messina. 'I first met Joyce at a tea party given for Joyce and Harold Grenfell's wife, Miriam,' remembers Mary Wilson, the wife of the managing director. 'The managers' wives arrived dressed in hats, stocking and gloves. Miriam and Joyce came in cotton frocks, bare legs and sandals.' Joyce felt stifled by the formality of all-white 'sundowners', 'brai-vleis' (barbecues) and dinner parties attended by nervous black butlers in white cotton gloves. A women's service at the local Dutch Reformed church required the donning of hats, gloves and stockings to listen to an hour of sermons in Afrikaans. Joyce's feelings about Afrikaners were as strong as theirs against black Africans: she thought they were narrow-minded with terrible accents. 'They take the vowels, iron them flat and then squeak them.' 'The Afrikaners go on fighting the Boer War,' she wrote in despair in 1959. 'Like elephants they never forget. They are as narrow as Calvin – totally un-loving, bitter, old-fashioned. It dictates the mood, which is hate of, and determined destruction of, everything British.'

Racial apartheid had become law in 1948 and was already causing major social and political problems. Joyce was aware that she had much to learn and listened to everybody's views but, whoever she talked to, she could not see the point of apartheid. When she and Miriam visited the local school they talked to the African school-teachers and children, who were ignored by the white women. During her first visit to Johannesburg Joyce went to hear Alan Paton speak about his novel *Cry, the Beloved Country*, which first exposed apartheid to the world.

In Johannesburg they came across a portrait photographer called Leon Levson and his wife Freda Troup, a writer and political activist. When Joyce met her in March 1953, Freda was on bail for walking with Mahatma Ghandi's son and thirty other people around a black township, without passes. Freda was the first white woman to be sentenced to imprisonment for her politics. The ANC put up her bail so that before she went to prison she could find a home for her younger sister, who had Down's syndrome. Joyce was impressed by her courage and they continued to meet in Johannesburg and then in London after Leon had died and Freda was deported from South Africa.

In 1964 she met Ruth Neale of the Institute of Race Relations in Johannesburg and was invited to perform in South Africa. Joyce liked the organisation because it was non-racial and non-violent, and agreed to do five performances the following year. She believed that she could use this opportunity to express her disapproval of apartheid. But William, a member of the British Musicians' Union, was bound by the cultural boycott and without him she could not put on a show. Secretly he was relieved – he did not want to break the boycott, but neither did he want to have a political argument with Joyce.

Joyce thought that Ian Smith's 1965 unilateral declaration of independence in Rhodesia was 'the most idiotic thing, pure folly'. 'The venal greed of white Africans and Rhodesians looms in a light as evil as that that shines on Captain Hook in Peter Pan,' she wrote to Katharine Moore.

'Oh there *is* a lot of horror in South Africa & one's blood does boil,' she wrote to Verily Anderson. 'Afrikaaners are peasant types, ignorant & cruel & they are the Gov just now & likely to be. There are v fearful & the reason for this has grown up out of their long history of misusing Africans. Thinking Africans know that time is on their side & their weight of numbers ensures final triumph. Meanwhile . . .?'

While in Johannesburg in 1968 Joyce made friends with Nobel Prize-winning writer Nadine Gordimer, whose novels about apartheid were banned in South Africa. Joyce was so pleased to find someone of intelligence and good taste to talk to. Over lunch they discussed the political situation, for which Gordimer could see no solution. 'Meeting Nadine Gordimer makes me realise what a colossal problem it is & I wonder how I'd tackle it if forced to produce a solution,' she wrote to BBC producer Jocelyn Ferguson. 'It wouldn't be apartheid but I do think the progressives are right in suggesting a sort of educational means test before any one, black or white, can vote, lots of whites would fail it – & a very good thing too.'

Nadine Gordimer was also impressed by Joyce's 'lively mind (off-stage as well as on) and her lack of any kind of human prejudice, whether of race, skin or creed. I doubt whether I influenced her ideas on apartheid – she will have seen it keenly for herself. The cultural boycott was a difficult matter for performers who were prepared to come out strongly against apartheid. But I was in favour of it since it shamed people who were fully prepared to come here and make money while tacitly supporting the regime by keeping their mouths shut in terms of making any criticism. It was ancillary to economic and trade sanctions, which I also supported, and without them apartheid would have survived much longer.'

Later that day Joyce met her Langhorne cousin James Fox, a twenty-two-year-old journalist on the liberal magazine *Drum*, who told her about the forced evictions and destruction of black Africans' homes. 'When I'm here [in London] it all seems so clear cut,' she wrote to Katharine Moore. 'When I'm there face to face with the problem it's all much more difficult. I can't breathe in Johannesburg, horrible place. But up country where we are, miles off, there are no troubles.'

Once Reggie had finished his business in Messina and Johannesburg, a favourite treat was to go and stay at Rawdon's Hotel, Lanzerac, near Cape Town – an elegant eighteenth-century Dutch-colonial farmhouse converted into a country-house hotel, well known for its food, style and spacious garden with a pool fed by mountain streams. Joyce made friends with the young manager, Michael Olivier, a white English-speaking liberal.

Each year many British visitors used to stay at Lanzerac – we called them the 'British swallows'. The servants would all bow and scrape and smile and happily accept the tips so generously handed out by these kind Britishers, so different from the Boer with whom they had to deal in the post offices and magistrates courts. And because they presented this ever-smiling face, many of the swallows thought that the blacks were happy and that all was well with the world.

I didn't know that Mrs Grenfell was a famous actress. I got to know Joyce the person, not Joyce the famous stage personality. Reggie was never 'Mr Joyce Grenfell', he was very much his own person and was never overshadowed by Joyce.

Reggie used to hire a huge Toyota and drive down to the sea, where Joyce enjoyed leaping in the giant rollers. Reggie never swam but sat in a deck-chair watching the birds. Michael sometimes took them for meals with his parents in nearby Gordon's Bay. 'Joyce was not a good passenger and was always saying, "You will drive carefully, won't you dear?" and "Not too fast now!" She told me that she always liked to "travel slowly and arrive early. It's just so restful don't you think?" After supper we would have our own private cabaret. My father egged Joyce on until we were dropping with laughter.'

When Michael went to London in 1975, he spent an afternoon with Joyce and Reggie at Elm Park Gardens, chatting about South Africa and his impressions of Britain. 'I loved the paintings, I loved the table with the little pots of flowers on it and I loved the just being there with this amazingly special woman with her very special husband.' Afterwards they walked down King's Road. 'She was greeted left and right by the barrow keepers – " 'Ello, Dahlin' " – and as we approached them she would start imitating *sotto voce* their accents and I was in such a state of giggles that I could hardly say good morning. When we got into Pont Street country, Joyce started talking like a Sloane Ranger, about the "hawsis" ridden by the "gels".'

Joyce was inspired by Michael to write a monologue about a young liberal South African visiting Britain and the prejudice he found against all white South Africans, whatever their beliefs. He wonders:

> How many of the protesters do anything constructive about race relations except yell? How many go to Wolverhampton or Notting Hill Gate or Birmingham to try to heal the misunderstanding, between ignorant white and innocent blacks? Apartheid is horrible when it means one law for A and another for B, one door for A and another for B. But how do we stop it unless we educate white opinions and educate black ignorance and all try to discover what man really is – eh?

When Michael read it twenty-six years later he said it was almost a transcript of his conversation with Joyce in 1975.

The monologue was never taken any further – she knew that there was no market for it in Britain. After visiting South Africa for over twenty years, Joyce had perfected various South African accents and their idiosyncrasies. She could mimic apologetic English-speaking whites, the mixed-race Cape Coloured people and the Afrikaans-speaking supporters of apartheid. But she could not include any of them in her repertory – at that time neither a British nor an American audience recognised a 'Sythe Effrikin ecksint' and certainly could not picture the life they led. A decade later they might have.

However, she did do a black South African – also her only mono-logue of a man. In 1968 a twenty-five-year-old black driver employed by Messina Mines drove her across Johannesburg. As with most people she met, she got into conversation with him and discovered that Nicodemus was a practising Methodist and read a lot of books. He preferred Maugham to D. H. Lawrence, loved Guy de Maupassant and Chekhov and was well versed in Shakespeare. Joyce found him charming and intelligent, with a poetic outlook. He reinforced her feelings about the lack of educational opportunities for Africans, but he used the time spent waiting for his employers to read. Although he could not leave South Africa, he told her, 'All the time I am travelling inside my head.' Joyce scribbled down his words the moment she left the car. She wrote them into a talking-song which she performed in half-light, clapping out a drum rhythm on her thighs.

By 1973 Joyce felt that:

This is a fascinating and tragic country but it is waking up and I see many changes for the better; more consideration, more awareness of man's dignity. Not *nearly* enough but it has to begin & I think it's madness to cut off all the lines of communication because one hates apartheid. What is needed is some under-standing of the colossal problems & encouragement of the liber-als here who are trying *hard* & establishing relationships of the mind and heart.

In 1976 Reggie, now seventy-three years old, retired as a director of Messina Mines and they made their last trip to Messina, which had grown into a town, sporting hotels, banks and even a Grenfell Street. They both felt quite sad at leaving the staff and the house they had known for twenty-six years. Joyce had watched the political situation and now noted 'enormous changes going on – *good* ones. Thank heavens.' However, she had been horrified by the shooting of school-children in Soweto that June. 'Despairing. What *is* the future?' she wrote to Virginia. 'The radio report says the hate felt by the children is a revelation to the SA government, what do they expect when freedom IS a right?' She wore a blue ribbon to support peaceful change. For Reggie's birthday treat they took the luxurious Blue Train from Pretoria to the Cape and were as thrilled as children to be upgraded to the VIP super de luxe suite with private bathroom, bedroom and air-conditioned sitting-room. But when the train passed lines of impoverished shacks, Joyce was reminded of the shocking living conditions of black South Africans.

– 24 –

THE MEDIUM THAT eventually brought Joyce most recognition in Britain was television. Although first broadcast in London in 1929, it got off to a slow start and by George VI's coronation in 1937 only two thousand sets had been bought. By 1938 there were live outside broadcasts of the Test Match, the Trooping of the Colour and Chamberlain holding aloft the fluttering peace agreement signed by Hitler. The normal range of reception was forty miles from Alexandra Palace – though occasionally BBC television was received as far away as New York. Television closed down the day war was declared in September 1939, and reopened for three hours a day on 9 June 1946. Joyce appeared just two days later, singing live in *Starlight*, but felt that 'television may develop one day but so far it is a waste of time'. She was right. After excerpts from *Tuppence Coloured* were broadcast three years later, the Head of Television, Cecil McGivern, complained about the appearance of the microphone. 'I think it fair to say that the presentation of this item was flat-footed in the extreme, and that the decor was terrible,' he wrote. 'Joyce Grenfell herself was charming.'

Joyce was not too happy either. She wrote to Norman Collins, Controller of Television, 'I wonder whether there might be some other way of feeding artists at Alexandra Palace than by the present method of slow queuing and wistful hoping for a table in those crowded and echo-y canteens? I never knew what concentration was until I did television revue! I don't believe I am a particularly over sensitive type but I do find a little cosseting before giving a perform-ance, and a little peace, is a help.' Collins replied that they were going to build a new canteen 'as soon as steel, labour and so forth become available'.

In 1950 Joyce was chosen as the first person to feature on *Women of*

Today, in which each week's guest talked about her life as it was reflected in her home decor. Joyce showed the viewers around her flat in King's Road and demonstrated how to make a salad.

As with radio, scripts had to be submitted to the censor before transmission. Joyce wrote to the BBC, 'I hate letting my stuff be seen on paper. It just lies there dead as mutton. I have got a beautiful new typewriter but no carbon paper and alas I am xtill [*sic*] a rotten typer on it.' For *Variety Show* in 1951 Viola agreed to accompany her, on condition she was out of camera shot. This caused considerable problems in the large echoing set at Alexandra Palace, as Joyce and Viola could not see each other. Reggie watched the programme on Virginia's set and said the lighting was so odd that Joyce looked as if she had one glass eye.

Three years later they performed together in a set cluttered with books, magazines, pictures, armchairs, sofas, vases of flowers and tea trays. The programme included an updated *Canteen*, *Shirley's Girl Friend* about hypnosis, and songs. The television crews were always impressed by Joyce's ability to retake a sketch or song in exactly the same way each time. After she had broadcast a series of four more shows with Daphne Oxenford and Elisabeth Welch in 1956, McGivern wrote to the producer, 'I found this polished, sophisticated and minority programme a welcome and refreshing change.' After this success, the Grenfells decided that it was time they bought their own television.

In 1958 Joyce received 150 guineas for *Music for You*, while Viola's fee had risen to fifteen guineas. By 1963 Joyce was one of the best-paid performers on television, receiving 250 guineas for an appearance in *The Billy Cotton Band Show*. When, a few months later, she was asked to write and present a forty-five-minute show for the same fee, her agent asked for £2,000. After the usual haggling, she accepted £750. For the next two years she received no television invitations and assumed she was no longer fashionable; in fact the accountants and producers were squabbling over her value. The accountants said her fees were too high and worried that if word got out, then all performers would want higher fees. The producers said she was a 'specialised performer' and eventually the accountants agreed to pay, on condition this did not set precedents. She was immediately invited to do two *Cabaret* shows for two thousand guineas each, which were watched by four million viewers. William Blezard's fee as composer and conductor rose from ten guineas to two hundred, and the orchestra of a dozen musicians had to make do with 240 guineas between them.

Joyce was also one of the best-paid contributors to *Woman's Hour*, receiving ten guineas for five-minute talks when others received only one. When she was asked to produce a whole *Woman's Hour* on her own in 1958, she chose 'Peace of Mind'. She had been at a cocktail party in New York when an East European man asked her and Greta Garbo which they would prefer – 'Peace of mind or a million dollars?' Joyce said she would forgo the money every time. The man was surprised, for he considered peace of mind to be death to a creative artist. Given that she did not have to choose between the two, Joyce had her usual row with the BBC over her fee – she wanted more than the fifty guineas they had offered her. For once, they won.

Joyce had been heard on *Woman's Hour* once or twice a year since 1949, talking about her career as an entertainer. The producer Joanna Scott-Moncrieff changed that when she asked Joyce to write a talk on the subject of 'Laughter' in 1961. From then on, Joyce wrote thoughtful talks and broadcast about once a month for over ten years. Given the subject 'Pleasures in Life', Joyce chose 'writing'; for 'Ambition' she wrote, 'I like the life I've got'; and for 'My Escape Route' she talked about the refuge she found in music and birdwatching. Her five-minute talks were, like her monologues, condensed pieces of writing that required considerable concentration. Each talk went through several drafts before she was satisfied; she always met deadlines but never rushed the writing.

Joyce admired Joanna Scott-Moncrieff's radio skills as much as she had Stephen Potter's, and they soon became friends. 'Joanna's vision of listeners' potential interests was reflected in the wide range of subjects she introduced,' Joyce said. 'She never imposed her views but made sure that you were making clear what you were trying to say. She always cut my opening paragraph. Always. And she was always right. As another colleague said, "She could take a lame item and turn it into a brilliant one with a few quick, constructive decisions." She made you so much better than you were.'

In 1961 Joyce was very surprised to be invited by Reginald Bevins, the Postmaster General, to join the Pilkington Commission, to explore the future of radio and television broadcasting, both state and commercial: 'a task of great interest, of first-class importance, and with far-reaching social and economic implications for the country as a whole'. Joyce thought there must have been a mistake. Why would they invite her, a comic entertainer, onto a serious government commission? But it was no mistake – she had been chosen for her knowledge of broadcasting and her ability to listen to others and articulate her thoughts. Although she had never sat on a political committee before and she represented no special interest group, she had been a regular listener for over thirty years and a broadcaster for over twenty. She was also a passionate believer in radio and television as a power for good.

The independent committee had eleven members chaired by Sir Harry Pilkington, an energetic industrialist from Lancashire, who was public-spirited, conventional, fair-minded and intelligent. Bevins considered that, with an average age of forty-nine years, the committee had an 'accent on youth'. University lecturer Richard Hoggart was already well known for his criticism of the potential consequences of expanding commercial television through his book *The Uses of Literacy*. The only other woman was Scottish social worker and broadcaster Elizabeth Whiteley, with whom Joyce got on very well. In addition to Billy Wright, the English football captain, there was also a headmaster, a trade unionist, a law professor, and a senior civil servant. Hoggart described them as 'a very mixed bunch – politically, by age and predispositions'. Sir Harry noticed that they all had one thing in common: 'None of us has an axe to grind. We are all passionate believers in truth.' The Christian press complained they were not represented – ignoring the fact that Pilkington was a lifelong Congregationalist, Joyce a committed Christian Scientist and other members were regular church-goers.

Joyce was the most unusual choice and critics claimed that she was only a token member, representing the lightweight taste of the middle classes and middle-aged theatre-goers. Hoggart observed that:

Her determination was fed by great seriousness combined with an excessive modesty because she had not been to university.

That was an accident of her upper-class background and time and meant little: she was an autodidact. She was not an intellectual but she had uncommon intelligence. If you convinced Joyce Grenfell about a point of view, you knew you had come through a very fine mill indeed. Once convinced, she stayed firm; flattery would not move her. She became the litmus paper, the Geiger-counter, the bench-mark of the sound sense and honesty of the committee's thinking.

When the Pilkington Commission began in September 1960, the ten most popular television programmes were all made by ITV and included *Emergency Ward 10*, *Take Your Pick* and *Sunday Night at the Palladium*. The BBC offered *Sooty*, *What's My Line?* and *Monitor*, and its most popular programme was *Juke Box Jury*. There were now just over ten million combined television and radio licence holders.

Joyce took her new role seriously and was conscientious about attending meetings. To reach the committee rooms she had to walk through a pedestrian tunnel under Waterloo Bridge, where she discovered to her delight that if she sang an arpeggio, it echoed back as a chord. Before every meeting, she held a solo concert under the archway. She always made sure that the committee looked presentable, so ties were checked for straightness and Hoggart was not allowed to take off his shoes during interviews.

'Sometimes Joyce was a bit like the head girl of St Trinian's,' Hoggart remembered.

Once, we were leaving Belfast Airport and we were at the barrier, with the plane across on the tarmac. There was a big man at the front who was the BBC sports commentator. 'There's going to be a real scramble here,' she said to me. Then, very quietly, 'Get me three coats.' So I collected three coats from the other Pilkington members. 'Watch me,' she said. 'The thing is to get out in front and if anybody tries to get past you, kick their ankles.' She streaked across that tarmac at a speed I would never have thought possible, especially with the coats. She beat the sports commentator hollow, straight up the stairs. When the rest of us got into the aircraft there she was, with all our seats booked, in the best places.

Commission members with salaries were seconded, so lost no income, but Joyce told Hoggart quite equably that this work had cost her several thousand pounds. The committee did receive expenses but even they had to be fought for. 'The Grand Hotel, Cardiff, only had one room with an attached bathroom,' Hoggart remembers. 'This was allocated to Joyce but the cost was more than the allowable daily rate. This seemed unfair, so the chairman wrote to the Postmaster General. Eventually a bureaucratic reply came saying that just this once they would repay the difference but members of the committee should remember that they were saving money by not being at home!'

The committee debated questions such as 'Should mass public taste dictate the quality of television programmes?', 'Could television refine and influence that taste upwards?' and 'How far does television influence manners and morals?'. They interviewed shopkeepers, politicians, teachers and engineers around the country. Over 150 organisations connected with broadcasting were included: trade unions, the film industry, the press, youth clubs and advertising companies. The committee was expected to grasp the intricacies of the management, financing and technical side of broadcasting. Joyce confessed she was no good at statistics or technology, but she was thrilled by colour television eight years before it was publicly broadcast and a direct television link with Yuri Gagarin being kissed by Khrushchev in Moscow. She was less keen on the commercial television companies, who claimed they wanted to make quality programmes 'but not at peak viewing hours'. The committee did not take kindly to one ITV director who explained the poor quality of his programmes by saying, 'People get the television they deserve.' Joyce found Lord Reith, the first BBC Director General, then aged seventy-one, arrogant and out of touch with modern viewers. Hoggart thought that he spoke 'as if the words were being cut out of granite during a thunderstorm'. The witness who impressed them most was T. S. Eliot – frail, elegant and articulate.

Every sentence was chewed over and thought through by the whole committee and, after seventy-eight meetings held over eighteen months, the Pilkington Commission reached a consensus and their report was published in June 1962. They knew that their radical proposals would not be liked by the government, but they believed in them, and were going to stick to them. Hoggart commented that he had never seen such a wide-ranging group 'so steadily and firmly reach a common mind'. The Pilkington Commission believed that viewers were capable of appreciating quality broadcasting. The BBC was upheld as the nation's broadcaster and rewarded with a second channel, while advertising on BBC continued to be rejected. Independent television was berated for poor-quality programmes and told it would have to improve before it could receive another channel, while advertising was to be reduced to seven minutes per hour. Their main proposal for improving commercial television was that the makers of programmes should not be the same people who sold advertising. The report stressed the importance of 'professionalism' – in all fields of broadcasting and entertainment. To the government's surprise, the commission had engaged in social philosophy and decided that 'triviality is worse for the soul than wickedness' and broadcasters should accept that they were in a constant relationship with the moral condition of society. Many interpreted this neutral statement as moralistic puritanism, whereas the tabloid press complained that middle-class academics were telling working people what to enjoy. An ITV company chairman burned an effigy of the report and another urged shareholders to complain to their MPs. Critics came from all quarters – the press, the broadcasting media, the Conservative government, the Opposition – but few of them read the report carefully.

After the press conference, the Postmaster General invited the committee to dinner at the Savoy – and then told them the government would not accept their recommendations. However, the report influenced debates about broadcasting for the next decade. Nearly twenty years later Joyce felt the chapter on the 'Purposes of Broadcasting' remained definitive, and thirty years later Hoggart still thought that chapter remained the finest statement in English on those issues and that the report had improved commercial television in the long term.

Joyce had put her mind and soul into the job and was disappointed by the government's reaction. However, she had enjoyed the stimulation of being part of a dedicated and professional committee, meeting large numbers of people, and was proud to have contributed to the future of entertainment in Britain.

When Hoggart and Joyce were made members of the BBC General Advisory Council from 1964 to 1970, he noticed that she always liked to be right in the middle of a good argument. She was in despair about the lowering of standards of the BBC's broadcasting. 'Quality has always marked the output of talks, discussions, features, plays and readings that we have learned to expect from the BBC.' She found a radio talk by a clergyman entitled 'Unyoung, Uncoloured and Unpoor' particularly distasteful and told the Chairman of the BBC, Lord Hill, in no uncertain terms.

Despite their differing political views, Joyce remained firm friends with Richard Hoggart and his family. 'During the commission Joyce made a conspiratorial effort with me to stop Richard smoking,' remembers Mary Hoggart. 'She used to drop me these little notes about his progress.'

'Joyce kept her friendships very well nourished, which is an unusual quality, especially for people who are so busy,' agrees Hoggart.

Once when Joyce and Reggie called on us in Leicester, they had had trouble with the car on the way. The man who stopped to help them turned out to be a big noise in the Football Association. He offered her tickets for the Cup Final, a week later. Joyce remembered that our two sons were very keen fans of Leicester City, who were in the final, so she sent them to us. Of course the boys were thrilled to bits and the tickets made us the stars of the street!

After the Pilkington Commission, Joyce's intellect and thoughtfulness were more widely recognised and she was invited onto serious programmes such as *Any Questions?*. 'At first the programme scared me silent,' she said. 'I had nothing to say about the Coal Board.' Then they were asked, 'What is the true function of the critic?' and Joyce was on home ground. 'The true function is "Did the playwright succeed in doing what he set out to?" The great mistake is that critics go on the first night. In an ideal world they should come to an early rehearsal and then come on a later date to see if you succeeded in what you tried to do. When you think of the work that goes into preparing a production you should give it courtesy.' In 1969 she travelled back from a transmission of *Any Questions?* in Eastbourne with panel members Enoch Powell and Bernard Levin and, after the political barracking during the programme, she steered the conversation onto music, books and holidays. She was surprised to find that in private they were delightful company. After two more *Any Questions?* programmes, with Gerald Nabarro, Tom Jackson and Malcolm Muggeridge, she decided she had had enough of being surrounded by opinionated men, and declined future invitations.

Although Joyce expected high fees, she remained resistant to commercial television and only appeared on it occasionally. In the USA she had no choice and had to compete with cars on *The Ed Sullivan Show* and cup-cakes on the game show *Make up Your Mind*. Despite frequent requests, Joyce never made a television commercial or advertised any product except her own.

All the same, her appearances on television greatly increased the number of people who recognised her in the streets. People were often surprised to find she was larger in real life than they expected and would say, 'I'd no idea you are so b— I mean tall.' It was even worse when they asked, 'Are you somebody? Should I know you?' But she was flattered by genuine, friendly recognition. In April 1979 she hailed a taxi in Sloane Square and the driver said, 'Fancy seeing you here.' He explained that they'd met in the Suez Canal Zone in 1952. 'I've never forgotten you,' he said. 'I tell my wife and children whenever we see you on TV, "That's the funniest woman in the world and I've sung a song with her on the stage."' Joyce was delighted with his chatter and even more pleased when, arriving in Elm Park Gardens, he said, 'This trip's on me.'

Even better were fans who were also Christian Scientists. Looking for shoes in a Sloane Street shop, Joyce chatted amiably to the young sales assistant. The next evening Joyce saw her in church. She told Joyce that it had been a terrible day in the shop and she was about to hand in her notice but Joyce had healed her with her 'strength of love and calm'.

Some aspects of her fame annoyed Joyce intensely. She was furious if she suspected that she had been invited to a party in order to provide free entertainment. She wanted to run a mile when hostesses clapped their hands for silence and said in loud voices, 'Joyce, dear, *do* do one of your funny little skits.' She was a professional entertainer, and she wanted everyone to appreciate that. She didn't mind spontaneous singing among close friends or professionals, but she hated being a performing dog.

Another irritation was amateur performers who were unaware of performing-fees or the laws of copyright. They often wrote to Joyce asking for copies of her scripts, as if they were books to be borrowed from the library. Unlike George Bernard Shaw, who had printed letters for such common problems, Joyce wrote to each fan individually, in longhand, explaining that her material was her personal tool and why didn't they have a go at writing their own sketches? She told John Betjeman that she replied to all fan letters, 'even if they are addressed to Miss Joan Grenville'.

Her fame had come through years of hard work and she was careful to preserve her reputation. According to Laurence Olivier, the qualities which make up a successful actor are 'Talent: this must develop into skill. Luck: you must see it has provided you with the right opportunities at the right times. Stamina: a gift seemingly not affected by disease, unless worn down by constant draughts.' Joyce certainly had all these.

In the 1968 *Show of the Week* she had twice as many television viewers as Joan Baez, but only half the number watching Dudley Moore and Peter Cook's *Not Only . . . But Also . . .*. The panel of viewers preferred her monologues to her songs and some felt she lacked her usual bounce and sparkle. A civil servant said, 'despite Miss Grenfell's undoubted mastery of her art, the show was never able to rise above a pleasant vicar's tea party interlude'. A fifth of the reporting audience felt it had a dated, old-fashioned air and was far too long for a one-woman show.

When Joyce performed the *Show of the Week* a year later, the viewers enjoyed it more. Even though many of the monologues were repeats, they were 'still just as fresh and vital as ever'; 'she has shown once again her shrewd but kindly observation of human foibles and frailties but there is always compassion in her humour'. A few found it too long and 'over-refined' and 'slightly reminiscent of a school elocution class or a Church Hall – Mrs. Whitehouse would have approved'. However, the 'Reaction Index' had gone up to 73 per cent – higher than for Harry Secombe, Terry Scott or even Val Doonican.

25

J OYCE'S FAVOURITE FORM of creative expression was music. She liked 'all types of music, as long as it was good' – Bach, Beethoven, Britten and Gershwin – and preferred chamber music to symphonies. She would rather go to a concert than the theatre, cinema or an exhibition.

In 1962 Viola introduced Joyce and Reggie to the Aldeburgh Music Festival, which Benjamin Britten and Peter Pears had established in 1948. Britten believed passionately in both his East Anglian roots and his duty to serve the community. 'I have tried to bring music *to* Aldeburgh in the shape of our local Festival; and all the music I write comes *from* it,' he said. The festival became one of the most successful in the country, mainly because the local community was involved, though not everyone liked so much music. One fisherman said in 1966: 'All bloody night all you could hear was violins in the house opposite.'

Aldeburgh is a pretty fishing-town, barely changed since its heyday in the early nineteenth century. The High Street is lined with interesting shops and the fishermen's cottages are painted in a variety of colours. Two or three concerts a day over three weeks took place in the Jubilee Hall, the parish church, the Baptist chapel, on the seafront and in the half-timbered cinema. From the first year she went, Joyce was thrilled with the Aldeburgh Festival, especially the opportunity to make and be with friends between concerts. 'The quality of the Aldeburgh Festival is not so much a series of performances as a gathering of friends – on both sides of the footlights,' wrote Bernard Levin. 'The performances are of the very highest standards, but everybody seems to be doing it for fun.' Reggie enjoyed it too – during the morning concerts he went birdwatching. They went every year and always stayed in the Wentworth Hotel, at the north end of the promenade where Joyce took a daily plunge into the

North Sea. 'June is a magical month in Suffolk,' she wrote. 'I will never forget the light as we drove to Orford for the first performance of Fiery Furnace – ditches full of Queen Anne's lace, wild roses, elderberry in full cream and a nightingale sang in the church yard, as we were going in! Such production!'

Although Reggie usually drove the car, Joyce set the pace. 'We like to drive slowly,' she said. 'Then we can see the flowers.'

'So damn slowly,' Reggie murmured, 'that we can see them growing.'

Suffolk was ideal for birdwatching, another interest they shared with Viola, Britten and Pears. In the autumn of 1969 the sea broke through at Aldeburgh and flooded Snape marshes where over one hundred species of birds breed, leaving the delicate flora and fauna at risk from permanent damage. Reggie wrote an article appealing to music lovers to donate the £8,000 needed to restore the river wall.

Nine miles along the coast from Aldeburgh is Minsmere Bird Reserve, formed accidentally in 1940 when the grazing-marshes were flooded as a defence against invasion. By the end of the war the reed-beds had attracted many species of birds, including marsh harriers, avocets and bitterns.

Herbert Axell, the warden, did much to improve Minsmere and masterminded the construction of the world's first man-made lagoon for birds. Joyce and Reggie would set off from the Wentworth Hotel armed with sandwiches, sketchbook and binoculars. Joyce watched birds the same way that she watched people – quietly, unobserved, taking mental notes and sometimes sketching them. She discovered that birdwatching is the perfect antidote to fame and a busy life, and fellow 'twitchers' were more interested in spotting birds than entertainers. 'A glorious day in June on the marsh has sometimes been too much for Joyce's *joie de vivre*, causing her to break forth into song,' Axell remembered. When he retired in 1972 the Grenfells bought him and his wife Joan a cottage near Minsmere and set up a trust to pay all the bills until his death.

After their second visit, Joyce wrote, 'Please may I say "Dear Ben" because it is so unnatural to put Dear Mr Britten after hearing everyone in Aldeburgh say Ben? Many thanks for yet another lovely and heartening festival. We came away nourished and refreshed.' Britten immediately invited Joyce to perform the following year. 'I feel truly honoured,' she replied. 'To be asked to be part of the best festival in the world gives me so much pleasure that I don't know how to say Thank you. It is the compliment I am more proud of than anything that has ever happened to me. I mean this. Your music past and present – and future – makes me feel as if I had been taken into space.'

Joyce performed her songs and monologues and the 1964 festival programme stated: 'for further information about Miss Grenfell the reader is referred to *Who's Who*, *Who's Who in America*, *Who's Who in Australia*, *Qui est Qui*, *Wer ist Wer (oder Was)* and *Chi e Chi*.'

Joyce's sell-out shows subsidised the more esoteric concerts and Britten wrote: 'It was a joy to have you here, & we are grateful to you for the incomparably funny and wise evening you gave us – we were the honoured ones! Come back again, both of you, & do another such evening for us – "as near the bone" as you like to make it. Love Ben.' Fidelity, Countess of Cranbrook chaired the Aldeburgh Festival for over thirty years. 'Joyce was an unusual choice for the festival, but she wasn't just a performer, she became part of Aldeburgh and got to know everyone.'

'Sometimes in the festival, the Joyce Grenfell character talking in between items in the next row would turn around and – what joy! – it *was* Joyce,' said writer John Amis. In the list of festival subscribers, Joyce modestly called herself 'Mrs R. Grenfell'.

In 1967 Britten's dream was fulfilled when the Snape Maltings, a derelict agricultural building a few miles inland from Aldeburgh, was converted into a 750-seat concert hall. The programme began with the official opening by the Queen and ended three weeks later with Purcell's *Fairy Queen*. Britten had also invited Joyce: 'it will be marvellous if you can step out of the audience on to the stage to celebrate being 20!' Joyce replied: 'There is something about the Aldeburgh Festival that makes you want to do far better than you have ever done before anywhere else in the world. It is a challenge to keep up to the standard you & Peter [Pears] give, that goes far beyond the line of duty!' Local resident Muffet Harrison was in the audience: 'Although the Maltings is very large, you could hear every word that Joyce said and every gesture was so plain.'

Joyce added a new character to her monologue *Artist's Room*. Marty Winderhaur, an American music student, advises the concert pianist that she quite liked the way you expose the contours of the sonata . . . Although it conflicts with interpretations I have familiarised myself with on disc. Still . . . I think it is valid, but would very much like to discuss with you the premises from which you tangentised your explorations. I think I could say I derived some intellectual satisfaction from your performance, but, urm, my emotions were only semi-engaged by your display of pyrotechnics.

Joyce also wrote Britten a surprise song, but since she did not like surprises herself, she and William visited Britten at home the morning before the concert. She said she 'just wanted to try something out'. It was a 'recitative' set to swing music by William, full of puns on 'Ben'. The middle verse went:

How Benevolent is the setting
Suffolk winds Benignly Blow
Benefiting all who came here
And to concerts go oh-oh-oh
Seats Benumb on Parish church Benches
But the Benefited Ear recognises Benediction
In the wonders it can hear
Ben-ee Bene Molto Bene.

Joyce was amazed by Britten's reaction. He was not just surprised, he was overwhelmed. When it finished he leaped up and embraced her, weeping.

Once back in London, Joyce and William recorded the song onto a disc and sent it to Britten. Three years later he wrote to Joyce: 'Peter & I were hunting for an ancient record in a seldom used cupboard, & to our great surprise, then delight, & then horror, we found a record you'd sent us, away back in 1967, which neither of us had seen before. I do hope that you will forgive my not having thanked for the precious copy of your handsome & delightful Tribute.' Joyce replied, 'Of course I understand & of course I forgive! What's more I can imagine the wave of horror you felt when you discovered the record and you have my deepest sympathy.'

Only two years after its opening, on the second day of the 1969 festival, Joyce and Reggie woke to the news that the Maltings had been destroyed by fire. The night before, they had been there, listening to the Trout Quintet with Britten at the piano. Reggie immediately went to help co-ordinate offers of assistance. Within twenty-four hours the programme had been rescheduled to Blythburgh and Orford Churches, and only one of the eighteen planned concerts was cancelled. In between the concerts Joyce helped open letters of condolence and donations and enough money was raised to make the new Maltings even better.

At the opening of the new Maltings in 1970 Colin Grahame, musical director of the festival, devised a seventieth-birthday tribute to Noël Coward, sung by Joyce, Cleo Laine and Ben Luxon. 'Joyce's sound was unforced in tune and true,' wrote Cleo Laine.

I found her to be as natural as her voice; a voice she was strangely unsure of, in a way that she most certainly was not about most things. We got on well together immediately, despite a certain disparity of age and background, often falling about like a couple of silly schoolgirls if anything tickled our fancy. At one rehearsal we were singing *Mad Dogs and Englishmen* and coming to the 'doo-wacka-doo' bit, a slip of the tongue from Joyce made the phrase sound a little risqué and even more nonsensical. We were all unable to contain ourselves, breaking down into hysterical, helpless, leg-crossing laughter. The more we tried, the worse we got, to the chagrin of Colin who had been directing and was sitting silently, patiently in the dark, waiting for the adult professionals up on the stage, behaving like one of Joyce's nursery school sketches, to pull themselves together. We tried to resume, only to break down in a heap again. Colin became very cross and boomed out of the stalls, 'Very well, get it out of your systems and then maybe we can get on?' It was a hard struggle before we regained control. Joyce was the oldest of us, but she was the most collapsible of the lot, enjoying a good laugh and disliking anyone with airs and graces.

Although Joyce and Reggie were never officially part of the Aldeburgh Festival, they intervened when they felt necessary. One year, after a row with the festival general manager, Stephen Reiss,

Britten had threatened to resign, which meant that Reiss would have to first. When Lady Cranbrook considered resigning too, in support of Reiss, Joyce and Reggie visited her. 'Joyce was a very level-headed person,' she remembers, 'and she couldn't bear the fighting. She could see the lasting damage if we didn't all make up and reminded us that the festival was bigger than these personal crises.' Their differences were patched up and when Reiss retired a few years later, Joyce organised a fund for his retirement and recommended him for an OBE, which he received in 1973.

Stephen and Mary Potter had moved to The Red House, on the out-skirts of Aldeburgh, in 1951 and Joyce remained friends with Mary after their divorce in 1955. Mary was also a close friend of Britten and Pears, who had a small cottage on the seafront. As their fame increased and the festival grew, the cottage became too public and too small, and Mary suggested swapping her large farmhouse for Britten's cottage, on condition she could still use the tennis court. The Grenfells often joined the Red House tennis parties with Mary, Britten, Pears and the van der Posts. Joyce and Reggie had first met playing tennis but it was not until middle age that they found their accuracy and energy had actually improved and it became a central part of their relaxation. On warm summer afternoons in London, Reggie would phone from his office suggesting a game before supper in Cadogan Gardens or at the Hurlingham Club. Joyce was once playing with a twelve-year-old boy when she pleaded, 'Do say, "Well played" occasionally instead of merely "*Run!*"' Joyce never ran – the ball had to come to her.

Over the years the Grenfells bought several of Mary's paintings. After Reggie bought a landscape in 1957, Joyce wrote:

The picture is so lovely I nearly wept when I saw it. What delight & *joy* your painting gives me. There is a tremendous atmosphere in all your work and it is as if that very first impulse that made you want to paint the picture is still vibrating. As in everything in life it is the *feeling* one has, that is the power. I mean you can talk till the cows come home, pray till your knees break but only when the feel happens is anything any good.

And *where* does that feel happen? In some sort of spiritual mind I rather think. Anyway I had a lovely feel at your exhibition & I'm *so* excited about the picture. Will you come & see it here one day?

Love Joyce.

In 1968 Joyce asked Mary if she would paint her portrait. Mary preferred doing still-lifes and landscapes but she agreed to do it in Aldeburgh, early in 1969. Mary was clear about her working conditions – no music, no talk and sitting only in the morning. In the afternoon she expected Joyce to go for a walk while 'I brood on it and tinker with it'. But Mary found it almost impossible to 'catch' Joyce in paint: 'I think the big one *is* like you, but not good enough, because it hasn't got enough life in it. My fault, not yours!' she wrote. Although she made three attempts, none of them really worked. There is a certain likeness but the features are too small and dainty. Reggie bought two, to prevent anyone else owning them.

Later that year, Stephen was diagnosed with bone cancer and then died from pneumonia. In her diary Joyce wrote, 'He was so talented, but he worshipped success and craved it, but his idleness ruled it out, even though his intelligence and gifts were more than adequate. He was kind, funny and clever, but very much a No 1 man, *only* concerned for SP.' Mary Potter wrote to Joyce, 'You are the only one of my friends who understood him – nearly as well as I did.'

Another old friend, Viola Tunnard, was a central attraction of Aldeburgh. As her classical reputation grew, so she tried to distance herself from having been Joyce's accompanist with ENSA, though she continued to play at hospital concerts with Joyce until 1957. Viola was rehearsal pianist for Herbert von Karajan and was a devoted member of Britten's musical team, working with singers like Janet Baker and Peter Pears and playing duets with Britten in concerts.

In the winter of 1969 Viola slipped on an icy pavement and hurt her leg. It did not get better and she walked with a limp for some months. When, during rehearsals of *Idomeneo* at Aldeburgh, she began to falter at the piano, Britten was angry with her for not trying. Viola had always been wilful and also very stoical, so for some time nobody realised how ill she was. Britten continued to expect her usual high standards and it upset Viola when she failed to meet them.

After a year, even Britten realised that something more than wilful-ness was affecting Viola's work. Once she received the diagnosis of motor neurone disease she knew that she would never be able to perform again, but she hoped she would be able to go on teaching music. It was a sad day for her when, at the end of 1970, she gave away her beloved Steinway grand piano. Viola moved in with Jean and Christopher Cowan, who ran the bookshop in the centre of Aldeburgh. She had her own front door for visitors, while the Cowans could give her the increasing care she needed. She never complained about her illness and was torn between wanting to see her friends, and not wanting them to see how disabled she had become.

Whether Viola wanted her to or not, Joyce visited as often as she could. At first she was convinced that if only Viola could understand Christian Science she could be cured. As the disease took hold, Viola tried any cure available – homeopathy, spinal injections – and finally asked Joyce for Christian Science help. Joyce pointed out that it would not work unless she truly believed in it.

Each time Joyce visited, she gave Jean Cowan 'picnic money', cheques for £100 to contribute towards Viola's keep, and also gave them a washing-machine and a colour television. 'Joyce was enor-mously compassionate towards Viola, and loved her like a child,' said Jean. 'But Viola found this irritating – she didn't want to be treated like a child.'

Joyce and Reggie arranged for Viola to visit Minsmere Bird Reserve in a wheelchair and in the last few weeks of her life, in 1974, Joyce sat beside her and read her the *Guardian* out loud. Joyce gave the first donation to the Viola Tunnard Memorial Trust, which funds student bursaries at the Britten-Pears Music School. In her obituary in *The Times*, Britten wrote that Viola was 'an unsparingly hard worker with very exacting standards. Her mercurial sense of humour never deserted her through the last years.'

Viola's illness and death strengthened rather than challenged Joyce's religious beliefs. In a letter to Britten shortly after Viola died, she wrote:

The sense of joy about her persists & it isn't just personal belief that her terrible time of illness is over, it is her actual *freedom*. I sense it totally & it has been a remarkable time of *not* grieving in a self pitying way, only a substantial certainty that all is well. I see Viola with her back to us, tall, & straight again as she was, so swift moving and free, looking towards light. She was such a talented, dedicated, difficult, rewarding, funny, generous, beautiful, demanding intellectually, companionable creature.'

Joyce was not afraid to say that she was glad when sick friends died and were now free. She finished a letter to Rupert Hart-Davis about a mutual friend who had just just died with 'Depressing cricket, isn't it?'

Soon after Britten had a heart attack in 1976, he wrote to Joyce, 'When I feel depressed I now go around murmuring "Ouch" to myself (at your suggestion) and it cheers me up a bit.' When he died later that year, Joyce wrote to Peter Pears from Australia:

When I think of Ben I get a feeling of light and great strength. His music is his memorial and that is evidence of all he was and this is his continuity. We are compounded of *qualities* rather than the inward & visible signs; these, I think, are what endure – we may think it is the look, touch, sound of the one we love, but I begin to realise that it is their humour, generosity, wisdom, loyalty, courage, honesty, etc. etc. that *are* the individual. These qualities are spiritual and therefore unchanging & eternal. This is a horrible time for you & I send my love and very real sympathy.

26

In 1972 Marmaduke Hussey, Reggie's nephew-in-law and the chief executive of *The Times*, arranged for Joyce *not* to be in *The Times* for her birthday, though she forgot about the *Daily Telegraph* and the *Express*. 'I really do not like birthdays & wish I could forget mine. Not because I'm 62 but because it is silly as one grows older.' Nevertheless she enjoyed her birthday outing to the musical *Godspell*, where she observed that 'The place was rigid with Bishops – Coggan, Coventry, Manchester, and three others!'

Joyce began the year with a four-part series for BBC television called *The Incomplete Collected Works of Joyce Grenfell*, in which she performed *Nursery School*; *Old Girl's School Reunion* (subtitle: 'Time Isn't Always a Great Healer'); and Blezard's spoof operetta compositions *Lillian, or The Woodland Princess* who meets a prince in the forest while she gathers berries, and *Freda and Eric* who sing a duet, 'Alone. Alone and weary.'

'I do not like watching myself, it is so strange,' Joyce said. 'My dress looked hideous. Oh little ego, how dim you are.' Soon after this she was offered a five-year contract in Hollywood for a television comedy called *The Snoopers* with Helen Hayes but it would mean spending twenty weeks a year away from Reggie and she turned it down.

Plans for 1973 were many – radio talks, television appearances, concerts in Birmingham and a three-month tour of Australia of sixty-eight concerts – quite a feat for a sixty-three-year old. But first, the Queen had asked Joyce to perform for her hundred guests at the Waterloo Dinner at Windsor Castle during Ascot Week. 'Nice to be asked,' Joyce wrote to Verily, 'but NOT my favourite audience – horsey, social upper-crust and not all that bright.' When she and Reggie were invited to the actual dinner as well, she decided to break her own golden rule and eat before a performance, but only if

William and Joan Blezard were invited to dine too. Diana Lyddon stage-managed the performance and had supper with the upper staff – hairdressers, valets and butlers.

'I had an upstairs-downstairs day,' she remembers.

The housekeeper warned me not to look out of the window when the Royal Family came back from the Ascot races in their horse-drawn carriages. A high-ranking army man helped me set up in the Green Drawing Room while somebody mended the curtains, which were in shreds. In the window, behind a platform for Joyce to stand on, was a statue of a racehorse and I asked if it could be moved. All round the walls were illuminated cabinets filled with china, and an equerry said the lights had to remain on. Maybe they were frightened the guests would pinch the china? When Joyce came in to test the lighting, I told her that it might spoil the effect. "Indeed it will," she said; "people should be able to fall asleep if they want to." The lights were turned off, but the horse remained. When Joyce finished *Eng. Lit.*, in which she wears a Marks and Sparks cardie, she put it on the horse, which made Princess Anne laugh.

Reggie's niece Sue Hussey, one of the Queen's ladies-in-waiting, lent Joyce her room to change into her pink silk frock designed by Clive Evans. The Green Drawing Room was filled with golden chairs for the guests and armchairs for the Royal Family, and she performed the numbers chosen in advance by the Queen. 'It was a tremendous honour,' said William Blezard. 'But I nearly blew it when I realised to my horror that I'd left my dilapidated, ancient copy of "The Battle March of Delhi" in the lady-in-waiting's quarters. People were brushed aside as I set off to the "Outer Hebrides" of Windsor Castle. I got back to the piano just in time.'

Though she did not know it at the time, the Waterloo Dinner was Joyce's last concert. The next day, she couldn't concentrate on Peter Pears singing *Death in Venice* at Aldeburgh and when they discovered that their hotel room had been double-booked she was relieved to go home early. She was very tired and her left eye was swollen.

The next day she went to see her Christian Science practitioner, Doris Henty, and confessed the 'discomfort' in her eye. Even in her diary, she never called it 'pain' and only referred to it as 'this damned rheumatism'. Doris urged Joyce to tell Reggie when he came in from work. Only five weeks earlier he had been furious with a Christian Scientist they met who had nearly lost the use of both her leg and her sight because she refused medical treatment. Now he was distressed that Joyce had said nothing before, and asked her to see his doctor, Patrick Woodcock, immediately. By eight o'clock that evening Woodcock had sent them on to see Mr John Winstanley, senior ophthalmologist at St Thomas's Hospital, who prescribed pills and drops to reduce the inflammation in the eye. He also told her she must rest for at least three months – all concerts and the tour of Australia had to be cancelled. For Reggie's sake, Joyce used the medicine, while maintaining her faith in Christian Science. Even so, she was relieved that Mary Baker Eddy had said in her book *Christian Healing* that if bodily pain was really bad then medication could be used, and if a doctor was employed he should be the best one available.

Joyce dreaded the publicity and possible criticism of her Christian Science beliefs. 'I have stood – I stand – as a student of C.S. & the criticism cannot touch God's idea,' she wrote in her diary. 'The sense of relief at not going to Australia is colossal. I don't know how much I feared it.' She felt 'bulldozed' by the medical instructions, the orders to stay quiet and the kindness of her friends. When Virginia sent her a bunch of flowers, she burst into tears. She was grateful that, having expected to be in Australia, her engagement diary was empty. Only a few people knew that she had not gone, so phone calls were rare.

For three weeks she felt so low that she wrote nothing in her diary. After a month Mr Winstanley reassured her that the inflammation was decreasing and by the end of the year she was feeling better, but was blind in her left eye. Early in 1974 she had a 'cosmetic contact lens' fitted in the blind eye which was so convincing that even those who knew about the problem couldn't work out which eye was affected. She wrote to Britten:

> I've had a bad eye so didn't go to Australia as planned but I am very well, though a bit of a cyclop. But I've had a great deal to be grateful for and when I was unable to think much or pray I was able to find a sort of place of peace and the comforting

realization that my being was entirely untouched and un-changed by what was going on in my body. This seemed to me to be a reinforcement of my certainty that one's spiritual being is the only real one!

She had frequent sessions with Doris Henty in order to overcome the general feeling of tiredness and ill-health. On really bad days she did not write anything in her diary – she did not want to report even to herself how she felt. Virginia must have realised as she was con-stantly driving Joyce around London, when previously she would have walked, driven herself or taken a bus.

Both Joyce and Reggie had always enjoyed good health. In sixty-three years, Joyce had never had any serious illness nor needed an operation. The worst that Reggie had had to cope with was varicose veins, which he had surgically treated in 1968. 'To my surprise,' he wrote to Rupert Hart-Davis, 'I found it a very peaceful interlude in my life which I shall always remember with happiness & gratitude. I turned out to be the freak of the varicose vein world – never had any pain or discomfort – came out on the Tuesday & was playing tennis within a week of my operation. Mighty lucky.' Joyce and Virginia claimed that his quick recovery was due to their work with Christian Science.

At the start of 1973 Joyce had said, 'I'm not going to retire, I plan gently to withdraw and do less,' but, with no regrets, she now decided that the time had come to retire from the stage. 'After thirty-five years of entertaining, and a lifetime of marvellous experiences playing all over the English-speaking world, I have a great deal to be grateful for,' she said on the radio.

I never set out with a plan – it's been an entirely unplanned life and career. My parents gave us the feeling that the sky is the limit – get out there and try your hand – man's potential is unlimited. Now it is time to stop and do something else.

I've got a husband and home and I've never been busier and I am fulfilled up to *here*. I didn't so much retire as change career. I got off the Inter-city and got on the local train. I'm fulfilled, I don't need an audience any more and I'm certainly not thirsty for more stroking of the ego.

In thirty-four years she had performed in front of King George VI and Queen Elizabeth, Queen Elizabeth II, Maurice Chevalier, Laurence Olivier, Igor Stravinsky and hundreds of thousands of other people on four continents. Millions had seen her on television. No other woman had written as much radio material as Joyce did between 1940 and 1979. Excerpts from her programmes were retransmitted on *Pick of the Week* eighteen times. During the war, she broadcast over a hundred programmes, and after it she could be heard on the radio over three hundred times, not counting repeats, an average of more than once a month during her working career. She was the only person to be featured on *Desert Island Discs* twice. On her first appearance in 1951, she was the ninety-ninth ship-wrecked person and chose Dvořák, Rachmaninov, an Oskar Strauss song, Purcell's *Nymphs and Shepherds*, two pieces by Bach, and Judy Garland singing *The Trolley Song*, written by her old friend Hugh Martin. Roy Plomley was struck by the modesty of her luxury – a pencil and paper so that she could write a play. Twenty years later, in 1971, her favourite pieces were Handel, Mozart, Bach, Mary O'Hara, and Frank Sinatra singing *You Make Me Feel So Young*, and her book was inevitably Mary Baker Eddy's *Science and Health*.

It may seem surprising that Joyce never featured as the subject of the television show *This Is Your Life*. Reggie was asked if he would co-operate in the secret preparations required but he turned the invitation down for three reasons – he could not keep such a secret from Joyce, she hated surprises, and he knew that she wanted to keep her personal life private. She was quite happy to be interviewed on radio, and later on television by people like Michael Parkinson, but only if she was in control of the topics covered.

Even though Joyce had announced her retirement, requests for openings, speeches and charity concerts continued to pour in. 'Endless saying No to invitations to work,' she wrote in her diary. 'I expect my plea for a year's quiet sounds a bit limp. I truly don't mind if I never work again. And that's a fact. Imagining the arrivals in cold halls, undoing the props – trying the mike – pianos etc. I can easily do without all that; and the affection of audiences & the pleasures of performing – because I've been given such a generous supply of it for so long.' A year later she told Virginia, 'I am actively enjoying *not* being a worker. No regrets, no wistful longings as I smell the size back-stage. Freedom. And gratitude.'

Joyce may have retired from the stage, but she did not retire from the limelight. On April Fool's Day 1974 she was interviewed on Radio Four about her first appearance in the theatre, at the end of the Victorian pier in the fictitious town of Fairpool. She claimed to have sung in a children's amateur talent contest: 'I wish I had a puppy with a curly-wurly tail; I'd call him Chummy, and he would be my pal.'

She often accepted invitations for public speaking, and although she never performed an entire monologue again she gave 'illustrated' talks. In 1976 she gave the opening speech at the Headmasters' Conference in Cambridge. She had felt apprehensive at the thought of such an audience, but the next day she wrote:

> It vanished into nothing as I observed the variations on a theme of headmaster and beheld their united friendliness. The memory I will always cherish was when I invited them to close their eyes & I would through my voice suggest I was an entirely different shape than the one they'd been looking at. And there they sat, obediently shut-eyed as I tried to evoke a small round Buckinghamshire country woman & then a very young deb of 40 years ago and smiles of recognition came on their nice faces! Very rewarding.

Joyce often played the 'Radio Game' to show the audience that they were actually doing most of the work. 'You must close your eyes, or it doesn't work,' she told them. First was a thin young woman at a literary party in the 1960s; then a stout middle-aged Scandinavian woman – 'Vee are going to Vestminster Abbey and zen to Mucksanspencer'; then an ancient folk singer of organic habits; and finally an old lady with no teeth in a London tenement. Asked which of the media that Joyce had worked in – radio, television, films, revue – she most enjoyed, she replied, 'A *live* audience, face to face, working in halls, theatres, barns, camps, hospital wards and in dining-halls . . . making it happen then and there without benefit of take or camera or wireless. There is no substitute for the actual live encounter of actor and audience, though I do have a weakness for the radio.

It's the next best thing to live work and that is because it calls on imagination.'

Joyce also continued with *Face the Music*, the television programme hosted by the pianist Joseph Cooper. She had first met him at a wartime lunch-hour concert in the National Gallery, and shortly afterwards he and Virginia wrote *No News Is Good News*, which Joyce sang in the revue *Light and Shade*. In 1955 Cooper chaired *Call the Tune*, a radio quiz programme which 'aimed to encourage an interest in serious music through spontaneous discussion by articulate and friendly people' such as Joyce, Gerard Hoffnung and Peter Scott. That same year, the BBC conductor Henry Hall hosted a television programme called *Face the Music*, with Joyce among the guests. The producer Walter Todds combined the radio panel game *Call the Tune* with Henry Hall's title, and *Face the Music* was born on Boxing Day 1966.

The idea of the 'hidden melody' was conceived when Cooper had played for radio 'smoking-concerts' just after the war, when he improvised a well-known tune in the style of another composer. In 1975 he wrote a collection of 'Hidden Melodies' for piano, which were published with cartoons by ffolkes. Joyce's portrait can be spotted on horseback, illustrating 'John Peel in the style of Mozart'.

The regular panel of 'informed amateurs' were Bernard Levin, David Attenborough, Richard Baker and Robin Ray. Joyce liked them all and noted in her diary: 'Robin and Bernard in top form and sparked each other off. I sat more soberly in the middle & was not too bad in my answers. Richard is a pleasant companion, quiet, undemanding, & friendly.' Richard Baker remembers Joyce's maternal side: 'The BBC offered "hospitality" between the lighting rehearsal and recording *Face the Music*. In common with some of my colleagues, I was probably imbibing a bit too freely and Joyce said to me, in her best Nanny style: "Now Dicky, one more gin and tonic and there'll be tears before bedtime."'

'Joyce had a great urge to organise people,' remembered Cooper. 'She was forever straightening ties, pulling down jackets, cajoling friends to smoke or drink less. But she never lost her sense of humour.' Joyce longed to straighten Patrick Moore's tie but realised that he liked the tousled look. She was annoyed at his false modesty: 'I'm absolutely hopeless at music.'

'But Patrick, haven't you written an opera?'

'Yes, but it's hopeless.'

'Patrick Moore is really rather a dear if you can get beyond the over-grown schoolboy slang & zest,' she wrote in her diary. André Previn was 'articulate and funny, intelligent and not conceited'.

The writer John Julius Norwich observed, 'Joyce had this habit of being frightfully good at a very very difficult question at the beginning of the game. This made us all nervous of her expertise, and then she would flunk a really easy question, so that we and the audience felt we must be clever after all.'

Robin Ray, the son of comedian Ted Ray, brought out the school prefect in Joyce. Young, handsome and irascible, he loved to shock Joyce. During one series he had just returned from a holiday in Morocco and wore an embroidered kaftan with strings of beads. Joyce was horrified: *Face the Music* was supposed to be a serious music programme, not music hall. His widow Susan Stranks remembers one of the perks of the programme:

Georg and Val Solti held an operatic fancy-dress party to which we were all invited. Robin and I went as Porgy and Bess, all blacked up. It wasn't very relaxing because the Soltis' home was entirely white – white sofas, tablecloths, everything. So for the whole evening we couldn't touch anything or sit down. There were lots of Peter Grimes present, in wellies and baggy jumpers with fishing gear. Joyce swept in, always the aristocratic lady rather than 'show business'. She wore an evening gown, and one white kid glove. She was 'Your Tiny Hand Is Frozen' from *La Bohème*.

The public and the press warmed to the informal, uncompetitive atmosphere of the programme, with no scores, and plenty of whispered cheating between panellists. The audience figures soon topped six million – very high for a 'minority interest' programme on BBC2. After her eye went blind, Joyce considered giving up television but Reggie encouraged her to try with her new cosmetic lens. With different lighting and camera angles, the producer declared that no one would notice. She also gave up wearing make-up on television. 'It's a very nice rest,' she said. 'The older you get, the better to leave your face alone.'

By 1973 Joyce appeared in eleven out of sixteen programmes in each series. Her only regret was that each team had two men and one woman on it, so she never met the other women panellists, such as Arianna Stassinopoulos. She admitted that she guessed many of the answers – she knew the century of a piece but not always the composer. 'Joyce was one of those rare people born with a marvellous ear for music,' said Joseph Cooper. 'She had a sense of pitch which was remarkable. One day I played one note, D flat an octave above middle C – straight away she knew it was Debussy's *The Girl With the Flaxen Hair*. There are very few musicians in the world who can do that. She was born with that fantastic ear and could sing pitch-perfect.'

Her wartime friend Stewart Perowne wrote: 'Darling Joyce, How splendidly you faced the music last night, clad in that wonderful cyclamen array! How remarkable of you to have spotted "La Fille au chevaux lin" just by its first note – its right up here, isn't it, ping, like that.'

'Inside Joyce were hundreds of tunes, absolutely perfectly contained,' remembered Cooper. 'But there was a tiny snag – she couldn't remember the names of them. She was unconsciously a star, she had a star quality about her. Her chief contribution to *Face the Music* was her lively sense of humour. But you never quite knew whether she was really being an idiot or if it was Joyce playing an idiot.'

After one programme she was standing outside the studio with the producer, his secretary and the director when her knickers fell down. 'Rather enjoyable somehow,' she related to Virginia. 'Plastic hood, evening dress over arm, crouched under umbrella with the producer's secretary, stepping out of panties into a puddle. It cheered us all up.'

Joyce's tours of American universities in the mid-1960s had reminded her of the importance and enjoyment of communication between generations. When she visited Cambridge University in 1967, she was pleased that she felt no distance between the generations, as there had been in her youth. When, aged seventeen, I visited Joyce for tea, she recorded in her diary, 'Janie and I had a deep talk about Life and the Bible. She is a real thinker.' My memory of the occasion is that

Joyce talked, and I agreed. I left under the *impression* that we had shared Deep Thoughts and thinking that, I if I tried harder, I might manage to be a better person.

Everyone wanted to please Joyce by doing better, which led to a certain amount of 'wishful thinking' in her friends' accounts of themselves or their children. For example, the letters to Joyce from my mother, Verily, recounting our exploits bear little resemblance to the reality of our teenage years. Our own letters, thanking for Christmas jerseys, emphasise the positive and omit the negative.

She enjoyed the beauty of young people – she loved the girls' flowing, hippy-style dresses and the men's long hair and Sergeant Pepper outfits. At my wedding in 1971, Joyce gave me the idea of linking the eight tiny bridesmaids and page boys with a rope garland of wild flowers, so none of them could get lost. She was amused by the guests – 'a mixture of Norfolk county in top-hats and peace-loving, if revolutionary-looking, students in rustic fancy-dress'. After her experience of Cliveden before the war, with its hundreds of servants and untold wealth, Joyce had always aspired towards an equal society. But as she entered her sixties her views seemed to revert to those of the schoolgirl in the 1920s: she had as little sympathy with the Miners' Strike of 1974 as she had had with the General Strike of 1926.

Maybe her views were changing because her blind eye made the world feel confusing. Pan's People, the dancers on *Top of the Pops*, were 'five sturdy girls who bump and grind & revolt me', she wrote in her diary in 1974. 'The men have hair in untidy formations and girls peer out from under deep wool bag hats. There is a lot of Hungarian fur, edging pseudo peasant leather coats. It is an age of ugliness & sloth. They are all so dirty, and, presumably, smelly.' Relating to young people became more difficult, and she was often disappointed. When I was twenty-one, Joyce's disapproval was provoked by my short haircut and my attempt to discuss Eastern religions with her. Nearly thirty years later, I learned from her diaries that she 'was saddened by Janie's whole stubborn attitude. I wonder why she is so un-gracious? She is a bit of a slut and has lost her looks.' Like her schoolfriend Betty Langley, who cut her hair into shingles in 1926, I had let the side down.

Joyce wanted young people to behave in the way she had forty years before, in silent obedience. She was shocked by Reggie's teenage nieces drinking wine and found it hard to understand her Phipps niece and nephew. After Sally graduated from college, she moved to London and worked in a women's refuge. Joyce was thrilled to have her niece living in London, but was irritated that Sally wore no make-up and rarely went to a hairdresser. She told Sally to treat the flat as her home – but banned bare feet and smoking. Sally decided to negotiate through Reggie, pointing out that in order to relax and feel at home, she needed to take her shoes off and smoke after the meal. Reggie relayed this and it was agreed that she could remove her shoes in the sitting-room and smoke out of the dining-room window.

Lang Phipps admits that he was a 'mixed-up teenager', drinking and dabbling in drugs but able to keep up a good front.

Few adults gave me the feeling that they were onto me, like Joyce. But I very much wanted her approval and it pained me that she might see me as a screw-up. One night I invited her into my room to listen to a piece of music I hoped she would like. It was Keith Jarrett's Köln Concert, a solo piano performance improvised before an audience. She sat and patiently took it in, and when it was through she told me in her frank, unsentimental way that it was rather self-indulgent, and self-absorbed. I was stung, but I asked her to listen again to one passage that I was particularly moved by, my favourite string of notes. This time she gave me her approval, saying it reminded her faintly of Rachmaninov. I was thrilled, remembering how she could peg great compositions after a bar or two on *Face the Music*.

When in 1974 Reggie's niece Helen Campbell-Preston became engaged, her bachelor uncle Harry Grenfell gave her £500 for a trousseau, on condition Joyce helped Helen to buy it. Joyce once described herself as 'about eight feet tall with a face like a reflection in a spoon', and so believed that dressing well was especially important. In spite of her childhood desire for frills, she learned that larger women look best in simple, clean lines without adornments and she wore little jewellery. She liked to keep clothes circulating, so whenever she bought herself a new suit or coat she would pass on something else, even if it was hardly worn, except for certain beloved garments. 'No girdle is as friendly as a middling old girdle still tough enough to discipline the stomach but old enough to allow easy breathing,' she wrote. But by now she 'put warmth and ease before elegance', preferring loose comfortable clothes, and was no longer interested in the latest fashions.

However, Harry did not know this, and so Helen squeezed her large aunt into her Mini car. They went to Dickens & Jones, Harrods, Fortnum & Mason and Selfridge's: none with clothes suited to Helen's age group. Joyce thought Helen should have a navy-blue coat, 'foundation garments', a white nightgown for the honeymoon and a 'morning dress' – all of which she fondly believed were 'un-dateable'. Helen wanted make-up, a bikini and some colourful summer frocks. Joyce thought that Helen was silent and shy, whilst in fact she was doing what she was told while hoping she might get something she could wear. At one shop the saleswoman understood the dilemma, and whispered to Helen that she could exchange the clothes the next day. They drove around central London for four days, and although most of the trousseau was never worn, Helen enjoyed the brief celebrity status of shopping with her famous aunt.

In the same year, Mary O'Hara left the Benedictine Order and visited Joyce in Elm Park Gardens. Joyce rejoiced at Mary's return to music and gave her two dresses designed by Clive Evans to wear on stage. 'We were the same height and I had them taken in, but sadly they were not really what a young folk singer could wear in 1975,' Mary admitted twenty-five years later.

27

'As you get older you enjoy fewer things,' said Joyce. 'But you enjoy them about a hundred times more than you did before: friends, flowers, music, birds.' These all came together in Joyce's favourite retreat in Cumbria. Back in 1958, while performing concerts with Viola, they had stayed in a small family-run hotel in a beautiful remote valley in the Lake District. There was something about Loweswater which filled her with joy, and she felt it was her spiritual home.

'Do you know Cumberland?' she wrote to the artist John Ward. 'R and I come regularly, if possible in May and we find it a place of tranquillity and charm, full of walks & little rivers and oak trees (acid green just now) and we stay in a very comfortable small hotel. It is full of light and hills and curlew & cuckoo & bluebells & the banks are full of buttoned-in primroses.' Every May they drove up in a leisurely way, stopping for picnics, and cups of tea with friends. Joyce felt that friends should be given at least twenty minutes' notice of a surprise visit. 'Then they have time to say, "Oh dear, I'm just going out."' Whatever make of car they owned, whether a Ford Zephyr or a Rover 2000, the numberplate was always J G 444. Joyce was slightly embarrassed by this, but Reggie had given it to her as a birthday present. In the car they always carried flower and bird books, country shoes, gumboots, a rug and cushions for picnics, a selection of maps, a pad and pencil for ideas, tissues and peppermints.

The Scalehill Hotel had all the ingredients that both Joyce and Reggie enjoyed for a holiday – traditional English food, comfort without luxury, other guests to talk to in the evenings – all set in wonderful countryside. They made friends with the local residents and went to the parish church on Sundays. They spent each day walking and birdwatching. 'I'm not an ornithologist but I am a birder,' said Joyce. 'I spot them, and Reggie tells me what I've spotted.' On warm days he would walk on with his binoculars, while Joyce sat on a grassy bank and sketched the view or the flowers growing beside her.

One year they invited John and Alison Ward to join them in Cumbria. 'Between us there was that bond of sketching,' John remembers.

We spent afternoons sitting on sketching stools dabbling away in the manner of old ladies. Joyce's shrewd perception quickly spotted the fact that art is a very unsentimental commodity. That although it is laudable to wish to paint GREAT works, unless one has the equipment, the results can be pretty ridiculous. That very minor works can have rightness – a fish-paste pot full of primroses well painted can have as serious a touch as the death of Dido on a six-foot canvas.

They were taken out by the local National Trust warden to fish trout on Loweswater and watch badgers feeding at dusk. Their visits to Cumbria were a confirmation of spring. 'One of the best moments is finding the first white violet of the year,' Joyce wrote. 'And a cowslip – the downy pink stem is very satisfactory, and the flower smells the way honey tastes.' The nearest Joyce and Reggie came to having a garden of their own was a few window boxes at Elm Park Gardens. They grew herbs on the kitchen windowsill, geraniums in the sitting-room windows and morning glory round the dining-room window.

The residents of Loweswater appreciated Joyce's determination not to give away the secret of the place for fear of encouraging an avalanche of visitors. Even in her autobiography she only gave the vaguest hint as to where it was. As their love of the place increased, so they became more keen to protect it. In 1963 the West Cumberland Water Board proposed building a treatment plant in the Loweswater Valley. Joyce asked Cliff Michelmore on BBC's *Tonight* to help the fight against 'this dastardly proposition. It is the most lovely unspoiled place, peaceful and beautiful. The idea of this waterworks building plum in the middle of the view is unthinkable and everyone is in a spin. We spend millions making weapons to destroy. Do let's spend a bit on saving something that gives joy to millions and will be lost for ever if it's not saved.' She also phoned local newspapers and coached the local vicar on presenting his views on television. The campaign was successful and the water board modified their plans.

Joyce's concern for the environment meant that in 1971 she told radio listeners not to use coloured lavatory paper because the dye would last for ever in the sea. The manufacturers of lavatory paper wrote and asked for her source: 'They felt they had gone to a lot of trouble to make sure that the dye would disintegrate,' she related. 'I had no idea who had told me this, so I will have to bow to their superior knowledge. But I still prefer white paper.'

Reading books was another pastime Joyce now had more time for. She woke early every morning to read first the daily CS lesson and then a book for instructive pleasure such as a new biography. By the mid-1960s she was often asked to review books on the radio and she read each one at least twice. On *Holiday Books* in 1965 with John Betjeman and Eric Newby, she chose *The Secret Garden*, Richard Hoggart's *The Uses of Literacy* and *The Brontë Story*. 'No one person has been The Great Influence,' she said, 'but many have added huge enjoyment and light in my awareness.' In 1968, '*Emma* made a perfect contrast to the elephants, hippos, and birds while we were in Kenya. I think Sir Edward Boyle is very unkind to inflict his tightly textured philosophy of law on us but I did my best and took in 15% perhaps.' Her heart sank when she was sent a book of *The Best Psychiatric Jokes*. 'So far I've raised one faint smile. There is something very daunting to me about joke books – about a pile-up of anecdotes *anywhere*. I will have to be honest with this book. It is dreadful – *full of dread*.'

Since the age of fifteen, Joyce had dreamed of writing a book herself and in 1962 confessed on the radio that she had one unfulfilled fantasy. 'It's about writing *the* book of the era, a wonderful book that everyone admires, a literary masterpiece. Everybody acclaims it for its wit and beauty and its sheer mastery of language, its poetry, its marvels.' From as early as 1945 she received two requests a year from authors and publishers who wanted to do her biography. Her answer was always the same: if anyone was going to write her life, it would be her. A few months before she retired from the stage, Joyce began to think about doing just that.

Although she had put 'Writer-Entertainer' in her passport for years, she had never written anything longer than monologues, songs and articles. For two years from 1950 she wrote monthly articles for *Everywoman* on topics such as 'Eating Habits', 'Personal Appearance', 'Tidiness' and 'Christmas Decorations'. She wrote in a jaunty, conversational style, as if she was a disorganised housewife with the usual preoccupations – cooking with scraps, worrying about electricity bills and finding suitable gifts for spinster aunts. These and articles for the *Spectator* and the *Christian Science Monitor* were a rehearsal for her autobiography, filled with memories and anecdotes.

Since 1957 Joyce had been the president of the Society of Women Writers and Journalists, judging writing-competitions and handing out prizes. In a bidding prayer for the society, she wrote, 'As women and as writers, may we continue to acknowledge our sense of love, and our trusting responsibility to our fellow man and woman, through our lives and our art, which is also a craft. May we be surprised by joy, delighted by wonder and grateful for all that is Good and therefore of God. And may we increase in understanding of that which is true.' This was also her aim for her new book, but the task seemed so big that she did not know where to begin.

'It's bloody difficult,' she wrote to Rupert Hart-Davis after three months. 'I suspect I shouldn't *try* too hard but swing more easily and say what I mean without too much self consciousness.' Reggie advised her not to think about a whole book, but simply to write down stories of her life, in any order she remembered them. For years Joyce had described herself as a 'peek and press' typist, and longed for someone to invent a typewriter which did not need loading with paper and carbon paper. Now she could afford to employ a typist. Lorna Andrade, a friend of Victor Stiebel, typed Joyce's spidery longhand, corrected the spelling and tactfully pointed out inconsistencies.

'How is it possible not to re-write every bit every day is my big question?' she wrote to Verily. 'I never do it right first time – Does one get better, I wonder? I'm so used to condensing & getting it all into a seven minute talk that I find it hard to allow myself to expand. I wonder if it has any quality at all?' She soon realised that there was so much to say it would fill at least two volumes. The first covered her life up to 1955, when she first appeared on Broadway, and the second covered the less eventful but more thoughtful remainder of her life. Although she enjoyed writing, she found it hard work and could do no more than two or three hours a day: letters to friends were so much easier.

Autobiography gave Joyce the opportunity to reflect on her life. She had no written evidence for the first fifteen years and admitted that her childhood memories were all of blue skies. Just before she died, Nora had returned all her letters from Joyce, who had only kept those that she liked. Even so, Joyce was shocked by their content: 'Disliking myself more & more for the endless pleasure I got from our songs and performances, recording every bouquet and smugly being amazed at how much success I had. I was genuinely amazed but I did go on about it,' she wrote in her diary. She felt deeply ashamed of her lack of thought for Reggie during the war. 'I was *totally* selfish – and *far* too busy with radio shows and concerts with Viola.' She was appalled at her attitude to her brother's decision to become a US citizen, and horrified to find anti-Semitic statements in her pre-war diaries. 'ME? Why? I don't remember feeling like that. What a horrid attitude.' Even so, her letters and diaries were not an accurate source, for she had already censored her experiences as she wrote them. During the war she rarely mentioned the Blitz or friends killed or missing. Her letters to Nora were written to cheer her up. Joyce's autobiography described the life she would have liked. Her parents' unhappy marriage, her mother's affairs, being a poor relation of the Astors and not having children were glossed over or not mentioned. As Virginia said, 'If the present wasn't very nice, Joyce looked round the corner for something nicer.' She omitted all mention of her and Reggie's enormous generosity and also left out anyone she did not like.

'I don't like a wallow and I hate self-indulgence,' she said at the time. 'I chose to leave the dark times out. There isn't a living soul who doesn't have them. I've had my share, but why dwell on them? They pass and they go. You may learn from them, but I want to write about this overwhelming sense of gratitude I have for the marvellous things that have come my way.'

The book reads fluently, as if Joyce is talking. But, as with her monologues, the easy style was the result of months of painstaking writing. Much of the editing was done by Reggie, who argued over every paragraph with her. From Reggie's methodical skill as an accountant emerged an unseen talent as an editor. Each night he took the carbon copy and, with scissors and tape, rearranged the material. In the morning Joyce would find the new version laid out on the dining-room table. After fifteen months she showed it to Rupert Hart-Davis, now retired from publishing.

Though they had known each other for fifty years, Joyce and Rupert did not particularly like each other. Joyce thought Rupert arrogant and autocratic, and after a visit in 1976 Rupert wrote that 'Joyce's bossiness has increased and she treats Reg like an under-privileged slave. She must always have the last word. Whenever I tell a funny story, she immediately caps it.' Joyce could as easily have written the same letter about Rupert: they were just too similar. But she trusted his judgement and was relieved that he was not only encouraging but also agreed to help edit it. They spent three hours a day 'in the business of ruthless pruning, cutting, and advice', from which Joyce emerged 'reeling but eternally grateful'. Rupert pointed out two important omissions – Reggie and Christian Science. 'I don't have to talk about Reggie – I *love* him,' she said. As for Christian Science:

I don't feel that this was the book for it. But I do want to write thoughtfully about my beliefs & my gratitude to the teaching of C.S. that has done so much for me. Part of my argument is that Roman Catholics, Buddhists and Baptists don't state their faiths unless they are specifically writing about the subject. I have always experienced the best understanding with like-minded people when neither of us know the denominations of the other & is free to explore without dogmas hampering the discussion. Noël Coward said a message is like a petticoat, it should not show.

The title of the book caused much discussion. Joyce suggested *When I Wasn't Looking* or *L for Learner*, but everyone else said it must have her name in it. Reggie suggested *Joyce Grenfell Requests the Pleasure*, after her first solo show, and she agreed because it held a 'modicum of modesty in the requests'.

Rupert introduced Joyce to the literary agent Richard Simon, who told Joyce he would need several weeks to read her manuscript. He telephoned two days later: 'I *love* it – I find it interesting, funny, moving and I like the writing.' Joyce assumed that literary agents said that to all aspiring authors.

Richard Simon chose Macmillan to publish Joyce's autobiography, and she liked the idea on the grounds that she shared a birthday with the chairman, Harold Macmillan. She was even more pleased when Richard Garnett, son of the Bloomsbury novelist David, was appointed her editor. During working lunches at their flat, Garnett enjoyed Joyce's stories, which were 'just a little earthier and more indiscreet than she liked to put in print'.

The first volume was published in September 1976, after three years of hard work. 'Apart from meeting Reggie, the best of all first-times happened when I held in my hands the first book I've ever written,' she said. 'There it was, the dear thing, handsomer than I had dreamed possible with its dark green cloth hardback covers and gilded title. It was unexpected and marvellous.'

Macmillan excelled themselves in promoting the book. Their mail was franked with a self-portrait of Joyce and she made a record for the sales reps on which the Nursery School Teacher, the Wife of the Vice-Chancellor and Mrs Moss spoke about it. In the month after publication Joyce did nine press interviews, ten radio interviews, six signing sessions, four television shows and nine literary lunches and dinners with up to five hundred guests at each, in a dozen different cities. At Foyle's lunch the *Guardian* observed 'a throng of women admirers in red straw hats, black trilbies and pill boxes that appeared to have been banged on with a hammer. One fervent lady admirer wore not only tweeds but also Wellington boots, which doesn't happen every day in the Dorchester Hotel ballroom.'

She found herself in a new and fascinating world, 'A macabre collection of faces – writers certainly come in funny shapes & sizes. Quentin Crisp with pale lilac mauve hair & full make-up; tiny Denise Robins in satin and fur neck piece; and Frank Muir in pink bow tie,' she recorded in her diary. At the 1977 Women of the Year Lunch she spoke in passing of one of her greatest pleasures – the sublime moment at the end of the day when she could remove her constricting undergarments. HAPPINESS IS TAKING OFF YOUR GIRDLE roared the *Times* headline. Newspapers all over the world picked up the remark, and she claimed to be annoyed that it made her more famous than anything else she had done. She had in fact said the same thing at the 1958 Women of the Year Lunch and she had been annoyed then, too, when the remark was repeated on *Woman's Hour.*

Richard Simon remembers that in addition to charm, Joyce had a less visible streak of steel. He took her to a literary lunch at Robert Carrier's hotel in Suffolk where her fellow-speaker was Edward Heath.

> During drinks she smiled fairly sweetly at Heath and said she was sure he would not mind her exercising her feminine prerogative to speak first. He puffed, and rather gracelessly, agreed. Joyce's speech went down a treat. Heath started off with a few political reminiscences, but his speech rapidly turned into a list of books and LPs, complete with publishers and catalogue numbers. During a slight pause, Joyce jumped up and announced that she too had just had an LP out, and rattled off some, most certainly spurious, catalogue number. The place erupted with cheers. During the book-signing Heath was alone at his table long before Joyce's queue had left with their treasured copies.

Joyce actively enjoyed these signing sessions, where her fans treated her like an old friend. In the Art Store in the Lake District, over three hundred customers lined up to have their books signed. The owner, Bruce Woods-Jack, was a Christian Scientist who had known Joyce as a student in London and she had lent him £100 to get the business going.

The journalists who came to interview her caused amusement and annoyance. Jane Watt of the *Guardian* noticed that Joyce's technique was to 'disarm us with tea, captivate us with voices, wash us clean of defences with an unending stream of talk: then have the face to interview us. Reggie sat on the sofa opposite, laughing not indulgently but with genuine amusement.'

One Sunday paper sent a young man who had not read her book. With some pleasure, she told him she had written a monologue eleven years before about just this situation. Sheridan Morley felt her displeasure when he called George from the *Nursery School* 'Cyril'. Her hackles rose because this small mistake reminded her of the countless journalists who had interviewed her about her work without having seen it. Another journalist asked, 'What makes you think you are important enough to write about your life?' 'I am not any more important than you,' Joyce replied. 'We are both absolutely totally unique, there is nobody like us. But I had a very happy, unexpected, unthought unplanned life, and I thought I'd like to write it down so I could read it.'

Joyce's book touched both reviewers and readers and it went to number one in the best-seller list a week after publication. It was the year in which civil wars continued in Lebanon, Northern Ireland and Rhodesia, the Tate Gallery showed a pile of bricks and the Sex Pistols swore on television. 'Oh it *is* good to read a happy book,' wrote John Ward. 'In this way your book is OUTRAGEOUS. None of the stock stuff, no misery, a good husband. No life in a garret, never a member of "the party" – oh la, you *are* in for it!'

'Your love of people shines like a light in this very darkened world,' wrote Laurier Lister. One of Nora's friends from North Carolina wrote: 'Your book is sheer delight. I savored each page as I used to eat ice cream, slowly, slowly, so it wouldn't waste out,' and Bunny Paine of Connecticut wrote, 'The pictures are lovely. Your beautiful teeth stand out & are a monument! How strong & reassuring is Paul's chin. Aunt Nancy is a splendid production.'

Several readers claimed the book had changed their lives. One woman related that, after seven years of childless marriage, she was delighted to find herself pregnant. But within weeks her husband had left her for another woman. Deeply distressed, only the prospect of her baby kept her going. The baby was born ten weeks premature by emergency Caesarean section, weighing only three pounds. He was taken to another hospital and died five days later, on Christmas Day. Her family lived on the other side of the country and were prevented by a blizzard from visiting her. Once discharged from hospital, she sat alone in her flat for two months, losing the will to live. A nurse at the hospital had given her a copy of Joyce's book.

'Then something wonderful happened,' she wrote.

I started to get interested. For the first time in eight weeks, my brain registered that there was something more to life than self pity and sorrow. The book has so much vitality – the sheer joy of living shouts from every page. I began to think constructively again. In other words, I picked myself up from the floor, and decided that enough was enough – I couldn't go on this way for ever.

I didn't even buy the book – and I'm sure you never meant it to be instant therapy for suicidal mental cripples. Please, Miss Grenfell look at this letter as I mean it to be – heartfelt thanks. You have given me the most precious thing that one person can give to another – the will to live. And you don't even know me, and probably never will.

She left no address. Joyce replied to them all, though could do nothing about the fan who wrote from a ship in such excitement that he forgot to sign the letter.

A month after publication, Joyce and Reggie flew to Johannesburg and then on to Australia, where in two weeks she did forty-two press and radio interviews, thirteen television shows and seven literary lunches, accompanied by the publisher Tim Hely Hutchinson on his first author-tour. 'She was tireless, funny, considerate and brilliant at putting a very green publicity person, and everyone else we met, at his ease,' he recalls. On New Year's Eve, a telegram arrived from Macmillan: 50 THOUSAND PLEASURES SOLD TODAY. The BBC repeated the *Woman's Hour* radio serialisation, read by Joyce, less than a year later when the paperback was published. In two months, over 250,000 copies were sold, one of the first books to be sold in supermarkets.

'It's Crazy!' wrote Joyce to Michael Olivier. 'But somehow so unexpected, that it is a joy! Huge tax of course – the accountant said we ought to go to Ireland for a year but I'd rather stay here & pay up.' She distributed her royalties to others. 'Please look on this, *as I do*, as a *sharing*,' Joyce wrote to Diana Lyddon. 'For that is what it is – and with the greatest joy at being able to do so. It is *such fun* to be able to share with those of whom one is fond. And please accept it in this spirit as it comes to you with love, Joyce. P.S. It is for being *enjoyed*.'

After the success of her autobiography, Joyce agreed to publish *George, Don't Do That*, a collection of the nursery-school monologues. She chose as her illustrator Royal Academician John Ward, who began his career with *Vogue* soon after the war. He and Joyce first met at the Festival of Britain in 1951 when he did a series of drawings for Stephen Potter, illustrating *English as She Is Spoke*.

'She asked me to come and draw her in her flat above a sweetshop in King's Road,' he recalls. 'I sat one side of the kitchen table, back to the sink, and she sat the other. Behind her was a dresser with some fine china, and gifts from schoolchildren which were not so fine but were dear to Joyce's heart. How enriching is such a juxtaposition – everlasting good taste can pall.' Although Joyce liked the picture, she asked for one more sitting so that Ward could make her 'look six months less old'. Ward was worried about the fee: he didn't want to charge too much but he had six children to support. 'If I charge you twenty-five guineas it is because we spend money like mad – the children eat it or something,' he wrote. Both for her own pleasure, and to help support the Ward family, Joyce commissioned him to draw friends, such as Victor and Virginia, her housekeepers and her parents-in-law.

'Joyce's friends were the pebbles in the portrait painter's pond which brought forth such lovely ripples,' he said. 'She never asked for just a portrait head, she realised that much of a person lies in the set of their elbows, or the way their knees touch their chins. All this I relished immensely.'

The Grenfells opened as many doors as they could for John Ward, but they didn't always warn him. One day they invited him to dinner.

It wasn't until I got to Elm Park Gardens that Joyce told me that the Queen Mother was coming too. As soon as the phone call came through that she had left Clarence House, Reggie and I had to dash down the four flights of stairs to hold the lift and a parking space. She was ushered into the building and Reggie hissed in my ear, 'There isn't room in the lift for more than two, I'll meet you at the top.' So I was squashed in the tiny lift with the Queen Mother, wondering whether I was allowed to speak or not. As the door opened, there was Reggie at the top again, pretending not to pant.

Ward spent several days sketching small children in Wye Primary School for *George, Don't Do That*. 'The teachers built me a barricade of desks and I sat in this fortress while the tides of children screamed and howled around me. I felt as if I was inside a Joyce Grenfell monologue: it was a clear case of nature imitating art.' His illustrations caught the mixture of the innocence and horror of small children, and *George, Don't Do That* sold fifty thousand hardback copies within three months. Normally, illustrators receive only a small fee, but Joyce insisted that she and Ward share the royalties equally.

28

ALTHOUGH JOYCE LIVED by her faith in Christian Science, she didn't talk much about it, partly because she knew that most people did not agree with it. But, as she wrote to Katharine Moore in 1964, 'It isn't as dotty as the world thinks it is – it *couldn't* be and work! It is a disciplined study and the *freedom* it gives me is the thing I am most grateful for. It answers all my questions, solves all my problems, is the climate in which I live. It requires constant practice, and now recently I have discovered it is worth the effort. I was brought up in it, but like anything else, it had to be discovered all over again when I began to *think*.' This required daily and disciplined study of the Bible and Mary Baker Eddy's *Science and Health*. Joyce sometimes read the Bible in three different versions if she didn't understand it sufficiently. Every Sunday morning or Wednesday evening she attended the First Church of Christ, Scientist in Sloane Terrace.

When Joanna Scott-Moncrieff moved from *Woman's Hour* to the BBC Religious Department, Joyce wrote many radio talks for *Ten to Eight* and *Thought For the Day*. She still did not want to reveal her Christian Science publicly but Joanna recognised that her values were shared by the majority of listeners, and Joyce did want to get faith and spirituality back into religious broadcasting. 'It's as if people are afraid of talking of such a delicate subject. But it *isn't* delicate. Spirit is *substance*!' she wrote in 1966. Thousands of Joyce's listeners wrote in for copies of the scripts, and she was especially thrilled by letters from agnostics. Her talk 'My Kind of Magic' was bought by the American journal *Woman's Day* and syndicated to magazines all over the English-speaking world.

Joyce was annoyed that the Church of Christ, Scientist was never properly acknowledged in Britain and that the established Church of England had so much power. 'Roll on the day when there are no more churches (small c),' she wrote to Paul Paget, 'And one great Church sans bricks, sans trappings but full to bursting with Love.'

Being a Christian Scientist in North America was much easier – with no established church, all denominations are accepted. 'Over here the CS church is just part of the scene and not something odd,' she wrote to Virginia. In New York, Joyce was thrilled that the man who ran the newspaper stand was a Christian Scientist and in Beverley Hills she visited fellow-believer Doris Day. In the Mother Church in Boston, Joyce was so overwhelmed to be there that she burst into tears during a hymn. 'Joy, I suppose,' she said. 'Not sad, just a great surge of wetness.'

In 1965 the Christian Science elders in Boston decided it was time to broadcast their message more widely but it took Joyce five years to publicise her faith in Christian Science. She liked and trusted the BBC radio interviewer Leslie Smith and invited him to her flat where they spent many hours planning his questions. 'I'm a *student* of Christian Science,' she said. 'You never stop studying. It's the very centre and foundation of my being. Blind faith isn't very practical – I must understand what I believe in order to make it work. Prayer is very important to me. It doesn't mean getting down on my knees. I mostly lie in bed praying, but it could be on a bus.'

Joyce's was not a personal god, with whom one had conversations and who granted wishes.

By God I mean all that is good, not some old man up there who says, 'You've been awfully good today, tomorrow you may have a nice cup of tea.' I don't converse with God. I try to acknowledge what I understand to be the ever-presence of Good. Good is already there, in everyone. If you recognise the good in somebody, you are recognising God.

God is Love, the very climate of harmony and truth. Love is *the* power; the *only* power and by golly it does work.

The feature that many people connect with Christian Science is the refusal of medicine. In 1970 Joyce had never been to a doctor for treatment. 'Of course I have been ill,' she said, 'but I have been able to overcome it without a doctor. You don't come in with a streaming cold and say, "I haven't a cold." The method is to acknowledge one's

spiritual reality which is untouched by the physical. The most important thing is believing in Good overcoming Evil. If you can touch it,
taste it, see it, then it isn't real – it's the spiritual that is actual, is now
and ever present.'

'To be brought up in Christian Science is a joyful and loving experience,' explains fellow-believer Bruce Woods-Jack. 'Some people try
to make it sound as though a C.S. childhood is abusive: "Not even an
aspirin in the house? How odd!" But if you have relied on God's
healing powers all your life, to find an aspirin in the house, well, that
would indeed be odd! This was Joyce's life too.'

Joyce was particularly fond of the verse in John's First Epistle, 'We
are called God's children and such we are.' 'It's the heart of the gospel
– that nothing and nobody can fall outside the love of God. I was tre-
mendously self-centred and selfish when I was young but I think I
have learned, quite often the hard way, that happiness comes in losing
your sense of self. The *pursuit* of happiness is a blind chase. You can
only *discover* happiness. Joy does not happen, it is the inevitable result
of certain rules followed and laws obeyed.'

One of Joyce's favourite quotations was from Marcus Aurelius:
'Man is made for kindness, and whenever he does an act of kindness
or otherwise helps forward the common good, he thereby fulfils the
law of his being and comes by his own.'

'Don't think I'm noble,' she told a *Daily Mail* reporter. 'I only do
my charity shows when I'm doing a season – I always try to do four
benefits in each tour. It's very difficult to know which charities to
help. I think people come first, yet suddenly you see a beautiful
building wants saving.'

'Seven Good Reasons' was a week in 1960 of performances at the
Scala Theatre in London which raised over £9,000 for Joyce's seven
favourite charities. 'I'm amazed and delighted,' she wrote to
Katharine Moore. 'Can you think of anything pleasanter than doing
a job you enjoy doing and on top of that making such a fat
Christmassy sum for some very good reasons?'

As well as the commercial shows, Diana Lyddon stage-managed
the charity concerts. 'Joyce had a long list of charities inviting her to
perform. When she planned a tour she would work out which she
could fit in. We always did one for the Commonwealth Blind.' At
Stratford-on-Avon, in the middle of a Shakespeare season, over

£1,400 was raised to build and equip an eye clinic in Swaziland. She gave all the royalties from her monologue *Nicodemus* to the charity Feed the Mind.

At the Chelsea Theatrical Garden Party in 1948 she helped Binkie Beaumont with his audition tent, where would-be actors paid 7s. 6d. to appear for two minutes in front of West End managers for their honest opinions. Joyce compèred the auditions for six hours, during which time two people were given contracts and £480 was raised for the Actors' Orphanage.

In the summer of 1951 she opened a bazaar every Saturday for three months. Her standard opening speech at fêtes was 'How I Would Do an Imitation of a Lady Opening a Bazaar if I Had to'. She came home with an extraordinary array of objects – knitted penguins, hand-painted bottles and purple crocheted tablemats. After she had opened a youth club in the East End, the *Daily Herald* reported that in addition to singing, Joyce had donned boxing-gloves and sparred with several young men. Joyce was so furious that she spent all day tracing the source of this libel: the reporter had spoken to a friend of a friend of Reggie's sister. Joyce insisted that the newspaper publish an apology: she had never boxed, would never box and hated all forms of boxing.

The House of St Barnabas, a hostel for women in Soho, named a dormitory after her after she had broadcast a radio appeal on their behalf in 1975. Two years later she supported PHAB – Physically Handicapped and Able Bodied – by lending her recorded voice as Mrs Jones the Policeman's Wife to the Dolphins' Puppet Theatre.

In 1968, *Woman's Hour* commissioned Joyce to talk about 'The Philosophy of Giving'. 'A fascinating subject,' she wrote to Verily Anderson.

It's not easy to do but I've been trained in a good school for I was on the receiving end of a very great deal of benevolence when I was young & I learned it isn't A (giver) and B (receiver) but A/B both receivers! For B gives A the opportunity and the acceptance and A gives the sense of sharing something good. I've also discovered what a nasty word 'taking' is – greedy & depressing – and what lovely words 'receiving' and above all 'accepting' are. Forward going and generous.

'Make sure no strings are left attached to whatever the generous gesture is,' she advised listeners.

From 1974 to 1979 Joyce served on the committee of the Churchill Memorial Fellowship Trust, deciding who should receive travel scholarships. Each year she read through hundreds of applications from older people with no qualifications, and enjoyed the interviews. 'We had train drivers, a stage carpenter, nurses and one fellow who wished to study "happenings" and quoted Oldenburg and Susan Sontag.' In 1975 it was her turn to chair the committee for teachers of the arts, and she read 550 submissions, shortlisted seventy, interviewed twenty-four and awarded nine places.

Christmas was Joyce's favourite time of year, when her faith, her creativity, her generosity and love of entertaining all came together. She loved the preparations, and 'fixin' up' her flat with American flair: home-made silver paper stars hanging from thread; ivy and red velvet ribbon festooning the fireplace; and hundreds of Christmas cards stuck into the books like a colourful mural. Each year she sent out several hundred Christmas cards, all hand-drawn and often portraits of herself. 'This is purely self-indulgence. My form of knitting while the telly is on,' she wrote.

Joyce's Christmas-present list was rarely less than a hundred people, but 'This cutlet-for-cutlet business over Christmas cards and presents is silly,' she wrote. 'It's a form of blackmail. If I feel like giving someone something why should I hesitate? Because it might make them feel they had to pay me back? Brrr. Why do we give grand presents to grand people instead of the biggest and best presents to the cosiest friends? The whole system is wrong.'

She did her best to right it. Virginia, her best friend but immensely rich, received no more than a Thermos jug or a shopping-bag. Reggie always got a book, a new pair of trousers and something useful like a travel rug or a tin opener. Presents for family and friends were mainly soap, cheese for men, or stockings for women. Young people got cheques for a few pounds. Overseas friends received subscriptions to the *Observer*, the *Listener* or the *Christian Science Monitor* and the postman, paperman and dustmen each received ten shillings. Large presents were given to those she felt needed them: a dishwasher was a nice surprise for the Blezard family, and the Andersons were delighted with a new twin-tub washing-machine. She bought presents in the January sales for later and admitted that, come December, not many of them matched her list of names, but she was always hopeful that this method would save time. The part Joyce enjoyed most was watching others enjoy Christmas. To her, giving was a greater pleasure than receiving. But she was always delighted with Reggie's presents, with their emphasis on thought rather than value. For Christmas 1947, he labelled each of Joyce's thirteen small presents with a single letter. When arranged correctly, they spelled 'MY BELOVED ONE!'.

Joyce and Reggie never had anyone to stay for Christmas, but always had two feasts for eight to ten people, one on Christmas Day and one on Boxing Day. Both days were a mixture of the Magic Circle, neighbours or Christian Scientists without families, and visitors from America or Australia. Mrs Gabe or Mrs Agos cooked most of the meal the day before, Joyce served it and Reggie was 'the vital assistant-cum-butler, washer-upper and moral supporter'.

Most of their Christmases were for adults, but sometimes they found children to share the fun with. When my mother was in hospital over Christmas in 1962, Joyce offered to have us for the day at Elm Park Gardens. Just as she had done for the soldiers at Cliveden Hospital during the war, Joyce did Verily's Christmas shopping too. She gave Joyce £5 to cover essential presents and five Christmas stockings.

When we woke on Christmas morning, we had the best stockings ever. How had our mother (whom we knew to be Father Christmas) managed it? A real manicure set, not a toy one; a reversible Alice band; nutcrackers to go with the nuts and a leather-bound diary – all wrapped to crackle enticingly. Joyce must have had as much fun choosing and wrapping them as we had opening them. Before my mother went to hospital, I had shown her in a shop window the party frock I hoped she would make me – navy-blue organza, trimmed with red velvet bows and white lace. There it was, hanging beside my bed, the identical one, from Harvey Nichols. But whereas my mother put home-made frocks into Harrods boxes, Joyce had cut out the label of this one and thrown away its box. We dressed in our new party clothes, brushed our hair and, after visiting our mother in hospital, arrived at Elm Park Gardens.

A huge lunch was served in the dining-room, the table glittering with gold-paper angels and candles. Reggie circulated with champagne for the grown-ups and fruit cup for us children and Joyce. I had no idea that Joyce was terrified of mice, and took my beloved pet, Sir Archibald Hurstmonceaux, tucked into the back of my hair. Only when I was grown up did I find out that she had kept her feet off the ground all day.

After lunch we were given more presents – the official ones from Joyce and Reggie. My older sisters and the other grown-ups received well-chosen luxuries like silk scarves; ours were more sensible – woolly cardigans, which didn't really go with my new frock.

We all behaved as Joyce expected children to – nicely spoken, with plenty of 'pleases' and 'thank yous'. When carols were asked for, Eddie, Alex and I obediently stood in a line and sang *Unto Us a Son Is Born*. Joyce described it to our mother:

> After giggling false-starts, wriggles
> And a moment of disintegration
> Each bright, young note made patterns in the air,
> The place was full of stars and sweetness
> And for a moment there was nothing interfering
> With the clear communication of sharp joy.

After tea Joyce organised us into two teams and we had to pass matchboxes down the line on our noses. Then we had to thread a key on the end of string through our clothes, binding the whole party into one. Fishing it out from the young men's trouser bottoms felt mildly daring. Reggie handed out prizes to everyone – we were all winners.

One of the guests was a young man with dirty fingernails who stood on his head on the tapestry rug. We thought he could do this because he came from Australia. Not until I heard the day described by him on the radio twenty years later did I discover that he was the writer Clive James.

'Joyce had a marvellous knack of putting young men right, without putting them down,' he said.

I was extremely arrogant: I thought the way to correct evil in the world was to remove the bad men who were ruling it and replace them with good men and everything would then come right. Until this could be arranged there was no point in charity. Joyce was the real revolutionary – her charitable activities were far beyond any glib talk about society's benefits being shared – she was out there doing it for real.

I slowly learned that she was engaged full time in thousands of small acts of charity. She had no belief in the world ever coming right and what she did was what she could, which was considerable. She was one of the few people I ever met who actually did good by stealth.

'I was taught from an early age to think of other people,' said Joyce. 'It took me a long time to actually know and do it. If you had a bar of chocolate you shared it – it was part of the training.' She responded to begging letters from strangers with a polite refusal because she felt it was bad manners for them to have asked. But to people she knew, even if only slightly, she gave without care and no strings. Her philanthropy was like W. C. Fields' bank accounts: after he died it was discovered he had a bank account in every town in America, all under assumed names. Few of those who benefited from Joyce's friendship and generosity ever knew about all the others.

Joyce was occasionally asked to preach in Anglican churches and always spent several weeks planning what she would say. After a talk in Truro Cathedral, a clergyman wrote to her:

Cornwall has been lifted up by your message and many of us who preach sermons twice every Sunday have seen our sins in a mirror. I cannot begin to describe to you the effect it has had in the corridors of County Hall, in little groups in the Cathedral Close, in offices, in shops and on street corners. People speak of your lecture with delight and with awe. We shall never fully realize what you have done for us. I think I shall now better understand the message and the impact made by the prophets in the Old Testament.

She particularly enjoyed taking part in the Bow Dialogues, run by the Rev. Joseph McCulloch. Following the reconsecration of St

Mary-le-Bow Church in the City of London in 1960, McCulloch had the bright idea of installing two pulpits, facing each other, and instigated lunchtime dialogues with leading thinkers and personalities. His aim was to restore a relationship between the Church and the World by an exploration of views. Not all the speakers were believers, but they all had strong opinions. Antonia Fraser talked about Good, Richard Crossmann about Truth, James Cameron and Malcolm Muggeridge were both rather gloomy prophets and Athene Seyler worried that death would find her 'unrehearsed'. Joyce was an ideal candidate – she held strong beliefs and could talk amusingly and cogently within the allotted thirty-five minutes. In all she was invited ten times between 1967 and 1979.

'As she came in to the church,' wrote McCulloch, 'the crowded audience erupted into a spontaneous applause of welcome. If ever there was anyone with whom they felt in personal rapport, it was certainly Joyce, the communicator par excellence. Whether the people with her are two or three gathered together, or thousands, she is the same radiant person, spontaneous, free, aware and very much alive, exceptionally gifted and utterly sincere, above all, a fundamentally happy woman.'

Joyce and McCulloch discussed a wide variety of subjects, including the meaning of Christmas, beauty and friendship. In 1970 she was asked what she thought of 'test-tube' babies – eight years before the first was born. 'There is nothing intrinsically wrong in this,' she said. 'It has nothing to do with where God is in the child.' What was more important was the quality of family life that the child received. 'Love you can't do alone – you have to include other people. Our identity includes the qualities of companionship and love; we are not out there fighting alone.'

McCulloch asked her to name her main virtue and she replied, 'Good nature. I wake up in the morning expecting good. I'm an optimist because my optimism is founded on some kind of truth, that there is continuity of Good in operation. Any small kindness is a sign of God in action.'

'Stand porter at the door of thought, admitting only Good,' Nora wrote to Joyce in 1935. In *First Flight*, one of the last monologues she wrote, she fulfilled a long ambition to write about someone who was essentially good, but not boring. 'Goodness is almost impossible to show on the stage,' she explained. 'It can appear dogmatic or opinionated. Not goody-goody, but sound as a nut, whole.' The inspiration for *First Flight* was an English widow going to see her son and daughter-in-law whom Joyce sat next to on a plane in 1963. Sometimes Joyce had great difficulty finding the right accent – the key to all her monologues. For *First Flight* she tried West Country, Buckinghamshire and south London accents but found a Northern accent created the feeling of honesty, integrity and directness that she wanted, and the story took off. There is a lovable vulnerability to the woman on her first ever flight, crossing the Atlantic to meet her Afro-American daughter-in-law and grandchildren. She is not racially prejudiced, but she knows that without careful thought she could be. 'I believe that it isn't *who* you are – it's what you are that matters.' As the plane descends, she says to the invisible passenger next to her, 'Oh I do hope I do it all right. I just want to do it right.'

'What can I do about all the hate and rage all over the world?' Joyce asked in 1972. 'I've come to the conclusion that we have to stop thinking about *them*. If I can't get on with the person next door to me, or in my office, or the annoying relation, I cannot heal the rest of the world. The cure for Northern Ireland has to start in my home. Have you noticed that a bus conductor in a bad mood seeps through the whole bus?'

After Joyce's death Virginia commented, 'She was like a sort of great spiritual cocktail. She thought *good* in any form was evidence of God's presence so she looked for good in everyone, and of course she found it. What stopped her being "too good" was her terrific sense of humour.'

Joyce's non-Christian Science friends were also aware of her spirituality. Celia Johnson observed, 'When she walked into the room it was full of light and joy and happiness. She brought a sort of aura with her, a sort of loveliness.'

– 29 –

JOYCE'S FINAL YEAR was incredibly busy. The manuscript of the second volume of her autobiography, *In Pleasant Places*, was delivered to the publisher on the 1st of January 1979. The title was from Psalms XVI, Chapter 6: 'The lines are fallen unto me in pleasant places; yea, I have a goodly heritage.'

'Vol. 2 is much more difficult,' she wrote to Verily in 1977. 'Vol 1 was lit with childhood sun; the giants were giants and seen from below, and they were very great. Now we're all the same size . . . and the light isn't quite as clear. I hope it can be written as another kind of book. More reflective, more like a collection of pieces than an adventure, as Vol 1, was.' This volume was indeed more serious, about her interests, philosophy and friends. 'I don't know how to solve the problem of loving too many people,' she wrote to Rupert Hart-Davis. 'Perhaps I should list them and then get on with the facts. The trouble is that *people* is what matter to me & it is *people* that make the Pleasant Places so pleasant. I'm reluctant to do as you ask and to cut you and June out altogether; it seems so unnatural to me. I think it's a pity to wait till people are dead before you praise them & thank them. The trouble is we really do have very deeply loved friends in a hellova lot of pleasant places.' As before, Reggie helped her to edit, proof-read and compile an index. John Ward's portrait of Joyce was used on the cover, with several more of his illustrations inside.

'I purr and purr! I gloat and dip and gloat again,' he wrote. 'There is no-one like you and you wove a fine thread of gold into my talent, years and years ago and what sparkle it has brought into the life of the Ward family! And strength too and there must be so many people who sing a better song because of your support, who catch the gladness and delight of your talent.'

Book promotion began in June, with a five-day tour of six cities, including Bristol, where she was delighted to be introduced on television as 'the Nation's Nanny'. Joyce had always refused to make television commercials, but was now keen to commend her own product. 'My grandmother must be spinning – she thought it very non-U to have one's picture in the paper on *any* pretext, but to advertise – never.' When the book came out on 30 August she had a full programme of bookshop signings, press interviews, radio and television shows. She spoke at several literary lunches, including her third for the *Yorkshire Post*, with 845 people attending and another three hundred waiting outside.

Once again Joyce's positive outlook cheered readers up and she wished that she had a secretary to cope with the huge piles of mail.

'The book is even more of a masterpiece than the first one – it's a pastmasterpiece,' wrote Stewart Perowne. 'The first one told us how you got there, and this one tells us who you are, now you are there. It's enthralling. You've told us so many things we thought we knew, and didn't really. I DID know that cleaning the bath is the most odious of all chores. But the great things of life, such as eternity, you've put it into sharp focus, for which among many thousands, I thank you most lovingly, dear Joyce.'

There were long queues outside bookshops for signing sessions, and some fans brought presents such as greengages or flowers. One man gave Joyce a pair of white gloves, to replace the ones ruined by ink when he had asked for her autograph thirty years before. In Cambridge, Howard Fergusson, from the wartime National Gallery concerts, queued up and presented Joyce with a camembert cheese. In Rye, Sussex, Paul McCartney came in with three children. 'Hello, Joyce,' he said, 'I want my daughters to meet you.' After they had gone Joyce said, 'Who was that?' Reggie explained that it was Paul McCartney, one of the richest musicians in Britain. 'I did wonder if it was a Beatle,' said Joyce. 'I thought it might be John Lennon. He was very friendly, but he might have at least bought a book.'

Joyce and Reggie's relationship had long since reached that happy state of easy contentment. In 1970 she had written to Virginia, 'Don't you think that love only really works between two people when both are revolving perfectly into one large revolution? If one leans, the structure wobbles.'

Apart from charity committees, Reggie's life was devoted to Joyce. 'Reggie's retirement is a lovely bonus for me,' Joyce wrote. 'He does the shopping & we live far better than when I did it. Butcher's meat and pink grape fruit & its fun being together so much more.' He had discovered that the secret of a relaxed retirement was wearing country clothes. He spent most afternoons watching sport on television and occasionally visited his club, Brooks', in St James's Street. He still did Joyce's accounts and she was amazed to learn how much money she was making from her books, records and the radio.

In February 1979 Joyce and Reggie took a three-week cruise up the River Nile on a Swan's Tour as their fiftieth wedding anniversary present to each other. It was a strenuous schedule of lectures and sightseeing, with early starts, long walks and even donkey rides. During dinner in Luxor Joyce was genuinely surprised when the lights were turned off and the passengers and crew sang 'Happy Birthday' to her by a candlelit cake. One evening she found herself on the same terrace where Prince Aly Khan had offered her the jewellery thirty-four years before. 'Standing up there just before sunset last night it all flashed back to me and I was very glad not to be vulnerable or young any more.' She remembered feeling very guilty but not having the energy to say no. 'Potent at the time. He had infinite charm and dynamism. I keep meaning to tell Reggie about it all & someday I will.' She never did.

They went to the Lake District and saw 'the great explosions of yellow dandelions and the thick clumps of cowslips – bigger & better than ever' and called on their many friends in the area for tea and chats about birds. On their way home they took eggs to Mrs Gabe in exchange for vegetables from her husband's allotment.

In April, Clive James asked himself to lunch. He had come a long way since Joyce described him as 'the wild, far-out 23 year old Australian boy' she had supported with clothes and cheques. As with most people, he wanted to please Joyce and was keen to tell her how well he was now doing, with a happy marriage, several books published and television shows written. He was about to begin a Saturday-night television chat show and knew 'everyone' in the media.

'He is portly and plump at 39 and his output is *enormous*,' she noted. 'He is both grateful & elated by his success. He has his cake and also his bread and butter. I like him – deplore some of his excesses of energy and his lack of resistance to the witty mot. Elegant in brown velveteen. He may well end on the side of the angels?' She was pleased that he had given up drinking and smoking but noticed that he ate all her chocolates. She was wearing her eyepatch and explained that she was waiting for a new cosmetic contact lens.

'I enjoyed lunch more than I can say,' James wrote to her. 'It was like dining with a very sweet, very civilised, transvestite version of Captain Hook. What a woman you are. When I think of how you have bothered to stay interested in me over the years I am almost cured of self-regard. Almost, but not quite. All my love, Clive.'

A few weeks later, he wrote again for no reason other than to say, 'I keep making a list in my mind of all I owe you, and the list is so long, so this letter is to shift a granule of the weight off my conscience, as well as to say hello. How did you ever put up with me at all? Your protégé, Clive.'

In the middle of June Joyce agreed to appear at Wavenden, the arts centre near Milton Keynes run by Cleo Laine and Johnny Dankworth. She was horrified to learn that Dankworth was to play jazz in the first half of the programme, followed by Joyce giving an 'illustrated talk' – she didn't think the two would mix. Much to her amazement, the two elements complemented each other and the audience gave her a standing ovation, a rare occurrence in Britain then.

Princess Margaret was there and Johnny Dankworth was talking to Joyce backstage when she approached. 'Joyce nudged me,' remembers Dankworth, and started telling a joke. It went like this:

There were two nuns on a train, one was doing a crossword puzzle and said, 'Sister Mary, help me. I'm not quite sure about two down, a form of intercourse, four letters, ends with K.'

'That's easy, Sister Josephine,' said Sister Mary. 'It's talk.'

'Oh yes, so it is. Can you lend me your rubber?'

It was quite obvious that Joyce told this joke to see whether Princess Margaret would be embarrassed. She wasn't.

Although officially retired, Joyce recorded her eighth series of *Face the Music*, made six radio programmes, reviewed Ruth Draper's letters and wrote for the *Observer* about her childhood. Discussions were under way for a BBC2 documentary to celebrate her seventieth birthday and during their September visit to Cumbria some filming was done. She was still being offered parts in films, but it was fifteen years since she had read a good script.

A long train journey took her to Newcastle to record a television interview about her favourite heroes. She chose the tennis champion Signorina D'Alvaraz, Frank Sinatra, Gertrude Lawrence, German theologian Dietrich Bonhoeffer and Jane Austen.

Joyce usually refused to co-operate with biographies but she agreed to take part in a television profile of Nancy Astor. Joyce felt that previous biographies had been too hard on her and not mentioned her generosity or humour. The programme featured recently rediscovered Astor home movies from the 1920s and 30s at Cliveden, showing George Bernard Shaw playing tennis in plus-fours, Nancy skating and a plump teenage Joyce in pigtails learning to use stilts. 'I felt all the old unrest but safely seen from the present.' She spent a day filming at Cliveden, talking about Nancy and the house parties where so many different people were invited and nobody was ever introduced. Standing in front of the huge fireplace, Joyce demonstrated how her aunt used to hitch up her skirt at the back on winter days. Joyce didn't enjoy returning to Cliveden, now an American college: the rooms were filled with desks and stacking-chairs; the flowerbeds were empty; the orangery was now a café; and the kitchen garden had been turned into a car park.

For over a year Joyce's blind eye had been inflamed and it was getting worse. She often felt tired, and in Aldeburgh she had passed out in the bathroom and Reggie had had to force the door open to get in to help her. Just as her father Paul had disguised his unhappiness when Nora left him, so Joyce ensured that none of her friends or relatives saw that she was in increasing pain. Only Mrs Agos her housekeeper witnessed her temper occasionally fraying and her diaries reveal increasing irritation with situations and people by the end of each day. Even the rhododendrons in full flower in the Lake District annoyed her – they reminded her of rain drips, heavy Victorian architecture and Tories. Her dreams were increasingly chaotic and frightening.

Joyce had great faith in Doris, her Christian Scientist practitioner, whom she telephoned often. She felt a failure because of her inability to overcome the pain in her eye. 'The thing has gone on for so long,' she wrote to Virginia, 'and is SO uncomfortable at times that it is a bit discouraging. Of course I don't study nearly enough. Must mend my ways. The thing has puffed up again . . . But I sleep well, am well.' Indeed she went on long walks most days and enjoyed weekends away with friends and family in the country. They usually walked several miles and, during a weekend with Reggie's sister Katie, they climbed the cliffs of Skomer Island.

Just as she had six years earlier, Joyce tried to keep her pain from Reggie. But by the middle of August she could no longer hide it from him and he insisted on her returning to the eye specialist, Mr Winstanley: he prescribed cortisone, which made no difference.

When Mr Winstanley went abroad he referred Joyce to Mr Michael Sanders, a consultant neuro-ophthalmologist at the National Hospital for Nervous Diseases, and Mr John Knight, the leading surgeon at Moorfield Eye Hospital. Joyce resented paying £12 for an X-ray and £16.50 for a blood test, but she liked the doctors: 'If one must consent to these treatments, one couldn't have pleasanter doctors. They are stars.' The X-ray was in fact the latest computer tomography, or CT scan, a more efficient and detailed technique for 'seeing' inside the body without surgery. The scan revealed that her eye had shrivelled up, and there was some 'abnormal tissue' spreading backwards from the eye. The doctors decided to remove it the following week.

Joyce and Reggie had planned a ten-week holiday in Australia and South Africa, leaving at the start of November. Reggie had booked them flights on Concorde as far as Singapore, and Joyce had already had a 'packing rehearsal' to ensure she could get everything into two suitcases. By postponing this trip by two weeks, she would have seven weeks in which to recover. To keep Reggie happy, Joyce agreed to the operation but carried on as normal: after seeing the doctors she went to two parties, one at the Royal Geographical Society and the other at Joseph Cooper's home, where she sang. The next day she made a speech at the Arthur Koestler Awards for prisoners' arts and crafts.

During the week before the operation she went by train to Manchester for the day to give two radio interviews and a talk at the

Liberty Theatre. The next day she and Reggie flew to Dublin for the weekend, where she signed books all afternoon and appeared on Gay Byrne's *The Late-Late Show* on Radio-Telefis Eirean.

Only Reggie's close family and friends were told about the impending operation. 'I'm not depressed about all this,' she wrote to June Hart-Davis. 'I'm just grateful for the love & care & skill that is being shown; & I'm very much supported by my faith.'

On Tuesday 16 October, Reggie drove Joyce to Moorfield Eye Hospital, where she was warmly welcomed by the nurses and settled into her private room. Her diary on this day reveals the extraordinary strength of both her faith and her relationship with Reggie. Here was a woman of sixty-nine who had never stayed in a hospital as a patient; who did not approve of medicine or doctors, yet found them charming and supportive; who had never worn a surgical gown and had no idea what a blood pressure machine was for, yet was completely calm. She wrote her diary in the usual detail about the weather (sunny and cheerful), the flowers (plentiful and bright) and the hospital food (roast lamb). Several doctors examined her and she was unable to tell them about her medical history – she had never taken any notice of it. She felt 'most lovingly cherished' and 'grateful for a feeling of support'. Any fear she felt was kept firmly in the background.

Reggie, too, showed enormous courage. Apart from his eyes filling with tears as he left her, he supported Joyce in the way he knew she needed – without fuss, well organised, patient and prompt. 'I love him v. much,' she underlined in her diary. Then she wrote to Virginia:

> Been visited by the doctors. The Irish matron's assistant is my avid fan. The anaesthetist and the registrar have all inspected me. I feel very removed and that is cause for immense gratitude. The thing is, I'm truly grateful for the sense of Love I find everywhere and realize it is God in action. Good is always a proof of God's presence.
>
> At a time like this one longs to make sure that those one loves really know just how much they are loved. In the case of R. and you it is 100% plus. More reasons for gratitude. Indeed 'the lines are fallen unto me in pleasant places.' Much love darling best friend. J.

After supper she listened to the last in the series of radio pro-grammes she had made about her favourite records. The following day, she woke after the operation and reported being pushed down corridors on a trolley and feeling as if it had happened to someone else. She was in no pain, with only slight bruising on her face. Her writing was slightly larger than the normal tiny spidery hand. 'I have felt wonderfully free throughout the day,' she wrote. 'I am so grateful for the clear feeling of Love and Support.' Reggie had been in twice with her post and more flowers, and returned home to phone his sisters and brother that all was well.

Two days later Joyce was discharged and within a week she was cooking meals and going for walks. The eye surgeon complimented her on her quick healing and said he did not want to see her until she returned from Australia in February. 'Very encouraging,' Joyce wrote to June Hart-Davis. 'I go to be fitted for new "orb" next week & *hope* they can make me one in time for our departure. Feel a bit battered. Never had an anaesthetic before & this was a massive one I gather. Feel as if I'd been run over by a bus! But the bruises are over & progress is made daily. Eating rather *too* well, we go for little walks and R is *marvellous* help.'

At first all appeared to be well, but even Christian Science could not overcome the increasing pain in her neck. Doris did her best, but the pain 'seems so *very* strong and very difficult', Joyce wrote in her diary. To Reggie she confessed only 'discomfort'. But he knew already that it was more than that. Tests on the removed growth had revealed choroidal malignant melanoma – cancer of the eye. This type of cancer normally fills the eye and is easily diagnosed. But in Joyce's case, having made her blind six years before, it grew back-wards into the optical nerve, where it could not be seen, and it had now spread to her spine. The doctors were amazed that she had lived with so little pain for six years.

Reggie was told that there was nothing medicine could do. She would probably live for about a year and he was advised to take her to Australia as planned. He discussed the diagnosis with Virginia. Should he tell Joyce or not? She believed that the doctors had removed 'some disturbance causing inflammation' and that all was now well. Virginia pointed out that as Joyce denied that any of her body was of importance she wouldn't be interested in a medical diagnosis. She was not afraid of death because she didn't believe in it. Life to her was everlasting: the time one spent in a human body was merely a speck in that continuum.

'No matter what happens to one's material body, it does not, cannot, touch the spiritual identity that is our eternal body,' she wrote in her diary. She believed that 'man is never separate from his creator and is spiritually whole wherever he is, in the air, on land, underground, in space – he is always contained and safe. We can learn to see beyond unhappy and distressing human conditions and ill-health to what we really are, here and now, for the kingdom of heaven is at hand now. And now is always.'

'Life *is* continuity,' she wrote when Verily's sister died a week later. 'And the going on is the point. I love the feeling that one can never be out of the range of Love/God because one is in fact the very expression of Love/God. I'm leading a normal but gloriously non-eventful life, beneficial and a "nice change"!' She was still making plans, having the new artificial eye made and accepting invitations to preach in churches the following year. She went to the hairdresser and persuaded Tracy to change the way she set her hair, in smaller, tighter rollers. Before the operation, Joyce had cancelled everything in her diary until 2 December, when they planned to fly to Australia. But she had forgotten to cancel a lunch for the Magazine Editors' Society. Rather than let them down, she rose from her sofa, put on her suit and made an after-lunch speech. The following day she wrote to Tommy with plans for their holiday together in France the following March.

On 9 November, Reggie drove Joyce to Aldeburgh for the weekend. Although the pain in her neck was increasing, they walked by the sea, enjoyed the blue skies and visited Herbert Axell at Minsmere. Joyce signed books in the bookshop and ordered new clothes for Australia from Hurren's, her favourite clothes shop. While there she phoned Muffet Harrison in Snape, who recalls, 'I don't know what it was but I clearly remember that there was something quite different about her during that conversation.'

Reggie showed enormous strength and love, with no clue in his behaviour towards her to give her any cause for concern. 'Reggie has been a tower – he has shopped, cooked and cared. It is idiotic not to be able to see through this mesmerism [cope with the pain]; it seems so *very* strong and very difficult.' She rejoiced that *The Times* was back in print after a year's strike and she could resume her favourite crossword puzzles. This, the 13th November, was the last day she ever wrote her diary, which she had written almost every day for forty years. Her final entry was, 'R has taken friends to theatre. I just couldn't make it.'

Two days later, Virginia organised a surprise golden-wedding party for Joyce and Reggie in her flat in Hyde Park Gardens. It was four weeks before the actual date, but by then Joyce and Reggie would be on their way to Australia. In 1942 Joyce had said of Reggie, 'Golly, the gods were good to me when they met me up with Reggie! I can't get over how truly lucky I am to be married to someone I am still dead in love with! I really am lucky to have a husband who is, apparently, entirely interested in all my doings, enjoys my career for me and is enthusiastic about all my attempts.'

Ten years earlier, for their fortieth anniversary, they had agreed that they wanted neither rubies nor a special celebration. However, on the morning, Reggie carried the breakfast tray to Joyce in bed, and over his pyjamas he was wearing the morning coat in which he had been married. They both laughed so much they couldn't go on with their cereal. 'Far better than rubies,' said Joyce.

Now, for their fiftieth anniversary, Joyce did not feel like going to a party, but Virginia noticed that 'as usual she wanted everyone else to be happy'. All the surviving 'old favourites' were there, including Reggie's sisters, niece and brother, Mrs Gabe and Mrs Agos, Athene Seyler, Norman Newell, and John Ward. I accompanied my mother, Verily. As the youngest guest I felt overawed by so many famous people and sat close to Joyce.

Celia Johnson read an ode and Diana Lyddon presented the Grenfells with a crystal vase which Virginia had had engraved with their favourite flowers and birds. 'I now find they are strongly opposed to the idea of presents,' she wrote to all the guests before the party, 'and indeed have forbidden their families to give them so much as a jar of Golden Shred marmalade.' Virginia invited everyone to contribute £1 towards the vase, 'unless you want to please them even more by not giving them anything!'.

William Blezard wrote a song, with a chorus in which everyone could join.

'Come on, Joyce,' called one of the guests from Virginia's grand piano, 'stand up and give us a song.'

'I'll sing from here, but you must all join in,' she replied in her best headmistress tone. Everyone sang with gusto, but I noticed that Joyce merely mimed. 'My neck's giving me hell,' she whispered to me.

'Have you tried aspirin?' I asked innocently.

'It's well past the aspirin stage, my old duck,' she said firmly.

Verily phoned Joyce the day after the party: 'She was very jaunty and said, "Would you believe it, I'm flat on my back? But I've got to get up tomorrow to wash the curtains." The next day I rang and she said, "I won't wash the curtains today. But the marvellous thing is that Reggie is doing all the cooking. So there's nothing to worry about at all."'

Mr Michael Sanders visited her at home and Dr Patrick Woodcock cared for her daily medical needs. The pain in her neck was now so bad that she could only lie flat on her back in bed. It was explained as a dislocated vertebra, probably caused during the operation. She accepted painkillers and the trip to Australia was cancelled. She continued to talk to friends on the phone and dictated letters to Reggie. St Andrew's University invited her to be their first woman rector, but reluctantly she turned it down – she was going to be away too much the following year. Less reluctantly she turned down the requests to talk at women's lunch clubs. 'I can't see the point of them. Money raisers are different & I will continue to do a few of those.' On 19 November a letter arrived from 10 Downing Street. It read, 'Her Majesty may be graciously pleased to approve that you be appointed a Dame Commander of the Order of the British Empire in the forthcoming list of New Year's honours.'

'Reggie's patience is miraculous because I am terribly slow at eating,' she dictated to Tommy. 'I don't read, but I listen to the radio, watch the television and talk a lot and Reggie reads out the newspapers.' After seeing her mother die of cancer and Viola Tunnard die of motor neurone disease, Joyce had a dread of long fatal illness.

Two days later Reggie wrote to Tommy: 'Poor Joyce is much the same. I am afraid I cannot give you any forecast as to when she will get better. She has a charming Trinidad nurse who comes every morning and washes her. Clean as Joyce has always been, she has never been cleaner than she is now. All love, Reggie.'

The next day, 27 November, Reggie decided that he would have to tell his close family the truth. He wrote to Tommy, 'The cancer seems to be progressing at an alarming rate. It might not be more (I would have thought less) than 5 or 6 weeks. She sleeps wonderfully at night, and snoozes quite peacefully most of the day. I have not told her – & at present have no intention of doing so. I myself, having got over the original shock, am quite all right.'

Reggie also told a few close friends. 'You need not keep it a secret,' he wrote to Leonard Gershe, 'just so long as all who know go on behaving normally. I hope it does not get into the press, but if it does, Joyce won't see it. Joyce lies in bed quite unquestioning, never looking worried or anxious. Leonard, Joyce *loves* getting your letters – so please go on writing and cheering her up.'

Despite her medical care, her Christian Scientist friends stayed close. Bruce Woods-Jack from Cumbria was one of the last friends to speak to her.

We had been planning for the signing of her second book when I received a call from Joyce. She didn't sound her usual self and mentioned that she was being challenged like never before with an illness. But after going through surgery she realised as a Christian Scientist that life was not in the body and her spiritual being was fully intact. I dashed out and sent her flowers and she rang again to thank me. We had a lovely chat about God and love and friendship.

The next day, 29 November, Virginia wrote to Rupert Hart-Davis:

I don't know if Reggie has written to you or not, but the sad news is that darling Joyce has cancer of the spine . . . She is very weak now, but completely out of pain, & one can only pray she will drift peacefully away; & for Reggie's sake, soon. She looks happy – starts a sentence & falls asleep in the middle of it. Reggie is doing everything, of course, though thank heaven there is now a nurse.

That evening Sue Hussey visited and chatted to Joyce. 'She looked beautiful with her creamy complexion and rich brown hair spilled out on her pillow.'

Joyce died a few hours later, on 30 November 1979, aged sixty-nine.

'It was miraculously marvellous,' Reggie wrote to Tommy.

At no time did Joyce even look questioning or anxious, for the last 3 days she was practically entirely out of all pain – it had left her; she didn't have to take pills to kill it. The little Trinidad nurse was a Godsend. On the last night I was alone here when Joyce's breathing seemed to get harder and faster. She didn't quite lose consciousness but just lay there, breathing rather heavily until at 3.30 her breathing got less & then stopped. It was *entirely peaceful*.

Reggie must have wondered whether Joyce would have lived longer if she had received medical treatment. This type of cancer is difficult to cure, and the disease might well have taken a similar path. 'Darlings,' continued Reggie, 'the form of cancer she had developed could be *agonising* & it could also go on a long time. It is extraordinary to think that she had had it for 7 years: in fact it was since she got it that Joyce had started her new career and written 2 best sellers.'

Bernard Levin wrote in the *Sunday Times*, 'Her faith, her work and her marriage; these were the three columns that held her life so serene and secure.' In her final year Joyce had enjoyed all three to the full.

'I always find it strange that people are afraid of the thought of eternity,' she had written twenty years before.

Why should it be awful? Why not perfection? It is, clearly, a spiritual state, and as such has no conflicts – for I take it that harmony is the rule and harmony is never dull. It is simply a human supposition that peace would be all ease and nullity. I have an idea peace is gloriously un-dull but cannot be perceived by the human mind, only by the spiritual awareness of the Divine Mind.

I believe that 'Eternity is now'.

– 30 –

If I should go before the rest of you
Break not a flower nor inscribe a stone
Nor when I'm gone speak in a Sunday voice
But be the usual selves that I have known.
Weep if you must,
Parting is hell,
But life goes on,
So sing as well.

Joyce Grenfell, 1940

'JOYCE'S LAST FEW days were extraordinary,' remembered Patrick Woodcock. 'She never saw impending death and was still accepting invitations to give lectures the following year.'

As soon as Reggie phoned her, Sue Hussey went to Elm Park Gardens. 'Reggie sat with tears streaming down his face, not sobbing, just quietly weeping. He was completely bereft, but immensely grateful that she had been in no pain and no fear. Joyce was his whole life, he fell further and further in love with her every year of their fifty years. Theirs truly was a fairy-tale love story.'

Tommy Phipps rang from Long Island for a morning chat with his sister – it was his sixty-sixth birthday. Reggie's attempts to soften the blow had failed – he had not yet received the letter about Joyce's illness. With no warning that she was even ill, Sue had to tell him that Joyce had just died. 'We had a very strong relationship,' he wrote. 'She was always rather secretly delighted – proud – amused – by my often outrageous romantic escapades. But of course, on the surface acted very governessy towards me!'

Sue phoned a friend at the BBC and Joyce's death was announced on the eleven o'clock news. By midday telegrams had been sent to friends all over the world. REGRET TO TELL YOU THAT DARLING JOYCE DIED TONIGHT. SHE DIED QUIETLY AND COMPLETELY AT PEACE LOVE REGGIE. The Queen sent a personal telegram to Reggie, and newspapers all over the world reported her death.

Cass Allen was rehearsing a musical with Elisabeth Welch at the Lyric, Hammersmith, when she heard. 'I opened my mouth to sing and only a huge sob came out. Joyce had listened to all my growing-up problems and had been the most influence on my career.'

When she was twenty-seven years old, Joyce had written to Virginia, 'I *loathe* funerals. Don't let me have one, will you? Just hire a professional man to get rid of my body and then you and a few right thinking friends can make some statements about Life, and leave it at that.' Four days after she died, Joyce's body was cremated after a small service at Golder's Green Crematorium, attended only by Reggie and three Christian Scientists: Virginia, Audrey Butterworth and Jean Gunn. They sang the hymn *Happy the Man Whose Heart Can Rest*, read from Psalms, Romans, *Science and Health* and Joyce's favourite quotation from William Penn: 'And life is eternal and love is immortal, and death is only a horizon, and a horizon is nothing save the limit of our sight.' Her ashes were not scattered in any special place – her life and work was her memorial.

Reggie received hundreds of letters from friends and fans, and insisted on replying by hand to most of them. 'I know that having been married to Joyce for just on 50 years, I have no reason – certainly no right – to be sad – & Joyce would have hated that anyway,' he wrote to Michael Olivier. 'And surprisingly, I am not sad. I just miss – terribly miss – not being able to tell her of the nice things that happen & of all the loving things written about her in the Press and in countless letters.'

Two weeks after Joyce died, Reggie invited her closest friends and his sisters to come and take away her clothes. Virginia had been dreading the occasion. 'Though I don't want to hurt Reggie's feelings I don't feel mine would stand the strain of meeting a lot of women dressed like Joyce!' she wrote to Tommy. 'I think all the protagonists feel pretty aghast at this party – which stemmed from J's description in her book of what fun it was trying on Nancy Lancaster's cast-offs.'

Mrs Agos greeted the dozen guests with kisses and tears, and served a buffet lunch with champagne. Joyce's clothes, shoes, handbags and coats were laid out in her sunlit bedroom for the guests to choose from. The women entered into the spirit of the occasion but Verily felt slightly embarrassed and wondered if she had taken too much. She chose two frocks, three pairs of size-seven shoes and several silk scarves for her four daughters. 'Here, take this hat for Janie,' said Reggie to her. I still have the straw boater with silk roses that Joyce wore in *Penny Plain* in 1951.

Jean Cowan took what was left to Aldeburgh. 'Joyce's friends had first pick and the rest went to a charity shop. I still see some of them being worn around Aldeburgh,' she said. Joyce had always believed that clothes should keep circulating, and they still are: this book was written wearing the patchwork jacket knitted for her by a fan.

Despite Joyce's request to have no church service, Reggie kept himself busy planning a thanksgiving service in Westminster Abbey, the only place large enough to hold all of Joyce's admirers, friends, relations and colleagues. Even so, the two thousand public tickets were snapped up almost immediately. Virginia accompanied Reggie to plan the service with the Dean of Westminster.

'I relish the incongruous,' she wrote to Tommy, 'and rather loved sitting in the Jerusalem Chamber which is where Richard II slept and Henry IV died, eating Huntly & Palmer assorted biscuits to the clinking of teacups, as we thrashed out the pros & cons of Vaughn Williams & Benjamin Britten. I won a tiny battle because "they" suggested muffled bells & the flag at half mast & I said Oy! This is supposed to be a *thanksgiving* – so now everything will be loud and clear.'

At the thanksgiving service on 7 February 1980, the flowers included Joyce's favourite catkins, pussy willows and wild lilies, and Joseph Cooper arranged the music. The Rev. Geoffrey White from Loweswater Valley gave the address. 'The simple truth is,' he said, 'Joyce Grenfell was the most spiritually-minded person I have ever met. My greatest and most abiding [memory] will be that I have known about her deep unshakable faith in God, and of her search for things eternal and true.'

'He was perfect,' wrote Reggie, 'exactly what I wanted – NOT theatre or smart, just simple and sincere. It was a wonderful occasion.'

The Phipps family came over from New York and sat beside Reggie as he wept unselfconsciously throughout the moving service.

He was especially sad that she did not live to become a Dame of the British Empire but, breaking the normal rules, the Prime Minister allowed it to be known that she had been nominated. Everyone worried about him living on his own, but his sister Frances moved down from Scotland and they shared the flat in Elm Park Gardens for the next thirteen years.

Joyce left £196,358, the equivalent in 2002 of over £1.5 million. Considering she had given away so much already, most of this must have been made in the last few years of her life. She left £20,000 to the First Church of Christ, Scientist in Sloane Street; £10,000 to the Viola Tunnard Memorial Trust for music students; £5,000 to Virginia's favourite charity, the Friends of the Elderly and Gentlefolk's Help; and £2,000 each to the House of St Barnabas in Soho and Family Service Units. Various friends such as Laurier Lister, her director; Lorna Andrade, her typist; Christine Harrison, a Christian Scientist friend; Connie Fite, her American stage manager; and Patrick Woodcock, Reggie's doctor, received £2,000 each. Diana Lyddon was thrilled and amazed to be left £5,000 and Rupert Hart-Davis was 'dumbfounded and overwhelmed' when he and June received £2,500 each. Other friends and godchildren received money or paintings. Reggie was left the most valuable part – the copyright of her works, which under current law remain in his family until 2049.

Reggie continued this generosity, and the Joyce Grenfell Trust still benefits charities such as the House of St Barnabas and the Chelsea Society. In 1980 he gave the money he had earned in Rhodesia to the Hampton family when we went to teach in newly independent Zimbabwe. It enabled us to buy a Land-Rover for delivering food to malnourished children, school library books and toys for the pre-school playgroup. A year later, Reggie stayed with us in Zimbabwe and visited the school and playgroup.

Within weeks of Joyce's death, Reggie began to assemble stories from friends and relations for the book *Joyce By Herself and Her Friends*. It was so successful that a collection of monologues called *Turn Back the Clock* followed, and then the letters between Joyce and Katharine Moore were published, showing the friendship unfolding over twenty-two years. Katharine continued writing and won a prize for Best First Novel when she was eighty-five. 'They were rather surprised and put out when they discovered my age,' she laughed. She died in 2001, aged 103.

Claremont Fan Court School, the descendant of the Christian Science school Joyce attended fifty years earlier, built a theatre called the Joyce Grenfell Centre. A gala charity concert in aid of this was directed by Wendy Toye, the choreographer of *Requests the Pleasure*, and featured many of her friends, including Cleo Laine and Richard Baker. Maureen Lipman performed *School Reunion*, which inspired her to mount *Re: Joyce*, which opened in 1988 and ran for over a year at the Fortune Theatre, where *Requests the Pleasure* had opened in 1954. While researching this solo show of Joyce's work, the playwright James Roose-Evans found Joyce's letters and diaries in her study and edited them into the books *Darling Ma: Letters to Her Mother* and *Time of My Life*, her wartime diaries. Reggie agreed that the BBC documentary about Joyce's life could go ahead, and *I Like Life* was watched by nearly three million viewers. He supported several 'tribute' shows to Joyce, including Margaret Baxter's in Zimbabwe in 1983, Jane Bower's in Cambridge and Jennifer Rose's, which sold out at the Edinburgh Festival in 1986.

Reggie continued to do everything that he and Joyce had done together, such as trips to Cumbria, Yorkshire and Aldeburgh and visits to the theatre. Whereas Joyce had kept all her friends, colleagues and relations in separate boxes, Reggie brought them together. Many found that though they had lost Joyce, they had gained new friends. Virginia died aged eighty-three, and Reggie died a month later on 31 March 1993, aged nearly ninety.

Joyce always said that 'Life is continuity,' and in her case it is true. Her work is remembered even twenty years after her death. Maureen Lipman performed more of Joyce's monologues and songs in the BBC radio series *Choice Grenfell* in 1997. In 1998 Joyce and five others were selected to commemorate British comedy with a caricature by Gerald Scarfe on a 37p stamp. The last BBC Radio Three serial of the millennium was the letters written between Joyce and Virginia, read by Maureen Lipman during Christmas week 1999. In May 2000, 'Joyce Grenfell' was the answer to a question on BBC television's *University Challenge*. Joyce loved the programme and would have been amazed that she was the answer to Jeremy Paxman's question, 'Who was the actress niece of Lady Astor who played a teacher called Miss Gossage in a film about a girls' school?'

Her creativity is still enjoyed by old and new fans – her songs and monologues are available on compact discs; her television and radio performances are repeated; and her professional style influences entertainers today. All understand the phrase 'very Joyce Grenfell'.

The last words in Joyce's final book are 'Zest, thank God for.'

Appendices

Joyce Grenfell's Homes

1910	Born in Knightsbridge, London
1911	Winnipeg and Vancouver, Canada
1913	New York
1914	Ford Manor, Surrey; Cliveden, Buckinghamshire
1918	Burton Court, Chelsea, London
1919	28 St Leonard's Terrace, Chelsea
1930	21 St Leonard's Terrace, Chelsea
1936	Parr's, Cliveden Estate
1943	London bases included: Virginia Graham, Cambridge Square; Reggie's parents, Beaufort Gardens; Pauline Spender-Clay, Ennismore Gardens
1945	Rectory Chambers, Old Church Street, Chelsea
1945	149 King's Road, Chelsea
1956–79	34 Elm Park Gardens, Chelsea

Stage Shows

1939–40	Farjeon's *Little Revue*, Little Theatre, London
1940–1	Farjeon's *Diversion*, Wyndham's Theatre, London
1942	ENSA tours of UK
1942	*Light and Shade*, Ambassador's Theatre, London
1944	ENSA tour of North Africa with Viola Tunnard
1944–5	ENSA tour of the Middle East and India with Viola Tunnard
1945–6	*Sigh No More*, Piccadilly Theatre, London, and tour
1947–8	*Tuppence Coloured*, UK tour followed by Lyric, Hammersmith, then Globe Theatre, Shaftesbury Avenue
1951–2	*Penny Plain*, St Martin's Theatre, London, and UK tour
1952	Six-week tour for British troops in Libya and Egypt with Viola Tunnard
1954–5	*Joyce Grenfell Requests the Pleasure*, UK tour, then Fortune Theatre, London, moved to St Martin's Theatre, then another UK tour with Three's Company and William Blezard
1955	*Joyce Grenfell Requests the Pleasure*, Bijou Theatre, Broadway, New York, with Three's Company
1956	*Joyce Grenfell at Home*, tour of Canada, Washington and Lyceum Theatre, New York, with George Bauer
1956	Tour of Northern Rhodesia (Zambia) with Viola Tunnard
1957	*Joyce Grenfell at Home*, tour of Dublin and UK provinces, then Lyric, Hammersmith
1958	*Joyce Grenfell Bids You Good Evening*, Broadway, then Canada and North America with George Bauer
1959	*Meet Joyce Grenfell*, Philip Street Theatre, Sydney, with William Blezard
1960	*Meet Joyce Grenfell*, tour of UK with William Blezard
1960	*Seven Good Reasons*, Scala Theatre, London

1962	*Joyce Grenfell*, Haymarket Theatre, London, followed by UK tour with William Blezard
1963	*Joyce Grenfell*, tour of Australia with William Blezard
1964	Tours of Canada, Switzerland and Hong Kong with William Blezard
1966	Tours of UK, Australia and New Zealand with William Blezard
1967	Tours of UK, Hong Kong, USA and Canada with William Blezard
1968	Tour of UK with William Blezard
1969	Tour of Australia and New Zealand with William Blezard
1970	Tours of UK and USA with William Blezard
1972	Tour of UK with William Blezard
1973	Waterloo Dinner, Windsor Castle

Films

A Letter from Home, director Carol Reed, 1941
The Lamp Still Burns, director Maurice Elvery, 1943
The Demi Paradise, director Anthony Asquith, 1943
While the Sun Shines, director Anthony Asquith, 1943
Design for Women, producer Alan Jarvis, screenplay by Joyce Grenfell and
     Stephen Potter, 1947
Poet's Pub, director Frederick Wilson, 1949
A Run for Your Money, director Charles Frend, 1949
Alice in Wonderland, director Dallas Bower, 1950
The Happiest Days of Your Life, director Frank Launder, 1950
Stage Fright, director Alfred Hitchcock, 1950
Laughter in Paradise, director Mario Lampi, 1951
The Magic Box, director Robert Boulting, 1951
The Galloping Major, director Henry Cornelius, 1951
The Pickwick Papers, director Noël Langley, 1952
Genevieve, director Henry Cornelius, 1953
The Belles of St Trinian's, director Frank Launder, 1954
Forbidden Cargo, director Harold French, 1954
The Million Pound Note, director Ronald Neame, 1954
The Good Companions, director J. Lee Thompson, 1957
Blue Murder at St Trinian's, director Frank Launder, 1957
Happy Is the Bride, director Roy Boulting, 1957
The Pure Hell of St Trinian's, director Frank Launder, 1960
The Old Dark House, director William Castle, 1962
The Americanisation of Emily, director Arthur Hiller, 1964
The Yellow Rolls-Royce, director Anthony Asquith, 1964

For more details of her films see www.imdb.com

Books

Nanny Says, Dobson, 1972 & 1987. Collection of sayings, introduced by Joyce.

Requests the Pleasure, Macmillan, 1973. First autobiography, up to 1954; serialised on BBC Radio Four.

George, Don't Do That, Macmillan, 1977. Nursery-school sketches.

Stately as a Galleon, Macmillan, 1977. More theatrical sketches and songs.

In Pleasant Places, Macmillan, 1979. Joyce's second autobiography, 1954–73.

Joyce By Herself and Her Friends, Macmillan, 1980. Poems and portraits by friends and relatives.

An Invisible Friendship, Macmillan, 1981. Letters between Joyce and Katharine Moore.

Turn Back the Clock, Macmillan, 1983. Monologues and songs.

Darling Ma: Letters to Joyce Grenfell's Mother, 1932–1944, edited by James Roose-Evans, Hodder & Stoughton, 1988.

The Time of My Life: Entertaining the Troops – Her Wartime Journals, edited by James Roose-Evans, Hodder & Stoughton, 1989.

Joyce and Ginnie: Letters of Joyce Grenfell and Virginia Graham, edited and introduced by Janie Hampton, Hodder & Stoughton, 1997; serialised on BBC Radio Three.

Hats Off! The Poetry and Drawings of Joyce Grenfell, edited and introduced by Janie Hampton, John Murray, 2000; serialised on BBC Radio Four.

Monologues

1939   *Useful and Acceptable Gifts. Different Kinds of Mother: Village Mother, American Mother, the Understanding and the English Mother. Head Girl. Committee.*

1940   *Canteen in Wartime. Local Library. Companion Pieces: The Friend Who Knits, The Friend Who Talks, The Friend Who Gets Lost at the Cinema.*

1942   *Cardboard Figures 1: End of Affair. Cardboard Figures 2: Her Ladyship's Maid. Cardboard Figures 3: Young Thing in a Straight Play. Woolgathering. Situation Vacant. The Voluntary Worker.*

1945   *Travelling Broadens the Mind* (revised 1955). *Nursery School – Nativity Play.*

1947   *Artist's Room – A Pair of Front Stalls, a Group of Balcony Tickets, a Pair of Complimentary Tickets, One Single Balcony Unreserved. Odyssey.*

1948   *Going Abroad for the Hols. Amateur Actress in a Costume Play.*

1949   *Nursery School – Going Home Time.*

1950   *Life and Literature. Thought for Today (Earth Ray Thought Forces). Nursery School – Flowers. Nursery School – Sing Song Time.*

1952   *Tristram* (the boy who went to church). *Nursery School – Biscuits and Milk. A Little Talk.*

1953   *Private Secretary* (first performed by Betty Marsden).

1954   *Women at Work 1 – Antique Shop. Women at Work 2 – Behind the Counter. Women at Work 3 – Writer of Children's Books. Young Musician, Before Her First London Recital. Mother and Daughter. Shirley's Girl Friend – Mr Pilchard's Discovery. Visitor – Cocktail Party. Fern Brixton (Extra Sensory Perception).*

1957   *Friend to Tea. Committee. Lady Wibberly. Shirley's Girl Friend – Fun Fair. Christmas Eve. Nursery School – Free Activity. Teacher* (first performed by Diana Churchill).

1959   *Life Story* (wife of famous musician). *Boat Train. Counter-wise. Simple Setting* (American woman having portrait painted). *Telephone Call* (first performed by Bettina Welch). *Shirley's Girl Friend – Beauty Through Body Control.*

1960   *Shirley's Girl Friend – Picnic Place.*

1962   *Fern Brixton – Dumb Friend. Speeches 1, 2 & 3. Shirley's Girl Friend – Foreign Feller. Nursery School – Story Time.*

1964   *It's Made All the Difference. Shirley's Girl Friend – Music Festival. Opera Interval.*

1965   *Lally Tullet. The Past is Present 1* (old boyfriend on Waterloo Station). *The Past is Present 2 – School Reunion. Eng. Lit. I – Interview.*

1967   *A Terrible Worrier. Eng. Lit. II – An Event. Good Old Jennifer. The Wedding is on Saturday.*

1968   *Nicodemus's Song. Eng. Lit. III – Anarchy.*

1969   *One is One and All Alone. First Flight.*

1971   *Mulgarth Street.*

Songs

(Composer in Brackets)

1940   *I'm in Love With a Gentleman* (Graham).

1942   *I'm Going to See You Today* (Addinsell). *Security Song* (Graham). *There is Nothing New to Tell You* (Addinsell). *Drifting* (Addinsell).

1943   *Turn Back the Clock* (Addinsell). *Someday* (Addinsell). *They're a Lovely Bunch of Boys* (Addinsell). *There But Anywhere in the World* (Addinsell).

1945   *Oh, Mr du Maurier!* (Addinsell). *After Dark in the Evening* (Addinsell). *You Put Me in Mind of My Dear Old Cockney Mum* (Addinsell).

1946   *When You Go* (Addinsell).

1947   *The Countess of Coteley* (Addinsell). *I Like Life* (Addinsell). *Echo Song* (Addinsell). *Learn to Loosen* (Addinsell). *Rainbow Nights* (Geoffrey Wright).

1948   *Teacher* (Addinsell).

1949   *The Wedding of Miss Duck* (Tunnard). *Charlie Parker's Flower Song* (Tunnard).

1951   *A Penny's Not a Penny Any More* (Addinsell). *Festival Calypso*, written by Graham & Grenfell (Addinsell). *Joyful Noise* (Donald Swann). *Running Commentary* (Addinsell). *Keepsake (Picture Postcard)*, written by Nicholas Phipps & Grenfell (Addinsell). *A Moment With Tennyson (or Maud)*, *Phipps & Grenfell* (Addinsell). *All Night, Angels Watching Over Thee. Sit Down Sister* (Tunnard). *Wrong Songs for Wrong Singers* (Tunnard). *Love at Last* (Addinsell).
Songs My Mother Taught Me: *Since Bacon Has Gone Up a Dollar a Pound; Fare Thee Well, Old Joe Clark; Never Mind the Weather; Yellow Rose of Texas; All the Pretty Little Horses; I'm Gwine Away t'Leave You; I'll Lend You My Horse; Hand Me Down My Bonnet; Rue de Provence; Seems Like Time; I Heard a Voice; Snowball; All Night, & Lord's Gin to Set This World on Fire* (Tunnard).

1952   *Teacher* (Geoffrey Wright). *Rainbow Nights* (Wright). *My Heart's as*

348

Light as Air (Addinsell). *I Don't Arf Love Yer* (Kenneth Mortimer and Addinsell). *Narcissus* (Nevion & Paramor).

1953   *Ordinary Morning* (Addinsell). *Old Willy Waddle* (Tunnard). *It's Almost Tomorrow* (Addinsell). *I was Born One Wet Whit Monday* (Donald Swann) for Moira Fraser in *Airs on a Shoestring*.

1954   *Songs of Many Lands* (Addinsell). *Career Girl* (Addinsell); first performed by Elisabeth Welch. *Ballad* (Addinsell). *Hostess* (Addinsell). *Ethel – Football Fan* (Addinsell). *The Music's Message* (Addinsell). *Encores* (Addinsell). *Three Brothers* (Addinsell). *Mrs Mendlicote* (Addinsell). *The Whizzer* (Addinsell); first performed by Elie and Doris Waters. *Palais Dancers* (Addinsell).

1957   *The Woman on the Bus* (Addinsell). Five *Songs to Make You Sick* (Addinsell). *All We Ask is Kindness* (Addinsell).

1958   *Numbers* (Addinsell). *London Scottische* (Grenfell).

1959   *You Don't Need More Than a Small, Bare Room* (Addinsell). *Dear François* (Addinsell). *Golden Wedding* (Addinsell). *Boat Train* (Addinsell). *French Bergerette* (Addinsell).

1962   *Old Tyme Dancing (Stately as a Galleon)* (Addinsell). *Time* (Addinsell). *Songs You Don't Want to Hear – Irish Volk Song* (Addinsell). *The Woodland Princess –* operetta (Blezard).

1964   *Visitor* (Blezard & Grenfell). *What Shall I Wear?* (Addinsell). *Pop-Song* (Addinsell). *Rockabye Lullaby* (Blezard). *Mediocre Song* (Blezard).

1965   *I Wouldn't Go Back to the World I Knew* (Addinsell). *Hymn* (Addinsell). *Bring Back the Silence* (Addinsell). *Ferry Boats of Sydney* (Blezard). *Come Catch Me* (Blezard).

1967   *Good Old Jennifer* (Blezard). *Unsuitable* (Blezard). *Bene Molto Bene* (Blezard). *Not in the Mood for News* (Blezard).

1969   *Private I* (Blezard). *Slow Down* (Blezard). *Thursdays* (Blezard).

1971   *In the Green Time of Moon Daisies* (Blezard).

1973   *See You Very Soon* (Blezard); performed at Windsor Castle.

Songs (Composer in Brackets)

Undated Songs

Songs of Gladdery of Joyage (Addinsell). *Kitchen Department* (Addinsell). *Urban Dweller's Wish Song* (Addinsell). *Middle-Aged Tennis* (Addinsell).

For more details of songs, records, films and references see www. bestweb.net/~foosie/grenfell.

Selected BBC Radio Programmes

Transatlantic Quiz, 1941–7
Monday Night at Eight, 1942–61
Henry Hall's Guest Night, 1942–57
Brains Trust, 1943–7
Cocktails, Kippers and Capers, The Whoopee Club, Let's Get Acquainted, Songtime in Laager, Jack's Dive, Palestine Half Hour, Middle East Merry-Go-Round, Here's Wishing You Well Again, Navy Mixture, 1942–3
Variety Band Box, 1942–4
Starlight, 1945–7
The Critics, 1945–67
In Town Tonight, 1946–65
Monday Night at Eight, 1945–7
We Beg to Differ, 1946–54
Waiting for ITMA, 1947
A Note With Music, series, 1947
Chronique des spectacles, BBC French Service, 1947
Woman's Hour, 1949–79 (over 150 times)
Festival of Britain Parade, 1951
Desert Island Discs, 1951, 1971
Saturday Night on the Light, 1953
The Wrong Shape for Dancing, three biographical talks, 1953
Younger Generation – Question Time, 1957
The Laughtermakers, No. 16: *The Art of Joyce Grenfell*, 1957
Pick of the Week, 1959–70 (eighteen times)
In Town Tonight, 1959–60
Any Questions, 1962, 1963, 1969, 1975
Five to Ten, Enjoying Christmas, 1964
Ten to Eight, 1965–70
Tribute to Stephen Potter, 1969

Selected BBC Radio Programmes

Subject for Sunday With Leslie Smith, 1970
Pause for Thought, 1970–2
Does God Make a Difference?, 1971
Joyce Grenfell on ENSA, The Entertainers: Joyce Grenfell, 1973
The Story of Revue, 1976
Grenfell and Bakewell, 1979
Joyce Grenfell, presented by Joseph Cooper, 1980
A Life of Blessings, presented by Richard Baker, 1989

Many of the above are held at the British Library Sound Archive.

How BBC Radio Programmes
Written With Stephen Potter

Each edition was a complete rewrite and new broadcast.

How to Apply for a Job, 1943
How to Talk to Children, 8 June, 27 July, 3 August 1943, 31 August 1944
How to Argue, 27 September 1943
How to Give a Party, 23 December 1943, 26 March 1950
How to Keep a Diary, 10 August 1944, 31 August 1944
How to Learn to Speak French, August 1944
How to Woo, 12 September 1944
How to Go to the Theatre, April 1945, 29 December 1950
How to Blow Your Own Trumpet, 19 April 1945, 14 March 1946, 24 May 1947
How to Be Good at Music, 24 June 1945
How to Talk to Young People, 14 November 1945
How to Make Friends, 20 November 1945
How to Deal With Christmas, 19 December 1945, November 1951
How to Move House, 3 April 1946
How to Go to the Ballet, August 1946
How to Listen, 20 and 30 September, 16 November 1946, 2 April 1950, July 1951, 18 September 1962
How to Salute the BBC, 1947
How to Be Good at Games, 24 December 1947, 25 December 1951
How to Travel, 19 July 1950
How to Deal With New Year, 1 January 1952
How to Broadcast, 28 September 1951
How to Cross the Atlantic First Class, 20 August 1955
How to Know America Really Well, 2 September 1955
How to Lead a Really Full Life, 17 May 1955

Selected Television Appearances

Starlight, BBC, 1946–50
Rainbow Nights in *Oranges and Lemons*, BBC, 1949
London Town, BBC, 1950
I Know What I Like, BBC, 1952
Face the Music, BBC, 1953–5, 1967–79
Panorama, BBC, 1954
The Ed Sullivan Show, USA, 1956
Chelsea at Nine, Granada, December 1957
Tonight with Cliff Michelmore, BBC, 1957–60
The Festival of Performing Arts – An Evening With Joyce Grenfell, USA, 1963
Call My Bluff, BBC, 1966
Pippi Longstocking, and five *Tales of Beatrix Potter, Jackanory*, BBC, 1968–9
Nature Spectacular, BBC, 1971
The Incomplete Collected Works of Joyce Grenfell and Composer Richard Addinsell
    With Recent Musical Additions of William Blezard, BBC, 1972
Michael Parkinson, BBC, 1976
A Time There Was: A Profile of Benjamin Britten, LWT, 1980
I Like Life: A Tribute to Joyce Grenfell, BBC, 1980

Selected Articles

'Housewife Into Actress', *Modern Living*, Winter 1950

'Turning Out', *Housewife*, 1951

'On Music, On Opening Bazaars, On Eating Habits, On Parties, On Innings, The Art of Not Being Bored, On Audiences, On Decorations, On Keeping a Diary, On Letter Writing, On Sleeping Habits, On Touring, On a Suitable Gift, On Buying a Dress', *Everywoman*, 1951–2

'An Ideal Husband', *News Chronicle*, 28 April 1952

'This Glorious Wall of Laughter', *London Calling*, 31 December 1953

'Myself When Young', *Everybody's*, 24 September 1955

'Ruth Draper' (obituary), *Daily Telegraph*, 31 December 1956

'Christmas is Children-Watching Time', *Christian Science Monitor*, 22 December 1964

'In Honour of Clemence Dane', *Woman Journalist*, Summer 1966

'Easter', in *Ten to Eight on Radio 4*, BBC, 1968

'Teachers Who Were in a Class of Their Own', *TV Times*, 10 February 1972

'Man Is Never Separated from God', *Christian Science Sentinel*, 14 October 1972

'First Times', *Christian Science Monitor*, 5 January 1977

'The Sights and Sounds of Seasides Long Ago', *Observer*, 1 December 1979

Selected Charities

Countess of Munster's Wool Fund, 1940
Free French, 1940
Land Army, 1943
Jewish Services Clubs, 1943
East Anglian floods, 1947
Pestalozzi Children's Village, 1951
Old People's Week, 1951
Kensington Beautiful Baby Competition, 1951
Girls' Friendly Society, 1951
Golder's Green Waifs and Strays Fund, 1951
Time and Talents Association, 1954
Yately Industries for Disabled Girls, 1956
St Andrew's Society for Helping Poor Ladies, 1957
Coventry Cathedral, 1962
Chichester Theatre, 1962
Family Planning Centre, Newcastle, 1964
Voluntary Services Overseas, 1967
Save the Children Fund, 1967
Lifeline (for European refugees), Cambridge, 1967
Shelter, 1968
National Library Week, 1969
Margaret Macmillan Children's Centre, Bradford, 1970
Council for the Preservation for Rural England, 1971
World Wildlife Fund, 1973
Women's International Decade, 1975
Royal National Lifeboat Institution, Cranster, 1977
Marriage Guidance Council, 1978
Rosehill Theatre, Cumbria, 1979

Selected Charities Supported by Joyce Grenfell

Serious Talks

British-American Fellowship Society (president), 1947
Lanchester College of Technology, 1967
Worshipful Company of Musicians, 1965
Heads of BBC departments, 1965
Society of Women Writers and Journalists (president), 1966
Southwark Cathedral, dedication of plaque to Oscar Hammerstein, 1966
Lucy Cavendish College, Cambridge (Honorary Fellow), 1968
St Olave's Church, London, 1970
Truro Cathedral, 1972
Dartington Hall, Devon, 1972
Young Christian Scientists, Keele, 1972
Manchester Polytechnic (Honorary Fellow), 1973
Churchill Fellowship Trust, 1974
Singing-teacher conference, Aldeburgh, 1976
Six Point Group (women's rights), 1977
Queen's Silver Jubilee Thanksgiving Service, Westminster Abbey, 1977
English Speaking Union, USA, 1977
Caravan Schools, Leeds, 1979
St Mary-le-Bow Church, London, 1967, 1968, 1970–7, 1979

Bibliography

Unless otherwise stated, all primary sources and letters are in private collections.

Abbreviations

BBC WAC	BBC Written Archive Centre, Caversham
BL SA	British Library Sound Archive
Bristol	University of Bristol Theatre Collection
LCC	Lucy Cavendish College, Cambridge
PRO	Public Records Office, Kew

Primary sources

Verily Anderson, diary, 1979
'Bristol, Joyce Grenfell', 1963–78, WE13/146/1, BBC WAC
'Contributors, Joyce Grenfell, Copyright File 1', 1940–62, BBC WAC
'Copyright, file 1, Stephen Potter', 1936–62, BBC WAC
'Entertainment, Joyce Grenfell Programmes', file R19/462, 1941–6, BBC WAC
'Entertainment, *How* series', 1942–55, BBC WAC
Eton Calendar Book, 1893, 1922 and 1931, Eton College Archive
Eton House Book, 1917–22, Eton College Archive
Herbert Farjeon, notes for a biography, pre-1945, Bristol
Herbert Farjeon, press cutting books, 1939–42, Bristol
Nora Flynn, notebook, c. 1930
Nora Flynn's visiting-book, 1932–49
Virginia Graham, photograph albums, 1927–90, LCC
Joyce Grenfell, diaries and notebooks, 1926–79, LCC
Joyce Grenfell, Manchester Luncheon Club speech, 1975, Bristol
Joyce Grenfell, *My Life*, notes, 1955, Bristol
Joyce Grenfell, notes about meeting Wynford Hicks, LCC
Joyce Grenfell, 'Pictures of Childhood', 1954, MS of article, Bristol
Reggie Grenfell file, 1921–94, Balliol College, Oxford
'Joyce Grenfell', Audience Research Department files, BBC WAC
Lord Killearn's manuscript diaries, 1944, St Anthony's College, Oxford
Killearn telegrams, 'file FO 371 – 1939', PRO
Killearn telegrams, 'file FO 954/5 – 1944' PRO
Janet Longcope, *Phipps Ancesters*, notebook, 1958
Diana Lyddon, theatre time-books, 1960–73
Matrimonial jurisdiction, Alexandria, 1944, 'file FO 847', PRO

Bibliography

John Constantine Phipps, *Phipps of Westbury Wiltshire*, 1980
Wilton Phipps, London scrapbook, 1889–1901
Stephen Potter and Joyce Grenfell, *Hurray for Books!*, Cheltenham Town Hall, 1949, Bristol
'Programmes, Joyce Grenfell', file ii, 1963–70, BBC WAC
'Programmes, Religion, Joyce Grenfell', file B/c 23–1969, BBC WAC
'Scriptwriters, Stephen Potter', file 1, 1936–62, BBC WAC
Slough Centre Nursery School, scrapbook, 1937–99
Slough Centre Nursery School, visitors' book, 1937
'Talks, Stephen Potter', 1947–62, BBC WAC
'TV, Joyce Grenfell, artists', file I, 1946–62, file ii, 1963–70, BBC WAC
'TV, Light Ent, Joyce Grenfell', 1951–65, file T12/187, BBC WAC

Collections of Manuscript Letters

Between JG and Herbert Farjeon, 1939–45, Bristol
JG to Rene Easden, 1943–1955
To JG from John Betjeman; George Henry Clews; Noël Coward; E.V. Dean, Blackpool; E. Dunston, Bombay; John Gielgud; Clive James; Ghulam Mahd; Sgt Ling, Maidstone; Laurence Olivier; Terence Rattigan; Capt Rogers, India; Sybil Thorndike, 1944–79, Bristol
Between JG and Verily Anderson, 1951–79
Between JG and Oliver Bernard, 1954–58
Between JG and Mary Potter, 1955–76
Between JG and Katharine Moore, 1957–79, LCC
JG to Michael Flanders, 1960–74, Flanders and Swann Estate
Between JG and Benjamin Britten, 1962–76, Britten-Pears Library and Bristol
JG to John Ward, 1962–79
JG to Leonard Gershe, 1963–79, LCC
JG to Priscilla Cunningham, 1963–79
Between JG and Janie Hampton, 1963–79
JG to Tommy and Mary Phipps, 1965–79
To JG from Eddie, Alex and Rachel Anderson, 1963–79
JG to Michael Olivier, 1966–79
JG to Sir Rupert and Lady Hart-Davis (June), 1968–79, LCC
JG to Lucia Arrighi, 1973–79
JG to Michael and April Falcon, 1975–78
JG to Eleanor Whitcombe, 1978–9, National Library of Australia
To Verily Anderson and Tommy Phipps from Virginia Graham, 1979
To JG from Prime Minister's PPS, 19 November 1979

Selected Newspaper References

'Accidental Heroes of the 20th Century', *Independent*, May 1999
'Actress Takes to the Pulpit', *Westminster, Pimlico & Chelsea News*, 18 June 1976
Alexander, Patrick, 'Silver Wedding For a Star', *Daily Sketch*, 3 December 1954
Anderson, Verily, *The Townsend*, December 1951

Askwith, Betty, and Benson, Theodora, 'Londoners Face Up to the Blitzkrieg', *The Sketch*, 6 November 1940

Barnes, George, *Listener*, 26 September 1946

Blanch, Lesley, *Leader*, 15 September 1945

'Both Sides of the Microphone', *Radio Times*, 13 April 1945

Brown, Ivor, *Observer*, 2 September 1945

Cookman, Anthony, *Tatler*, 5 September 1945

Darlington, W. A., *Daily Telegraph*, 23 August 1945

Darlington, W. A., *New York Times*, 2 September 1945

Davies, Victor, 'The Invisible Composer' (Addinsell), *Saga*, June 1999

'*Dekho!*', *Burma Star Association Journal*, Winter 2000

Dez Weekley News in *Band Wagon*, 1 November 1944

Entwistle, Frank, 'The Heart Warmers', *Evening Standard*, 4 April 1962

Grenfell, Reginald, 'Maltings Birds', Aldeburgh festival programme, 1969

Guy, John, 'Elevenses With Joyce Grenfell', *Everybody's*, 1955

Hobson, Harold, *Christian Science Monitor*, 27 August 1945

Iraq Times, April 1944, LCC

'Mistress of Monologue', *Tatler and Bystander*, 24 October 1945

Obituary of Paul Phipps, *The Times*, 24 August 1953

'Plays and Pictures', *New Statesman*, 5 September 1945

Pleiades, 'She Just Oozes With Talent', *Hobart Mercury*, 15 September 1969

Scott, Esme, 'Joyce Grenfell is Quite at Home in Chelsea', *TV Times*, 13 December 1957

Seymour, Anne, 'After 40 Club', *Housewife*, 1954

Slough Express, 31 October 1997

Slough News Chronicle, 31 October 1997

Standora, Leo, 'Comic Star Dies in London', *New York Post*, 30 November 1979

Sunday Chronicle, 12 November 1939

Sunday Times, 23 April 1939

Syal, Meera, 'Goodness Gracious', *Independent on Sunday*, 18 February 2001

Taylor, Nora E., 'Monologist Without Malice', *Christian Science Monitor*, 1 April 1958

Trewin, J. C., 'Look Back in Laughter', *Birmingham Post*, 18 September 1976

Trewin, J. C., *Punch or The London Charivari*, 5 September 1945

Trunk Call, 10 April, 17 April, 5 November 1944, LCC

The Week, 30 March 1938

'The Younger Generation – Into a New World', *Radio Times*, 11 January 1955

Watts, Jane, *Guardian*, 17 September 1976

Selected Books

Aldeburgh Festival Programme books, 1962–79

Anderson, Verily, *Scrambled Eggs For Christmas*, London, Hodder & Stoughton, 1970

Annual Report 1937–8, Slough, Slough Social Centre, 1938

Astor, Michael, *Tribal Feeling*, London, John Murray, 1963

Axell, Herbert, and Hosking, Eric, *Minsmere: Portrait of a Bird Reserve*, London, Hutchinson, 1977

Bibliography

Beaton, Cecil, *The Years Between: Diaries 1939–44*, London, Weidenfeld & Nicolson, 1965

Becker, Robert, *Nancy Lancaster*, New York, Alfred A. Knopf, 1996

Bernard, Oliver, *Getting Over It*, London, Peter Owen, 1992

Blum, Daniel, *Theatre World Season 1955–56*, New York, Greenberg, 1956

Bogarde, Dirk, *A Postillion Struck by Lightning*, London, Chatto & Windus, 1977

Briggs, Asa, *The BBC: The First Fifty Years*, Oxford, Oxford University Press, 1985

Bruccoli, Matthew, *Some Sort of Epic Grandeur: The Life of F. Scott Fitzgerald*, London, Hodder & Stoughton, 1981

Carmichael, Ian, *Will the Real Ian Carmichael?*, London, Macmillan, 1979

Carpenter, Humphrey, *Benjamin Britten: A Biography*, London, Faber & Faber, 1992

Coleman, Elliot, *Poetry*, New York, Dutton, 1936

Cooper, Artemis, *Cairo in the War*, London, Hamish Hamilton, 1989

Cooper, Joseph, *Facing the Music: An Autobiography*, London, Weidenfeld & Nicolson, 1979

Coward, Noël, *Middle East Diary*, London, Heinemann, 1944

Dean, Basil, *Theatre at War*, London, Harrap, 1956

Eddy, Mary Baker, *Christian Healing*, Boston, 1886

Science and Health With Key to the Scriptures, Boston, 1891

Elliott, Ivo, ed., *Balliol College Register 1833–1933*, Oxford, Balliol College, 1934

Etiquette For Ladies: A Guide to the Observance of Good Society, London, Ward, Lock & Co., 1930

Farjeon, Herbert, *Omnibus*, London, Hutchinson, *c.* 1943

Fitzgerald, F. Scott, 'The Intimate Strangers', in *The Last Uncollected Stories*, London, Quartet Books, 1979

Fleming, Kate, *Celia Johnson: A Biography*, London, Weidenfeld & Nicolson, 1991

Fleming, Peter, *Invasion 1940*, London, Rupert Hart-Davis, 1958

Fox, James, *The Langhorne Sisters*, London, Granta, 1998

Gilbert, Martin, ed., *The Churchill Papers: Never Surrender*, Vol. 2, London, Heinemann, 1994

Gray, Charlotte, *Flint and Feather: The Life and Times of E. Pauline Johnson*, London, HarperCollins, 2002

Hart-Davis, Rupert, *The Arms of Time*, London, Hamish Hamilton, 1979

Harrison, Rosina, *Rose: My Life in Service*, London, Cassell, 1975

Hillier, Bevis, *Young Betjeman*, London, John Murray, 1988

Hoggart, Richard, *An Imagined Life, 1959–91*, London, Chatto & Windus, 1992

Jones, J. D. F., *Storyteller: The Many Lives of Laurens van der Post*, London, John Murray, 2001

Jones, Thomas, *A Diary With Letters, 1931–1950*, Oxford, Oxford University Press, 1954

Laine, Cleo, *Cleo*, London, Simon & Schuster, 1994

Lord, Graham, *Just the One: The Wives and Times of Jeffrey Bernard*, London, Sinclair-Stevenson, 1992

Oliver, Lyttelton, *The Memoirs of Lord Chandos*, London, Bodley Head, 1962

Macmillan, Harold, *War Diaries 1943–45*, London, Macmillan, 1989

McCulloch, Joseph, *Under Bow Bells*, London, Sheldon Press, 1974

Mortimer, Favell Lee, *Reading Without Tears*, London, Hatchard's, 1861

Bibliography

Mosely and Sanders, *Computerized Tomography in Neuro-Ophthalmology*, London, Chapman & Hall, 1982

Niven, David, *The Moon's a Balloon*, London, Hamish Hamilton, 1971

O'Hara, Mary, *The Scent of Roses*, London, Michael Joseph, 1980

Payn, Graham, and Morley, Sheridan, eds., *The Noël Coward Diaries*, London, Weidenfeld & Nicolson, 1982

Pearson, Hesketh, *Bernard Shaw*, Glasgow, Collins & Co., 1942

Plomley, Roy, *Desert Island Discs*, London, William Kimber, 1975

Potter, Julian, *Mary Potter: A Life of Painting*, Ilkley, Scolar Press, 1998

Rose, Norman, *The Cliveden Set*, London, Jonathan Cape, 2000

Sheridan, Dorothy, *Wartime Women, Mass-Observation*, London, Heinemann, 1990

John Singer Sargent, exhibition guide, London, Tate Gallery, 1998

Taylor, Eric, *Front-Line: British Nurses in World War II*, London, Robert Hale, 1997

Turnbull, Andrew, ed., *The Letters of F. Scott Fitzgerald*, London, Bodley Head, 1963

Ustinov, Peter, *Dear Me*, London, Heinemann, 1977

Vogue's Gallery of Famous Authors and Artists, London, Condé Nast, 1962

Ward, John, *The Paintings of John Ward*, Newton Abbot, David & Charles, 1991

Warren, Dorothy, ed., *The Letters of Ruth Draper: Self-Portrait of an Actress 1920–1956*, Chicago, Southern Illinois University Press, 1979

Williams, Emrys, *Bodyguard: My Twenty Years as Aly Khan's Shadow*, London, Golden Pegasus, 1960

Winn, Alice, *Always a Virginian: The Colourful Langhornes of Mirador, Lady Astor and Their Kin*, Lynchburg, VA, Kenmore Association, 1982

Year Books, London, BBC, 1936–47

Zabel, Morton Dauwen, *The Art of Ruth Draper*, London, Oxford University Press, 1960

INDEX

Index

Note: JG = Joyce Grenfell; RG = Reggie Grenfell

Addinsell, Richard ('Dick'), 171;
friendship with Clemence Dane,
164, 177; health, 115–16, 126; JG's
friendship with, 182, 212–13; *Joyce
Grenfell Requests the Pleasure*, 198;
songs, 114–15, 120, 178, 184, 189,
191, 203, 226

Adrian, Max, 108, 109, 203; *Penny
Plain*, 185; *Tuppence Coloured*, 177,
179, 181

African National Congress (ANC),
260–1

Aga Khan, 146

Agate, James, 79

Age of Consent, The (film), 232

Agos, Mrs (housekeeper), 215, 314,
322, 328, 333–4

Air Ministry, 87

Albert Herring (Britten), 178

'Alcoholic Case, An' (Fitzgerald), 55

Aldeburgh, Suffolk, 216, 327, 334, 336;
Music Festival, 226, 277–81, 282,
322

Alderly Park, 52

Alderson, Connie (*later* Fite), 247, 335

Alexan, Alphonse, 142

Alexander, Patrick, 204

Alexandra, Princess, 221

Alexandra Palace, 266, 267

Algiers, ENSA tour (1944), 128–33

Alice in Wonderland (book), 21

Alice in Wonderland (film), 194

Alington, Hester, 242

Allen, Cass, 208–9, 333

Aly Khan, Prince, 142, 152, 154, 212,
321; and JG, 145–6, 148–51, 153

Ambassador's Theatre, London, 107

American Civil War (1861-5), 1, 2

American in Augustland, An (poem), 171

Americanisation of Emily, The (film),
230–2

American Musicians' Union, 203

Amis, John, 278

Anderson, Janie (*later* Hampton), 219,
293, 294, 328, 329, 334

Anderson, Rachel, 219–21

Anderson, Verily (*later* Paget), 218–21,
242, 294, 314, 328, 329, 334

Anderson family, 219, 314–15

Andrade, Lorna, 300, 335

Andrews, Harry, 201

Andrews, Julie, 230, 231

Antrim, Peg, Countess of, 30, 118

Any Questions? (radio series), 273–4

Aquitania (liner), 57

Armstrong Jones, Anthony, 221, 225–6

Arthur Koestler Awards, 324

Artist's Room (monologue), 178–9, 233,
278–9

'Art of Writership, The' (book), 174

Arts Store, Lake District, 304

Ashcroft, Peggy, 91, 189

Ashton, Winifred *see* Dane, Clemence

Askey, Arthur, 164

Astaire, Fred, 30

Astor, Bill (cousin), 36, 165, 248

Astor, David, 19, 165

Astor, Gavin, 139

Astor, Jakie, 165
Astor, Michael, 85, 165
Astor, Nancy (*née* Langhorne), 1, 4, 5,
    50, 95, 97, 107, 108, 117, 166;
    Christian Science, 25, 62; dressing
    up, 36; generosity, 9, 47, 51, 59, 63;
    JG and, 47, 48, 59, 62, 63, 76, 90,
    96, 98, 248; and Nora, 7, 8, 171,
    202; and nursery schools, 63, 64–5;
    political career, 62, 63–4, 83, 168;
    TV profile, 322
Astor, Waldorf, 4–5, 10, 35; builds
    Cliveden Hospital, 94; Christian
    Science, 26; and 1945 election, 168;
    and Nora Phipps, 19, 34; political
    career, 67, 83
Astor, William (Waldorf's father), 5
Astor, Wiss (*later* Willoughby de
    Eresby), 32, 37, 41, 42, 48, 165
Astor family, 4–5, 83
As You Like It, school performance, 23
Atlantic Monthly, 58
Attenborough, David, 291
Attlee, Clement, 168
Australia, tours, 251–8, 285, 287
Austria, RG in, 45
Avery, Miss (teacher), 27
Axell, Herbert, 277, 327

Bach, J S, 31, 67, 68, 103
Baddeley, Hermione, 76, 77, 90, 135
Baghdad, ENSA tour (1944), 135, 142
Bahrain, ENSA tour (1944), 157
Baker, Janet, 282
Baker, Richard, 291, 336
Balliol College, Oxford, 45
Banbury, Frith, 107–8
Bangalore, ENSA tour (1944), 159
Bankoff, Dr, 90
Bari, ENSA tour (1944), 135
Barnes, George, 173
Barnes, Kenneth, 39
Barry, Sir Charles, 5
Bauer, George, 203, 247
Baxter, Margaret, 336
BBC, 69, 81, 124–5, 169, 173–4, 187,
    268; Forces Programme, 155;
    General Advisory Council, 273;

Home Service, 169; JG as
    performer, 110–12, 116, 155–6,
    273–4; Third Programme, 173–4
BBC Television, 266–8, 270, 272
Beaton, Cecil, 6, 162, 179, 203
Beaton, Peggy, 28
Beaumont, Binkie, 178, 180, 312
Beerbohm, Max, 173
Beethoven, Ludwig van, 84, 103
Belfast, Christian Science Church, 120
Belles of St Trinian's, The (film), 195, 196
Benson, E F, 27
Benson, George, 175
Bernard, Dora ('Fedora Roselli'), 207
Bernard, Jeffrey, 207
Bernard, Oliver, 207–8
Betjeman, John, 178, 213, 221, 236,
    256, 299
Bevins, Reginald, 268, 269
Beyond the Fringe (revue), 238
Bijou Theatre, New York, 203–4,
    205–6
Billy Budd (opera), 182
Billy Cotton Band Show, The (TV series),
    267
Billy Higgs Studio, London, 66
Blackburn, Aubrey, 124, 169
Blezard, Joan, 226, 286
Blezard, William, 203, 236, 261, 314,
    328–9; as accompanist, 226–7,
    248–9, 250, 251–2, 255–6, 279; *Joyce
    Grenfell Requests the Pleasure*, 198,
    285, 268; at Windsor Castle, 286
Blickling Hall, Norfolk, 52
Blithe Spirit (musical), 256
Blitz (1940), 92, 93–4, 98, 99–100, 117
Blue Murder at St Trinian's (film), 195
Blum, Daniel, 204
Bogarde, Dirk (Derek Bogaerde),
    99–101
Bombay, ENSA tour (1944), 157
Boulting, Roy, 185, 196, 197
Boulting brothers, 185
Bourhill, Mary, 51–2, 59
Bournemouth, *Tuppence Coloured* tour,
    180
Bow Dialogues, 316–18
Bowes-Lyon, David, 104

Bowes-Lyon, Nancy, 23
Bowes-Lyon, Rachel, 221
Box of Tricks, A (revue), 20
Boyle, Sir Edward, 299
Brand, Jim, 165
Brand, Phyllis (*née* Langhorne), 58, 61
Brand, Virginia (*later* Ford), 48, 181
Brighton, *Tuppence Coloured* tour, 180
'Bright Spots,' 53
Brimm, Anna *see* Gabe
Brimm, Reg, 170
British Non-Ferrous Metals, 87
Britten, Benjamin, 178, 276, 277, 278,
    279, 280, 281, 282
Broadway, *Joyce Grenfell Requests the
    Pleasure*, 203–6
Broady, Ann, 2
Brook, Peter, 180
Brookes, Mrs, 192
Brooks, Peter, 165
Brooks, Phyllis (*née* Langhorne), 4, 6,
    11, 54
Brooks, Winkie, 11, 32, 61, 165
Brown, Ivor, 97, 200
Brown Beans, 15
Buckinghamshire Education
    Committee, 64
Burman, Miss, school, 1555
Burton, Christabel (*later* Bielenberg),
    41
Bushell, Arthur, 36, 61
Butler family, 8
Butterworth, Audrey, 333
Byrne, Gay, 325
Byrne, Gwen, 118, 120

Cabaret (TV series), 267–8
Cairo, ENSA tour (1944), 137–8,
    139–42, 145–7, 148–51, 154
Calcutta, ENSA tour 1944, 161
California University, 251
Call the Tune (radio series), 187, 291
Calthrop, Gladys, 164, 166, 177,
    179–80
'Calypso' (song), 185
Cambridge University, 293
Cameron, James, 317
Campbell, Judy, 121, 166

Campbell, Mrs Patrick, 21, 34
Campbell-Preston, Frances (*née*
    Grenfell) 44, 47, 48, 105, 335
Campbell-Preston, Helen, 295–6
Campbell-Preston, Patrick, 105
Canada, Phipps family in (1911), 11–12
Canteen (monologue), 97
Cardboard Figures (monologue), 108
Carey, Joyce, 124
Carlson, Miss (headmistress), 23
Carmichael, Ian, 74, 176, 196
Carrier, Robert, 304
Carry On films, 230
Castle, Irene and Vernon, 14
Cavendish, Diana, 32
Central Office of Information, 193
Chamberlain, Neville, 84
Chapell-Harms (music publishers), 171
Charles, Ray, 205
Charlottesville, Virginia, 2
Chelsea, Phipps family in, 8, 15–17
Chelsea Palace Theatre panto, 20
Chelsea Society, 335
Chelsea Theatrical Garden Party, 21–2,
    80–1, 312
Cheltenham Literary Festival (1949),
    174, 179
Chesapeake & Ohio Railway, 2
Chesham Place, Grenfell family at, 51
Chester, JG performs in, 125
Chetwode, Penelope, 15, 41
Chevalier, Maurice, 289
Choice Grenfell (radio series), 336
Chorleywood, Hampshire, 17
Christian Science, 25–6, 38, 52, 70,
    116, 211, 283, 309, 310–11, 335
Christian Science Monitor, 168, 300
Christmas, 33–7, 313–15
Chuck (Nora's boyfriend), 191, 192
Churchill, Diana, 189
Churchill, Winston, 62, 83, 92, 93,
    102, 168
Churchill Memorial Fellowship Trust,
    313
Church of Christ Scientist, 25–6
Claremont Fan Court School, 336
Claridge's Hotel, London, 88
Clark, Kenneth, 102, 104

Clearview School, Norwood, 26–9, 32

Clemens, Samuel Langhorne (Mark Twain), 1

Clements, John, 175, 176

Clews, George Henry, 210–11

Clitheroe, Lancs, JG performs in, 125

Cliveden, Bucks; Christmas house parties, 33–7; First World War (1914-18), 13; life at, 5, 60–1, 62, 63, 67–8, 83, 248, 294, 322; Phippses honeymoon at, 9; Second World War, 84–6, 92–3; Slough Nursery School visits, 65; *Yellow Rolls-Royce* shot at, 232

Cliveden Hospital: First World War, 91, 94; Second World War, 94–6, 107, 117, 135, 314

Cockburn, Claud, 83

Coke, Lady Silvia (*later* Combe), 41, 42, 93

Colchester, Halsey, 129

Colditz Castle, 105

Cole, George, 123, 196

Colefax & Fowler (company), 170

Coleman, Elliot, 56, 171–2, 212

Collins, Norman, 155, 266

Comilla, East Bengal, ENSA tour (1944), 160–1

Conder, Derek, 116–17

Connolly, Cyril, 45

Cooke, Alistair, 69, 204

Cooke, Gwen, 84–6

Cookham Home Guard, 105

Cooper, Lady Diana, 130

Cooper, Duff, 130

Cooper, Gladys, 21, 31, 200

Cooper, Joseph, 108, 291, 293, 324, 334

Countess of Coteley, The (monologue), 179, 180, 239, 247

Country Life (magazine), 67

Cowan, Christopher, 283

Cowan, Jean, 283, 334

Coward, Noël, 21, 81, 121, 124, 177, 203, 221; *Lyric Revue*, 184; and Middle East, 126, 135, 141, 144; *Sigh No More* (revue), 161, 162,

165–8, 170; songs, recording, 177; 70th birthday tribute, 280

Cranbrook, Fidelity, Countess of, 278, 281

Cranford (book), 27

Craxton, Harold, 103

Creed, Mrs (cook), 17

Crisham, Walter ('Wally'), 97, 99, 135

Crisp, Quentin, 303

Crossman, Richard, 317

Cumbria, Grenfells visit, 297–8, 322, 336

Cummings, Constance, 187

Curzon, Georgina, 41

Curzon, Lady Cynthia, 22

Dacca, ENSA tour (1944), 160

Daily Express, 174

Daily Herald, 79, 100, 312

Daily Mail, 79, 201, 239, 311

Daily Sketch, 91, 97, 98, 204, 225–6

Daily Telegraph, 79, 89, 168

Daily Worker, 112

Damascus, ENSA tour (1944), 156

Dana, Viola (*later* Flynn), 49

Dane, Clemence (Winifred Ashton), 95, 114, 115, 177, 180

Dankworth, John, 216–17, 322

Darns, Frank, 158

Davies, Betty Ann, 108

Davies, Irving, 198, 199, 204, 205

Davies, Sir Walford, 91, 103

Day, Doris, 310

Dean, Basil, 117–18, 126

Dear François (song), 152

de la Mare, Walter, 236

Delhi, ENSA tour (1944), 162

Delmar-Morgan, Rachel, 23

Desborough, Lady, 36

Desert Island Discs (radio series), 187, 190, 191, 289

DEZ Weekly News, 156

Dickson, Dorothy, 99, 102

Directorate of Army Psychiatry, 101

Disneyland, California, 249

Ditchley Park, 52, 102

Diversion (revue), 97–9, 239

Diversion No 2 (revue), 99–101, 102

Dollamore, Miss (teacher), 28
Douglas, General, 2
Draper, Phyllis, 202
Draper, Ruth, 35, 55, 76, 239, 253,
    322; JG compared to, 79, 100, 225
Drum (magazine), 262
Dublin: Grenfells visit, 325; JG visits,
    120, 200
du Maurier, George, 166
Dvořák, Antonin, 103

Easden, Rene, 59, 85, 86, 95, 98, 105
Echo Song, 179
Eddy, Mary Baker, 25, 203, 216, 287,
    289, 309
Eden, Anthony, 146, 147
Edinburgh, JG visits (1942), 121
'Ed Sullivan Show', 204–5, 206, 247,
    274
Edwards, Mary, 13, 17
Egypt: ENSA tour (1944), 137–8,
    139–42, 145–7; River Nile cruise
    (1979), 321
Eliot, T S, 271
Elizabeth, Queen Consort, 64, 95;
    dines with Grenfells, 307; JG dines
    with, 181, 221, 289; JG performs
    for, 81, 104, 189
Elizabeth Garrett Anderson Hospital,
    London, 126
Elizabeth II, Queen, 285–6, 289, 333
Elm Park Gardens flat, 222–4, 298, 332,
    335; Christmas at, 314–15
Elphinstone, Lord, 6
Emett, Rowland, 178
EMI records, 190–1
Empire Theatre, Holborn, 43
Eng Lit (monologues), 242–4
ENSA, 117–18; in India (1944–5), 157;
    Malta/Italy tour (1944), 134–7;
    Middle East tours (1944–5), 126–7,
    137–45, 154–62; North Africa tour
    (1944), 128–34; Northern Ireland
    tour (1941), 118–21; North of
    England tour (1942), 125; and
    Victory Parade, 165
Entertainment Calcutta (magazine),
    160

Entertainment National Service
    Association *see* ENSA
Equity (trade union), 75
Eton College, 44–5, 49, 51
Evans, Clive, 229–30, 286, 296
Evans, Edith, 27, 91, 98, 99, 102
Evans, Sgt, 162
Evening News, 79
Everybody's Weekly, 225
Everywoman, 300

Face the Music (TV series), 291–3,
    322
Fairbanks, Douglas, 20
Family Service Units, 335
Farjeon, Eleanor, 73, 108
Farjeon, Gervase, 77, 98
Farjeon, Harry, 108
Farjeon, Herbert, 100, 178; death, 109;
    and JG, 73, 74, 81, 127; *Diversion*,
    97, 98; *Light and Shade*, 107–9; *Little
    Revue*, 75–81, 88–90, 95
Farjeon, Joan, 73
Farjeon, Jocelyn, 108
Farouk, King of Egypt, 139
Fergusson, Bernard, 256
Fergusson, Howard, 103, 104, 320
Festival of Britain (1951), 185
Festival of Performing Arts, The (TV
    show), 248
First Church of Christ, Scientist *see*
    Christian Science
First Flight (monologue), 317–18
First World War (1914–18), 11–12, 13
Fitch, Julia, 213
Fitch, Lillian, 213–14
Fitzgerald, F Scott, 55, 56, 247
Fitzgerald, Zelda Sayre, 55, 56
Five Children and It (book), 21
Flanders, Michael, 185, 186, 189, 199
Fleming, Lucy, 218
Fleming, Peter, 60, 90, 162
Flynn, Blanche (*née* Palmer), 49
Flynn, Maurice ('Lefty'): divorce from
    Nora, 191–2, 250; JG and, 54, 171;
    marriage to Nora, 54–6; Nora
    elopes with (1913), 12–13; Nora
    elopes with (1930), 49–51

Folkestone, *Joyce Grenfell Requests the Pleasure* tour, 200
Followers of Bonnie Prince Charlie, 15
Ford, Edward, 181
Fordham, Catherine, 48
Ford Manor, Sussex, 14–15, 30, 38
Foreign Office, 87
Formby, George, 115
Fortune Theatre, London, 200, 201, 336
Fougasse, Mr, 67
Fountain, Winston, 2
Fox, James, 62, 63–4, 262
Francis Holland School, Chelsea, 23–4
Fraser, Antonia, 317
Freda and Eric (duet), 285
Frick Collection, New York, 44
Friends of the Elderly and Gentlefolks Trust, 335
Fry, Stephen, 171

Gabe, Mrs (Anna Gavrieldes), 170, 188, 189, 215, 314, 328
Gabor, Zsa Zsa, 152
Gachet, Alice, 39
Gamesmanship . . . (book), 174
Garland, Judy, 152
Garnett, Richard, 303
Garvin, James Louis, 67–9, 75
Gary Cooper (dog), 60
Gater, Irene, Lady, 104
Gavrieldes, Anna *see* Gabe, Mrs
General Strike (1926), 31, 294
Genevieve (film), 125
George, Don't Do That (monologue), 306–8
George V, King, 22, 40, 41
George VI, King, 64, 81, 181, 189, 266, 289
Geraldo and Orchestra, 116
Gershe, Leonard, 213, 230–1, 232, 249
Ghulam Mahid, 157, 159, 162
Gibbons, Caroll, 66
Gibson, Charles Dana, 6, 12, 55
Gibson, Irene (*née* Langhorne), 43
Gielgud, John, 35, 91, 100, 179, 184, 200, 249, 252
Gielgud, Val, 68, 69, 111

Gilliatt, Sydney, 195
Glasgow: *Joyce Grenfell Requests the Pleasure*, 199; *Penny Plain*, 186
Glenarm Castle, Co Antrim, 118
Globe Theatre, London, 181
Godolphin & Latymer School, Hammersmith, 84, 86
Godspell (musical), 285
Golden Doom, The (play), 26–7
Golden Stallion, The (film), 49
Golden-Wedding Party, 328–9
Golders Green Crematorium, 333
Good Music Company, 159
Gordimer, Nadine, 261–2
Gould, Diana, 117
Graham, Harry, 30
Graham, Virginia (*later* Thesiger), 30, 48, 125, 203, 336; Christian Science, 257, 288; Christmas presents, 313; generosity, 212–13, 229; invests in *Penny Plain*, 187, 189; on JG, 233–4, 301, 318, 326–7, 330; and JG's death, 333, 334; JG's friendship with, 67, 89, 182, 211–12, 216; JG's letters to, 67, 255; on Nancy Astor, 107; sends JG's verse to *Punch*, 67; songs, 61, 66, 73, 100, 108, 185, 291; and Stiebel, 212–13, 229; and *Tuppence Coloured*, 180, 181; in wartime, 84, 88, 105
Grahame, Colin, 280
Granger, Stewart, 123
Grassin, 'Le Joli Garçon,' (driver), 130, 133, 155
Greene, Graham, 45, 99
Greenwich, Connecticut, 51
Grenfell, Lt-Col Arthur Morton, 44
Grenfell, Harold (cousin-in-law), 170, 295, 296
Grenfell, Harry (brother-in-law), 44, 47, 165
Grenfell, Hilda (*née* Lyttelton), 44, 46, 95, 216; Middle East tour (1944), 135, 140
Grenfell, Joyce Irene (*née* Phipps)
Life: family background, 1–9; childhood, 10–11, 12, 13–14, 15, 16–17, 18–22, 323; early

performances, 12, 13–14, 26–7,
29; education, 23–5, 26–9, 31–2,
37–9; Christian Science, 25, 28,
38, 52, 62, 120, 124, 133, 149,
158, 249, 255, 287, 302, 309–11;
meets Reggie Grenfell (1927),
38–9, 43; engagement (1929), 43,
45–6; marriage (1929), 47–9, 57,
107, 328; parents' divorce, 49–50;
travels (1930s), 53–7; financial
problems (1936), 58, 59; moves
to Parr's (1936), 59–61, 66, 294;
childlessness, 60; as *Observer* radio
critic, 67–9, 71–2, 88; Second
World War, 83–7, 88–94, 102–7,
110, 117, 122–3, 125, 128; radio
performances, 110–14, 116,
155–6, 273–4, 289; film parts,
123–4, 193–7; monologues,
233–4, 306; television work,
266–8; records, 190, 191; charity
concerts (1960), 311–12;
religious broadcasting, 309–11,
316–17; updates monologues,
238–9, 240–1; eye trouble,
286–8, 323–4, 326–30, 331;
retires from stage (1973), 288–90;
writing, 67, 86, 299, 300, 306,
319–20; nominated Dame, 329,
335; death, 330–1, 332–5
Other references: accents, 238, 239,
241, 242, 251, 318; birdwatching,
277, 297–8; character, 252,
274–5, 284, 291, 293, 326–7;
earnings, 98; encores, 248;
environment, 298–9; fans, 115,
116, 175, 274–5; favourite
characters, 240, 241, 242; fees,
124–5, 187, 268, 274; food, 215;
friendships, 15, 25, 30, 38, 39, 41,
89, 101–2, 102–3, 182, 207–14,
216–21, 273; generosity, 187–8,
207–9, 210–11, 212–13, 219–20,
244, 246, 311–16, 335; heroes,
322; interests, 52, 53, 215–16,
223; letters, 216, 335–6; methods,
228–9, 234, 235–6, 238; mimicry,
36, 52–3, 263; music, 30, 31, 103,
104, 276; observation of people,
233; as organiser, 182;
perfectionism, 185; personal
appearance, 14, 22, 27–8, 38, 40,
162, 194, 198–9; politics, 238,
241–2; priggishness, 37, 63, 80;
reading tastes, 27, 66–7, 127, 218,
299; relationship with RG, 57,
93, 127, 137, 148, 151, 152, 154,
205, 212, 259, 320–1, 325;
respect for audience, 80; social
class, 31–2, 239; views on 1970s
youth, 294–6; voice, 248–9
Grenfell, Katie (*later* Lort-Philips), 44,
54, 323
Grenfell, Laura (*later* Fergusson), 44,
47, 48, 95, 165, 256
Grenfell, Mary (*later* Waldegrave), 44,
48
Grenfell, Reggie: family background,
44; education, 44–5, 49; meets JG
(1927), 38–9, 43; engagement
(1929), 43, 45–6; marriage, 47–9;
career, 49–50, 53, 54, 170; JG's stage
career, 75, 124, 181–2; Second
World War, 87, 92–3, 95, 99, 105,
107, 154; and Aly Khan, 152; and
Elliot Coleman, 171; and *Tuppence
Coloured*, 180, 181; as JG's financial
manager, 187, 189, 205, 245, 321;
invests in *Penny Plain*, 186–7, 189;
personality, 187, 214, 288;
relationship with JG, 137, 205, 223,
259, 313, 314, 320–1; overseas tours
with JG, 203, 245, 256, 257; and JG's
health, 287, 292; birdwatching,
297–8; and JG's writing, 300, 301–2,
319; and JG's death, 330–1, 332,
334–5; death, 336
Grenfell, Vera, 44, 95, 165
Grenfell, Victoria (*née* Grey), 44
Grenfell & Co (investment company),
49–50
Grenfell family, 44, 45, 46; and JG's
stage debut, 76
Grey, Owsley, 57
Griffin, Miss (lady's maid), 17
Griffiths, Miss, school, 14–15

'Groans About Touring in Northern Ireland' (poem), 119
Guardian, 79, 303, 304
Guinness, Alec, 193
Guinness, Bryan, 52, 154, 156
Gunn, Jean, 333

Haifa, ENSA tour (1944), 155
Haley, Sir William, 173
Hall, Henry, 110, 291
Hammerstein, Oscar, 181, 203
Hammond, Kay, 175, 176
Handl, Irene, 196
Hannen, Beau, 212
Hansel and Gretel (Cliveden pantomime), 13–14
Happiest Days of Your Life, The (film), 194
Happiest Days of Your Life, The (school play), 257
Happy Hours Club, 15
Happy Is the Bride (film), 196–7
Harding, Gilbert, 175, 176
Harold Holt Ltd, 227, 228
Harper's Bazaar, 225
Harris, Clinton, 36
Harrison, Christine, 335
Harrison, Muffet, 278, 327
Harrison, Rosina, 36, 171
Hart-Davis, Deirdre, 41, 48
Hart-Davis, June, 335
Hart-Davis, Rupert, 216, 302, 335
Hartnell, Norman, 41
Hawkins, Jack, 157
Haydn, Joseph, 104
Hayes, Helen, 285
Haymarket Theatre, London, 230
Hayworth, Rita, 152, 160
Head Girl (monologue), 32, 110
Headmasters' Conference, Cambridge, 290
Heath, Edward, 304
Henn-Collins, Patience, 23
Henry Hall's Guest Night (radio series), 110
Henty, Doris, 286, 287, 288
Here's Wishing You Well Again (radio series), 155

Hess, Myra, 102–4, 203
Hever Castle, Kent, 5
Hewson, Miss, 26, 27, 31
Hicks, Wynford, 243, 244
Highfield Preparatory School, 24
Hill, Charles (*later* Lord), 175, 273
Hiller, Arthur, 231
Himalayas, 161
Hippodrome Theatre, London, 99, 100
Hitler, Adolf, 83, 84
H M Tennant (company), 178, 184
Hobart Mercury, 257
Hobson, Harold, 167, 200
Hodson, Margaret, 160, 201
Hoffnung, Gerard, 291
Hoggart, Mary, 273
Hoggart, Richard, 269–71, 272, 273, 299
Holiday Books (radio series), 299
Holmes, Leslie, 128
Holyroodhouse, Palace of, 181
Hope, Vida, 100, 108
Horne, Kenneth, 165
House of Regrets (play), 101
House of St Barnabas, Soho, 312, 335
Housewife magazine, 199, 223
Howard, Leslie, 91
How (radio series), 112–14, 167, 173–4, 190, 240, 242; *How to Apply for a Job*, 113; *How Not to Broadcast*, 190; *How to Cross the Atlantic First Class*, 112; *How to Deal with Christmas*, 113–14, 240; *How to Give a Party*, 113; *How to Go to the Ballet*, 167; *How to Listen*, 173–4; *How to Talk to Children*, 240; *How to Woo*, 112
Humphrey, Leslie, 239
Humphries, Barry, 256
Hussey, Marmaduke, 285
Hussey, Susan, 286, 330, 332
Huxley, Julian, 63
Hyderabad, ENSA tour (1944), 158
'Hymn to the Hoover' (song), 115–16

'I Don't Arf Love Yer' (song), 191
I Like Life (TV documentary), 336
'I'm Going to *See* You Today' (song), 115

Index

Incomplete Collected Works of Joyce Grenfell (TV series), 285
India, ENSA tour (1944), 154, 156–62
In Pleasant Places (autobiography Vol II), 319–20
'Intimate Strangers, The' (short story), 55
Intoxicating Liquor Bill (1923), 63
Iraq, ENSA tour (1944), 142–5
Iraq Times, 143
Italy, ENSA tour (1944), 135–7
ITV, 270, 272
Ivy (parlour maid), 51
'I Wouldn't Go Back to the World I Knew' (song), 168

Jackson, Maurice, 117
Jackson, Tom, 274
James, Clive, 244, 253–4, 315, 321–2
James, Henry, 8, 35, 173, 239
Jeffries, (retired gardener), 61
Jewish Chronicle, 167
Jewison, Norman, 232
JG Productions Ltd, 189
Joan Khan, Princess, 142, 146, 149, 150
Johannesburg, JG visits, 261–2
John, Augustus, 104
John, Rosamund, 123
Johnson, Celia (*later* Fleming), 114, 119, 124, 164, 218, 221, 318, 328; JG's friendship with, 39, 60, 182; in wartime, 88, 95, 101–2
Johnstone, Betty, 113
Jones, Lady Evelyn, 126
Jones, J D F, 214
Jones, Thomas, 34
Joyce By Herself and Her Friends (book), 335
Joyce Grenfell at Home (show), 224–6
Joyce Grenfell Requests the Pleasure (autobiography Vol I), 299–302
Joyce Grenfell Requests the Pleasure (show), 198–201, 203–6, 207, 208, 238
Joyce Grenfell (show), 230
Joyce Grenfell Trust, 335
'Joyful Noise' (song), 185
Junior Miss (play), 124

Karajan, Herbert von, 282
Kaye, Beryl, 198, 199–200, 207
Keene, Nanaire Witcher, 2, 4
Kelly, Grace, 152
Kennedy, Charles A, 197
Kennedy, John F, 232
Kent, Mr (sweetshop keeper), 169, 170, 188, 189
Kester, Mr (BBC producer), 66
Kiddle, Miss (teacher), 24
Killearn, Miles Lampson, Lord, 139–42, 145, 154; and Aly Khan, 146, 147, 148, 150, 151
Kinchinjunga mountain, 161
King's Road flat, 169–70, 178, 222, 307
King's Royal Rifle Corps, 92, 105
Kitchen Quartet, 103
Knight, John, 323
Knightsbridge, Grenfells in, 122–3
Knox, Edmund Valpy, 67
Kut, ENSA tour (1944), 144

Ladbrooke, Ida, 180
Laine, Cleo, 216–17, 280, 322, 336
Lake District, Grenfells visit, 297–8, 321, 322
Lally Tullet (monologue), 153, 225, 236–7
Lampson, Graham, 142, 149
Lamp Still Burns, The (film), 123–4
Lancaster, Nancy *see* Tree
Langhorne, Buck, 3, 35–6
Langhorne, Chiswell Dabney ('Chillie'), 1–3, 4, 6, 7, 9, 12; Trust, 18, 19, 202
Langhorne, Irene (*later* Gibson), 4
Langhorne, Keene, 3
Langhorne, Lizzie (*later* Perkins), 3, 12
Langhorne, Nanaire (*née* Keene), 2, 4
Langhorne, Nora *see* Phipps
Langhorne family, 1–9
Langley, Betty, 31, 294
Larner, Lionel, 232, 248
Late-Late Show, The (RTE TV series), 325
Lauder, Frank, 195
Laughter in Paradise (film), 194

Lawford, Patricia, 232
Lawrence, Gertrude, 21
Lawrence, T E, 98
Leach, Mr (chauffeur), 17
League of Nations, 63
Learn to Loosen (monologue), 233
Lee, Edwin, 33, 34
Legge, Walter, 118
Leigh, Charlotte, 74, 75, 76, 78, 80, 81, 92, 218
Lesley, Cole, 177
Letter from England (film), 101–2
Levin, Bernard, 274, 291, 331
Levson, Leon, 260
Lewis, Rosa, 44
Life and Literature (monologue), 184
Lifemanship (book), 174
Life Story (monologue), 152–3, 236
Light and Shade (revue), 107–9, 291
Lillian, or The Woodland Princess (spoof operetta), 285
Lillie, Beatrice, 21, 53, 57, 84, 91, 95
Lindo, Harold, 91, 162
Linklater, Eric, 193
Lipman, Maureen, 336
Listener, The, 68, 112
Lister, Laurier, 305, 335; *Joyce Grenfell At Home*, 224; *Joyce Grenfell Requests the Pleasure*, 198; *Penny Plain*, 184, 185, 186; *Tuppence Coloured*, 177, 178, 180
Lister, Moira, 193
Little Revue, 75–81, 82, 84, 88–90, 95, 108–9, 134, 224
Little Theatre, London, JG's debut, 78–9
Liverpool, JG performs in, 125
Living Space (monologue), 110
Lloyd, Marie, 22
Local Library (monologue), 99, 100, 110
London, Blitz , 92, 93–4, 98, 99–100, 117
London County Council, 95
'Love's Melody' (Fitzgerald), 55
Loweswater, Cumbria, 298
Lutyens, Sir Edwin, 7, 52
Luxon, Benjamin, 280

Lyddon, Diana, 235–6, 328, 335; as stage manager, 227–8, 249–50, 311–12; at Windsor Castle, 286
Lynn, Vera, 156
Lyric Revue, 189
Lyric Theatre, Hammersmith, 180, 189, 224
Lyttelton, Dame Edith, 47
Lyttelton, Hilda (*later* Grenfell), 44
Lyttelton, Sir Neville, 44
Lyttelton, Oliver (*later* Lord Chandos), 87
Lyttelton, Rev, 48

McCall's magazine, 55
McCartney, Paul, 320
McCulloch, Rev Joseph, 316–17
MacDonald, Miss (housemaid), 17
McDonell, Rose (*later* Baring), 32, 48
McGivern, Cecil, 266, 267
Macmillan, Harold, 129, 130, 137, 303
Macmillan Publishers, 303
Madden, Cecil, 156
Madras, ENSA tour (1944), 159–60
Magic Box, The (film), 185
Make Up Your Mind (TV game show), 274
Makins, Roger, 129, 130, 137
Malta, ENSA tour (1944), 134
Manchester, JG performs in, 125, 324–5
Manchester Guardian see Guardian
Marcus Aurelius, 311
Margaret, Princess, 181, 203, 221, 322; dines with Grenfells, 188–9
Marie, Queen of Romania, 19, 54
Marshall, Sophie, 218
Martin, Hugh, 185, 256
Mary, Queen Consort, 40, 41, 64
Mauritania, RMS, 203
Meet Joyce Grenfell (show), 227–8
Menges, Isolde, 104
Messina Copper Mines, Transvaal, 170, 259–62, 264–5
Meynell, Francis, 73
Michelmore, Cliff, 298
Middle East, ENSA tour (1944), 126–7, 154–7

Middle East Merry-Go-Round (radio series), 155
Middleton, Molly, 48
Midsummer Night's Dream, A, 179
Miller, Glenn, 155
Miller, Max, 43
Million Pound Note, The (film), 195
Milne, A A, 34
Miners' Strike (1974), 294
Minsmere Bird Reserve, 277, 283, 327
Mirador, Virginia, 2–3, 11
Mitchie, Mr (BBC producer), 66
Mitford, Diana (*later* Guinness and Mosley), 38, 41, 52
Mitford, Nancy, 32
Moiseiwitsch, Benno, 104
Moment With Tennyson, A (monologue), 184
Monday Night at Eight (radio series), 164
Monroe, Marilyn, 19
Monte Cassino, battle, 135–6
Montmartre (nightclub), New York, 57
Moonlight and Splash (radio series), 110
Moore, Katherine, 217–18, 335–6
Moore, Patrick, 291–2
Moorfields Eye Hospital, London, 324, 325–6
Morgan, Mrs, 236
Morley, Sheridan, 69, 237, 304
Morrison, Miss (teacher), 23
Moseley, Sydney O, 68
Mosley, Oswald, 22
Mosley, Vivienne, 48
Moyne, Lord, 154
'Mrs Mendlicote' (song), 199
'Much-Binding-in-the-Marsh', 165
Muggeridge, Malcolm, 274, 317
Muir, Frank, 236, 303
Murray-White family, 187–8
Music for You (TV series), 267
'Music's Message, The' (song), 208
Music You Love (company), 118–21
My Beautiful Career (film), 232
Myers, Baldwin, 5, 6
'My Heart Is as Light as Air' (song), 115

Nabarro, Gerald, 274
Nannau (dog), 60

Nannau (North Wales), 53
Naples, ENSA tour (1944), 134, 136
'Narcissus' (song), 190–1
National Gallery, London, wartime recitals, 102–3, 104
National Health Service, 170
Nazism, 83
Neale, Ruth, 261
Neame, Ronald, 195
Nesbit, Edith, 21
Neville, Angela, 41
Newby, Eric, 299
Newell, Norman, 190–1, 328
News Chronicle, 174, 205
New Statesman, 174, 200
New Theatre, Oxford, 102
New York, 11, 56–7, 192, 251; *Joyce Grenfell Requests the Pleasure*, 202–6
New Yorker (magazine), 58
New York Times, 54, 167
New Zealand, Grenfells visit, 256
Nice Song, 179
Nicholls, Phyllis (*née* Spender-Clay), 72
Nicholson, Robin, 161
Nicodemus (driver), 264
Nicodemus (monologue), 264, 312
Nine Sharp (revue), 74
Niven, David, 54, 101
'No News is Good News' (song), 291
North Africa, ENSA tour (1944), 128–34
Northern England, ENSA tour, 125–6
Northern Ireland, 318; ENSA tour (1942), 118–21, 165
Norwich, John Julius, 292
Note With Music, A (radio series), 175
Novello, Ivor, 21, 81, 185
nuclear research, 87
Nursery School (monologue), 182, 205, 225, 240–1, 285
nursery schools, 63, 64–5

OBE, 171
Obelensky, Prince George, 30
Observer, 88, 112, 165, 200, 322; JG as radio critic, 68–9, 71–2; JG's verse published in, 67
Odyssey (monologue), 179

O'Hara, Mary, 252–3, 296
Oh Boy! (film), 49
'Oh! Mr du Maurier' (song), 166
Olav V, King of Norway, 45
Old Church St, Chelsea, 169
Old Girl's School Reunion (monologue), 285, 336
Olivier, Laurence, 123, 275, 289
Olivier, Michael, 262–3, 264
'On Hearing Myra Hess Playing HF's Sonata,' (poem) 104
Open All Night (film), 49
Opera Interval (monologue), 233
Orr, William, 252
Oxenford, Daphne, 179, 192, 218, 267
Oxford, *Penny Plain* tour, 185–6
Oxford University, 45
Ozanne sisters, 38

Paget, Paul, 221
'Paiforce,' ENSA tour (1944), 135, 137, 142–5, 154–7
Paine, Bunny, 305
Palace Theatre, London, 91
Palestine Half-Hour (radio series), 155
Palmer, Bud, 54
Pangbourne Nautical College, 207
Pan's People, 294
Paramor, Norrie, 191
Paris, 37–9
Parker, Cecil, 196
Parker, Mr (butler), 17
Park Wall Infant School, Chelsea, 240
Parr's (Cliveden cottage): Grenfells at (1936–42), 59–62, 89, 95, 97, 122
Past is Present, The (monologue), 152
Pate, John, 2
Paton, Alan, 260
Paxman, Jeremy, 337
Payn, Graham, 177, 184, 189
Peace Ballot (1935), 83
Pearl Harbor, bombing (1941), 106
Pears, Peter, 179, 276, 277, 278, 279, 281, 282, 286
Peck, Gregory, 195
Penn, William, 333
Penny Plain (revue), 184–9, 190, 218
Perkins, Lizzie (*née* Langhorne), 3, 12

Perkins, Moncure, 12
Perowne, Bishop of Bradford, 48, 143
Perowne, Leslie, 110, 143
Perowne, Stewart, 143, 224–5, 293, 320
Petty-Fitzmaurice, Lady Margaret Mercer Nairne, 48
Philip Street Theatre, Sydney, 251–5
Phipps, Ann, 48
Phipps, Betty, 70–1, 186
Phipps, Donrue (*née* Leyton), 94, 171
Phipps, Edmund, 15
Phipps, Jessie Percy Butler (*née* Duncan), 7–8, 15, 16–17; Sargent portrait, 8, 17, 192, 223
Phipps, Joyce Irene *see* Grenfell
Phipps, Margaret, 15
Phipps, Mary (*née* Cheseboro), 203, 245, 246
Phipps, Nicholas, 79, 100, 178, 179, 180, 184
Phipps, Nora (*née* Langhorne): advice, 133, 151, 317; beauty, 5, 6; Christian Science, 26; death, 201–2, 329; dressing up, 36; elopes with Lefty Flynn (1913/1930), 12–13, 49–51; family background, 1, 3–4; First World War, 13–4; and Fitzgerald, 55, 56, 247; friendships, 21; General Strike (1926), 31; generosity, 31, 61, 182, 202; London visits, 61, 182, 191–2, 200; marriage to Lefty Flynn, 54–6; marriage to Paul Phipps, 8–9, 15; mimicry, 18; as mother, 18, 19, 28, 29, 171, 195, 202; personality, 18–20, 34, 55; philanthropy, 15; as practical joker, 30; Second World War, 94, 123; in Tryon, 54
Phipps, Pamela, 216
Phipps, Paul, 6–7, 8, 20; architectural career, 7, 10–11, 15; Christian Science, 25, 26, 52, 70, 71; commissions, 52, 59, 60, 102; death, 192; family background, 7–8; as father, 28, 29; First World War, 11–12, 13, 14; friendships, 21; General Strike (1926), 31; on

Grenfells, 52; health, 182, 192, 322; marriage, 8–9, 15; as parent, 20; renovates Parr's, 59; Second World War, 83, 95; in Washington, 14, 15
Phipps, Rachel (*later* Lampson), 139
Phipps, Sally, 203, 246–7, 294–5
Phipps, Simon, 48, 200
Phipps, Thomas Langhorne ('Lang'), 246, 295
Phipps, Thomas Wilton, 11, 13, 17, 49, 50, 94, 171, 195; childhood, 22; in Hollywood (1938), 70; on JG, 332; marries Mary Cheseboro, 203; in New York, 56–7; at *New York Times*, 54; prep school, 24; Second World War, 106–7; settles in America, 51; stage plays, 245
Phipps, Wilton (grandfather), 8
Phipps, Wilton (nephew), 70, 71, 89, 171, 186; death, 254–5
Phipps family, 1, 7, 15, 26
Physically Handicapped and Able Bodied (PHAB), 312
Piaf, Edith, 205
Pickford, Mary, 20
Pick of the Week (radio series), 289
Pickwick Papers, The (film), 194
Pie, Eliza, 3, 11, 192
Pilkington, Sir Harry, 269
Pilkington Commission (1961–2), 269–72
Piper, John, 178
Plomley, Roy, 113, 173, 175, 190
Poet's Pub (film), 193
Poona, ENSA tour (1944), 157–8
Potter, Mary, 73, 190, 213, 224, 281–2
Potter, Stephen, 112, 114, 174, 184, 213; *Design for Women* (film), 193; divorce, 190, 281; *How* radio series, 111, 112–13, 167, 173, 190; illness and death, 282; on JG, 100; meets JG, 72–4; *Tuppence Coloured*, 178, 181
Powell, Anthony, 45
Powell, Enoch, 274
Presley, Elvis, 247
Preston, Lancs, JG performs in, 125
Previn, André, 292

Princess Patricia's Canadian Light Infantry, 12, 13
Proctor family, 106
Profumo, John, 248
Punch, 67, 68, 86, 97, 99, 104, 105, 168
Pure Hell of St Trinian's, The (film), 195–6

Queen magazine, 225
Queen's Hall, London, 31
Queen Victoria Hospital, East Grinstead, 93

'Radio Game,' 290
Radio Times, 68, 89
Rawdon's Hotel, Lanzerac, South Africa, 262–3
Rawson, Mildred, 78, 90
Ray, Robin, 291, 292
Reading, Baroness, 88
Reading Without Tears (book), 15
Red, White and Blue ENSA concert party, 159
Red Cross: American, 120; British, 107; Canadian, 94, 107
Redgrave, Michael, 91
Red House, Aldeburgh, 281
Reed, Carol, 101
Rees, William, 147
Reiss, Stephen, 280–1
Reith, Lord, 271
Renoir, Claude, 194
Rest Harrow, Kent, 10
Rhodesia, 261 *see* Zimbabwe
Ribbentrop, Joachim von, 63
Richard, Cyril, 77, 167
Richardson, Ralph, 91
Richmond, Virginia, 2
Robins, Denise, 303
Robinson, Carley, 25, 52, 127, 152, 172, 220
Rogers, Capt, 155
Roose-Evans, James, 336
Rose, Jennifer, 336
Roselli, Fedora *see* Bernard, Dora
Royal Academy of Dramatic Arts (RADA), 39–40
Royal Army Ordnance Corps, 144

Index

Royal Avenue, Chelsea, 51
Royal Command Matinée (1939), 91
Royal Shakespeare Company, 184
Run For Your Money, A (film), 193
Russians Are Coming, The (film), 232
Rutherford, Margaret, 194
Ruthless Rhymes for Heartless Homes
   (book), 30

Sackville-West, Edward, 173
St Andrews University, 329
St-Germain-en-Laye, Paris, 37–8
St James's Square, Piccadilly, 10, 42, 47,
   63, 92, 93
St Leonard's Terrace, Chelsea, 15–17,
   25, 51–3, 58, 59, 95, 169, 222
St Margaret's, Westminster, 47
St Martin's Theatre, London, 186, 201
St Mary-le-Bow, London, 316–17
St Paul's Cathedral, 95, 100
St Trinian's films, 194, 195–6
Salur Jung, Nawab, 159–60
Sampson, Aggie, 11
Sampson, Lucy, 29, 60, 82; as nanny,
   10, 11, 13; as nursery-governess,
   17–18, 24
Sanders, Michael, 323, 329
Sargent, Emily, 8
Sargent, John Singer, 6, 8, 17, 192, 223
Sargent, Malcolm, 103
Sargent, Violet, 8
Sarony, Leslie, 128
Saturday Afternoon (radio series), 124–5
Savoy Hotel, London, 48
Scalehill Hotel, Cumbria, 297
Scarfe, Gerald, 336
Scharrer, Irene, 104
Schubert, Franz, 25
Schumann, Robert, 104
Science and Health (book), 26
Scott, Peter, 291
Scott-Moncrieff, Joanna, 268, 309
Scrambled Eggs for Christmas (book), 220
Searle, Ronald, 186, 195, 196
Second World War (1939–45), 83–94,
   110, 122–3
Secunderabad, ENSA tour (1944),
   158–9, 159–60

Selig, Richard, 253
'Seven Good Reasons' (charity
   concerts), 311–12
Seyler, Athene, 196, 209, 212, 317, 328
Seymour, Nancy, 218
Shaw, Bobbie, 5, 14, 36, 116, 165
Shaw, Charlotte, 33
Shaw, George Bernard, 33–4, 39, 58,
   87–8, 98, 110, 275, 322
Shaw, Robert Gould, 4
Shenley, Bucks, 101
Shevekiar, Princess, 142
Shirley's Girl Friend (monologue), 182,
   200, 204, 237
Shopping – East-side New York
   (monologue), 110
Show of the Week (TV series), 275
Shuaibah, ENSA tour (1944), 144–5
Sicily, ENSA tour (1944), 135
Sigh No More (revue), 161, 162, 165–8,
   170
Sim, Alistair, 194, 195
Simon, Richard, 302–3, 304
Situation Vacant (monologue), 106, 108
Sitwell, Osbert, 178
Skomer Island, 323
Skopje, Grenfells visit (1936), 53–4
Sloboskya, Oda, 185
Slough Nursery School, 64–5, 240
Slough Social Centre, 64
Smith, Ian, 261
Smith, Leslie, 310
Smuts, Field Marshal J C, 173
Snape Maltings, Suffolk, 278, 279–80
Snoopers, The (TV comedy), 285
Society of Women Writers and
   Journalists, 300
'Someday' (song), 115
'Songs My Mother Taught Me,' 192,
   204
South Africa: apartheid, 260; cultural
   boycott, 259, 261; Grenfells in, 170,
   259–65
Southsea, *Penny Plain* tour, 185
Soviet Union, Nancy Astor in, 64
Spectator, 99, 207, 300
Spender-Clay, Pauline (*née* Astor), 14,
   92, 122

Spender-Clay, Rachel (*later* Bowes-
  Lyon), 104
Spindels, Dr (dentist), 29
Stalin, Joseph, 64
Stapylton, Barbara Chetwynd, 23
Starlight (TV series), 125, 266
Stassinopoulos, Arianna, 293
'Stately as a Galleon' (song), 227, 286
Stiebel, Victor, 164, 177, 180, 203, 221;
  as designer, 127, 198–9, 227, 229;
  JG's friendship with, 116, 182,
  212–13
Stoll, Oswald, 87
Stone, Paddy, 198, 199
Strachey, James, 66–7
Strachey, Lytton, 66
Strachey, Marjorie, 66
Strand Theatre, London, 91
Stranks, Susan, 292
Stratford-on-Avon, 311–12
Strathmore, SS, 128
Stravinsky, Igor, 289
Strickland, Margot, 235
Sullivan, Ed, 204–5, 206, 252
Sunday Chronicle, 88
Sunday Pictorial, 167
Sunday Times, 79, 331
Swann, Donald, 185, 198, 199
Sydney, JG tours, 251–6

Tatler and Bystander, 97, 225
Television, early, 266
Tennyson, Lord, 66–7
Ten to Eight (radio series), 309
Ten Year Plan for Children, 63–4
Terry, Ellen, 21
Theater World Annual, 204
Theatre Royal, Drury Lane, 117
'There Is Nothing New to Tell You'
  (song), 115, 132
Thesiger, Tony, 84, 88, 212, 257
'They're a Lovely Bunch of Boys'
  (song), 115
Third Sherwood Foresters, 13
This Demi-Paradise (film), 123
This Happy Breed (film), 124
This is the End of the News
  (monologue), 168

This Is Your Life (TV series), 289
Thomas, Terry, 195
Thought for the Day (radio series), 309
Thought for Today (monologue), 184,
  186, 204
'Three Brothers' (song), 201
Three Mothers (monologue), 76
Three's Company (dancers), 203, 204,
  205
Times, The, 40, 41, 47, 87, 109, 167,
  200, 283, 303, 328
'Time' (song), 53
Time to Waste (monologue), 250
Titian, 44
Tobruk, ENSA tour (1944), 138
Todds, Walter, 291
Tonight (TV series), 298–9
Townsend, Peter, 181
Toye, Wendy, 198, 336
Travelling Broadens the Mind
  (monologue), 165–6, 167, 204
Tree, Michael, 48, 139
Tree, Nancy (*née* Perkins, *later*
  Lancaster), 14, 40, 58, 102, 170, 201,
  334
Tree, Ronald, 102
Trewin, J C, 168, 238
'Tribute to a Treasure' (poem), 105–6
Trinder, Tommy, 115
Troup, Freda (*also* Levson), 260
Trunk Call (newspaper), 143
Truro Cathedral, 316
Tryon, North Carolina, 54, 55, 94, 171,
  202
Tunis, ENSA tour (1944), 133–4
Tunnard, Peter, 137, 144, 150
Tunnard, Viola, 167, 189, 192; as
  accompanist, 126, 129, 267, 282; at
  Aldeburgh, 276, 282–3; at Ballet
  Rambert, 198; coaches JG, 182–3;
  ENSA tours, 126, 127, 128–34,
  134–7, 135, 137–8, 139–42, 142–5,
  145, 150, 151, 154–5, 157–62, 171;
  illness and death, 283, 329
Tuppence Coloured (revue), 177–81, 182,
  184, 224, 266
'Turn Back the Clock' (song), 115, 116
Turner, Alfred, 145

Twain, Mark, 1
Tyler, James Grant, 166
Tynan, Kenneth, 236

United States, Second World War,
106–7; (1946) 170–2
University Challenge (TV series), 336–7
Useful and Acceptable Gifts (monologue),
72, 74, 81
Ustinov, Peter, 99, 100–1;
US tours (1956/58/60/63), 246–8,
249–51, 293

Valentino, Rudolf, 21, 30
Valpy, Mr, of Dawlish, 5–6
Vancouver, Phipps family in (1911), 11
van der Post, Ingaret, 214
van der Post, Laurens, 214, 281
Variety Show (radio series), 169, 267
Varnel, Marcel, 124
Veeny (Mirador servant), 3
Vesuvius, Mount, 136–7
Viola Tunnard Memorial Trust, 283,
335
Vivian, Lettice, 23
Vogue magazine, 181
Voluntary Aid Detachment (VAD),
13

Wallis, Margaret, 85, 86
Walmsley, Sgt Fred, 161
Walton, William, 178
Ward, Alison, 298
Ward, John, 222, 298, 305, 319, 328
Ward, Stephen, 248
War Office, 13, 87
Warsaw Concerto (Addinsell), 114, 120,
131
Waterloo Dinner, Windsor Castle,
285–6
Watt, A P, 58, 67
Watt, Jane, 304
Waugh, Evelyn, 174
Wavell, Lord, 162
Wavenden Arts Centre, 217, 322
Weatherill, Corporal Sid, 155, 156,
157
We Beg to Differ (radio series), 175–7

Welch, Elisabeth, 179, 180, 181, 185,
187, 267, 333
Wellesley, Anne, 41
West, Rebecca, 201
Westminster Abbey, thanksgiving
service, 334
'What Shall I Wear?' (song), 227
'When You Go' (song), 115
While the Sun Shines (film), 123
White, Rev Geoffrey, 334
Whiteley, Elizabeth, 269
Whitfield, June, 185
Wigmore Hall, piano lessons, 17
William and Mary University, Virginia,
237
Williams, Emlyn, 141
Williams, Emrys, 148
Wilson, A E, 200
Wilson, Mary, 260
Windsor, Edward, Duke of, 206
Winn, Alice (*née* Perkins), 3–4, 5, 10,
12, 13, 37, 72, 92, 122
Winn, Anne, 92
Winn, Elizabeth, 48, 92, 222
Winn, Reggie, 50
Winnipeg: JG tours (1970), 249; Phipps
family in (1911), 11
Winstanley, John, 287, 323
Winter in Torquay (sketch), 77–8
Wintle, Mrs (nursery school leader),
64–5
Wisdom, Norman, 191
Wodehouse, P G, 27
Woman's Day (journal), 309
Woman's Hour (radio series), 238, 268,
304, 312
Women of Today (TV series), 266–7
Women's Institute: Cliveden, 59–60,
72; in wartime, 85
Women's Land Army, 86
Women's Voluntary Service (WVS),
88, 105
Wood, Sir Henry, 31
Woodcock, Patrick, 116, 198–9, 212,
236, 287, 329, 332, 335
Woods-Jack, Bruce, 304, 311,
330
Woolgathering (monologue), 110

Worsley, T C, 200
Wright, Billy, 269
Wright, Geoffrey, 178, 179, 180
Wye Primary School, 307–8
Wyndham's Theatre, 98, 99

Yank at Oxford, A (film), 195
Yellow Rolls-Royce, The (film), 232

Yorkshire, Grenfells visit, 336
Yorkshire Post, 320
Young, Gladys, 175
Younger Generation, The (radio series), 208
Ypres, battle, 13

Zimbabwe, 335